Glossator: Practice and Theory of the Commentary

We do nothing but comment upon one another
—Michel de Montaigne

All our so-called consciousness is a more or less fantastic commentary on an unknown, perhaps unknowable, but felt text
—Friedrich Nietzsche

Not system but commentary is the legitimate form through which truth is approached
—Gershom Scholem

COPYRIGHT NOTICE

This work is Open Access, a print version of the online open-access journal *Glossator* (http://glossator.org). It is licensed under a *Creative Commons Attribution 3.0 United States License*. This means that:

You are free:
- to Share – to copy, distribute and transmit the work
- to Remix – to adapt the work

Under the following conditions:
- Attribution – You must attribute the work in the manner specified by the author or licensor (but not in any way that suggests that they endorse you or your use of the work).

With the understanding that:
- Waiver – Any of the above conditions can be waived if you get permission from the copyright holder.

Other Rights – In no way are any of the following rights affected by the license:
- Your fair dealing or fair use rights;
- Apart from the remix rights granted under this license, the author's moral rights;
- Rights other persons may have either in the work itself or in how the work
- is used, such as publicity or privacy rights.

Notice – For any reuse or distribution, you must make clear to others the license terms of this work. The best way to do this is with a link <http://creativecommons.org/licenses/by/3.0/us/>.

Attribution may be made to the authors following the conventions of journal citation.

Questions may be directed to:

Nicola Masciandaro, Editor
Glossator: Practice and Theory of the Commentary
Department of English
Brooklyn College
The City University of New York
2900 Bedford Ave.
Brooklyn, NY 11210
glossatori@gmail.com

GLOSSATOR

Practice and Theory of the Commentary

Volume One

Edited by

Ryan Dobran, Nicola Masciandaro, and Karl Steel

http://glossator.org

Glossator 1 (2009)

Table of Contents

Nicola Masciandaro, *Introduction*..i

Erik Butler, *Benjamin at the Barricades: The* Arcades Project *as Combat and Intrigue*...........1

Alan Ramón Clinton, *Rayond Roussel's Self Help Notes (A Commentary on Bob Perelman's "Chronic Meanings")*..19

Bruno Gullì, *The Sovereign Exception: Notes on Schmitt's Word that Sovereign is He who Decides on the Exception*..23

Stephanie A. Viereck Gibbs Kamath, *Periphery and Purpose: The Fifteenth-Century Rubrication of the* Pilgrimage of Human Life..31

Anna Kłosowsksa & Nicola Masciandaro, *Beyond the Sphere: A Dialogic Commentary on the Ultimate Sonetto of Dante's* Vita Nuova..47

J. H. Prynne, *Tintern Abbey, Once Again*..81

Daniel C. Remein, *New Work: A Prosimetrum*..89

Adam Rosen, *Prelude to a Reading of Aristotle's* Metaphysics*: Beta One, Paragraph One*...129

Michael Stone-Richards, *A Commentary on Theresa Hak Kyung Cha's* Dictée................145

INTRODUCTION
Nicola Masciandaro

The "task of the commentator" is neither to describe the world, nor to change it, but to confound the illusions by which its contingencies assume the air of inevitability.
—Erik Butler

The perfect place to write a great work of literature would be a **symbiosis of home and prison**.
—Alan Clinton

[T]here is no real paradox in deciding against the decision, provided that the one who decides is not sovereign, but *anyone* who chooses freedom and dignity over domination.
—Bruno Gullì

Surviving manuscript copies suggest that the marginal Latin commentary was an integral part of the translation in its circulation, and probably in its composition.
—Stephanie A. Viereck Gibbs Kamath

You know this. It does not require commentary.
—Anna Klosowska & Nicola Masciandaro

To recognise is to confirm by second looks, and to experience why such recognition may move the soul is to feel each just pleasure in confirming a hunger for acknowledgment which, until thus confirmed, might have never been admitted or even registered.
—J. H. Prynne

The comment must not worry too much about getting its final codes right if it is going to participate in the poem, if it is going to always already be the radiance that is the romance of the poem—the sprouting antler sprouting more in the shape of an infinity of codes.
—Dan Remein

ISSN 1942-3381

> Perhaps what is at stake is less a methodologically regulated path to a predetermined end than an "ethical" reorientation, a concomitant change in the character of the inquirer and the inquiry.
>
> —Adam Rosen

> . . . a double channel work of sound and image, which then allows one *to hear* that commentary spoken as, indeed, a form of *dictation*—and *commentaire*
>
> —Michael Stone-Richards

Take these epigraphs as a small garland, a chain of flowers collected from *Glossator*'s first volume, presented here both in gratitude to their authors and for the reader, as a poetic suggestion of the work their contributions are doing, individually and collectively. Read them closely and you will find that they comment on each other, even conduct a subtle conversation (found or made?), a dialogue composed—like all commentary—of a mysterious intersection between a reading subject and a textual object. This dialogue concerns especially the ambivalent *creativity* of commentary, its operation as a complex formal space defined by decidedly mixed characteristics and impulses: exposure, critique, renewal, freedom, possession, constraint, superfluity, belatedness, excess, irrelevance, openness . . .

According to Giorgio Agamben's diagnosis, it is precisely the "loss of commentary and the gloss as creative forms" that attests to the impossibility of "any healing" in Western culture "between *Halacha* and *Aggada*, between *shari'at* and *haqīqat*, between subject matter and truth content."[1] To this schism we may add, as a rough parallel, that between *practice* and *theory*, the proportionally inseparable variables included in this journal's title with deliberate emphasis on the priority of the former as what holds the key to both (practice founds theory). In light of this priority—we want *commentary*, really, send us COMMENTARIES!—the primary editorial challenges of this volume lay in negotiating the minority of submissions employing the apparatus of formal, running commentary and the unexpected number of hybrid submissions: commentarial work addressing commentary. A volume neatly divided into writings *about* commentary and *actual* commentaries turned out to be impossible. But this impossibility now appears as a more propitious start than the editors could have planned, the index of a less predictable and more authentic desire for commentary, a creative beginning.

---

[1] Giorgio Agamben, *Infancy and History: On the Destruction of Experience*, trans. Liz Heron (Verso: New York, 1993), 160.

BENJAMIN AT THE BARRICADES: THE *ARCADES PROJECT* AS COMBAT AND INTRIGUE
Erik Butler

Die Mystifikation ist . . . ein apotropäischer Zauber
[Mystification . . . is an apotropaic magic][1]

The real pathos of Benjamin's life—and death—should not cast a shadow on the bright and variegated tapestry that is the *Arcades Project*. As Beatrice Hanssen has justly observed, "it is well known that National Socialism forced Benjamin into exile, into an enforced nomadic existence in Paris, where he would wander from one borrowed room and apartment to the next. Less a topic of consideration, however, is the fact that during the Weimar years, Benjamin practiced the fine art of travel, gravitating to Paris like his affluent intellectual friends."[2] Benjamin's zigzag course through the Parisian arcades is in large part animated by what Edgar Allan Poe called the "imp of the perverse."[3] If Benjamin sought "secular illumination,"[4] this ambition does not preclude his also undertaking operations intended to produce quasi-religious amazement without insight.

---

[1] References to the *Arcades Project* (from which this quotation is taken) follow the text found in Walter Benjamin, *Gesammelte Schriften*, ed. Rolf Tiedemann (Frankfurt a. M.: Suhrkamp, 1982), Volume V. English translations are from Walter Benjamin, *The Arcades Project*, trans. Howard Eiland and Kevin McLaughlin (Cambridge: Harvard University Press, 1999). Hereafter, they will occur parenthetically. For the epigraph, see pages 422 and 335.

[2] Beatrice Hanssen, "Physiognomy of a Flâneur: Walter Benjamin's Peregrinations through Paris in Search of a New Imaginary," *Walter Benjamin and The Arcades Project*, ed. Beatrice Hanssen (London: Continuum, 2006), 1.

[3] Against the "pure arrogance of reason," Poe proposed that one acknowledge "a radical, primitive, irreducible sentiment . . . overlooked by all the moralists," which "we might . . . deem . . . a direct instigation of the Arch-Fiend, were it not occasionally known to operate in furtherance of good" (Edgar Allan Poe, *Poetry and Tales*, ed. Patrick F. Quinn [New York: The Library of America, 1984], 826, 829). This diabolical streak is also displayed by Benjamin, who approvingly quotes Valéry's remarks about Poe's invention of novel literary forms—a "phenomenon" (295/224) which, like the Devil's ruses, relies upon finding new ways to orchestrate perception, toy with expectations, and lure into complicity.

[4] Norbert W. Bolz and Richard Faber, eds., *Walter Benjamin: Profane Erleuchtung und rettende Kritik* (Würzburg: Königshausen & Neumann, 1985) offers a number of approaches to the topic. For an excellent treatment of Benjamin's aims and the *Arcades Project* in particular, see James Rolleston, "The Politics of Quotation: Walter Benjamin's *Arcades Project*," *PMLA* 104 (1989), 13-27.

ISSN 1942-3381   Erik Butler

It is difficult in the case of Benjamin to draw a sharp line dividing autobiography and the other forms of writing he practiced, notably the *essai*. From Montaigne on, this hybrid genre has permitted writers to conceal themselves in quotations and irony in order to play a game of hide-and-seek with readers, and experiment with form and intention to ends often unknown even to themselves.[5] The problems of demarcation characteristic of this kind of literature present themselves especially acutely in the *Arcades Project*, which consists of bits and pieces taken from elsewhere and alternately commentated or left to stand "as is." Even in the latter case, the works of others bear the mark of the author's style, if in muted form.[6] Some parts of the *Arcades Project* are visibly more complete than others, having received, in the words of editor Rolf Tiedemann, the "mortar" of Benjamin's own words.[7] Had Benjamin lived to complete his undertaking, more such verbal cement would presumably hold together the rest of the text. But the *Arcades Project* was never finished.[8]

The discussion at hand leaves in place the rough edges of the *Arcades Project*, for in their unfinished state, they perform an obstructive function that demands attention and generates engagement.[9] Oddly-proportioned spaces, detours, clandestine points of assembly, and dead ends shape the work. The commentary-on-commentary offered here eschews the hermeneutic task of unveiling meaning in an effort to connect with the spirit of intellectual combativeness that echoes in the glorious ruin that is the *Arcades Project*. These reflections, like Benjamin's fighting words, affirm the joys of life in danger. While such an existence is hardly an ideal state of being, sometimes there is nothing better to expect. The "task of the commentator" is neither to describe the world, nor to change it, but to confound the illusions by which its contingencies assume the air of inevitability.

The open-ended text mirrors its subject matter. Benjamin writes of Paris:

> *Die Stadt ist nur scheinbar gleichförmig. Sogar ihr Name nimmt verschiedenen Klang in verschiedenen Teilen an. Nirgends, es sei denn in Träumen, ist noch ursprünglicher das Phänomen der Grenze zu erfahren als in Städten. Sie kennen heißt jene Linien, die längs der Eisenbahnüberführungen, quer durch Häuser, innerhalb*

---

[5] For a rewarding discussion of this topic of long standing, see Ann Hartle, *Montaigne: Accidental Philosopher* (Cambridge: University of Cambridge Press, 2003), 62-90.

[6] On citation-as-authorship (as exemplified by Montaigne), see Antoine Compagnon, *La seconde main, ou, Le travail de la citation* (Paris: Seuil, 1979), 13-45 and *passim*.

[7] Rolf Tiedemann, "Einleitung des Herausgebers," in Walter Benjamin, *Gesammelte Schriften* (Frankfurt a.M.: Suhrkamp, 1982), V, 13. When not otherwise credited, translations are my own.

[8] Tiedemann presents the evidence concerning the work's genesis in Benjamin, *Gesammelte Schriften*, 11-41. Cf. the "Translators' Forward" in the English edition, pp. ix-xiv and Margaret Cohen, "Benjamin's Phantasmagoria: The *Arcades Project*," *The Cambridge Companion to Walter Benjamin*, ed. David Ferris (Cambridge: Cambridge University Press, 2004), 199-200. An indispensable guide for orientation in the *Arcades Project* is Susan Buck-Morss, *The Dialectics of Seeing: Walter Benjamin and the Arcades Project* (Cambridge: The MIT Press, 1991).

[9] In this regard, Benjamin reveals his affinity for contemporary movements in politics and the arts. See Michael Jennings, "Walter Benjamin and the European Avant-garde," *The Cambridge Companion*, 18-34. On the reception of Benjamin's writings and their power to occasion further commentary and discourse, see Detlev Schöttker, *Konstruktiver Fragmentarismus. Form und Rezeption der Schriften Walter Benjamins* (Frankfurt a.M.: Suhrkamp, 2002).

des Parks, am Ufer des Flusses entlang als Grenzscheiden verlaufen, wissen; heißt diese Grenzen wie auch die Enklaven der verschiedenen Gebiete kennen. Als Schwelle zieht die Grenze über Straßen; ein neuer Rayon fängt an wie ein Schritt ins Leere, als sei man auf eine tiefe Stufe getreten, die man nicht sah.

(The city is only apparently homogeneous. Even its name takes on a different sound from one district to the next. Nowhere, unless perhaps in dreams, can the phenomenon of the boundary be experienced in a more originary way than in cities. To know them means to understand those lines that, running alongside railroad crossings and across privately owned lots, within the park and along the riverbank, function as limits; it means to know these confines, together with the enclaves of the various districts. As threshold, the boundary stretches across streets; a new precinct begins like a step into the void—as though one had unexpectedly cleared a low step on a flight of stairs [141/88]).

These words about Paris apply equally well to the *Arcades Project* itself, which also "takes on a different sound from one district to the next." Some parts are more peaceful than other, more turbulent areas. The text is divided by borders that run along the lines of theme, lexicon, and source (among other things). By following their uneven course, one constantly finds oneself making a "step into the void" and landing at another plane of elevation and in a new frame of reference. Indeed, though he has Paris in mind here, Benjamin presents a vision of urban space that holds true of cities in general, which always possess numerous strata to explore. Paris is the privileged site of Benjamin's reflections not just because it is the "Capital of the Nineteenth Century," as the introductory section of the *Arcades Project* declares, but also because of the accidents of biography and the contingencies of individual taste. A strong element of personal fantasy pervades Benjamin's work.

There is no model for the *Arcades Project*, except, perhaps, that of "life" or "history" itself—unclear points of reference, at best. Therefore, the words mustered here in commentary follow the signs posted by Benjamin's work in much the same way that one generally heeds the rules of traffic but occasionally breaks them. Infractions, after all, are something that city planners must anticipate, just as criminality is the necessary companion of law and order. Nothing in the text—or in Benjamin's biography, for that matter—encourages readers to stick to a "straight and narrow" course of interpretation for long.

To employ a phrase of recent scholarship, Benjamin's *Arcades Project* is comprised of "topographies of memory."[10] But the memory in question is both personal and cultural, intimate and distant. On the one hand, the text draws on Benjamin's lived experience of Paris, and, on the other, the author's vast readings about the city. How should one orient oneself? The *flâneur*—the figure providing the work with a theme and representing the author himself in his oblique writing trajectory—wanders through an expanse of images that belong to different, but contiguous and also overlapping worlds. The reader may follow "the man in the crowd,"[11] but only at constant peril of losing sight of him. Benjamin plunges his reader into an open page of history, which is still in the making. He writes: *Die Rede vom Buch der Natur weist darauf hin, daß man das Wirkliche wie einen Text lesen kann. So soll es hier mit der Wirklichkeit des neunzehnten Jahrhunderts gehalten werden. Wir schlagen das Buch des*

---

[10] Bernd Witte, ed., *Topographien der Erinnerung: Zu Walter Benjamins Passagen* (Würzburg: Königshausen & Neumann, 2008).

[11] Benjamin refers this figure from Poe at numerous points, e.g. 151/96-7; 526/418.

Erik Butler

Geschehenen auf (The expression "the book of nature" indicates that one can read the real like a text. And that is how the reality of the nineteenth century will be treated here. We open the book of what happened [580/464]). *Das Geschehene*, like the *Arcades Project*, belongs to the past, but it is also in large part still unwritten inasmuch as its contents flow into the present and the future.

Den Flanierenden leitet die Straße in eine entschwundene Zeit. (The street conducts the flâneur into a vanished time [524/417].) Almost every element of this sentence may be read allegorically as a kind of reflection on the composition of the *Arcades Project*. Baudelaire, about whom these words are written, becomes Benjamin's stand-in; the nineteenth-century witness of, and participant in, history, is made to speak for his twentieth-century commentator. Baudelaire, the exemplary *flâneur*, is Benjamin. The "street" is a poem. The "vanished time" is not a historical event so much as a literary scene created by another author, whose vision is equal parts observation and literary embellishment. The statement is also the self-commentary of the *hypocrite lecteur* whom the author of *Fleurs du Mal* apostrophizes[12]—that is, of Benjamin himself, glossator of Baudelaire. Benjamin, the avid reader, is also a "hypocrite" in that, when writing, he does not state unequivocally what he means, but instead prefers allusions, juxtapositions, and circuitous paths toward meaning.

The reader must endeavor to share, as best s/he can, Baudelaire and Benjamin's dissimulation. *Diese Arbeit muß die Kunst, ohne Anführungszeichen zu zitieren, zur höchsten Höhe entwickeln. Ihre Theorie hängt aufs engste mit der der Montage zusammen* (This work has to develop to the highest degree the art of citing without quotation marks. Its theory is intimately related to that of montage [572/458])[13]. The *Arcades Project* mimics what it commentates and fans the sparks generated by the resulting interference; otherwise, history would be a dead letter.

Without wishing to discredit the author, we should note that Benjamin is not an unimpeachable source of information. Just as often than not, he can only lay claim to "memories" that have no index in his own experience. But what interests Benjamin is everything that has gone missing, anyway—what no one, even contemporaries of events, could possibly take into full possession and transmit as actual fact. Benjamin's pursuit concerns the "aura," "appearance," and "surface" of things—what one might call "the objectivity of the subjective." This is also why, throughout his writings, he takes up the pseudo-scientific language of Johann Kaspar Lavater's physiognomy. Subtracting the latter's essentializing, ontological claims, Benjamin recognizes a method of description that offers a rich phenomenological lexicon. Hence, he gives sections headings such as "Exhibitions," "Advertising," and "Modes of Lighting"—projections outward which quickly land in an inner space. Benjamin means to rally the illusions besetting him—and all others who wander the streets of modernity—for a counteroffensive against the forces that command these deceptive visions.

Sofern der Flaneur sich auf dem Markt ausstellt, bildet seine Flanerie die Fluktuationen der Ware nach (Insofar as the flâneur presents himself in the marketplace, his flânerie reflects the fluctuations of commodities [464/367]). In the universe that Benjamin evokes—with a polemical surplus-value for the twentieth century—people and things have become relay-points for transmigrating souls, which wander between the reified human beings, on the one hand, and uncannily animate objects, on the other. The metempsychosis of disembodied spirits under capitalism determines the life of the senses: *Die Liebe zur Prostituierten ist die Apotheose der Einfühlung in die Ware*

---

[12] Charles Baudelaire, "Au lecteur," *Oeuvres complètes*, ed. Y.-G. Le Dantec (Paris: Gallimard, 1954), 82.

[13] The relationship between this principle and what Benjamin calls *gesteigerte Anschaulichkeit* (heightened perceptibility or vividness) is explored by Brigid Doherty, "'The Colportage Phenomenon of Space' and the Place of Montage in The *Arcades Project*," in Hanssen (2006), 157-83.

(Love for the prostitute is the apotheosis of empathy with the commodity [475/375]). Such statements are, in equal measure, appreciations of occult aspects of modern life and warnings to the alienated subject.

As the simultaneously desired and feared reverse of a hallucinatory world, flatness, monotony, automation, mass production, and boredom form the backdrop of Benjamin's reflections.[14] This is why transient appearances, precisely to the extent that they are illusory, command his attention. The task of the commentator, for Benjamin, is to be alert to the shocks and violent interruptions that occasionally disrupt the decorous dullness, however ephemeral and unfulfilling these diversions may be.[15] And to this end, he employs whatever means are available. *Ich habe nichts zu sagen. Nur zu zeigen. . . . [D]ie Lumpen, den Abfall: die will ich . . . auf die einzig mögliche Weise zu ihrem Rechte komme lassen: sie verwenden* (I needn't *say* anything. Merely show. . . . [T]he rags, the refuse—these I will . . . allow, in the only way possible, to come into their own: by making use of them [574/460]). Much has been written about the mourning and melancholy that pervades Benjamin's work.[16] Such observations are certainly not wrong, but the author of the *Arcades Project* also displays an appetite for the "cheap thrills" of casual sex, drugs, and shopping when he writes of prostitution, hashish, and the enticing display of consumer goods. Benjamin often seems undecided about how to judge affairs, but he clearly believes that boredom demands a strong antidote.[17]

This is why Benjamin also likes the heady wine of nineteenth-century extremists. He discusses the figure of Louis-Auguste Blanqui not just to reveal Baudelaire's poetic invention as having one of its sources in political radicalism, but also to enliven a vision of his own. *Die Verwertung der Traumelemente ist der Kanon der Dialektik* (The realization of dream elements is the canon of dialectics [580/464]). What else is the idea of revolution but a dream? Benjamin's prose alternates between somnambulistic citation and frenzied efforts to wake up from what, after all, may in fact be a nightmare.

When the historical night had apparently fallen forever on Blanqui, the first professional revolutionary, the latter's fantasy ignited a flame of unprecedented intensity. It burns in the pages of *[d]ie Schrift, die . . . [er] in seinem letzten Gefängnis als seine letzte geschrieben hat* ([his] last work, written during his last imprisonment [169/112]). Benjamin commentates this text, *L'éternité par les astres* (1872), as follows:

> *Es ist eine kosmologische Spekulation. . . . Die kosmische Weltansicht, die Blanqui darin entwirft, indem er der mechanistischen Naturwissenschaft der bürgerlichen Gesellschaft seine Daten entnimmt, ist eine infernalische—ist zugleich ein Komplement der Gesellschaft, die B<lanqui> an seinem Lebensabend als Sieger über sich zu erkennen gezwungen war. . . . Es ist eine vorbehaltslose Unterwerfung, zugleich aber die furchtbarste Anklage gegen eine Gesellschaft, die dieses Bild des Kosmos als ihre Projektion an den Himmel wirft.*

---

[14] Benjamin, 156-78; 101-19. For a discussion in context of nineteenth- and twentieth-century intellectual history, see Elizabeth S. Goodstein, *Experience without Qualities: Boredom and Modernity* (Stanford: Stanford University Press, 2004), 108ff.

[15] For Baudelaire, Benjamin's literary companion, they are often bloody: *l'Ennui . . . rêve d'échafauds en fumant son houka* (Boredom . . . dreams of the scaffolds, smoking his hookah) ("Au lecteur," 82).

[16] For a discussion focusing on Benjamin's early writings, see Max Pensky, *Melancholy Dialectics: Walter Benjamin and the Play of Mourning* (Amherst: University of Massachusetts Press, 2001). A relevant work that deserves more attention from English-language critics is Karl Heinz Bohrer, *Der Abschied. Theorie der Trauer: Baudelaire, Goethe, Nietzsche, Benjamin* (Frankfurt a. M.: Suhrkamp, 1996).

[17] Cf. Richard Wolin "A Metaphysical Materialist," *The Nation* October 16, 2006, Vol. 283, Issue 12, 30-35.

(It is a cosmological speculation. . . . The cosmic vision of the world which Blanqui lays out, taking his data from the mechanistic natural science of bourgeois society, is an infernal vision. At the same time, it is a complement of the society to which Blanqui, in his old age, was forced to concede victory. . . . It is an unconditional surrender, but it is simultaneously the most terrible indictment of a society that projects this image of the cosmos—understood as an image of itself—across the heavens [169/112]).

Blanqui's work stages a *coup d'état* on bourgeois society down on earth through a siege on the City of God up in the heavens by laying hold of modern Laplacian theory in order to demonstrate the full import of a materialist understanding of the universe. Few are inclined to follow him in his cosmic flight of vengeance. Blanqui's *L'éternité par les astres*, Benjamin observes, *ist . . . bis heute gänzlich unbeachtet geblieben* (has remained entirely unnoticed up to now [169/112]). The statement basically holds true in the twenty-first century, too.[18]

Stated summarily, Blanqui's argument is as follows. According to modern science, the universe is infinite, but a finite number of elements constitute it. In the limitless expanse of the sky, countless other worlds exist. By necessity, then, not only are these planets like the earth—life on them has assumed forms identical to the world we know. Ergo, somewhere, among the host of celestial doubles, the revolution has been won and "Blanqui" and his cause have been vindicated. Benjamin qualifies this vision as "infernal," whereby he has Blanqui's contemporary Baudelaire in mind. Like the verse of the *poète maudit*, the revolutionary's discourse appropriates and parodies the language and pacifying cant of his day. Baudelaire openly embraces Satanism, albeit with reservations that appear readily to the reader sufficiently familiar with dissimulation to have earned the confidential titles of *semblable* and *frère*. To similar ends, Benjamin argues, Blanqui embraces positive science. The truth that Blanqui declares, like the dark secrets that Baudelaire intimates to his readers, is audible only to the heightened senses of fellow conspirators and sympathizers; however, a noble end can justify a falsehood.[19]

Poetry and politics move, in Benjamin's Paris, in the shadows of a triumphant world of commerce, which conceals its cruelty in opulence. The wretched urban poor—the rag-pickers, petty criminals, and prostitutes whom Baudelaire hymned, like the proletariat of June 1848, in whose name Blanqui struggled—led an existence of virtual invisibility, either dying or already dead. But when recoded as "the specter haunting Europe" of which Marx and Engels wrote in the *Communist Manifesto*, these ghosts materialize and slake their thirst on the blood of their oppressors. Benjamin passes from Baudelaire to Blanqui and then to Nietzsche, the theorist of *ressentiment* and the Eternal Return; the latter harbored destructive fantasies whose attractions the author of the *Arcades Project* certainly appreciated.

Hence, it is perhaps less surprising than one might first think that Benjamin, the critic of violence,[20] quotes passages from Joseph de Maistre's somber *Soirées de Saint-Pétersbourg*. Maistre and Poe, Baudelaire wrote,

---

[18] However, the work has been republished; see Auguste Blanqui, *L'éternité par les astres* (Paris: Les impressions nouvelles, 2002). Benjamin draws heavily of Gustave Geffroy's 1897 biography of Blanqui, (reprinted under the original title, *L'enfermé* [Lausanne: Éditions rencontre, n.d.], 211-23).

[19] Cf. the *Arcades Project* 745-63/603-19.

[20] A discussion of Benjamin's critique, its implications, and afterlife can be found in Beatrice Hanssen, *Critique of Violence: Between Poststructuralism and Critical Theory* (London: Routledge, 2000).

m'ont appris à raisonner (taught me how to reason/argue).[21] Benjamin chooses the most merciless words of Maistre, the apologist of counterrevolution and defender of the Church Eternal:

> *La terre entière, continuellement imbibée de sang, n'est qu'un autel immense où tout ce qui vit doit être immolé sans fin, sans mesure, sans relâche, jusqu'à la consommation des choses, jusqu'à l'extinction du mal, jusqu'à la mort de la mort.*

> (The whole earth, continually steeped in blood, is nothing but an immense altar on which every living thing must be sacrificed without end, without restraint, without respite, until the consummation of the world, the extinction of evil, the death of death [434/344]).

Maistre believes that blood, if only enough is spilled, can wash away blood. His position, though opposed to that of "the left," shares with many of its soldiers a messianic vision and eagerness to accelerate the End of History. Hence, if only in ironic quotation, he is Benjamin's tactical ally.

At many points, the author of the *Arcades Project* affirms that he wants only to state the facts, not to take sides.[22] Such declarations are not to be credited. The disjointed, fragmentary nature of Benjamin's work represents the fits and starts of a mind unsettled by its own dreams, uncertain which impressions to trust, but desirous of adventure. In the *Traumstadt Paris* (Paris the dream city [517/410]), *das Kollektivbewußtsein [versinkt] in immer tieferem Schlafe* (the collective consciousness sinks into ever deeper sleep [491/389]), and the figures that interest Benjamin, like the wandering spirits of murdered men, do not rest more soundly than he does.

In den Gebieten, mit denen wir es zu tun haben, gibt es Erkenntnis nur blitzhaft (In the fields with which we are concerned, knowledge comes only in lightning flashes [570/456]). Benjamin looks to the skies and see the City of Light as a refuge from the gathering clouds of National Socialism. His Paris consists of images, whether verbal or graphic, taken both from first-hand experience and extracted from readings. Paris is not Benjamin's native Berlin, but rather a counterweight to the Prussian capital on the march toward its own destiny.[23] There was no place for Benjamin in the 1000-year empire that was supposed to emerge in Germany. Over cosmopolitan Paris hung a different firmament; even unlucky stars had the advantage of belonging to another world, where, a tourist of the imaginary, Benjamin could still feel secure.

Benjamin praises the gates of Paris:

> *Wichtig ist ihre Zweiheit: Grenzpforten und Triumphtore, Geheimnis des ins Innere der Stadt einbezogenen Grenzsteins, der ehemals den Ort markierte, wo sie zu Ende war.—Auf der anderen Seite der Triumphbogen. . . . . Aus dem Erfahrungskreise der Schwelle hat das Tor sich entwickelt, das den verwandelt, der unter seine Wölbung hindurchschreitet.*

---

[21] Baudelaire, 1234 ("Mon coeur mis à nu").

[22] E.g., Benjamin's marginal remark on methodology: *Vordringen mit der geschliffenen Axt der Vernunft und ohne rechts noch links zu sehen. . .* (Forge ahead with the whetted axe of reason, looking neither right nor left. . . [570/456]).

[23] Cf. Bernd Witte, "Paris–Berlin–Paris. Zum Zusammenhang von individueller, literarischer und gesellschaftlicher Erfahrung in Walter Benjamins Spätwerk," *Passagen: Walter Benjamins Urgeschichte des XIX. Jahrhunderts*, ed. Norbert Bolz and Bernd Witte (Munich: Fink, 1984), 17-26.

Erik Butler

(Important is their duality: border gates and triumphal arches. Mystery of the boundary stone which, although located in the heart of the city, once marked the point at which it ended.—On the other hand, the Arc de Triomphe. . . . Out of the field of experience proper to the threshold evolved the gateway that transforms whoever passes under its arch [139/86-7]).

The curvature of the Arc de Triomphe is like a second sky that covers and protects the wanderer and his shadow. The monument commemorates those who have fallen for France, especially on Napoleon's campaigns; its iconography contrasts the bloom of French youth with an armor-plated, medieval Germanic soldiery. It is as if the gate has been erected to express Benjamin's nostalgia for the revolutionary spirit of French yesteryear, which contrasts so sharply with the contemporary German longing for an even earlier time, the dream-world of a sleeping Barbarossa.[24]

As Roland Barthes observed for another generation, "myth," in a modern context, does not refer to antiquity, but rather to the world of illusions that sustain life in bourgeois society.[25] This was already Benjamin's insight—and Marx's, too, in the preceding century. Benjamin taps into a vital current of his forebear's thought when he takes up the supernatural imagery that abounds in the polemical language of *Capital* and other works.[26] His concern is to illuminate the struggle that takes place not just in the arena of relations of production (the "material" realm), but also on the seemingly more immaterial terrain of culture.

To overstate the case somewhat, Benjamin, like the poetic and political radicals he commentates, loves trouble. His textual *praxis* engineers tension and conflict, for they are the wellspring of the revolutionary spirit. In its textual "barricades," the *Arcades Project* opens onto multiple layers of time that intersect and diverge—both on a "vertical," properly chronological axis and on the "horizontal" plane of the city street, which opens onto the recesses of history.

> *Paris steht über einem Höhlensystem, aus dem Geräusche der Métro und Eisenbahnen heraufdröhnen, in dem jeder Omnibus, jeder Lastwagen langausgehaltenen Widerhall erweckt. Und dieses große technische Straßen- und Röhrensystem durchkreuzt sich mit den altertümlichen Gewölben, den Kalksteinbrüchen, Grotten, Katakomben. . . . Noch heute kann man gegen zwei Franken Entgelt sich seine Eintrittskarte zum Besuche dieses nächtlichsten Paris lösen, das so viel billiger und ungefährlicher als das der Oberwelt ist.*

(Paris is built over a system of caverns from which the din of the Métro and railroad mounts to the surface, and in which every passing omnibus or truck sets up a prolonged echo. And this great technological system of tunnels and thoroughfares interconnects with the ancient vaults, the limestone quarries, the grottoes and catacombs.

---

[24] For a comparative analysis of opposing systems of cultural memory, see Stefan Goebel, "Re-membered and Re-mobilized: the 'Sleeping Dead' in Interwar Germany and Britain," *Journal of Contemporary History*, Oct 2004, Vol. 39: 487 - 501.

[25] Roland Barthes, *Mythologies*, trans. Annette Lavers (New York: Hill & Wang, 1972).

[26] Terrell Carver, *The Postmodern Marx* (University Park: Pennsylvania State University Press, 1998) discusses Marx's figural language in relation to political theories that do not share his assumptions about class struggle and modes of production.

Even today, for the price of two francs, one can buy a ticket of admission to this most nocturnal Paris, so much less expensive and less hazardous than the Paris of the upper world [137/85]).

The surface world echoes with the din of constructions belonging to what one might call, in grammatical terms, the "historical present perfect"–the network of trains constructed in the nineteenth century, whose modernity is such that they seem to date only "from yesterday." On this level, phenomena crowd the senses, for the entrances and exits to the Métro spit out and swallow human traffic at a rate exceeding the powers of cognition.

The quarries, grottos, and catacombs around which this web is spun seem calmer, but they, too, have the power to overwhelm:

Das Mitttelalter hat es anders gesehen. Aus Quellen wissen wir, daß . . . sich kluge Leute sich erbötig machten, gegen hohe Bezahlung und Schweigegelübde ihren Mitbürgern dort unten den Teufel in seiner höllischen Macht zu zeigen. . . . Der Schmuggelverkehr im sechzehnten und achtzehnten Jahrhundert ging zum großen Teil unter der Erde vor sich. Wir wissen auch, daß in Zeiten öffentlicher Erregung sehr schnell unheimliche Gerüchte über die Katakomben umliefen.... Am Tage nach der Flucht Ludwigs XVI verbreitete die Revolutionsregierung Plakate, in denen sie genaueste Durchsuchung dieser Gänge anordnete.

(The Middle Ages saw it differently. Sources tell us that there were clever persons who. . . , after exacting a considerable sum and a vow of silence, undertook to guide their fellow citizens underground and show them the Devil in his infernal majesty. . . . In the sixteenth and eighteenth centuries smuggling operations went on for the most part below ground. We also know that in times of public commotion mysterious rumors traveled very quickly via the catacombs. . . . On the day after Louis XVI fled Paris, the revolutionary government issued bills ordering a thorough search of these passages [137/85]).

Benjamin seems almost, in the manner of one of his sources, Michelet, to officiate at a summoning of ancestral voices from the past.[27] The scenes he evokes are alive with the occult forces that move history–black masses, crime, conspiracy, rumor, and political paranoia. The archeology of the Parisian underground reveals the tectonic instability of life in bygone ages. The passage concludes: . . . *ein paar Jahre später ging unversehens das Gerücht durch die Massen, einige Stadtviertel seien dem Einbruch nahe* (. . . a few years later a rumor suddenly spread through the population that certain areas of town were about to cave in [137/85]). These dormant tensions can reemerge and pull the city into the depths of terror once more.

The *Arcades Project* is less analytic than synthetic in ambition. Not just because of Benjamin's death, but also because of his critical methodology, the text branches off into unwritten chapters that still belong within its scope. In the spirit of the logic underlying Benjamin's project, we now turn to an alleyway that the author almost certainly knew about, but which he did not himself wander down in the pages he left behind.

---

[27] Roland Barthes, *Michelet*, trans. Richard Howard (New York: Farrar, Straus and Giroux, 1987), 81-87. On this topic, see also the brilliant essay by Philippe Muray, *Le XIXe siècle à travers les ages* (Paris: Denoël, 1984), 309-23, 451-73, 480-510.

The name *Champfleury*, the pseudonym of Jules François Félix Husson (1821-1889), recurs throughout the *Arcades Project*. Champfleury, the friend of Baudelaire[28] and Courbet, spent the last sixteen years of his life as the Chief of Collections at the Sèvres porcelain factory; today, he is best known as an art historian. He also composed sketches from the *vie de bohème* that he led in younger years. One such picture in prose is "L'homme aux figures de cire" (The Wax-Figure Man) (1849).

Champfleury presents his work as a slice of life[29] from mid-century Paris. The story begins with the narrator calling to mind a *spectacle . . . d'un extérieur morne et dégradé* (sight . . . with a gloomy and worn exterior) that one might have seen in walking from the Place de la Concorde to the Arc de Triomphe. On the other hand, it might have escaped notice, being *trop peu engageant pour le public des Champs-Élysées* (too uninteresting for the public of the Champs Élysées).[30] Significantly, the flâneur might have stumbled upon this attraction in the revolutionary year of 1848. There, one would have found two wax figures beckoning to passersby.

Une femme de cire vêtue en saltimbanque, que le [propriétaire] s'était imaginé pouvoir figurer une puissante princesse, tournait les yeux tantôt à droite, tantôt à gauche, par un mécanisme grossier. . . . L'autre figure de cire représentait un criminel sans titre, vêtu d'un modeste habit noir, les bras tendus en avant, comme pour engager le public à entrer. Ma longue étude de cet art populaire me donne aujourd'hui à penser que celui que j'appelle le criminel *n'était autre chose que le témoin d'un crime. J'entends par là que l'homme en habit noir avait été sans aucun doute détaché d'un groupe représentant un assassinat.*

(A woman in wax dressed as a circus performer, which the owner had thought might represent a powerful princess, turned her eyes alternately to the right and the left by means of a crude mechanism. . . . The other wax figure portrayed a criminal of an uncertain kind, dressed in humble clothing, extending his arms forward as if to encourage the public to enter. My lengthy study of this form of popular art makes me think, today, that the figure I am calling the *criminal* was nothing other than the witness of a crime. By that, I mean that the man in black dress had, without a doubt, been detached from a group of figures portraying a murder.)[31]

The female figure, clothed as a kind of clown, is supposed to have the commanding presence of a princess, although her eyes turn from right to left and back again, as if she were uncertain where to look for parties to support the royal cause. The male effigy, the narrator surmises, has been taken from another scene, in which "he" was the witness of a crime; now, he beckons to customers. *Les beaux bras qu'il faisait pour attirer le public furent anciennement un geste d'horreur; et cette bouche, qui jadis semblait crier: au meurtre! devint le pendant mécanique des oeillades de la princesse* (The striking gesture that he made to attract the public had formerly been an expression of horror; and that mouth, which once seemed to cry out "Murder!" became the mechanical counterpart to the princess's

---

[28] Baudelaire devotes a section of *L'art romantique* (VII [pp. 955-57]) to "Les contes de Champfleury."

[29] Cf. his 1857 study, *Le réalisme* (Geneva: Slatkine, 1967).

[30] Champfleury, *L'homme aux figures de cire* (Paris: Gallimard, 2004), 7; the tale first appeared as part of the second volume *Les Excentriques* (1852), which is subtitled "Les grands hommes du ruisseau" (The Great Men of the Gutter).

[31] Champfleury, 8.

Erik Butler

winks.)[32] A criminal quality still adheres to the dummy, as if by contagion—only at present, it taints the commercial spectacle as a whole.

On n'était pas encore sous la République (We were not yet living under the Republic),[33] the narrator observes. It is all the more remarkable, then, that the wax figures' human counterparts, who operate the sideshow, display inside their hutch unflattering representations of Bourbon kings and, moreover, indulge in diatribes against the contemporary Orléanist regime. They are also every bit as odd as the dummies that advertise for them: the man looks shifty and menacing, and the woman has no legs. The initial encounter prompts numerous subsequent visits, but, alas, *[l]a révolution de février arriva, qui coupa brusquement le carnaval en deux* (the Revolution of February came, which abruptly cut the carnival in two[34]). The *cabinet de cire* closes. In the second year of the new government, the storyteller once again finds himself promenading in Paris in search of diversion—this time, at the *folles saturnales* of the idle rich disporting themselves at masked balls.

> . . . *je sortis d'un de ces terribles endroits, quasi hallucinés, ne me connaissant plus, ayant remarqué des confusions des sexes, des hommes et des femmes hybrides dont les sculptures et peintures licentieuses des antiques ne peuvent donner aucune idée.*
>
> (. . . I exited from one of those terrible places, which seemed almost a hallucination, no longer knowing myself after observing the jumbles of the sexes, hybrid men and women of which the licentious sculptures and paintings of antiquity cannot give the slightest idea.)[35]

The new society exceeds ancient Rome in its decadence. Suddenly, *un homme qui se disputait avec une vieille femme* (a man quarreling with an old woman) bids the narrator to enter a building in a curious fashion: *Entrez donc. . . vous n'avez pas peur qu'on vous assassine. . . . [V]ous . . . aimez le curieux* (Come on in, then . . . you're not afraid of being murdered? . . . [Y]ou . . . appreciate unusual things.)[36] Caught off-guard by this strange confidence, our hero agrees to follow. After five minutes in dark passageways, he realizes that he has again encountered the odd couple he met previously. *Je suis mon maître à présent* (I'm my own boss now),[37] explains the *homme bizarre*: on the condition that he marry the *femme cul-de-jatte*, his employer bequeathed the dummies to him, which now stand in greater disrepair than ever in the deepest recesses of their new home.

With the events of 1848, the world of business has changed as much as the political order. In this context, the strange old man who has come into possession of the wax cabinet is a figure of the bourgeoisie, which now controls government and finance alike. Like the class he represents, the new capitalist has a single, driving concern: *Il ne me manque plus qu'une chose* (Only one thing remains to be done), he excitedly tells his visitor, *c'est de nettoyer les figures, on ferait de l'or avec, bien exploitées* (that is to clean the figures—one could make a lot of money.)[38]

---

[32] Champfleury, 9.
[33] Champfleury, 10.
[34] Champfleury, 21.
[35] Champfleury, 22.
[36] Champfleury, 23-24.
[37] Champfleury, 26.
[38] Champfleury, 28.

Erik Butler

Champfleury's narrative alter ego reacts with fascinated horror:

. . . je regardai cet homme plus curieux que tout son musée. Ses habits semblaient avoir servi à des pièces de la collection, mises au rebut. Sa figure était pâle et jaune. . . . L'oeil était vitreux, d'un bleu clair ressemblant à de certaines porcelaines. Si on avait pu retrancher la voix, cet homme eût pu passer pour une figure de cire; car ces gestes avaient le décousu et la raideur. Sa physiognomie génerale n'offrait rien d'humain, il semblait sortir du moule où se coulent les criminels.

(. . . I looked at this man, who was stranger than his entire museum. His clothing seemed to have been part of the collection, cast-offs. His face was pale and yellow. . . . His gaze was vitreous, the bright blue of certain kinds of china. If it had been possible to remove his voice, this man could have passed for a wax dummy, for his gestures had a disjointed and stiff quality. His physiognomy, in general, presented nothing human; he seemed to come from the mold where criminals are made.)[39]

Earlier, the dummy beckoning to visitors near the Champs-Élysées was transformed from the witness of a misdeed into a mannequin radiating criminality; now, the weird man who is his human equivalent has changed from a lowly role managing the cabinet of curiosities into its owner and orchestrator. In the process, it is as if he has shed his humanity for a waxen and mechanical body. Just as dummies can seemingly come alive, people can lose their soul and become inanimate.

[N]ous n'avons pas de temps à perdre ([W]e have no time to lose),[40] the hellish entrepreneur declares, once he learns that he is in the company of parties whose artistic abilities can help him revive his wax figures. *[N]ous retournons aux Champs-Élysées où il y a du beau monde* ([W]e're going back to the Champs-Élysées, where there's high society)[41]: already, he envisions a return that will consecrate his status in the new order.

The story's "punch line" is that the freakish entrepreneur, before he can remobilize his waxen army to march upon the Elysian Fields in a terrifying display of false immortality, absconds with the likeness of a particularly beautiful woman—a dummy he has named "Julie"[42]—leaving his amputated wife behind with the rest of the broken bodies in his gallery. When the narrator and his friends return some two weeks later to treat themselves to another look at the spectacle, the *femme cul-de-jatte* indignantly tells them that it is no more: she caught her husband in bed with the *gueuse* (tramp,)[43] and the pair stole away in the night.

Benjamin, who sought the archaic in the modern and the modern in the archaic, wrote the continuation of works begun a century earlier by others. The *Arcades Project* is his version of the Eternal Return: like his forebears Blanqui and Nietzsche, Benjamin envisions a world in which he is not the plaything of historical fatality, but instead the master of his destiny. This underlying fantasy defies whatever god(s) may exist.

---

[39] Champfleury, 31.

[40] Champfleury, 29.

[41] Champfleury, 29.

[42] This figure, *la reine des belles* (the queen of the beauties [33]) clearly implies a parody of Rousseau's *Nouvelle Héloïse* and its optimistic vision of humanity.

[43] Champfleury, 37.

An exhaustive tour of Benjamin's phantasmagorical Paris would be exhausting, and indeed, like the "talking cure" proposed by Freud, interminable. It is, however, necessary that we cease our wanderings at some point. In the spirit of the labyrinthine *Arcades Project*, and having passed the halfway point of our walk, we now turn to a diptych of the monsters that, like modern minotaurs, lurk in the pages of Benjamin's Paris and, like Champfleury's hellish entrepreneur of 1848, offer reflections of earlier and later revolutionary climates.

Benjamin makes passing reference to Pétrus Borel (1809-1859) and Isidore Ducasse, "Comte de Lautréamont" (1846-1870).[44] The latter, especially thanks to his "rediscovery" by the Surrealists, now enjoys a fixed—if eccentric—position in the French literary canon; the former remains largely unknown outside of a limited circle of specialists. These authors are significant not just because their period of artistic ferment coincides with times of revolutionary upheaval (1830 and 1870), but also because of the self-stylization they engineered in their works, whose mystifying results can be seen as analogues to Benjamin's cryptic mode of writing. Borel made himself known as "the Lycanthrope," and Lautréamont as "the Vampire."

Borel and his friends, who became known as the *Bousingots*, formed the Romantic avant-garde at the famous theater riots surrounding Victor Hugo's *Hernani* (1830).[45] Baudelaire wrote appreciatively of his predecessor, who represented for him the *expression la plus. . . paradoxale* (most paradoxical expression) of the new poetic *esprit* in his *haine aristocratique. . . contre les rois et contre la bourgeoisie* (aristocratic hatred. . . for kings and the bourgeoisie) under Louis Philippe's rule.[46] Nominally a republican—before the word came to signify the status quo of the ruling classes—Borel, like Baudelaire, was essentially a keen-eyed misanthrope (and, also like Baudelaire, he led a squalid, largely unrecognized life before dying prematurely and in penury).

Borel used his works to fashion an outrageous persona he intended to be mistaken for his true identity. *Champavert* (1833) was not only the title of a book—provocatively subtitled *Contes immoraux* (Immoral Tales)—but also the name of the work's "author." That is, Borel adopted a mask when he took the stage of publication. Or, to be more precise—and also more confusing—in another book that appeared the same year as *Champavert*, Borel assumed the appellation "Champavert" for himself. In the "Notice sur Champavert" appended to the second edition of *Rhapsodies*, a volume of poetry, "Champavert," the "same" party who had committed suicide in the eponymous story, revealed himself as the "true" author and "Pétrus Borel" as a pseudonym. In other words, "Pétrus Borel" was supposed to have killed himself, not "Champavert." Borel thereby declared the fictitious persona to be real and himself to be a fake (notwithstanding the impossibility that a man might record his own death).[47] Pétrus Borel, a.k.a. Champavert, a.k.a. *le Lycanthrope*, played a game of mystification by presenting a double work of fiction—made-up stories vouched for by a made-up person who enacted the "death of the author" over one hundred years before literary criticism caught on to the concept—as an authentic record of fact.[48] The spurious persona thereby fashioned, whose every word points back to his impossible

---

[44] Borel: 335/260, 353/276, 931/772. Lautréamont: 87/37, 120/71, 682/549.

[45] Enid Starkie, *Petrus Borel: the Lycanthrope: His Life and Times* (New York: New Directions, 1954) contains a vivid account of the author's milieu and exploits.

[46] Quoted in Benjamin 931/772. Cf. Baudelaire, 1104-7 (*L'art romantique*, "Réflexions sur quelques-un de mes contemporains," V).

[47] Jean-Luc Steinmetz, "Le retour du lycanthrope," in Pétrus Borel, *Champavert: Contes immoraux* (Paris: Phébus, 2002), 9-26.

[48] Or, to put matters in somewhat different terms, Borel trumps literary theory by multiplying the sites of authorial identity and literalizing, in advance, what Roland Barthes would speak of metaphorically.

(auto)biography, does not vanish behind the tales he tells so much as appears, spectrally, among them. Champavert, the supposed suicide, outlived the man who invented him. . . .

The lycanthrope's literary kinsman, the vampire, is the product of similar trickery and artifice. Factually, the author of *Les chants de Maldoror* was Isidore Ducasse—a young transplant from Uruguay who sought his literary fortunes in Paris some forty years after Borel. However, in the sphere of illusion that Ducasse created on the pages of the *Chants*—and bequeathed to his readers and commentators—matters are considerably more convoluted. Ducasse's game of vampiric personation occurs through the equation of Lautréamont, the work's fictive "author," on the one hand, and Maldoror, the "protagonist," on the other. Writer and character merge, diverge, merge again, and so on, in the space opened by writing.

> *[Maldoror] s'aperçut. . . qu'il était né méchant. . . . Il n'était pas menteur, il avouait la vérité et disait qu'il était cruel. Humains, avez vous entendu? Il ose le redire avec cette plume qui tremble!*
>
> ([Maldoror] perceived he was born wicked. . . . No liar, he confessed the truth, admitting he was cruel. Mankind, did you hear? He dares repeat it with this quivering quill!)[49]

This passage initially discusses Maldoror in the third person and situates him in the past through a detached narrative voice. Then, as the (anti)hero's acknowledgement of his inherent evil is described, the voice aligns itself with him. Protagonist and author meet up in the moment of written confession.[50]

Rumors—excited whispers breathlessly passed from one person to another like a disease—surround Maldoror.

> *Les uns disent qu'il est accablé d'une espèce de folie originelle, depuis son enfance. D'autres croient savoir qu'il est d'une cruauté extrême et instinctive, . . .et que ses parents en sont morts de douleur. Il y en a qui prétendent qu'on l'a flétri d'un surnom dans sa jeunesse. . . . Ce surnom était le* vampire*!*
>
> (Some say he has been stricken since childhood by a type of inherited madness. Others hold that he is of an extreme and instinctive cruelty. . . and that his parents died of grief because of it. There are those who maintain that he was branded with a nickname in his youth. . . . This nickname was *the vampire!*)[51]

The surname "vampire" is just one designation among others; it is a mark applied from without, rather than an emanation of inner essence. Yet Maldoror *has* no inner essence; he exists only in perpetual opposition to God and His World. The titles that the Adversary of the *Chants* receives present him as a remorseless, parasitic

---

[49] Isidore Ducasse/Comte de Lautréamont, *Oeuvres complètes*, ed. Hubert Juin (Paris: Gallimard, 1973), 19-20; *Maldoror and the Complete Works of the Comte de Lautréamont*, trans. Alexis Lykiard (Cambridge, MA: Exact Change, 1994), 29.

[50] That is, as Derrida would observe, an infinite deferral of the present—a "space" outside time, never given to experience.

[51] Lautréamont, 42/46. Cf. Jean Michel Olivier, *Lautréamont: le texte du vampire* (Lausanne: L'âge d'homme, 1981).

creature with a toxic embrace, e.g., *celui qui ne sait pas pleurer* (he who does not know how to cry), *le frère de la sangsue* (the brother of the leech), and *l'homme aux lèvres de soufre* (the man with lips of sulfur). Contagion is his core, and it spreads from his mouth and hand.

Thus, of all the names Maldoror receives, *vampire* comes closest to capturing his formless, seething substance. Lautréamont appears where Maldoror takes up the pen, and vice-versa: *je jette un long regard de satisfaction sur la dualité qui me compose* (I cast a long look of satisfaction upon the duality that composes me.)[52]

Ducasse's bizarre work culminates in the appropriately outrageous act of self-canonization among the patron saints of French letters by means of murder. The key to the intrigue is an epistolary exchange reproducing, in miniature, the dangers that the *Chants* hold for the reader in general.[53] Mervyn, a comely adolescent, catches Maldoror's attention, and the latter sends him a confidential missive. The missive concludes with *une tâche de sang* (a bloodstain) and *trois étoiles* (three stars).[54] Mervyn writes back a *lettre coupable* (guilty letter).[55] The boy expresses shameful lust, but even more importantly, he performs an action just like Maldoror's: *Je me dispense de signer et en cela je vous imite* (I excuse myself from signing, and in that I imitate you),[56] he writes. This move is fatal for it sets the boy adrift in the mysterious element of non-identity that his seducer amphibiously[57] inhabits.

When Mervyn finally meets his correspondent in person, the latter throws him unceremoniously—and in almost slapstick fashion—into a bag and beats him within an inch of his life. Maldoror then hangs the boy headfirst from the Vendôme Column and swings him through a series of mounting and expanding revolutions until his body is traveling on a plane perpendicular to the obelisk. The fiend releases the rope, and Mervyn goes flying across the river to the Left Bank.

---

[52] Lautréamont, 246/203.

[53] Hence the words of warning with which the book begins: *Plût au ciel que le lecteur, enhardi et devenu momentanément féroce comme ce qu'il lit, trouve, sans se désorienter, son chemin abrupt et sauvage, à travers les marécages désolés de ces pages sombres et pleines de poison; car, à moins qu'il n'apporte dans sa lecture une logique rigoureuse et une tension d'esprit égale au moins à sa défiance, les émanations mortelles de ce livre imbiberont son âme comme l'eau le sucre. Il n'est pas bon que tout le monde lise les pages qui vont suivre: quelques-uns seuls savoureront ce fruit amer sans danger.* (May it please heaven that the reader, emboldened, and become momentarily as fierce as what he reads, find without loss of bearings a wild and abrupt way across the desolate swamps of these sombre, poison-filled pages. For unless he bring to his reading a rigorous logic and mental application at least tough enough to balance his distrust, the deadly issues of this book will lap up his soul as water does sugar. It would not be good for everyone to read the pages which follow; only the few may relish this bitter fruit without danger [17/27].)

[54] Lautréamont, 241/199.

[55] Lautréamont, 245/202.

[56] Lautréamont, 245/202.

[57] Gaston Bachelard, *Lautréamont*, trans. Robert S. Dupree (Dallas: The Dallas Institute of Humanities and Culture, 1986), 13-32. Cf. Alain Paris, "Le bestiaire des *Chants de Maldoror*," in Philippe Fédy, Alain Paris, Jean-Marc Poiron, Lucienne Rochon, *Quatre lectures de Lautréamont* (Paris: A.-G. Nizet, 1972), 79-144; pp. 84-7 of this study provide a list of over 120 real and fantastic animals with which Maldoror overlaps at various points of the *Chants* (e.g., eagle, basilisk, crab, toad, snail, hornet, rat, and shark).

Erik Butler

> *Mervyn… ressemble à une comète trainant après elle sa queue flamboyante. . . . Dans le parcours de sa parabole, le condamné à mort fend l'atmosphère. . . et son corps va frapper le dôme du Panthéon, tandis que la corde étreint, en partie, de ses replis, la paroi de l'immense coupole. C'est sur sa superficie sphérique et convexe . . . qu'on voit, à toute heure du jour, un squelette desséché, resté suspendu.*
>
> (Mervyn . . . resembles a comet trailing after it its flaming tail. . . In the course of his parabola, the doomed one cleaves the air. . . and his body hits the dome of the Panthéon while the rope's coils partly lasso the superstructure of the vast cupola. There upon its spherical and convex surface area . . . at any hour of the day a wasted skeleton may be seen, stuck hanging.)[58]

This finale, which leaves words behind and writes itself immediately into the real, ratifies the power of vampiric writing. Not only does the exchange of letters, by delivering Mervyn into Maldoror's clutches, make the *tour de force* possible; this operation alters the landscape in which it inscribes itself: "at any hour of the day," supposedly, the boy's remains are still visible as the signature of the vampire's immortality.

Mervyn's correspondence with the fiend leads to his physical annihilation, but also to an afterlife. His fractured body eternally scars the summit of the Panthéon. This structure, which was originally built as a church, came to house the remains of the gods of French letters. In effect, Maldoror forcibly lodges the youth among the "Immortals." Because Mervyn has fatefully imitated Maldoror and become like him, his remains read as the apotheosis of the vampire, whose name in turn reveals itself as a coded description of the triumph of evil: the *Mal d'Aurore*.[59] And because Lautréamont is Maldoror's alter ego, the diabolical Count ascends to the heavens at the same moment.

What is the relationship between Benjamin and the werewolf Champavert, the conjuror of undead automata Champfleury, and the vampiric Comte de Lautréamont? The author of the *Arcades Project* also published under pseudonyms,[60] and, notwithstanding his readers' assumptions, he also, as I hope to have demonstrated, had an affinity for the perverse amply on display in the pages of his masterwork. Benjamin's fondness for occult subjects and his predilection to adopt a riddling style are also matters of fact. It would speak to his resourcefulness and genius if, at the time of National Socialism, he made his own the dissimulation and ruse of authors who, in the revolutionary years of 1830, 1848, and 1870, employed the pen as a sword to perform operations on a social reality like the ones they, too, found oppressive. At any rate, Benjamin never sought the dogmatic affirmation of any creed, religious or political, but instead appreciated the struggle of dialectical encounters with the deeply unjust world in which he found himself.

The *Arcades Project*, a sprawling mass of bricks and mortar, does not yield a choir singing the *Marseillaise*, the *Internationale*, or any other revolutionary hymn. The voices that echo in and between its fragments are closer to the whispers of conspirators seeking influence and power.[61] Notwithstanding the status Benjamin's

---

[58] Lautréamont, 265-66/218; translation slightly modified.

[59] A pun first pointed out by René Crevel, "Lautréamont, ta bague d'aurore nous protège," *Le Disque vert*, 1925 (text reproduced in Marie-Louise Terray, ed., *Commentaire des Chants de Maldoror, Lettres, Poésies I et II* (Paris: Gallimard/Folio, 1997), 114.

[60] "Ardor," in his first articles, for the journal *Der Anfang*; toward the end of his life, as "O. E. Tal" and "Detlef Holz."

[61] Cf. 745-63/603-19.

writings have achieved in the critical canon, his work—and especially the *Arcades Project*—offers more practice than theory. Even Benjamin's critical essays engage with their subject matter and the reader in a way that, for the most part, avoids analysis in favor of gnomic statements, provocative formulations, and aphorisms. This mode of writing demands of readers that they face the text as a series of obstacles; Benjamin's thought does not always unfold clearly, and it therefore becomes necessary to revisit a passage several times or to strike out on a course of nonlinear reading that uncovers points of contact and communication between isolated parts of his works.

The *Arcades Project* spins a web of intrigue inherited from earlier generations. The reader of Benjamin's work, today, must disentangle many knots in order to move through the text. Some of these points of confusion cannot be resolved, for an exhaustive commentary would mean that the past, present, and future have all been disclosed to finite human understanding—an ahistorical and, notwithstanding Benjamin's flirtations with dark powers, a blasphemous notion.

"Mystification . . . is an apotropaic magic," this essay's epigraph reads. As has been remarked on more than one occasion, Benjamin does not come out and say what he means, but rather skirts the issue, coyly gesturing toward a truth that has little reassuring about it, anyway. The *Arcades Project* presents as many obstacles to understanding as it offers insights, but these barriers are not simply impasses: instead, they represent points of resistance, where images are mobilized both to confound the enemy and to beckon to allies who still find themselves "on the other side." The examples offered by Benjamin's favorites, Baudelaire and Blanqui, as well as those of kindred authors (Borel, Champfleury, Lautréamont), reveal a creative perversity—or, if one prefers, a seditiousness—that forms the most substantive aspect of Benjamin's work.

Erik Butler teaches German and comparative literature at Emory University. He has written two books: *Metamorphoses of the Vampire: Cultural Transformation and the Modern Monster, 1732-1933*, and *The Bellum Grammaticale and the Rise of European Literature*; both titles are scheduled to appear in 2010.

RAYMOND ROUSSEL'S SELF HELP NOTES (A COMMENTARY ON BOB PERELMAN'S "CHRONIC MEANINGS")

Alan Ramón Clinton

If I could at least find some meaning for my chronic symptoms, even if I can't cure them. Reducing them all to **the single fact is matter**[1] for fantasy, but I would settle for a thread of some kind. Already people are coming to me, unsolicited, and asking advice on interface. But, it's like I'm sending telegrams to myself, and **five words can say only** so much. Ordinary things like **black sky at night, reasonably** integrated into the logic of cause and affect, have the power to fill me with an utter sense of dread. No matter what I say **I am, the irrational residue** of what I'm not haunts me more than anything.

When I was a kid, my friends and I stumbled on a **blown up chain link fence.** We knew at the time it wasn't really blown up, but we began to believe our own lie and the thought that it might really have been blown up returned **next morning stronger than ever.** And by **midnight the pain is almost** palpable, we think that we're the chain link fence in the act of being blown up. **The train seems practically expressive** as it goes by, mocking us.

It's a story familiar as a story can be. **Society has broken into bands the nineteenth century was sure** would end up burning **characters in the withering capital.**

The heroic figure straddled the globe—my father. **The clouds enveloped the tallest** mountains, rendering his reaction to the death of his own father invisible. **Tens of thousands of drops** of rain could have fallen and I would have been unable to know if he was crying. **The monster struggled with Milton** Bradley, and it all depended on a roll of the dice.

I thought that **on our wedding night I** would broach the subject of my fear concerning fathering a retarded child. I could tell it as a Gothic Romance, "**The sorrow burned deeper than** the fjords of Norway. **Grimly I pursed what violence** destiny had chosen for me, **a trap, a catch, a** zine." **Fans stand up, yelling their** approval of the stage version. **Lights go off in houses** as couples are inspired to at least have the chance of avoiding the birth canal. It would be neither an essay nor a novel, **a fictional look, not quite** a fiction. The royalties are not important. **To be able to talk** about it is reward enough.

---

[1] Bob Perelman, "Chronic Meanings," in *Postmodern American Poetry* (New York: Norton, 1994), 501-504. The words in bold represent the lines of Perelman's poem, in order, which in the original all begin with capital letters and end in periods.

The coffee sounds intriguing but looks even more so under the expert hand of Jean Luc Godard. **She put her cards on** the table and admitted that boredom had driven her to this point. **What had been comfortable subjectivity** suddenly degenerated into a very awkward conversation. **The lesson we can each** take from this is to always load the burning deck.

An hour a day is **not enough time to thoroughly** exhaust my resources. **Structure announces structure and takes** structure as its structure. **He caught his breath in** spades. **The vista disclosed no immediate** problems.

Another Saturday night, **alone with a pun in** the oven. **The clock face and the** mountain face were my only company. Although I could have leaned on the **rock of ages, a modern** prosthetic seemed more in order. **I think I had better** have a plan A.

I know all about globalism and multinational, cosmetic-driven satellite empire, but just **now this particular mall seemed** different. **The bag of groceries had** a way of forcing you to decide just what your life would become, **whether a biographical junkheap or** something that would make people tremble. **In no sense do I** condone turning to a vegetable, but **these fields make me feel** like opening up, admit that I once proposed to **Mount Rushmore in a sonnet.** Some in the party tried sestinas, **so it's not as if** my scheme was completely harebrained.

That always happened until one day **she spread her arms and** asked **the sky if anything grew which left a lot of** one's evenings and weekends free.

No one could help it fulfill the dreams its father had for the future. **I ran farther than I** had ever run before, and when I got there I died. **That wasn't a good one. Now put down your pencils.**

They won't pull that over two or three yards. **Standing up to the Empire** requires the aid of a professional like Hans Haacke. Even so, your wife may silence everyone–**stop it, screaming in a** voice reserved for medieval torture and well-done porno. The calm before the storm comes with **the smell of pine needles.**

I've thought about psychotherapy, but **economics is not my strong** point. **Until one of us reads** the instructions, this argument is pointless. **I took a breath, then** ran into the burning building. **The singular heroic vision, unilaterally** inspired, came at the wrong moment.

Gregorian **voices imitate the very words** used at Greg's funeral: "His **bed was one place where** he always mixed business and pleasure. He knew what summed up **a personal life, a toaster. Memorized experience can't be completely** faithful to an individual as mysterious as he."

Sometimes, while reading about the paradigm shift enacted by quantification of the speed of light, I'm paralyzed by **the impossibility of the simplest** procedures, like not being punched in the face by an angry motorist, losing my balance, and falling headfirst into traffic. Now someone might say, "You obviously can't handle books of such a specialized nature, **so shut the fucking thing** and realize that the world is divided into

Alan Ramón Clinton

two types of people, those who read primary texts and those who read secondary texts." But that same person, upon starting to see me tear, would then say, "**Now I've gone and put** my foot in your mouth, **but that makes the world** go round."

The point I am trying to make, in case one day I should become someone's Dr. Schreber, is that I feel like my life has been wasted **like a cartoon worm on** benzedrine, which has speech without a physical mouth, when all I ever really wanted was to be a real man on quaaludes, having **a physical mouth without speech. If taken to an extreme**, this conceit could lead to Manicheism.

"**The phone is for someone** who really knows how to use it," I proclaimed in a moment of rare charisma, "like Dr. Freud." At the moment I uttered the statement, it walked away from me like a distant woman in a train station, and yet **the next second it seemed** trite. **But did that really mean** I thought the statement was stale or hackneyed? I tried to ignore the ramifications, **yet Los Angeles is full** of agoraphobic dandies just like me.

Naturally enough I turn to writing as an escape from life, thus rendering questionable its efficacy as a form of therapy. When it comes to the mind, **some things are reversible, some** are not. We should be happy for even that malleability. With physical laws, **you don't have that choice. I'm going to Jo's for** comfort food.

Now I've heard everything, he said in a tone that made one believe the statement was not only not stale, but not even quoted. **One time when I used** quotes in the transcript of one of his speeches, he threatened to sue me for **the amount of dissatisfaction involved.** Believe me, when you've seriously considered life at the whim of the elements, you'll discover **the weather isn't all it's** purported to be.

You'd think people would have a "category e," **or that they would invent** one in order to justify whatever they want to do. **At least if the emotional** elements of the problem were properly addressed, no one in their right mind would begrudge **the presence of an illusion.**

The perfect place to write a great work of literature would be a **symbiosis of home and prison. Then, having become superfluous, time** could really come into its own. **One has to give to** maintain appearances, prioritize. For instance, there are only two things I want to **taste: the first and last.**

I remember the look in my mother's eyes when I told her I wanted to make impressions of Africa for future use. **It was the first time** she had ever grimaced and I had **some gorgeous swelling feeling that** the **success which owes its fortune** to hard work would soon be a thing of the past.

Come what may it can't be any worse than that. **There are a number of** ways to make a rebus **but there is only one** way to tame one. **That's why I want to** declare a moratorium on comparison and contrast.

ISSN 1942-3381

Alan Ramón Clinton

Alan Ramón Clinton is the author of a scholarly monograph, *Mechanical Occult: Automatism, Modernism, and the Specter of Politics* (Peter Lang: 2004), and a volume of poetry, *Horatio Alger's Keys* (BlazeVox: 2008). He currently lectures at the University of Miami.

THE SOVEREIGN EXCEPTION: NOTES ON SCHMITT'S WORD THAT SOVEREIGN IS HE WHO DECIDES ON THE EXCEPTION
Bruno Gullì

"Sovereign is he who decides on the exception"–this is how *Political Theology* famously starts (2005: 5). For Carl Schmitt, who follows Hobbes, the concept of sovereignty, as used in political philosophy and in juridical theory, is the secularization of a theological concept–but of a decisionist rather than rational theology. Sovereignty is decision and domination. It is not simply a technical concept in state theory (which could be understood according to its internal and external aspects)[1] but rather the personal privilege of the ruler. But what is it, precisely, to decide on the exception? In a sense, the answer is contained in the paradoxical figure of the sovereign, in sovereignty as a "borderline concept," "one pertaining to the outermost sphere" (*ibid.*) Schmitt says that although the sovereign "stands outside the normally valid legal system, he nevertheless belongs to it" (p.7). He belongs to it precisely in virtue of his capacity to decide on the exception. As Tracy B. Strong notes in his foreword to the 2005 edition of *Political Theology* from Chicago University Press, for Schmitt "it is the essence of sovereignty *both* to decide what is an exception *and* to make the decisions appropriate to that exception" (p.xii). Here one sees the complexity of this apparently simple and straightforward truth. The question is: What enables the sovereign to decide on the exception and thus be sovereign? The answer is found not in Schmitt, but in Walter Benjamin: violence, and the violence always "implicated in the problematic nature of the law itself" (1978: 287). But let us pursue this more slowly. The question I just posed can also be rephrased as follows: What gives the sovereign that special capacity to see that there is an exception, a state of emergency, and consequently decide on it? Does the sovereign become sovereign because he can decide on the exception, or is it rather the case that he can decide on it because he is already sovereign? Depending on the answer, the hyperbolic truth enunciated by Schmitt acquires a different meaning. In the first case, any person with special powers (or even simply a special sensibility) could be recognized as sovereign. This would be an honorary status conferred on him. The implication here would be that there actually is, objectively speaking, an exception and the sovereign is he who can recognize and handle it. But of course Schmitt does not speak of any sense of recognition, understanding, and judgment, but only of decision–though one would think that a decision can only come after a judgment is made on rational grounds, or, as Aristotle says in *Nicomachean Ethics*, after deliberation. It is perhaps the concept of "genuine decision," of which Schmitt speaks in the Preface to the second edition of *Political Theology* (p.3), which comes close to this first sense of the statement. A genuine

---

[1] As David Held says, "The doctrine of sovereignty has . . . two distinct dimensions: the first concerned with the 'internal' aspect of sovereignty; the second concerned with the external . . . The former involves the belief that a political body established as sovereign rightly exercises the 'supreme command' over a particular society. . . . The latter, external, dimension involves the claim that here is no final and absolute authority above and beyond the sovereign state" (1995: 100).

decision is not necessarily that which is made by those who have the legal, constitutional power to decide. In fact, they can be, and most of the times are, completely mistaken in their decisions. A genuine decision requires some inherent and special powers. In this case, the decision would decide of the sovereign. In making the decision, X would rise to the status of sovereign.

In the second case, the sovereign is he who has the power (in the strictly political, institutional sense–a power always grounded in violence) to decide on the exception. This is, for instance, the case of G. W. Bush rebuking the UN before attacking Iraq: "We don't need permission," or his decision to open the detention camp at Guantanamo. As I write (June 12, 2008) a divided US Supreme Court has ruled that the Guantanamo "enemy combatants" have the right to challenge their detention. The Associated Press reports that Justice Anthony Kennedy, writing for the court, said: "The laws and constitution are designed to survive, and remain in force, in *extraordinary* times" (emphasis added). This is a blow to Bush's sovereignty and a challenge to the Schmittian notion of sovereignty. To be sure, it would challenge only the second of the two meanings of Schmitt's truth given by Strong, that is, the sovereign may very well decide on what constitutes an exception, but he has to listen to other institutional voices and sites of power before deciding on the appropriate measures – he can disagree, but he has to abide. Thus, the sovereign is sovereign only to an extent. Probably, Schmitt would blame this state of affairs on constitutional liberalism and the rule of democracy. In any case, it would be difficult to prove here that (and if) the decision made by the sovereign is a genuine one. In fact, the exception itself can be a mere fabrication of the sovereign, which acquires dubious legitimacy on the basis neither of ethics nor of a violence travestied as force of law, but of mere and raw violence. In this case, it is not the exception, the state of emergency, which calls forth the sovereign decision, but the other way around, the sovereign decision creates the exception, or state of emergency. Then, the state of emergency is not, in Benjamin's sense, a *real* one. In Strong's important explication of Schmitt's truth, it is the first meaning of "decide" (which is also the least apparent), which lends Schmitt's theory of sovereignty an ontological, rather than simply technical (i.e., juridical), dimension. Although, contrary to Strong, I doubt that Schmitt's decisionism can be weakened on that account.

The assumption in Schmitt (both on a logical and on an existential level) is that the exception is an essential part of the order of things. However, there are philosophies that have no use for the concept of the exception. For instance, in Leibniz's philosophy of individuality there is no exception, and this is so because every individual being is complete, unique, and thus exceptional. But when the exception can be so generalized, it also loses its meaning and reason to be. It is no coincidence that Leibniz offers one of the earliest critiques of the concept of sovereignty and of Hobbes's philosophy in general. In Schmitt, on the contrary, the concept of the exception makes sense because it is contained in the concept of the sovereign; it *is* the sovereign. Using Leibniz's language, one could say that the exception is the predicate of the sovereign subject. Thus, it is not the case that the sovereign realizes that there is an objective state of need and thereupon he acts decisively. Instead, the sovereign chooses which state is to be raised to the level of the exception, or simply fabricates it. An illustration would be the war on terror, and particularly the war against Iraq. One would think that there are many other more urgent situations in the world that require attention and perhaps intervention, for instance, poverty, child labor, inadequate education. Yet, none of these are raised to the status of the exception, and the reason for this neglect must be sought precisely in the fact that they are not contained in the concept of the person of the sovereign, as a predicate in a subject. They are other than the sovereign; in fact, they are instances of bare life.[2]

It is easy to see that, despite its brilliance[3] and internal logical coherence, Schmitt's doctrine is also deeply flawed. It says that the decision on the exception is a privilege of the sovereign, that the sovereign is a sovereign precisely in virtue of his capacity to decide; yet, it does not say how he receives this capacity nor why is this capacity not generalized to become a privilege of each and every individual, the dignity of individuation,[4] which is probably the only *real* exception. Ultimately, the justification for Schmitt's theory is the fear determined by the supposedly evil character of human nature. In the last chapter of *Political Theology*, he says:

> Every political idea in one way or another takes a position on the "nature" of man and presupposes that he is either "by nature good" or "by nature evil." (p.56)

However, this is not correct, and not only today when the question of human nature has ceased to have the importance it did have in the 17th, 18th, and 19th centuries. Long before, even Aristotle's political science was built on the idea that the human being is by nature endowed with the twofold capacity of being good or evil, and that this capacity changed into a state depending on the decision one made and on the habit built thereafter. But by nature, one is neither good nor evil, as this would eliminate the possibility for change and freedom, because what is by nature in one condition cannot be brought into another condition:

> A stone, for instance, by nature moves downwards, and habituation could not make it move upwards, not even if you threw it up ten thousand times to habituate it. (Aristotle 1999: 1103a 21-23)

It is true that Schmitt intends to meet this objection when he adds:

> The issue [of human nature] can only be clouded by pedagogic and economic explanations, but not evaded. (p.56; brackets added)

Yet, I think that the objection still stands. In the case of Aristotle, for instance, the importance of education does not simply explain away the issue of human nature; more fundamentally, it provides a structure for the practice of human freedom (and of the responsibility that comes with it), which Schmitt of course intends to dispense with. We have already seen Schmitt's concept of "genuine decision" (p.3). This is to be found in the context of the notion that "the political is the total" (p.2) and of the description of the three types of legal thinking: normativist, institutional, and decisionist. The first emphasizes impersonal rules and leads to the bureaucratization of society; the second "leads to the pluralism characteristic of a feudal-corporate growth that

---

[2] On the relationship between sovereign power and bare life, see Agamben (1998).

[3] See Schwab's introduction to *Political Theology*.

[4] I have been studying the concept of dignity of individuation in relation to Leibniz's writings on political philosophy and ethics. I should be able to present the results of this study in a forthcoming book on labor and sovereignty.

is devoid of sovereignty" (p.3); the third, which relies on personal decision and which Schmitt opts for, needs to be able to determine what a *genuine* decision is. For Schmitt, "genuine" does not have anything to do with an ethical or politico-ontological situation, or with existential authenticity. It is political in the Schmittian sense of the distinction of friend and enemy. However, despite Schmitt's assertion to the contrary, this is not the only possible sense of the political. I do not disagree with Schmitt's critique of liberalism. Yet, "political" should not be seen as an either/or between Schmitt's totalistic conception (which in principle is not incorrect) and liberalism. In fact, besides this either/or (and one could say: at the level of neither/nor, i.e., of potentiality), "political" also addresses the capacity for social transformation. This can be utopian, anarchist, yet it is the modality of the political that has no use of sovereignty. It is not that which calls forth a normativist or institutional legal theory, both of which risk trampling the individual, nor is it individualistic; rather, it highlights the tension between what-is and what-could-be, the moment of non-law, that is, a world devoid of any law which is not the one of the dignity of individuation. Of course, Schmitt would find the idea of a radical transformation of the social completely unrealistic. Yet, his defense of sovereignty is, realistically, unable to bring about security for all–given that this is ultimately its main aim. Thus, in *The Concept of the Political*, starting from the premise of an irreducible antagonism between friend and enemy, Schmitt very logically shows the impossibility of perpetual peace (though he is not addressing Kant's concept here). The fact is that for Schmitt the permanent regime of war, which seems to be a natural foundation of the social and the political, could only be ended by "a war against war" (1996: 36)–in other words, a paradox. That would be a war of the pacifists against the nonpacifists, but still a war, and, as such, a political position and a political act. Interestingly, the end of war is also the end of the political, and the situation becomes really paradoxical: "the last absolute war of humanity." Schmitt continues:

> Such a war is necessarily unusually intense and inhuman because, by transcending the limits of the political framework, it simultaneously degrades the enemy into moral and other categories and is forced to make him a monster that must not only be defeated but also utterly destroyed. (p.36)

Thus, there is no exit from war. A regime of war, understood as the antagonism of friend and enemy, is preferable to the end of war with the utter destruction of the enemy. Schmitt does not see any alternative for humanity to emerge from the logic of violence and domination that is apparently connatural to it. As a consequence, he chooses to give a theoretical justification for this fact. To an extent, this might be understandable, as Schmitt was writing *The Concept of the Political* and *Political Theology* in the aftermath of World War I. However, with World War II the notion of the utter destruction of the enemy became tragically concrete,[5] both with the Nazi final solution and with the American (sovereign) decision to use the atomic bomb against Japan.[6] What Schmitt had articulated as the paradox of pacifism became the utmost degree of the total war. This makes Schmitt's partisan philosophy of the political prophetic and realistic on the one hand, yet also difficult to accept on the other. The state of the exception, from Auschwitz and Hiroshima to Guantanamo and

---

[5] The notion of the utter destruction of the enemy is of course not completely novel in history. Schmitt himself mentions, in this context, the extermination of the Indians of North America (1996: 54).

[6] The initial name of "Operation Infinite Justice" for the war on terror started in 2001, soon changed to "Operation Enduring Freedom," evidently belongs to the same logic of the utter destruction of the enemy.

Abu Ghraib, proves to be outside of the political, in the realm that belongs to violence, cruelty, gangsterism, and criminal justice.

There is no alternative for humanity because, as Schmitt says, "Humanity is not a political concept" (p.55). Humanity "has no enemy" (p.54). But what if humanity's enemy is precisely something like this logic of sovereignty that seems to be unassailable and necessary? From Schmitt's position, it follows logically (again) that humanity "as such cannot wage a war" and this "because the enemy does not cease to be a human being" (*ibid.*). But what if humanity's war is not simply political in the Schmittian sense, but politico-philosophical, that is, ontological, in the sense of aiming at reconstituting the essence of humanity itself? In other words, what if the enemy is not a group of particular, concrete human beings, but the conditions of possibility of violence, domination, and the very antagonism of friend and enemy? Indeed, physically eliminating human beings perceived and conceived as enemies is what gangsters and the various mafias do very well. One does not need a theory of the political for that. Certainly, there is more than this in what Schmitt says. He says that the word humanity is confiscated, invoked and monopolized by one state or an alliance of states to wage war against an enemy who is denied "the quality of being human" (p.54). He is correct in saying:

> When a state fights its political enemy in the name of humanity, it is not a war for the sake of humanity, but a war wherein a particular state seeks to usurp a universal concept against its military opponent. (*ibid.*)

It is in this context that he refers to the extermination of the Native Americans—and it is evident how relevant this type of rhetoric is today with the notion of humanitarian war. But again, against Schmitt's extreme realism, or cynicism, one can hold on to the idea, advanced by many, that, with an incredible amount of work and commitment, there is hope for humanity to exit the logic of war, of politics in the Schmittian sense, of violence and domination. For this to happen, however, the concept of sovereignty must be discarded, or even utterly destroyed.

If politics is antagonism and war, or the ever-present possibility of war, if this antagonism cannot be eradicated, and if "justice does not belong to the concept of war" (p.49), then the possibility of a world of social justice is ruled out *a priori*. As I have said, I agree with the critique of liberalism, but not necessarily for the reasons given by Schmitt (e.g., liberalism entails the end of the political)—or perhaps I would not characterize liberalism in exactly the same way. I agree with this critique insofar as it presents a clear exposition of the limits and flaws of individualism. Yet, individualism should not be confused with the theory of individuality, grounded in singularity and the dignity of individuation, which makes possible the full development of the individual. Under liberalism, for Schmitt, the "state turns into society" (p.72) and politics (the politics of antagonism) is abandoned. Yet, precisely, he says, "State and politics cannot be exterminated" (p.78). True, Schmitt points out the hypocrisy of liberal rhetoric, and of pacifism in particular:

> War is condemned but executions, sanctions, punitive expeditions, pacifications, protection of treaties, international police, and measures to assure peace remain. (p.79)

This is indeed an accurate description of the new world order of the last two decades. Schmitt continues:

> The adversary is thus no longer called an enemy but a disturber of peace and is thereby designated to be an outlaw of humanity. (*ibid.*)

The consequence is the notion of the last war of humanity, which I have discussed above. In sum, there is no exit from the friend/enemy distinction, and an

> allegedly non-political and apparently even antipolitical system serves existing or newly emerging friend-and-enemy groupings and cannot escape the logic of the political. (p.79)

Schmitt is criticizing in particular the attempt at dissolving the political into the ethical on the one hand and the economic on the other. For him, this would be an impossible task. But let us consider what might be the most fundamental friend-and-enemy relation, that between labor and capital. First of all, it must be noted that there is here no reduction of the political to the economic, as is often understood and Schmitt himself seems to understand. The antagonism of labor and capital is in fact fully political, even in the narrow sense given to the word by Schmitt. Capital tries to assert its sovereignty over labor, and labor, in its most radical expression, tries to free itself from the yoke of capital. But labor has two enemies: capital and the productive form of labor, that is, the form of labor that produces and increases capital. For Marx, the struggle of the proletariat is the struggle for the dissolution of all classes, including the dissolution of the proletariat itself as a class. From the point of view of labor, the enemy is certainly not a group of people that must be physically eliminated, but rather practical categories and structures of domination equal to the very form of the political antagonism. This should say clearly that the aim of the political struggle is the overcoming of the political, or perhaps its redefinition along lines that are neither those of the friend-and-enemy split, nor those of the split between economic competition on the one hand and the (legal) construction of ethical and cultural patterns of discourse on the other. Rather, the aim of the political struggle is to open up the potential by enduring the tension between what-is and what-could-be. The real enemy is this what-is, which Schmitt sees as unavoidable and necessary, the apparently unsurpassable structure of the empirically given. But Schmitt does not consider the moment of contingency.

At the end of his critique of the state of exception, Giorgio Agamben addresses the question of contingency, which is very important in all of his work, when, with a reference to Benjamin, he speaks of "the urgency of the state of exception 'in which we live'" (2005: 86).[7] This is also to be understood as the restricted sense of *the real* imposed on life as "an empty space, in which a human action with no relation to law stands before a norm with no relation to life" (*ibid.*). It is the paradox of a state of exception become permanent. The exit for Agamben is a redefinition, or recuperation, of politics, that is, a *space for human action* without regard to the law. He says:

> Politics has suffered a lasting eclipse because it has been contaminated by law, seeing itself, at best, as constituent power (that is, violence that makes the law), when it is not reduced to merely the power to negotiate with the law. The only truly political action, however, is that which severs the nexus between violence and law. (p.88)

---

[7] I have dealt more fully with Agamben's study of the state of exception in another work (Gullì, 2007).

In his eighth thesis on the philosophy of history, Walter Benjamin says:

> The tradition of the oppressed teaches us that the 'state of emergency' in which we live is not the exception but the rule. We must attain to a conception of history that is in keeping with this insight. Then we shall clearly realize that it is our task to bring about *a real state of emergency*. (1968: 257; emphasis added)

Both Agamben and Benjamin challenge the logic of sovereignty that Schmitt defends. Benjamin's *real* emergency, which conceptually also pertains to Agamben, is the exit from the exception that has become a rule. This real emergency is not what suspends the law, but what destroys it, what opens a space for existence other than the law. For Benjamin, what destroys the law is divine violence, or (still) sovereign violence (Benjamin 1978: 300). As William Rasch says in his concise and clear exposition of the main distinction in the work of Schmitt, Benjamin, and Agamben:

> Whereas Schmitt locates himself firmly within the political as defined by the sovereign exception, both Benjamin and Agamben imagine the possibility of a politics that exceeds the political. (2007: 99)

Rasch continues saying that, however, neither Benjamin nor Agamben can say what this post-sovereign politics really is. They only say, according to Rasch, that "if and when it comes, it will come with an all consuming but bloodless violence that, in Benjamin's terms, will be divine . . . neither law-making nor law-preserving" (*ibid.*), but precisely law-destroying (Benjamin 1978: 297).

The paradoxical regime of a permanent state of exception, more evident in our time, is a general feature of the logic of sovereignty and domination, of the antagonism that for Schmitt characterizes the political. As Machiavelli says, the fundamental antagonism is between those who want to dominate and those who do not want to be dominated.[8] The aim of the latter group, which is called *more honest*[9] by Machiavelli, evidently points toward the end of domination as such, that is, of a world in which the law is not necessary because "good habit" (buona consuetudine) suffices.[10] But this would amount to *deciding against the decision*, which at the end of *Political Theology* Schmitt derides Bakunin for doing. Thus he says:

> the odd paradox whereby Bakunin, the greatest anarchist of the nineteenth century, had to become in theory the theologian of the antitheological and in practice the dictator of an antidictatorship. (2005: 66)

---

[8] See Machiavelli's *Discourses* (I, V) and *The Prince* (IX).

[9] *The Prince* (IX).

[10] See *Discourses* (I, III). Of course, Machiavelli is not saying that this is the actual state of affairs, and, he starts this chapter of the *Discourses* with the notion that the sovereign should consider all subjects bad or guilty ("è necessario a chi dispone una repubblica ed ordina leggi in quella, presuppore tutti gli uomini rei"). Consequently, he says that the law is usually necessary. But then, relying on common knowledge ("Però si dice : Yet people say"), he adds that "where things work well without the law, the law itself is not necessary. But when such good habit (buona consuetudine) is lacking, then the law immediately becomes necessary" (p.118).

However, leaving Bakunin aside, there is no real paradox in deciding against the decision, provided that the one who decides is not sovereign, but *anyone* who chooses freedom and dignity over domination.

WORKS CITED

Agamben, Giorgio. 1998. *Homo Sacer: Sovereign Power and Bare Life*, trans. Daniel Heller- Roazen. Stanford, CA: Stanford University Press.

———. 2005. *State of Exception*, trans. Kevin Attel. Chicago and London: The University of Chicago Press.

Aristotle. 1999. *Nicomachean Ethics*, trans. Terence Irwin. Indianapolis and Cambridge: Hackett Publishing Company.

Benjamin, Walter. 1968. "Theses on the Philosophy of History," in *Illuminations*, trans. Harry Zohn. New York: Schocken Books.

———. 1978. "Critique of Violence," in *Reflections*, trans. Edmund Jephcott. New York: Schocken Books.

Calarco, Matthew and Steven DeCaroli., eds. 2007. *Giorgio Agamben: Sovereignty and Life*. Stanford, CA: Stanford University Press.

Gullì, Bruno. 2007. "The Ontology and Politics of Exception," in Matthew Calarco and Steven DeCaroli eds., *Giorgio Agamben: Sovereignty and Life*. Stanford, CA: Stanford University Press.

Held, David. 1995. *Democracy and the Global Order: From the Modern State to Cosmopolitan Governance*. Stanford: Stanford University Press.

Machiavelli, Niccolò.1976. *Il principe e altre opere politiche*. Milano: Garzanti.

Rasch, William. 2007. "From Sovereign Ban to Banning Sovereignty," in Matthew Calarco and Steven DeCaroli eds., *Giorgio Agamben: Sovereignty and Life*. Stanford, CA: Stanford University Press.

Schmitt, Carl. 1996. *The Concept of the Political*, trans. George Schwab. Chicago: The University of Chicago Press.

———. 2005. *Political Theology: Four Chapters on the Concept of Sovereignty*, trans. George Schwab. Chicago and London: The University of Chicago Press.

Bruno Gullì is an adjunct professor of philosophy at Long Island University, Brooklyn Campus.

PERIPHERY AND PURPOSE: THE FIFTEENTH-CENTURY RUBRICATION OF THE *PILGRIMAGE OF HUMAN LIFE*

Stephanie A. Viereck Gibbs Kamath

Commentary is never far from the activity of translation, as both efforts seek to transport meaning from a source into a new context.[1] For European writers of the late Middle Ages, the idea of transporting meaning jointly through the practices of commentary and translation held particular cultural force, as the powerful *translatio imperii* narrative of westward-moving world hegemony underwrote the tremendous energy surrounding the notion of a *translatio studii*, a movement of learning from earlier times and more central places into the vernacular languages of new locations.[2] In translation, authoritative works such as the Christian scriptures and patristic doctrine, along with classical literature, attracted not only extensive expository commentary but also allegoresis, a form of interpretative commentary that presumes the source signifies at multiple levels and conveys a meaning that exceeds its denotative expression.[3] The expectation that a

---

I am grateful to members of the London Old and Middle English Seminar, who offered feedback on a presentation containing a portion of this work, and to the editors and anonymous reviewers of *Glossator* for their comments and suggestions. Modern English translations provided within this essay are my own.

[1] Maryvonne Boisseau underscores this similarity in the two practices, the way both "supposent un prétexte" [are predicated upon a prior text], in her introduction to a new volume on the subject, with a predominant focus on modern texts; see "Présentation," *De la traduction comme commentaire au commentaire de traduction*, ed. Maryvonne Boisseau, Palimpsestes 20 (Paris: Presses Sorbonne Nouvelle, 2007), 11-19, at 11.

[2] 'Central' in this context refers to the region of the Mediterranean, a name literally meaning 'middle of the earth', the core of medieval maps. For more extended study of medieval mapping and the importance of geographic narratives of center and periphery to England's literature, see Kathy Lavezzo, *Angels on the Edge of the World: Geography, Literature, and English Community, 1000-1534* (Ithaca: Cornell University Press, 2006).

[3] In the case of pagan mythography, the term *integumentum*, rather than allegoresis, is at times employed for this form of interpretative commentary and its subject, in order to distinguish commentary on texts considered to be fictive at the literal level, rather than true, as in the case of scriptural works. Rita Copeland notes that "allegoresis proposes itself as co-extensive with the text," as this particular form of commentary aims to expose layers of meaning already present within the text; Martin Irvine describes the process by declaring that "in allegory one can distinguish the level of expression or rhetorical form from the level of content or additional signification . . . the text and the necessary supplement that discloses what the text signifies." See Rita Copeland, *Rhetoric, Hermeneutics, and Translation in the Middle Ages: Academic Traditions and Vernacular Texts* (Cambridge: Cambridge University Press, 1991), 81, and Martin Irvine, *The Making of Textual Culture: 'Grammatica' and Literary Theory 350-1100* (Cambridge: Cambridge University Press, 2006, rpt. 2004), 248.

translator's task should encompass rendering commentary and allegoresis was well established by the opening of the fifteenth century, and such enriched translation was perceived as support for the transmission of cultural and political authority. Christine de Pizan, for example, declares that Charles V of France merited praise and benefited France since he "fist . . . translater de latin en françois tous les plus notables livres, si comme la Bible en .iii. manieres, c'est assavoir: le texte, et puis le texte et les gloses ensemble, et puis d'une autre maniere alegorisée" [caused . . . the most notable books to be translated from Latin into French, such as the Bible translated in three manners, which is to say, a translation of the text, then the text and the glosses together, and then allegorized in another manner].[4] Medieval thinkers, including Christine, assigned considerable value to the vernacular translation of the commentaries and allegoresis accompanying the most notable works of Latinity, and modern scholarship on the translation of Latin literature into European vernaculars during the Middle Ages has traced significant correlation between this practice and claims of cultural authority.[5] This essay seeks to trace the influence of the theoretical model underpinning the vernacular translations of authoritative Latin works, with its emphasis on rendering commentary and allegoresis, in a case of translation between two vernaculars, when the transportation of meaning transpires between texts far less distant in space, time, and cultural context. Rather than the ancient wisdom of Jerusalem or Greece and its commentaries, the translator who crafted the mid-fifteenth-century English poem *The Pilgrimage of Human Life* chose to render a source already endowed with internal allegoresis and created less than a single century earlier, just across the Channel, in the vernacular of continental France. Nonetheless, the additional notes, or rubrication, found in the surviving manuscripts containing the *Pilgrimage* suggest that the translator's interest in interpretative commentary was the most visible aspect of a translation presented as service to an English earl in the context of the Hundred Years War.

Although scholars recognize the efflorescence of translations from French to English during the late Middle Ages, the connection between the overarching narrative of the *translatio studii* and the practice of intra-vernacular translation remains understudied, particularly in the case of medieval compositions without roots in early Latin or Greek literature.[6] The *Pilgrimage* presents such a case, as it translates the *Pèlerinage de la vie humaine*

---

[4] Christine de Pisan, *Livre des fais et bonnes meurs du sage roy Charles V*, ed. S. Solente (Paris: H. Champion, 1936), II, 43. The spelling 'Pizan' has been adopted in modern scholarship. For discussion of this method of translation as a model for Christine's own use of tripartite composition structure and its direct imitation in England, see G. Parussa, introduction to the *Epistre d'Othéa*, by Christine de Pizan (Geneva: Droz, 1999), 13, and S. A. V. Gibbs [Kamath], "Christine de Pizan's *Epistre d'Othéa* in England: The Manuscript Tradition of Stephen Scrope's Translation," in *Contexts and Continuities: Proceedings of the IVth International Colloquium on Christine de Pizan*, ed. A. J. Kennedy et al. (Glasgow: University of Glasgow Press, 2002), 397-408.

[5] One seminal consideration of medieval translation in relation to Latinate authority and the vernacular can be found in Copeland, *Rhetoric, Hermeneutics, and Translation in the Middle Ages*.

[6] Samuel Workman's classic *Fifteenth-Century Translation as an Influence on English Prose* (Princeton: Princeton University Press, 1940) demonstrates the extensive translation from French sources transpiring in late medieval England, but direct translations from compositions in French typically receive less individual attention than translations of classical or pseudo-classical works relying on French translations as intermediaries. For example, Humphrey of Gloucester's patronage of translations rooted in classical literature has been the subject of a number of worthwhile studies. See Alessandra Petrina, *Cultural Politics in Fifteenth-Century England: The Case of Humphrey, Duke of Gloucester* (Leiden: Brill, 2004) and Daniel Wakelin, *Humanism, Reading, and English Literature,*

[*Pilgrimage of human life*], a French allegory written by the Cistercian monk Guillaume de Digulleville.[7] Popular across Europe for several hundred years, Digulleville's allegory was recognized as a production of the Middle Ages and never attributed a more authoritative origin, in contrast to other popular late medieval texts, such as the pseudo-Ovidian *De vetula*. The *Pèlerinage* is the first text in a trilogy of allegorical pilgrimage poems, and far from any pretense of ancient origins, the composition date of 1331 is indicated within the poem.[8] In the 1350s Diguilleville expanded the *Pèlerinage* with several thousand more lines, including Latin lyrics, and added an opening prologue that complained the text had circulated before he had completed it.[9] This later version of the *Pèlerinage* is the source for the English verse translation, commonly attributed to the Benedictine monk John Lydgate, which acknowledges its French source in an additional prologue, surviving in two manuscripts.[10] The additional prologue of the *Pilgrimage* dates the translation to 1426 and identifies its patron as Thomas Monacute, the earl of Salisbury, commending the earl's victorious campaigns against the French. Although the translation renders a medieval vernacular composition rather than an ancient text, the theoretical expectations guiding the translation of notable Latin works seem present in this prologue, which pairs the transfer of meaning in translation with the transfer of political power. The English earl's "comavndement / Thys seydë book in Englysshe for to make" [commandment to make this aforesaid book in English] (133-4) coincides with his assumption of command in France; the date of the translation is introduced with the phrase "My lord that tymë beyng at Parys" (157).[11] To what extent, then, does the practice of the translator reflect the emphasis on

---

1430-1530 (Oxford: Oxford University Press, 2007). Since John Lydgate may be the translator of the English verse *Pilgrimage*, Wakelin's suggestion that John Lydgate may have created Latin scholarly notes for several of his 'humanist' translations for Humphrey is of interest to this study; see Wakelin 39-43.

[7] The spelling 'Deguileville' is also current in modern scholarship. For a list of manuscripts containing Guillaume de Digulleville's French texts, French adaptations, and English, Dutch, German, and Latin translations, see Guillaume de Digulleville, *The Pilgrimage of Human Life*, trans. and intro. Eugene Clasby (New York: Garland, 1992). A more complete and up-to-date list of manuscripts containing the French texts appears in *Guillaume de Digulleville: Les Pèlerinages allégoriques, Actes du colloque de Cerisy-la-Salle, 5-8 octobre 2006*, eds. Frédéric Duval and Fabienne Pomel (Rennes: Presses Universitaires de Rennes, 2008).

[8] The subsequent texts of the trilogy are the *Pèlerinage de l'âme* [*Pilgrimage of the soul*], dated to 1355, and the *Pèlerinage de Jesus Christ* [*Pilgrimage of Jesus Christ*], dated to 1358.

[9] Roughly 7,000 and 8,000 additional lines of verse appear, although the lack of a modern critical edition of Digulleville's recension text prevents an exact count.

[10] The argument concerning authorship can be found in Kathryn Walls, "Did Lydgate Translate the '*Pèlerinage de Vie Humaine*'?" *Notes and Queries* 222 (1977), 103-105 and Richard Firth Green, "Lydgate and Deguileville Once More," *Notes and Queries* 223 (1978), 105-106. Derek Pearsall sums up the current scholarly view: "There has been debate about the attribution including the possibility that Lydgate may have employed help for this huge translation, completed very quickly under pressure of many other commitments, but there can be no real doubt that Lydgate was commissioned to write it and had a major hand in it." See Pearsall, *John Lydgate (1371-1449): A Bio-bibliography*, English Literary Studies Monograph Series, No. 71 (Victoria, BC: University of Victoria, 1997), 27-8. The identification of the translator as John Lydgate is not an essential component of the analysis presented here.

[11] All quotations from the English translation refer by line number to John Lydgate (?), *The Pilgrimage of the Life of Man*, eds. F. J. Furnivall and Katharine B. Locock, 3 vols., Early English Text Society e.s. 77, 83, 92

the addition and display of interpretative commentary found in the translation of 'the most notable books', sources that could lay claim to the patristic or antique authority of Latin literature?

Recent studies of the *Pilgrimage* have drawn attention to the particular resonance that the religious themes and artisanal figures of the French poem assume in their new English context without undertaking close study of the translator's pattern of practice in rendering the entire poem.[12] Such consideration may appear a daunting task, as the English *Pilgrimage* is roughly twice the length of its French source and the translator's prologue offers no direct description of the translation's relation to commentary and interpretation that lie beyond the immediate source. The prologue praises the patron and asserts the moral worth of the text but does not explain textual practice in a way comparable to Christine's enumeration of the manners of biblical translation.[13] Instead of direct explanatory statements, evidence revealing the importance of interpretative commentary to this translation from one vernacular language to another appears in the periphery of the manuscript page. Short notes placed in the margins or in the blank spaces between sections of text identify not only the dedicatory prologue but four specific textual passages as the translator's own additions, and these notes and marked passages focus attention on the translator's ability to enrich the source text with interpretative commentary. To trace the influence exerted by the medieval concept of a grand translation of learning and power from the world's center to its periphery, then, we need to pay attention to the paratextual matter that surrounds the central text in surviving manuscripts. When we do so, we find that the interlinear notes that purport to distinguish the translator's prologue from the source also establish a resemblance between the voices of the English translator and French author, taking advantage of the text's allegorical structure to present translation as another, integral layer in the text's interpretative process. The marginal notes that isolate particular contributions to the text made by the translator similarly lend emphasis to the passages in which the translator assumes the authority to expand the text with interpretative commentary, emulating the author's composition process, as opposed to the passages that enlarge the text with comments predicated on the differences between the French and English languages. Finally, the visual features and language of the marginal notes suggest connections between the translation and authoritative texts that lie beyond the immediate French source. These notes have not received much scholarly attention to date, but their presence signifies an interest in transcending the relationship between source text and translation that is still at issue today; indeed, one

---

(London: Kegan Paul, et al., 1899, 1901, 1904). Rubrics and notes are not assigned line numbers in this edition; where necessary, I provide the closest possible line number.

[12] Michael Camille, for example, claims Lydgate's translation "sought to emphasize orthodox attitudes" through imagery; see "The Iconoclast's Desire: Deguileville's Idolatry in France and England," in *Images, Idolatry, and Iconoclasm in Late Medieval England: Textuality and the Visual Image*, ed. Jeremy Dimmick et al. (Oxford: Oxford University Press, 2002), 151–71, at 167. Lisa Cooper examines the significance of how artisanal figures were translated in "'Markys . . . off the Workman': Heresy, Hagiography, and the Heavens in *The Pilgrimage of the Life of Man*," in *Lydgate Matters: Poetry and Material Culture in the Fifteenth Century*, ed. Lisa H. Cooper and Andrea Denny-Brown (Palgrave Macmillan, 2007), 89-112.

[13] A greater amount of overt theorization concerns the transmission of Greek or Latin texts into English, although there are late medieval discussions of translation that describe or allude to translation from French. A collection of texts relevant to theorizing vernacular composition and translation can be found in *The Idea of the Vernacular: An Anthology of Middle English Literary Theory, 1280-1520*, ed. Jocelyn Wogan-Browne et al. (University Park: Pennsylvania State University Press, 1999).

recent analysis of the role played by translator's notes in modern practice links the implications of the apparatus to the medieval tradition of combining the practices of the commentary, interpretation, and translation.[14] Regardless of the provenance of the immediate source, the notes calling attention to the translator's ability to serve as a hermeneutic guide rather than simply a provider of interlinguistic equivalence allow this late medieval intra-vernacular translation to claim the power and authority of the wider *translatio studii* movement.

Scholars have long recognized the importance of interlinear and marginal glosses, notes, and rubrication to the way medieval readers navigated texts. The thirteenth century saw an explosion of artwork and decoration in marginal spaces, which could serve as mnemonics, helping readers to remember or to locate quickly particular textual passages within a manuscript or, at times, serve alternative functions; Michael Camille's study of the development argues that "things written or drawn in the margins add an extra dimension, a supplement, that is able to gloss, parody, modernize and problematize the text's authority while never totally undermining it."[15] Malcolm Parkes also identifies the thirteenth century as a key turning point in textual presentation, noting how manuscripts across Western Europe showcase far more regular and complex use of features such as headings, running titles, subdivisions, lists of contents, and notes. Although such "compilation was not new . . . what was new was the amount of thought and industry that was put into it, and the refinement that this thought and industry produced."[16] Parkes identifies this development as reflecting a transition from meditative reading practices to more discontinuous styles of reading, categorizing texts more precisely and drawing upon sections for reference purposes; Parkes observes, however, that the apparatus thus developing in academic scholastic commentaries on the Bible soon spread to the manuscript design employed for more popular vernacular compositions. Studies examining the paratextual matter in late medieval English manuscripts are most frequently concerned with works composed in English, particularly by canonical authors such as Geoffrey Chaucer and John Gower.[17] In the case of translations, it is frequently assumed, often rightly

---

[14] Pascal Sardin's approach to the question "que *fait* la note du traducteur au texte en traduction?" [what effect does the note of the translator have upon the text in translation?] insists that the ability of notes to represent the translator's voice and practice leads us back "à l'époque médiévale notamment, lorsque les translateurs étaient aussi des exégètes et que leurs remarques et ajouts se mêlaient au texte des auteurs qu'ils translataient" [notably to the medieval epoch, when translators were also exegetes and their remarks and additions mingled with the texts of the authors they translated]; see "De la note du traducteur comme commentaire: entre texte paratexte et prétexte," in *De la traduction comme commentaire*, ed. Boisseau, 121-135, at 123 and 130.

[15] Michael Camille, *Image on the Edge: the Margins of Medieval Art* (Cambridge, MA: Harvard University Press, 1992), 10.

[16] M. B. Parkes, "The Influence of the Concepts of *Ordinatio* and *Compliatio* on the Development of the Book," in *Scribes, Scripts, and Readers: Studies in the Communication, Presentation and Dissemination of Medieval Texts* (London: Hambledon Press, 1991), 35-70, at 58.

[17] Christopher Baswell studies the effects of the Latin references accompanying Chaucer's Wife of Bath's Prologue and Tale, one of the most heavily glossed tales in manuscripts of *The Canterbury Tales*; see "Talking Back to the Text: Marginal Voices in Medieval Secular Literature," in *The Uses of Manuscripts in Literary Studies: Essays in Memory of Judson Boyce Allen*, eds. Charlotte Morse, Penelope Reed Doob, and Marjorie Curry Woods (Kalamazoo: Medieval Institute, 1992), 121-60; Steven Partridge offers more precise description of the entirety

so, that the note systems accompanying the text borrow from source manuscripts. In the case of the *Pilgrimage*, however, the notes surrounding the translation, both interspersed with text and on edges of page, direct attention to the translator's own efforts, serving as a guide to what the translation aims to accomplish.

A quick consideration of the three interlinear rubrics, notes written in red, dividing the two prologues and the opening of the text in the two most complete surviving manuscripts demonstrates how these external markings differentiate what the translator adds to the text yet invite recognition of a resemblance between the translator and the author as providers of allegoresis.[18] The last line of the English translator's prologue employs deictic language asking the reader to observe the moment as the start of the translation: "Wyth yowrë gracë thus I wyll be-gynne" [with your grace thus I will begin] (184). But what immediately follows is not the translation proper but the two rubrics, "Here endyth the prologue off the translatour" and "Her be-gynneth the prologue of the auctour." The beginning of the translator's task is thus the assumption of the author's voice. The author's voice does not continue without interruption, however; another rubric appears in the text, marking the close of the authorial prologue translated from Digulleville's recension. This rubric differentiates the voice of the author from the voice of the central character who narrates the allegorical poem, labeled in these manuscripts as 'the pilgrim'. The translator is thus not the only figure presented as offering introductory commentary external to the narrative. The voice of the author is also set apart from the voice of the narrating character who records the allegory, since the rubric "Here begynneth the pilgrime" appears immediately after the authorial prologue ends (303). The rubrics mark boundaries between the voices of the translator, author, and pilgrim, but suggest that the first-person voice of the text is doubly encased: both translator and author can introduce and comment upon the narrating voice delimited by the frame of the allegory's dream vision.[19] The desire to create such an analogy may even have prompted the employment of rubrics differentiating the voice of the author from the pilgrim character at the end of the prologue. The differentiating rubric at this point appears to be the innovation of the English translator or scribe: I have examined all but one of the extant

---

of the *Canterbury* glosses, arguing that Chaucer himself was responsible for a certain set, in *The Manuscript Glosses to the* Canterbury Tales (Woodbridge: Boydell and Brewer, 2002). Ardis Butterfield has studied the implications of the headings and divisions appearing in manuscripts of Chaucer's *Troilus* as well as the authorial claims advanced by the apparatus of John Gower's *Confessio Amantis*; see "Articulating the Author: Gower and the French Vernacular Codex," *Yearbook of English Studies* 33 (2003): 80-96, and "Mise-en-page in the *Troilus* Manuscripts: Chaucer and French Manuscript Culture," *Huntington Library Quarterly* 58.1 (1996): 49-80.

[18] The manuscripts are London, British Library, Cotton MS Vitellius C.xiii and London, British Library, Stowe MS 952. Sizable portions of the translation text also appear in the fragmentary London, British Library, Cotton MS Tiberius A.vii. A dedicatory drawing, without text, appears in London, British Library, Harley MS 4826.

[19] Such simultaneous indication of difference and resemblance is a notable feature of textual commentary *writ large* as well as the specific course of medieval translation. Christina Shuttleworth Kraus, for example, notes how commentary can both "serve" and "direct our attention away from the text"; see "Reading Commentaries / Commentaries as Reading," in *The Classical Commentary*, eds. Roy K. Gibson and Christina Shuttleworth Kraus (Leiden: Brill, 2002), 1-28, at 1. Rita Copeland similarly observes that "vernacular exegetical translation forges new links with the Latin cultures of antiquity and the Middle Ages by replicating them at the same time that it registers a profound difference with them"; see Copeland, *Rhetoric, Hermeneutics, and Translation in the Middle Ages*, 106.

French recension manuscripts that have been identified to date, and none features a rubric that distinguishes between an 'authorial' voice and that of the internal 'pilgrim' at this key point in the text.[20]

The differentiating rubrics at the text's beginning establish the first-person voice narrating the English text as a collaborative voice, mediated for the reader by the commentary of both the author and the translator. The text of the translator's prologue heightens this effect by praising the author for gathering the wisdom of other sources into his allegory, declaring the *Pèlerinage* is worth translating into English because "the auctour, wych that dyde hyt ffyrst compyle, / So vertuously spent ther-on hys whyle" [the author who first compiled it spent his time on it very effectively] (139-140). The textual activity of the author as well as the translator is envisioned as compilation, folding together multiple textual voices, with Digulleville being distinguished only as the "ffyrst" to undertake the labor. The opening rubrics and prologues, setting out this role for the translator, work in concert with the series of Latin notes appearing in the margins of surviving manuscripts. The marginal notes connect the English text with quoted (and often cited) scriptural, patristic, and classical writings, identifying the exterior sources the French author may have employed in compiling the allegory. But the marginal notes also specifically remind readers of the role of the translator in compiling the voice of the text: the marginal Latin note, 'verba translatoris,' identifies four passages as moments when the first-person text expresses 'the words of the translator.'

Surviving manuscript copies suggest that the marginal Latin commentary was an integral part of the translation in its circulation, and probably in its composition. The schema of Latin commentary appears in all three extant manuscripts of the translation, now housed in the British Library. Two of the manuscripts use the phrase 'verba translatoris' to mark the same four passages of text; the third lacks large segments of text, including the passages marked with this phrase in the other manuscripts.[21] The earlier manuscript to employ this phrase may have been consulted in the copying of the other manuscript, although they are not exact copies in other senses.[22] The small number of manuscripts and unfortunate lacunae thus do not allow a stronger claim for the relation of the Latin commentary to the text than the statement that the commentary circulated with the

---

[20] There are nine French manuscripts of the recension text known to be extant: Cherbourg, Bibliothèque Municipale, MS 42; Paris, Bibliothèque de l'Arsenal, MS 3646; Paris, Bibliothèque nationale de France, MSS F. Fr. 377, F. Fr. 825, F. Fr. 829, F. Fr. 1138 (missing start of text), F. Fr. 12466; Paris, Institut de France, MS 9 (fragmentary, missing start of text); St. Petersburg, Российская национальная библиотека, F.p.XIV.11. With the exception of the St. Petersburg MS, I have consulted all of the surviving manuscripts. None contain a rubric dividing between the voices of author and character after the newly added prologue, even in the manuscripts which contain rubrics indicating speaker voice elsewhere or which draw attention to the beginning of the dream in another fashion, with a decorated capital letter or an illumination. Nor is such a rubric found in the two early printed editions of the French text created in the sixteenth century.

[21] The manuscripts containing the 'verba translatoris' rubric are London, British Library, Cotton MS Vitellius C.xiii and London, British Library, Stowe MS 952. The fragmentary London, British Library, Cotton MS Tiberius A.vii is missing these sections of text.

[22] London, British Library, Cotton MS Vitellius C.xiii is the earlier manuscript, dated to the mid-fifteenth century; London, British Library, Stowe MS 952 is dated to the late fifteenth or early sixteenth century. For studies of owner and scribe John Stowe's influence in textual transmission, see *John Stowe (1525-1605) and the Making of the English Past*, eds. Ian Gadd and Alexandra Gillespie (London: The British Library Publishing Division, 2004).

three relatively contemporary copies that survived. The likelihood that this schema was original to the translation appears stronger, however, when considered in conjunction with the comparable manuscript tradition of *Reson and Sensuallyte*, another fifteenth-century English verse translation of a French allegorical text often attributed to John Lydgate. Although Lydgate's authorship of the *Pilgrimage*, as well as *Reson and Sensuallyte*, has been disputed, scholars have agreed that the same translator who wrote the *Pilgrimage* created *Reson and Sensuallyte*, an unfinished English verse translation of the fourteenth-century French allegory *Les Echecs Amoureux*. Latin notes appear in the margins beside the text of *Reson and Sensuallyte* and also mark certain passages as the translator's (e.g., 'Ista sunt verba translatoris'). Scholarship on this text has generally concurred with the text's early editor, Ernst Sieper, who noted more than a century ago that the Latin rubrics, including the 'verba translatoris' phrases, were likely to be the translator's own, arguing that "if Lydgate did not write the marginal notes himself, they originate from a man who knew perfectly all the conditions of his work."[23]

Setting aside the question of the translator's biographical identity, I investigate a different form of attributed identity by considering closely the moments at which the 'verba translatoris' notes appear in the *Pilgrimage*. As noted above, the *Pilgrimage* is almost twice the length of its French source; of all the additional material in the new verse rendering, why did the four passages marked by these notes require such a visual sign of their production by the translator? Examining the passages identified as the translator's words can aid us in determining what medieval readers saw as the role of the English translator when rendering a text written in another vernacular. Analysis reveals that the passages marked as the 'verba translatoris' do not call attention to the French nature of the source or to the French to English linguistic transposition, even though such passages can be found within the translation. For example, the personification of 'Rude Entendement' [Poor Understanding], described in the original text as carrying "vng baston de corneillier" [a club of dogwood] (fol. 47r), has the description of his "gret staff" extended in the English translation, which offers a linguistic gloss, explaining the staff was "yhewe out off A tre / Callyd in ffrench A cornowler" [hewn from a tree called in French a *cornowler*] (10336, 10338-9).[24] Such versified explanations of retained French vocabulary draw attention to the work's French source and tendencies towards lexicon expansion; these passages sustain the interest in France displayed in the setting described in the translator's prologue. But no passage of this kind is rubricated as the words of the translator.

The passages that Latin rubrics render distinct, as the translator's alone, do not emphasize the multiple vernaculars of the text, but rather mark the shift between the literal and hermeneutic levels of the allegory, adding to the interpretative commentary or allegoresis present in the original text. The emphasis on what is new within the English translation falls upon such allegoresis rather than the transition between French and English. Indeed, certain of these passages attempt to identify the translation as closely with Latin texts as with the French source, emphasizing direct contact with authoritative ancient wisdom. The choice of Latin as the

---

[23] Ernst Sieper, Introduction to *Reson and Sensuallyte*, by John Lydgate (?), 2 vols., Early English Text Society e.s. 84, 89 (London: Kegan Paul, Trench, Trübner & Co., 1901, 1903), I.4.

[24] For ease of reference, this paper refers by folio number to one of the earliest printed editions, *Le Romant des trois Pelerinaiges*, printed circa 1510-1511 or 1514-1518 in Paris by Barthole Rembolt and Jean Petit. For a discussion of the relative dating of this edition and the 1511 *Pelerinage de l'homme* printed in Paris by Anthoine Vérard, see Edmond Faral, "Guillaume de Digulleville, Jean Galloppes et Pierre Virgin," in *Études romanes dédiées à Mario Roques* (Paris: Droz, 1946), 96-7, note 2. I have compared the early printed edition for sense agreement with multiple medieval manuscripts of the recension.

language for these notes itself contributes to this effect. The insistence on the translator's ability to offer interpretative commentary is most pronounced in the first and final passages noted as the translator's, whereas the two central marked passages forge a stronger connection between the translator and external authorities. Although the first additional passage marked by a Latin marginal note is far longer than the last, which is a mere couplet in length, both issue similar invitations to readers to engage in textual interpretation, asking those "who lyst lere" [who desire to learn] (457) and those "who espye kan" [who can perceive] (4057) for their close attention. Each also focuses on a particular figurative image in the text, and considering each in turn reveals how the words specially identified as belonging to the translator present commentary that aids complex interpretation of the source's meaning.

Near the beginning of the French source, the narrator views for the first time a beautiful city, figuring the heavenly Jerusalem, his ultimate goal as a pilgrim. The first city gate he sees has a portcullis stained with blood, indicating that those who enter the city through this gate do so by suffering violence. After noting that he saw none pass that way while he was watching, the narrator describes the guardian of the gate. The gate, as depicted in French text, can thus be interpreted as representing the martyrdom suffered by early Christians. But the English translation inserts between the narrator's vision of the bloodstained gate and his description of its guardian a figurative interpretation of the violence needed to enter heaven, replacing the observation of the source text's narrator that he saw none enter this gate. In a passage marginally marked as the 'verba translatoris', the narrator explains that "who that loke a-ryht" [those who examine rightly] (450) can see "that gret vyolence & myght" [that great violence and power] (449) is the strength a mortal requires to break into heaven. Explanation of this declaration expands into a microcosm of the entire text, a mini-allegory of personifications on pilgrimage: the text declares "thys is to seyne, who lyst lere" [to those who wish to learn, this means] (457) only virtue can "makyth a man conquere" [make a man conquer], and Virtue (suddenly personified) must have her mistress, Reason, as her guide "to lede hyr also and to dresse / in hyr pylgrymage" [to lead her and to prepare her for her pilgrimage] (464-5) to attain heaven. Rather than representing the martyrdom of the past, by which few now enter heaven, the gate described in the English translation represents the entire text's message, recapitulating in miniature the poem's pilgrimage structure as well as the personifications of Reason and Moral Virtue, who appear as characters in later passages within the poem.[25] The words of the translator, when thus visually separated from voices of the author and narrating character, still resemble the work of Digulleville, presenting elaborations on the allegory and commentary on its meaning as well as inviting readers to interpret. The importance of the translator as an interpretative guide is underscored by the placement of Latin rubric indicating the translator's efforts beside the invocation of readers "who lyst lere" [who wish to learn] the text's meaning.

The same role is granted to the translator when the text is describing the personification of Penitence, the last passage to contain words specially identified as the translator's own. In the French text, immediately after Penitence names herself, she declares that she is the guardian of a secret isle and describes her function of

---

[25] One part of the addition made by the English translator to this passage, the incorporation of a Latin phrase from the gospel of Matthew into the verse, finds a parallel in the 1511 printed edition of the French text, which places the same Latin quotation in the textual margin beside the passage (fol. 2v). But nothing like the personification allegory added to the English translation appears in the French printed edition. Likewise, the English translation features none of the six other marginal notes that appear beside this passage in the French printed edition (referring the reader to passages in Genesis, Acts, Hebrews, and the book of Wisdom).

ISSN 1942-3381   Stephanie A. Viereck Gibbs Kamath

cleansing all filth from her domain, much later identified as the house of which Grace Dieu (the Grace of God) is mistress—that is to say, the soul. The passage added to the English text at this point and marked as the translator's words emphasizes the need for interpretation and for supplying interpreting readers with guiding commentary, as in the earlier instance. Penitence's declaration of her guardianship, a single line in the French, is extended in the translation by a phrase inviting close examination of this figure, specifically invoking those who wish to see her true role. In an aside the nineteenth-century editors of the text set apart in parentheses, the English 'Dame Penance' says that she is "the cheff wardeyn (who lyst se), / Off thylkë ylë most secre" [the chief warden of that most secret isle (whoever desires to see)] (4055-6). Immediately thereafter, in the additional couplet marked as the translator's words, she offers an aside very similar to the one appearing in the couplet above: "The wych (who espyë kan,) / Ys yhyd *with*-Inne a man" [which is hidden within a man (whoever wishes to perceive)] (4057-8). The marginal rubric 'verba translatoris' envisions the translator not as a source for explanations of unfamiliar French phrases, but rather as an exegetical guide who directs readers towards the allegorical meaning of the secret island, the model of the human soul, or of the salvific pilgrimage, the journey of human life. The The differing lengths of the additional passages related to the island of Penitence and to the heavenly gate, both marked as 'verba translatoris,' makes clear that they have not been distinguished as the words of the translator because they are longer interpolations than, say, the added definitions of retained French vocabulary, phrases, or customs. Instead, what these passages have in common is their role in extending attention to the hermeneutic system of the text.

This depiction of the translator as the interpreter and expander of the source text's allegory also underlies the other passages marginally marked as the translator's words. Although these two passages appear to be more directly connected to literary and linguistic explication, their focus is not upon French but rather Latin words and works, specifically those important to the text's rhetoric of authority and allegorical signification. For example, the English translator expands a reference to the Aristotelian treatise on sophistic rhetorical fallacies, designed to explain how mercy is concealed within the symbols of the earthly Church's power to punish, by naming the author and elaborating upon his authority. At this point in the French allegory, the narrator describes a dialogue between the personification Reason and a character with the attributes of both Moses and the Pope, representing the earthly church. The character, noting he has horns and a sharp staff, has asked Reason whether this means he should be very fierce. Reason gives an extended answer in the form of a sermon about wearing horns on the outside but having mercy inside, an answer that includes a couplet declaring that a fallacy of sophistic rhetoric can be taken as a true model in this case: "Et fallace delenche faire / Peuz bien ycy sans toy meffaire" [The fallacy of *elenchus* can be well enacted here, without you acting wrongly] (fol. 8r).[26] The English translator inserts almost thirty lines into Reason's response after this reference, explaining the meaning of the sophistic fallacies described by Aristotle (such as the discord in inner meaning and external appearance) and attributing to Aristotle a concrete example of deceptive appearance (a

---

[26] This reference at the moment of disclosing the allegorical meaning of the horns of wisdom that are the traditional attributes of the patriarch Moses may be a subtle invocation of the classic 'horned man' dilemma of the sophistic rhetoric developed by the Stoics: "If you never lost something, you have it still; but you never lost horns, *ergo* you have horns," as expressed in Diogenes Laertius, *Lives of Eminent Philosophers*, trans. R. D. Hicks, 2 vols., Loeb Classical Library Nos. 184, 185 (Cambridge, MA: Harvard University Press, 1938), II 7.187. Alternatively, the couplet may simply refer to the general idea that making things seem to be what they are not is a rhetorical ploy of the Sophists.

bull's gall can make a mark that looks like gold).[27] In the earlier extant manuscript containing the 'verba translatoris' note (London, British Library, Cotton MS Vitellius C.xiii), the passage is thrice marked with paraphs in addition to the Latin marginal notes, and at each point, these markings pick out an invitation to interpretation: the first picks out lines declaring that these "wordës fewe" [few words] are "an exaumple ful notable / To folk that be not rekkeles" [a noteworthy example to people who pay attention to advice], the second draws attention to the claim that the example can be understood by "who that lokë wel" [whoever considers well] (1691), and the third gives emphasis to the final reminder that this is an example to "han in mynde" [keep in mind] (1696).

That this passage is not a simple expansion of a brief intertextual allusion in the source but rather a development of the text's allegory and a newly urgent demand for interpretation becomes even more apparent in light of the narrative that follows Reason's sermon in the Digulleville's French text. After the French allegory recounts Reason's sermon and the church ordination process, it describes the administration of the Eucharist as a miraculous dinner. The personified Grace of God responds to the pilgrim narrator's questions on the subject by recounting a story of how Reason and Nature send their disciple Aristotle to debate at length with Wisdom concerning the nature of this marvelous feast. Like the passage marked as the translator's words that presented the personifications of Reason and Virtue prior to their first appearance as characters in the source allegory, the passage discussed here similarly foreshadows the appearance of a character encountered in a later passage of the French allegory, developing the exemplary role of Aristotle as an authority who is nonetheless subject to divine will.

Specially marked additional commentary on the part of the English translator also introduces a far more contemporary Latin authority into Digulleville's poem. The English translator inserts a reference to John of Genoa's thirteenth-century *Catholicon*, one of the earliest Latin-Greek dictionaries, into a passage in the French allegory that employs linguistic definition and stories of etymological derivation in the service of the allegory. Reason, continuing her sermon to the church official, explains the meaning of the sword that the Grace of God has given him in order to defend the heavenly city. She does so by noting that a "glaive" (sword) is so called because it divides the "gueulle" (throat), signifying that judges should truly divide by the throat, giving judgment according to the oral testimony they hear and not for other reasons such as bribes.[28] This passage presents a seemingly straightforward dilemma for an English translator, and one would expect the translation to retain the French terms here and explain their meaning, as is done in other passages, so that the

---

[27] It may be worth noting that the question of what exactly 'elenchus' means, especially in relation to Socrates, is still at issue in modern philosophical scholarship and the subject of extensive commentary in English. See Gary Alan Scott, introduction to *Does Socrates Have a Method?: Rethinking the* Elenchus *in Plato's Dialogues and Beyond*, ed. Gary Alan Scott (University Park: Pennsylvania State University Press, 2002), 1-16, esp. 4-5.

[28] "Glaiue comme on trouue en escript / Gueulle diuisant si est dit" (fol. 9r). In contrast to the earlier printed edition, the 1511 printed edition of the French text features a citation of the *Catholicon*, placing the Latin note "Gladius dicitur guladius quia gula(m) diuidit. Ut ioha(n)nes iauue(n)sis inquit" in the left margin of the page beside this passage (fol. 10v). But five other marginal notes appear beside this column of text alone on the page, referring the reader to such sources as the Psalms, Tobias, and Acts, and these references are not incorporated into the English translation. If the marginal notes of the later printed edition had an early source that was known to the English translator, the choices made in translation are thus still distinctive.

Stephanie A. Viereck Gibbs Kamath

name of the instrument and its etymology can continue to act as a sign of the ideal administration of justice represented in the French allegory. Rather than simply explaining the terms of the French text, however, the translator inserts into Reason's speech a citation of the *Catholicon*.[29] The citation allows the translator to provide the Latin words for sword and throat as the basis for interpretation, in place of the words of the French source. The citation concludes with the words "ffor throte yn Ynglyssh (thys the ffyn) / Ys callyd Gula in Latyn, / Wher-off Glayvë took hys name" [For (this is the point) 'throat' in English is called 'gula' in Latin, from which 'glaive' takes its name] (2459-61). These lines put English first in the narrative order of the terms and present the French term of Digulleville's text as a secondary derivation. Following this emphasis on the Latin underlying the French, the translator reshapes Reason's interpretation of the sword's meaning of throat as signifying the judge's need to rely on spoken witness. The English verse translation instead emphasizes the parts into which the throat is divided when cut, since the judge's powers of interpretation to "discerne" and to "seke and enqueryn" become important as a means to understand the "outher part" (2468-71). This passage, specially marked as the translator's words, thus differs from the many unmarked instances in which the translator chooses to retain and to define some of vocabulary found in the French source. This additional passage, like the three considered above, gives greater emphasis to the interpretive system necessary to find understanding—seeking, looking, enquiring, slicing apart layers of meaning—and associates the translator's voice with this reading process. Like the new interpretation of the gate dividing heaven from earth, the new etymological source allows the translator to claim greater authority by expanding and altering the source's existing allegoresis.

Moreover, the schema of Latin commentary that marks these passages as the words of the translator also visually allies the translator with the other Latin authorities cited in the text's margin (and, in this instance, also within the text). The resemblance is particularly strong in the earlier extant manuscript containing the 'verba translatoris' rubric (London, British Library, Cotton MS Vitellius C.xiii). At moments when there is an intertextual allusion in the text for which the Latin source text and author are given in the accompanying commentary, the scribe often writes the Latin author's name to the right of the Latin quotation; a curving bracket between the name and citation and a red flourish on the first letter of the author's name draw more attention to these instances of naming. This presentation looks remarkably similar to the visual relation of the text and the phrase 'verba translatoris', which occurs four times in this manuscript, each time with a curving bracket linking it to the text and a red flourish at its start. The authority of the translator in explicating the

---

[29] On the complex manuscript history of John of Genoa's dictionary, see Gerhardt Powitz, "Le *Catholicon*—esquisse de son histoire" in *Les manuscrits des lexiques et glossaires de l'antiquité tardive à la fin du moyen âge*, ed. Jacqueline Hamesse, Textes et études du Moyen Age 4 (Louvain-la-Neuve: Fédération internationale des instituts d'études médiévales, 1996), 299-336. The nature of the citation draws attention to the (relatively) contemporary nature of the source, beginning "By record off Ianuence / (Thys was nat ful yere agon) / In hys book Catholicon" (2450-2452). The currency of the *Catholicon* as a source in England is also witnessed by the adoption of the same title, in a colophon dated to 1483, for a English to Latin word list, which includes 'glaudia' under the header of 'swerde' and 'gula' under 'throte'. See *Catholicon Anglicum*, ed. Sidney Herrtage, Early English Texts Society 75 (London: Trüber and co., 1881), ix, 373, 386. In this context, it seems interesting that *Catholicon* defines *interpretatio* in a fashion that allies translation and exegesis, defining the role of the interpreter as interlinguistic translation but also as the expounding of sacred mysteries; see Copeland, *Rhetoric, Hermeneutics, and Translation in the Middle Ages*, 90.

deeper senses of the text is thus bolstered visually, placed on a par with, for example, St. Chrysostom, as a source revealing the inner sense of these moments.[30]

Like the replacement of French terms with Latin terms in a passage marked as the translator's words, the marginal addition of Latin citations along the sides of the English translation serves to depict the French allegory's author, Digulleville, as a translator and complier of Latin sources. The manner in which manuscripts of the English translation incorporate Latin, even in passages not marked as the translator's words, is not a simple equivalent of any of the other adaptations of Digulleville's verse that made use of the Latin language. Digulleville's French allegory perhaps most closely resembles a compilation from Latinate authoritative texts in a manuscript of Digulleville's second pilgrimage text, *Le Pèlerinage de l'âme*. This manuscript contains Latin glosses in the margins beside the verse text, and it could have been prepared for the great French patron of translation, Charles V, according to Michael Camille's early study. Camille suggests that glosses may have been planned for all three of Digulleville's texts, although no manuscript containing a glossed trilogy is now extant.[31] Another notable instance of French to Latin movement is the translation of the second pilgrimage text entirely into Latin for the English regent, the Duke of Bedford, in the 1420s; an independent Latin translation of the entire trilogy does survive, although the earliest witness is a manuscript dating from 1504.[32] Early print editions of the French text, also dating to the sixteenth century, apply Latin glosses to the *Pèlerinage de la vie humaine*, in both its initial form and its recension. These glosses sometimes overlap with the commentary found in the English translation manuscripts, although the commentary differs enough to be clearly distinct and the print editions of the recension in French, although they may reflect lost manuscripts, were produced a good half century later than the English translation. While the question of influence remains uncertain, the overall pattern of the English translation manuscripts is distinctive. At times deploying marginal Latin glosses separate from the body of the text and at times replacing the French terms of text with Latin equivalents, this translation demonstrates a particular sensitivity to new English passages of hermeneutic guidance and commentary.

Indeed, the English translation replaces the French vocabulary of the source with Latin terms in the passages most concentrated upon defining levels of understanding. This technique makes the French text draw

---

[30] The similarity can be seen clearly on the facing folios 8v and 9r, from which this example is drawn.

[31] Paris, BnF, MS F. fr. 1648. See Michael Camille, "The Illustrated Manuscripts of Guillaume de Deguileville's 'Pèlerinages', 1330-1426" (Ph.D. Dissertation, University of Cambridge, 1985), 66-77.

[32] The Latin translation of the *Ame* survives in London, Lambeth Palace Library, MS 326 (formerly housed in the Sion Abbey collection). Jenny Stratford argues that this manuscript was not the presentation copy in "The manuscripts of John, Duke of Bedford: Library and Chapel," in *England in the Fifteenth Century: Proceedings of the 1986 Harlaxton Symposium*, ed. Daniel Williams (Woodbridge: Boydell Press, 1987), 329-350, and Frédéric Duval draws attention to the sophistication of Digulleville's own Latin compositions in contrast to the rather simple Latin translation of the *Ame* in "Deux prières latines de Guillaume de Digulleville à saint Michel et à son ange gardien," in *Guillaume de Digulleville: Les Pèlerinages allégoriques*, 185-211. For a brief discussion of context of the sixteenth-century manuscript containing a Latin translation of the entire trilogy (Paris, Bibliothèque de l'Arsenal, MS 507), see Florence Bourgne, "Medieval Mirrors and Later Vanitas Paintings," in *The Middle Ages after the Middle Ages in the English-Speaking World*, eds. Marie-Françoise Alamichel and Derek Brewer (Cambridge: D. S. Brewer, 1997), 79-90. Bourgne notes differences between the earlier Latin translation of the *Ame* and this one, which appears to translate not Digulleville's verse but rather a fifteenth-century French prose adaptation of the text.

ISSN 1942-3381

Stephanie A. Viereck Gibbs Kamath

more prominently upon Latin authorities, emphasizing resemblance between the author and the English translator as compilers, much in the manner of the analogy set out by the opening rubric. The debate mentioned earlier in this essay, in which the characters of Aristotle and Wisdom argue about the interpretation of the Eucharist, offers an example of the changes to vocabulary made in the English translation. The English verse translation uses the Latin terms "Vertualiter," "Corporaliter," "Realiter," "Presencialiter," and "Veraciter" (6050, 6053, 6054, 6055, 6056) in place of the French terms "vertuablement," "corporelment," "reaument," "presentement," and "vraiment" (fol. 19r) in one passage of contention concerning the nature of the divine presence in material substance. An independent English prose translation of the earlier, shorter *Pèlerinage* text, generally believed to have been composed less than five years after the verse translation of the recension, finds English equivalents for the French terms, such as "vertualliche," "bodiliche," "rialliche," "presentliche," and "verreyliche" (I.1767-1768).[33] The English verse translation thus chooses to emphasize the Latinate basis of this text's hermeneutic system even as it makes interpretation more elaborately present in English.[34] In effect, the translator represents his task as commentary on the notable texts and terms of Latin academic discourse, even when engaging in vernacular translation, by depicting the vernacular source text as a product of the same practice.

Thus far, this study has remained silent on the subject of the new passage added to the English *Pilgrimage* that has drawn the most critical attention to this text in past scholarship: the praise of Geoffrey Chaucer evidently intended to precede an interpolation of Chaucer's own translation from Digulleville's poetry, an acrostic lyric known as the "ABC."[35] It is true that one manuscript does contain an English rubric, "the translator," above the passage containing Chaucer's praise. Yet the rubric appears to be a late addition, part of the text written in the bibliophile John Stowe's hand, and unfortunately the other manuscripts are missing pages or have incomplete rubrics as this point, making the verification of Stowe's choice as reflective of the rubrics in earlier manuscripts impossible. I hope that in devoting my primary attention to the passages more certainly presented to the eyes of medieval readers as the translator's words, I have produced a better understanding of the function envisioned for the medieval translator. Certainly, this approach suggests that inserted references to Latin sources and an emphasis on interpretative commentary may have played quite as significant a role in valorizing the translator's labors as this allusion to translation from the same allegory by "the noble poete off Breteyne" [the noble poet of Britain] (19754), Geoffrey Chaucer. The translator emulates Chaucer's earlier translation by selecting the same contemporary French text as a source. But the translator

---

[33] Quotations are cited by volume and line number from *The Pilgrimage of the Lyfe of the Manhode*, ed. Avril Henry, EETS o.s. 288, 292, 2 vols. (Oxford: Oxford University Press, 1985-1988).

[34] This difference may also reflect the overall effect of the changes Digulleville made in revising his text: although this passage is relatively unchanged between the two versions, the recension does contain Latin insertions elsewhere, as noted earlier.

[35] Unfortunately, none of the extant manuscripts containing the English verse *Pilgrimage* actually contain the Chaucerian lyric discussed. The cultural stakes of comparison with Chaucer have not always generated analysis focused on the intratextual significance of the passage. One scholar quotes the passage of dedication in full simply as a demonstration of how Lydgate's "spongy line-filling" turns "bracing narrative into laxness"; see Kay Gilligan Stevenson, "Medieval rereading and rewriting: The context of Chaucer's 'ABC'," *'Divers toyes mengled': Essays on Medieval and Renaissance Culture in honour of André Lascombes*, ed. Michel Bitot (Tours: Université François Rabelais, 1996), 27-42, at 29.

also emulates the style of translations from the notable works of antiquity, and the manner in which the translation is displayed upon the page calls as much attention to this aspect of the translator's endeavor as to the emulation of Chaucer's prior effort.

In conclusion, I want to suggest that this vision of the English translator's role is not necessarily restricted to one text and its manuscript tradition. I mentioned *Reson and Sensuallyte* earlier as the example which seems most immediately comparable to the translation examined here, and the marginal notes "Ista sunt verba translatoris" and "Huc vsque verba translatoris" in a manuscript of *Reson and Sensuallyte* similarly draw attention to a moment of added attention to textual allegoresis.[36] The goddess Pallas, who tries to win the dreamer away from the worship of Venus in this text, is described as having swans flying about her, and the English translator provides an explanation of the swan's Christological-moral significance. This explanation is not present in the French source, which describes Pallas as surrounded by owls. In fact, the swans the translator allegorizes may have been influenced by a misreading of the word *chieuete*, meaning owl (a much more typical attribute for Pallas Athena) as the word *chienette*, similar to the English word for swan 'cynets'.[37] Latin marginal notes not only mark the allegorical interpretation of the swan as the translator's, but also provide the addition with accompanying Latin quotations from St. Paul's Philippians and Alan de Lille's *De Planctu Naturae*, underwriting the medieval text with patristic and neo-classical authorities.[38] Like my brief review of the passages marked as 'verba translatoris' within the fifteenth-century verse translation of Digulleville's poem, the transformed 'ugly duckling' of *Reson and Sensuallyte* suggests that the most visible role at least one fifteenth-

---

[36] See Oxford, Bodleian Library, Fairfax MS16, fol. 219r. By way of a contrast, the note 'uerba translatoris' in San Marino, Huntington Library EL 26 A.13, 6r, serves a function similar to the rubrics dividing the prologues of the *Pilgrimage*; the text introduced by this rubric, John Lydgate's *Dance of Death*, a translation of French verses displayed in a churchyard, is in stanza form, divided into a dialogue between characters' voices after the initial introductory commentary.

[37] Ernst Sieper, Introduction to *Reson and Sensuallyte*, by John Lydgate (?), 2 vols., Early English Text Society e.s. 84, 89 (London: Kegan Paul, Trench, Trübner & Co., 1901, 1903), II.viii. Sieper's thesis of influence was challenged by Joseph Mettlich, as noted by Caroline Boucher and Jean-Pascal Pouzet in their "'La matière des *Échecs amoureux*', d'Évrart de Conty à *Reson and Sensuallyte*," forthcoming in *The Medieval Translator / Traduire au Moyen Age*, eds. Denis Renevey and Christiania Whitehead (Turnhout: Brepols, 2009), 157-71. Boucher and Pouzet do not propose an alternative explanation for the alteration of Pallas' bird, instead drawing attention to the similar interest in mortality found in the French prose commentary designed to accompany the source poem's reference to Pallas' owl and in the glosses that accompany the figure of the swan found in the English verse translation; I am grateful to the authors for sharing their work with me in advance of its publication. Karl Steel of Brooklyn College suggested to me in personal communication that the alteration may have been influenced by negative portrayal of the owl in contemporary medieval literature. See, for example, Jan Ziolkowski, "Avatars of Ugliness in Medieval Litature," *MLR* 79 (1984): 1-20, at 13.

[38] The association of the addition with Alain de Lille's allusion to the swan's death song in *De Planctu Naturae*, Prosa 1, may also be an instance of imitating Geoffrey Chaucer's citation and translation practice, since Chaucer alludes to Alain de Lille's *De Planctu Naturae* less than thirty lines before describing the swan's death song in the *Parliament of Fowls* (line 342), a detail Chaucer also incorporates into Dido's final speech in his *Legend of Good Women* (line 1355). Line numbers are drawn from *The Riverside Chaucer*, ed. Larry D. Benson, 3rd ed. (Boston: Houghton Mifflin, 1987).

Stephanie A. Viereck Gibbs Kamath

century translator working between vernaculars assumed was not so much the linguistic transition of the French into English—indeed, the owl-swan switch in *Reson and Sensuallyte* is far from the only moment of deviation from a French source—but rather the task of commentary, the enlargement of the text's hermeneutic system in a wider context than the vernacular source alone. Analysis of the notes on the periphery of these medieval texts reveals that translations of contemporary vernacular texts, just as much as translations drawn from the classics of antiquity or scripture and patristic doctrine, found their purpose in the translator's interpretative labor, reshaping the allegorical narrative to bring Latinate authority and meaning into English.

Stephanie A. Viereck Gibbs Kamath is an assistant professor at the University of Massachusetts, Boston. Her translation work includes the first full modern English translation of René d'Anjou's *Le livre du cuer d'amours espris*, co-authored with Kathryn Karczewska (New York: Routledge, 2001), and her current research in the field of medieval allegory and its vernacular translation is supported by awards from the British Academy's Neil Ker Memorial Fund and the Huntington Library.

BEYOND THE SPHERE: A DIALOGIC COMMENTARY ON THE ULTIMATE SONETTO OF DANTE'S *VITA NUOVA*

Anna Kłosowska & Nicola Masciandaro

Revolutions: The turning movement through the images of this sonetto involves several eddying, (micro)cosmic motions. We begin already beyond the widest sphere, then penetrate it from this side via love's weeping in a motion that is virtually re-initiated from the heart in a kind of syntactic time-warp. Then comes the thought-sigh's arrival before the lady and its getting lost in the epicycles of honor and splendor and gazing. Then his subtle retelling of the gaze caused by a secondary motion of the heart that first moved it. Then the mystical understanding of the *pensero*'s unintelligible speech through the apophatic anamnesis of the beloved's name. Finally, a gracious love-boast gently expanding towards those who have understanding of love.

Con-sider our commentary a love-driven constellation, a double star (binary or optical?) gravitationally caught within these motions, like the subtle turnings of an ungraspable celestial tress.

THE HAND that begins to write is in a messy and tactile landscape where only poems can reach *oltre mer*/beyond the sea.[1] There, lives my beloved. Here, I die of grief. Dante and Nicola decree a transcendent, astrolabe-like, cosmic landscape: the page holds us holding the sphere, both inside and outside the farthest trajectory, both on earth and in heaven. Spheres are made of quintessence (fifth element), with stars (in seventh sphere/firmament), planets, and moon (in spheres below) embedded as gems. If our hands caress this *spera*, *primum mobile*, 'first-moved,' the farthest sphere, ninth, crystal heaven, then we are *Oltre*/beyond, in *empireum*, the abode of God. We're immovable, the mover: we are calling it a hand maybe for the last time, all distinctions slowly dissipating but not lost: these pages keep them. We have distinctions merely to multiply and expand experience, *che più larga gira*. As one side calls the sphere/*spera* 'the one that spins farthest,' *oltre*/the other *la spera*/wishes/hopes 'that it spins farthest.' One steps *oltre*/beyond *l'aspera*/troubles—better than *per aspera ad astra* (through rough paths, wilderness, troubles, bitterness, to the stars), *oltre*/another *l'aspira*/breathes in, blows, aspires, hopes. We have split our brains and exchanged the halves: Dante and Nicola share an analytical brain able to name, divide, pass beyond/*oltre*, draw, predict the movement of the spheres. They prefer punctuation, 'situation and figure or form': Dante in *Quaestio de aqua et terra*, treating of the nature of the two Elements, Water and Earth, declaring in favor of Earth in a dispute 'whether the Water in its own sphere, that is in its natural circumference, might be in any part higher than the Earth, which emerges out of the waters.'[2] 'Spherical ambivalence: which sphere is within which?' (N) Touching the outermost from the outside in a world of musical, gyrating spheres, we resolve the anguish of the impossible sea crossings, *oltre mer*: no longer confined in and on surfaces, we follow ways through them. [A]

EMPYREAN CONSPIRACY, intimate relation to the ultimate exterior. The line speaks (us) as already present past a boundary we could never count to, at the open end of an unimaginable sum, on the other side of *più*. Medievally knowing it as the ninth in no way diminishes the supreme distance of its perfect superlative, the wonder of reaching by comparison comparison's death, its passing away. The sphere we are beyond, 'che tutto quanto rape / l'altro universo seco, corrisponde / al cerchio che più ama e che più sape' (*Paradiso* 28.70-2) [which sweeps along with it all the rest of the universe, corresponds to the circle which loves most and knows most].[3] The logic of *più*, of more, of n+1 handlessly draws the geometry of desire, operates as the unceasing engine introducing into all things an incalculable, incommensurable angle, their invisible eternal individuating spin. It gives, *is* the most in every more. 'You will not die. For God knows that when you eat of it your eyes will be opened, and you will be like God, knowing good and evil' (Genesis 3:4-5). There is no arrival here, no landing on this shore, no seizing what owns every seizure, what ravishes (*rape*) every possession. 'La bufera infernal, che mai non resta, / mena li spiriti con la sua rapina' (*Inferno* 5.31-2) [The hellish hurricane, never resting, sweeps along the spirits with its rapine]. We see beyond only from desire's most secret, largest within. 'Infinity is not the "object" of a cognition . . . but is the desirable, that which arouses Desire, that is, that which is approachable by a thought that at each instant *thinks more than it thinks*.'[4] Saying what we can never not say. Speaking in the imperishable sweetness of our most spontaneous passivity. It is not that we know. We hear, celestially, self-forgetfully, the here. 'For me—how could there be something outside me? There is no outside! But we forget this with all sounds; how lovely it is that we forget! . . . In every Instant being begins; round every Here rolls the ball. There. The middle is everywhere. Crooked is the path of eternity.'[5] [N]

Oltre la spera che più larga gira

Anna Kłosowska & Nicola Masciandaro

CORAM TE COR MEUM *et recordatio mea* [open to you are my heart and my memory].[6] *Coram*, an adverb of manner (openly) or place (before) is of the heart. *Recordatio* (memory) seems an aspect, the temporal flow of the body/heart/*core*. This, assuming *core* is a verb: and if so, which verb is it?– To L/love: to learn by heart, to (re)member in the body: the body always knows love better, sooner, stronger, louder, it is not easily swayed, and slow if ever able to forget, rebellious in a near-silent and obvious acknowledgment of its truth. Avicenna's translators use *recordatio* for *dh-k-r* (admonishing), a specifically human ability: animals possess memory, but only man can recall principles once known and now forgotten.[7] The proximity between admonishing and sighing is cruelly remembered: dying for a month of wounds received in a duel he provoked, the king's beloved Quélus scandalously forgets God and all saints and remembers 'my king': *Il passa de ce monde en l'autre, aiant toujours en la bouche ces mots, mesme entre ses derniers souspirs qu'il jettoit avec grande force et grand regret: 'Ah! Mon roy, mon roy!' sans parler autrement de Dieu ne de sa Mere* [he passed from this world into the other, having always in his mouth these words, even among his last sighs, which he threw with great force and great regret: 'Oh! My king, my king!' without speaking otherwise of God or his Mother].[8] The words *among* the sighs: are words and sighs distinct? How does a sigh issue from my heart? 'A sigh knows how to leave the body and travel on its own, it doesn't need provisions or a map' (N). Dante and Nicola's *sospiro* seem part of the original world that Augustine does not leave in departing from it, a world where *recordatio* is of the heart, not of the admonition. *Molto mio, tutto mio*: in *De vulgari eloquentia*, Dante uses *mio* as *caro*, and so does Petrarch: *o dolce mia guerrera* [o my sweet foe].[9] My all, my king, my foe: if in Levinas we know only in relation to the other, in Dante we love as if our own, *mio* the episteme of *caro*. [A]

Passa 'l sospiro ch'esce del mio core:

EXITING THROUGH THE SINGULAR. This sigh, my sigh, the simple word-breath of the flesh possessed, spoken for but not to someone, said to none and heard (therefore) by everything, issues in the limbo of love, and having no place, finds space beyond it. 'And there is a third nature, which is space [*chōra*] and is eternal . . . and is apprehended when all sense is absent, by a kind of spurious reason [*logismō tini nothō*]' (*Timaeus* 52b).[10] Such extreme apprehension, such touching of innermost and outermost, which happens *from* the heart (my me, possessed possessor, given giver), *through* the breath (medium of body and soul), and *towards* nowhere (utopia, placeless place), indicates the way, forms the shape of being's return to itself. Some, thinking soul as in the body, say sigh is exhalation. More properly, sigh is your being breathed in, the in-spiration of individuated life by the supersoma, the big body, the corpus-cosmos that also is mine, ALL MINE!!![11] The sigh's knowing where it's going, its seminal passive surpassing, is the hither side of this inbreathing, beauty's effect everywhere being, whether from above or below, incubus or angel, to *take your breath away*. So also the sigh (actuality of Plato's bastard logos, the chora-seeking sound Socrates's body really makes) is illegitimate, both as monstrous, non-made word and as lost, misspent spirit. And it is exactly *this* should-not-have-been, the pure negativity pertaining to the specificity of my single sigh's being, that holds it, perfectly homeless, in supreme relation to what is beyond place. Many sighs is infernal: 'Quivi sospiri, pianti et alti guai / risonavan per l'aere sanza stele' (*Inferno* 3.22-3, cf. Argento's *Suspiria*). No sigh is ideal: 'those who sigh loudly and weep and wail have yet to experience love. Love sets on fire the one who finds it. At the same time it seals his lips so that no smoke comes out.'[12] But a singular human sigh, momently opening and airing the event of oneself, is *perfect*: 'Beyond the sphere passeth the arrow of our sigh. Hafiz! Silence' (*Divan*, 10.9). [N]

Anna Kłosowska & Nicola Masciandaro

AMOR che ne la mente mi ragiona: in *Convivio*, Love reasons from within my mind. What s/he says (*dice*, 18) moves things in me (*move cose. . . meco*), deviates my intellect ('*ntelletto . . . disvia*, 4), my *debole intelletto* (16).[13] Empyrean *ogni intelletto* (23), *intelligenza* that Dante associates with (sun)light does not necessarily presuppose—is not limited to—mental or rational exchange, or use of language. If Amor is an angel or a demon, s/he does not need to use language (*loqui*), a trait s/he shares with God and 'inferior animals,' as opposed to humans (*De vulgari*, 1.ii.2).[14] Angels communicate (*pando*, spread out, unfold, unwind, akin to Pandarus and to *pandus*, crooked, wound) without time (promptly, from *promo*, to bring forth emotions) and space (ineffably, from *effero*, to bring forth news): they impart intelligence without words. In the tripartite hierarchy of cognition (reasoning, intelligence, contemplation), intelligence links the lowest to the highest term. Derived from *intus legere*, reading within (oneself), or less frequently, from *inter legere*, reading between, intelligence exceeds speculation, leads to loving contemplation, mystical union, unimpeded by differences between God and humans. Both angels and demons have intellect, an inalienable though corruptible part of their nature.[15] Dante sometimes describes how wordless communication works: either intelligence, like ether, makes angels 'totally known to one another by itself' (*alter alteri totaliter inotescit per se*), or they apprehend each other because they are all reflected in the 'resplendent mirror' (*De vulgari*, 1.ii.3). Non-rational animals of the same species communicate wordlessly; non-individuated, they're guided by instinct and identical acts and passions (1.ii.5). Similarly, languages at the building site of Babel are split between the different 'species' (occupations; those who carried stones by sea *vs.* by land, etc.: 1.vii.7). Human language: reason imparted by touch: *de una ratione in aliam nichil deferri possit nisi per medium sensuale* (1.iii.2).[16] **[A]**

intelligenza nova, che l'Amore

EVAPORATION OF THE EARTHLY. Intelligence, new, rises from the earth, from all that stays in self-touching. Long before it becomes ris*ing*, before it finds verb, intelligence is there, new before its own newness, with Love behind it, leading the way. Earth, *tellus*, is immanent (*in-manere*) to in*tel*ligence, bearing it from within: 'thinking takes place in the relationship of territory and earth' (D & G).[17] Ergo the gravity between scholars and rocks (e.g. *suiseki*, lit. 'water rock,' an idea-vaporizing machine), between stone (Caillois's *l'orée du songe*) and con-templation, our self-ordering (*ratio*) geo-metry and love's taking place (*para-deisos*, *locus amoenus*). *Pace* the Aristotelian substance/accident structure of the language ('alcuna cagione del mio essere,' *Convivio* 1.13.4) that Dante emerges from/into, newness is not a property of intelligence but its essential natality, its always being *born*, which means, as with our own births (life, I can't believe it's really happening), being always at once *ex nihilo* and from somewhere, an *avvenimento* (event-as-eventing) whose curse is necessarily *ad omnes*: 'Bestemmiavano Dio e lor parenti / l'umana spezie e 'l loco e 'l tempo e 'l seme / di lor semenza e di lor nascimenti' (*Inferno* 3.103-5) [They cursed God and their parents, the human race and the place and the time and the seed of their origin and of their birth].[18] Here we hear, via the echoing etymological bestial voice that Big Mouth's commentary encompasses ('Fa qui l'autore imitare a quelle anime il bestiale costume di molti uomini che . . .), the infinite sublimity, via terror, of intelligence's newness, the eternal ground of rationality's blaspheming of the animal: '. . . until in the animal-form this instinct is fully manifested as one of the finite aspects of the finite mental form of the soul. Gradually this instinct is further and completely transformed into intellect, this being the highest finite aspect of the manifestation of the mental form in the human-form of the gross-conscious human soul experiencing the gross world.'[19] **[N]**

Anna Kłosowska & Nicola Masciandaro

LITTLE WRETCH (*misella*), drunk, the luckiest lover is s/he who is the most open: only tears bring on kisses: *et dulcis pueri ebrios ocellos/ illo purpureo ore suauiata* (Catullus 45.11-12: 'the dear drunken eyes of the sweet boy, caressed with that purple mouth').[20] In Catullus's little poem, the lovers who could not be happier (*beatiores*, 25), devoted (*unuam*, 21, *uno*, 23, only), exchange vows sealed by Amor's sneezes, 'in entwined passion, loving, loved' *mutuis animis amant amantur* (20). *Quand en pleurant ma Maîtresse s'ennuye,/ Voyant s'amye avoir mille douleurs,/ L'enfant Amour se baigne dans ses pleurs,/ Et dans ses yeux ses larmes il essuye:* when my beloved, weeping, torments herself, seeing his darling have a thousand pains, the child Love comes to bathe in her laments, and from her eyes wipes away all the tears (Ronsard, II, 429).[21] Like rain, tears flow freely and, like the farthest sphere, they are beyond count: 'The quality of mercy is not strain'd, / It droppeth as the gentle raine from heaven' (*The Merchant of Venice*, 2095-6). Desire, love, rain, *calculus* (sand), stars, tears all participate in the immeasurable beyond, as in Guillaume de Machaut's *True Story* (*Voir Dit*), ballade 33 (ca. 1362): *Nes que on porroit les estoilles nombrer, / Quant on les voit luire plus clerement, / Et les goutes de pluie et de la mer, / Et la greve seur quoy elle s'estent, / Et compasser le tour dou firmament, / Ne porroit on penser ne concevoir / Le grant desir que j'ay de vous veoir* (Just as no one can count stars, although they seem to shine more brightly, or drops of rain or sea, or gravel on which she extends, or encompass the curve of the firmament—so, no one can think or conceive my great desire to see you).[22] It is also s/he who implores: *Ploures, dames, ploures votre servant . . . Vestes vous de noir pour mi* (*Ballade* 32: Ladies, weep for your servant. . . wear black for me), for only they can save the lover: *en vous de bien a tant/ que dou peril . . . me geterez* (there's so much good in you that you will thrust me far from peril).[23] [A]

piangendo mette in lui, pur su lo tira.

'ONLY LOVE / Can bring the rain / That makes you yearn to the sky. / Only love / Can bring the rain / That falls like tears from on high. / Love reign o'er me' (The Who).[24] Drawn upward by what beats down, driven onward by what remains behind. From *plangere*, noisy beating, thus the self-striking of lamentation, ergo weeping as self-affliction, hence tears = anti-gravitational soul-goading. Warning: reading the personification allegory unidirectionally (i.e. backwards) kills its phenomenology. Love's weeping putting into one's sphere-passing sigh a new intelligence drawing it ever upward is more *real* than whatever it means. It (poetry), like the tear a cosmos-reflecting almost-nothing, here finds the echoing repetitional *space* (stanza) of weeping itself, the cavernous place where it happens (vide, audi Uaral, 'Uaral,' *Sounds of Pain*). Now comes the homology between love's tear and the 'li miroers perilleus / Ou Narcisus li orguilleus / Mira sa face e ses iaus vairs' [perilous mirror where proud Narcisus gazed at his face and his brilliant eyes].[25] Tear and mirror are twins, such that in weeping, one is on the *inside* of the reflection, or becomes reflection itself, the principle of in-sight.[26] So only in love's weeping is there real self-love, the irreplaceable worrilessness of *being* in love (thank God I am weeping, thank me for loving). Only the blinding tear reopens and lights the world, re-se(e)izes it as mirror or poiesis-zone where love keeps *turning* into new intelligence. Only letting the tears pour in, praying for rain, is there chance of seeing *through*, of finding what Narcissus dies to see, how much the image loves him, how truly your reflection, mistaken for another, really loves you. One never weeps, is never crying's secret agent. Weeping is the weather, the atmospheric condition, of love's working, its limitless secluded labor. 'Thus we are nothing, neither you nor I, beside burning words which could pass from me to you, imprinted on a page: for I would only have lived in order to write them, and, if it is true that . . .'[27] [N]

Anna Kłosowska & Nicola Masciandaro

LUX MEA *qua viva vivere dulce mihi est* (Cat. 68. 160): my light whose burning makes it sweet to live. Jacques Roubaud, the 'composer of mathematics and poetry,' glossator of the Occitan tradition from which Dante emerges, speaks of the suicide of his brother and the death of his wife as the two shores/edges/*bords*: the first brought him into *speaking in his manner, that is poetry*, the second into silence the more complete since poetry preceded it.[28] It is as if silence was the most extreme poetry, and poetry balanced on the edge of silence, in a loving, unintelligible sigh.[29] The interstice between poetry and silence, death and silence, is immeasurably small, just as the lover's desire to see, to be where s/he desires, to be joined/*giunto*/*coniunx* is immeasurable. In this equation, death finds substitutes: love, desire, even beauty can so completely still us.[30] Lost love, separation and death bring physical pain that is only relieved by tears or by nearness, touching or speaking. At the death of Eurydice, the dryad choirs fill the highest peaks with their cry, immeasurably vast lands mourn, *flerunt Rhodopeaie arces . . . et Actias Orithyia* (Virgil, *Georgics*, IV, 460-63). The cosmic mourning collapses into the hollow of Orpheus's lyre that soothes the bitterness of love, *cava solans aegrum testudine amorem* (464), a song to you, sweet *coniunx*, you and him alone (*solo*, 465), but You cosmically expanded into day and night, time immeasurable, *te ueniente die, te decedente canebat* (466), and unto hell. Hearts that do not soften at human prayer, weak shadows and lightless ghosts, monsters and larvae are stilled, and the souls like a flight of a thousand frightened birds are flushed upwards by Orpheus's singing. The ink-stained waters yield Eurydice, he retraces his steps, but coming to the upper world (*superas . . . ad auras*, 485), the careless lover is seized with madness, easy to overlook if ghosts knew how to forgive. Having emerged into the light, forgetful, exhausted, he stops and looks back at Eurydice.[31] **[A]**

Quand'elli è giunto là dove disira,

NO ARRIVAL (but this one), NO LOVE (but this one). The *when* of the sigh's arriving is the place of desire's Dasein, the *there* of its being at issue for itself. Who arrives where desire goes? Who follows it *là*? Only you, the one who never *had* and who *is* desire, only the flowing thing that is barely you. Whence the story of the musk deer finally finding what it wants only when arriving at itself as its source.[32] There is the real fragrance, the sweet self-presence of the perfectly dying, the *odor sanctitatis* of the ultimate philoputrefaction or consummate nuptial complicity with anonymous materials.[33] The place where desire wants to be is the *there* where love already is: 'Ego tanquam centrum circuli . . . tu autem non sic.'[34] But this *there* is the very *here* of desire, where it takes place, i.e. in the unity of the double meaning of *dove disira*. This *giunto*, the becoming endless of the identity between desire's *to* and desire's *from*, is love. *Ergo* love's intelligibility only as eccentricity, as the heart's being where *you* are not: 'Where your treasure is, there is your heart also' (Matt 6:21). Here the lover lives, in the utopia of the infinite sphere (see Empedocles et al.), forever translating (*opus suspirii*) the no-where of the circumference into the center's now-here.[35] Love's irresistible gravity, drawing things towards each other via invisible curvatures, is the always-arriving flow of this eccentricity: 'l'amor che move il sole e l'altre stele' (*Paradiso* 33.145). Nota Bene: in the non-finality of their innumerable multiplicity, the *other* stars have the final word. Being-in-love is belonging to what flows beyond, possessing one's possession by the unpossessable: 'there is indeed a belonging to the rivers . . . It is precisely that which tears onward more surely in the rivers' own path that tears human beings out of the habitual midst of their lives, so that they may be in a center outside of themselves, that is, be excentric. The prelude to inhering in the excentric midst of human existence, this "centric" and "central"' abode in the excentric, is love.'[36] Cf. Joy Division's 'Love Will Tear Us Apart.' **[N]**

Anna Kłosowska & Nicola Masciandaro

NULLA potest mulier tantum se dicere amatam / uere (Cat. 87.1-2): no woman can say she is loved as much, truly, as . . .[37] Dante's *riceve onore* echoes the lines on the first night of love in the 13th c. romance of *Flamenca*, imprisoned in a tower by a jealous husband, freed by Guillaume de Nevers, who falls in love before he sees her.[38] We surprise her receiving honor: *vede* before *riceve*. If, as *Flamenca* and I want, to give and receive honor is to share caresses and kisses, it is a very sensuous scene: 'looks for nothing, asks nothing, / but that which his lady, *si dons*, offered him, / who was not slow to give pleasure, / but did him much honor and good, *ains li fes mas honors e bens*' (5962-5): *uere*, Arnaut Daniel's 'double joy in Paradise for his soul / if ever man entered it for loving well,' *q'en paradis n'aura doble ioi m'arma, / si ja nuills hom per ben amar lai intra* (*Sestina*, 35-6). *Il miglior fabbro*, Arnaut greets Dante in Occitan in *Purg.* 26. His *Canso* anticipates Dante's sonnet: Love that rains/weeps in my heart, *l'amors q'inz el cor mi plou* (13), instantly perfects (*plan*, to smooth out, perfect) and inspires (*d'aura*, fills with breath) my song that moves from him or her (*de liei mou*) who keeps and governs worth: *Amors marves plan'e daura / mon chantar, que de liei mou / qui pretz manten e governa* (5-8). But Dante's *onore* is for the dead, from the undead: *mai, se non dopo la morte*: sung so the war would not remain enclosed within the miserable one who feels it, *e acciò che questa battaglia che io avea meco non rimanesse saputa pur dal misero che la sentia* (*VN* 37:3); Arnaut, but also *VN* 35-8, an attempt to love someone else, precede it: '*Voi non dovreste mai, se non per morte, / la vostra donna, ch'è morta, obliare.' / Così dice l'meo core, e poi sospira* (37:8): my eyes, you must never forget your lady that is dead, except by dying. So said my heart, and sighed. Constant heart and inconstant eyes (37), soul/reason and heart/passion (38): 'my desire turns all towards [the new lady], *lo mio desiderio si volge tutto verso lei*. . . the soul/reason says to heart/appetite . . . he responds.'[39] **[A]**

vede una donna, che riceve onore,

TRANSCRIBING SECRETS, the present tense of *vede* produces the presence of what it sees. So the sonetto insists throughout on its present, on the being-without-beginning-and-without-end of its when (*quando*). Nothing happens—everything is happening: the sigh's circling beyond and back from the sphere to the heart it exits, the lady's shining upon and receiving from those who see her splendor, the sorrowing heart's hearing whom it causes to speak . . . Every event traces a flowing beyond and a returning back. All things circulate themselves, producing time from a somewhere beyond the sphere. 'If . . . the Soul withdrew, sinking itself again into its primal unity, Time would disappear: the origin of Time . . . is to be traced to the first stir of the Soul's tendency towards the production of the sensible Universe' (Plotinus, *Enneads*, 3.7.12). The sigh's seeing a lady turns the heart that shares its light to the movement of this first stir, to the scene of the first look of love. Here we record the *ocular* origin point of cosmos (janua coeli, oculus mundi), the fact that it is happening, not in a static place, but in an ecstatic erotic stir that remains visible in our looking, in the spontaneous giving-receiving of seeing which miraculously exceeds by staying within itself: 'the very cause of the universe . . . is also carried outside of himself . . . He is . . . beguiled by goodness, by love, and by yearning and is enticed away from his transcendent dwelling place and comes to abide within all things, and he does so by virtue of his supernatural and ecstatic capacity to remain, nevertheless, within himself' (Pseudo-Dionysius, *Divine Names*, 4.13).[40] Love at first sight is only the reseeing of original vision. 'The process of perception runs parallel to the process of creation, and the reversing of the process of perception without obliterating consciousness amounts to realising the nothingness of the universe as a separate entity' (*Discourses* II.98). As if love is a seeing that receives itself in surplus from the seen. As if the widest sphere is the eye. **[N]**

Anna Kłosowska & Nicola Masciandaro

QUE *n'est tout mon corps en pensers transformé?* O, let my body be all thought . . . At parting, the lover's eyes send a mist into the mind; seized with it, reason lets herself slip into dream, a constant vision of the beloved, tormenting heart and soul with the desire to see the absent lover. Sometimes, the mind returns, only to fetch the heart and go see the lover together; the soul runs after the heart to fetch it back, but instead, she herself is taken in by that pleasant place, and forgets to return (Ronsard, *Elegy II*).[41] Dante's sigh, lover's dream, travels freely, seeing, speaking, hearing, breathing the lines in and out, like a body, like a lovers' kiss. This line, like love, is in flight: it takes off and lands nowhere, it changes everything, it begins everywhere: *luce*/*riceve*, *splendore*/*onore*, *suo*/*mio*, like Diotima's Love, *metaxy*/between gods and mortals, of one and the other: *suo* of the lover and splendor, and of me who adores/*mira*; *mio* of me and the body, and of the lover/*caro*. *Pur su*/*per lo suo*: logic, condition, and direction confounded. Like tears, they have no agent: light is the weather of loving, loving is the condition of rising, tears are the opening of loving. A sigh that senses light: a sigh/t, at first sight, endlessly there in my love's eyes. What takes the breath away is the fullness of the loved one, beauty, goodness and brilliance; but what captures the heart, and makes me want to make love to him is, like her light, without agent, beyond his control. Both are love, both moved by him, but the second is desire: like sacrifice, in excess, irrational. That, but first, what makes me love is his incandescence at the sight of me. Love at first sight is circular, without origin (who looked first?) The always cosmic event where the soul, beguiled by goodness, creates body/universe/all things to love in infinitely more ways. So, in flowing-circulation, the sigh that leaves the body is being embodied again in seeing. Love speaks light: *guardi le stelle che tremano d'amore . . . il mio mistero è chiuso in me: sulla tua bocca lo dirò, quando la luce splenderà*.[42] **[A]**

e luce sì, che per lo suo splendore

SPECTACULAR INTIMACY, or, the brightness of light becoming itself. Splendor is not a quality, but the condition of the overcoming of quality. It is not something seen, but the visible approach of the place where seeing becomes the seen.[43] 'In this state of absorbed contemplation there is no longer question of holding an object: the vision is continuous so that seeing and seen are one thing; object and act of vision have become identical; of all that until then filled the eye no memory remains. . . . the vision floods the eyes with light, but it is not a light showing some other object, the light is itself the vision.'[44] Syntactically, the line temporalizes splendor, traces the becoming substantial of the relation between seeing and seen as a time delay within their distinction. Suspended in this light-filled air, can I say what splendor is? Luckily Dante, being one who breathes love back into philology (the exhale of his taking note when love inspires), is here to help.[45] Commenting on the descent of divine power as sight (*In lei discende la virtù divina / sì come face in angelo, che 'l vede*), he explains splendor via Avicenna as not only reflected light, but the visible/visual becoming of a thing toward the virtue shining on it.[46] Seeing is not simply splendor's external measuring tool, but the very efficiency of its cause. To see someone's splendor, to experience how she shines, is to witness her becoming like what she sees and thus belong by parallel process to her being. Splendor is the ideal form of seeing as participation, the term of beauty's neither-subjective-nor-objective being in the eye of the beholder, the self-forgetful love-seeing or ocular 'erotic anamnesis . . . that transports the object not toward another thing or another place, but toward its own taking place—toward the Idea.'[47] So the sigh returns in the lady's splendor to its own very cause.[48] So is splendor what speaks the being of love: 'Non per aver a sé di bene aquisto, / ch'esser no può, ma perché suo splendore / potesse, risplendendo, dir "Subsisto," . . . / s'aperse in nuovi amor l'etterno amore' (*Paradiso* 29.13-8).[49] **[N]**

Anna Kłosowska & Nicola Masciandaro

EX ALTA *providentiae specula*: Boethius's *Consolation* and Dante's sigh/t coincide where the pilgrim spirit arrives.[50] Whether distanced from philosophy/theology or safely wrapped in it, like a mantle, this line, in recognizing weariness (*peregrino*) and concrete happiness of the lover's presence within the sight of the beloved (*la mira*), speaks my quiet becoming-joy, unlike the abstract *giunto* and *desira* of the line whose rhyme/mirror this is (*mira/desira*). Or rather, the indeterminate *quando* and *la dove* in that earlier line where love was still only a promise, made me tremble: *Ch è questa che vèn, ch'ogn'om la mira, / che fa tremar di chiaritate l'àre* (Guido Cavalcanti, *Rime* 4: who is she that comes, that every man looks at, that makes air tremble with brightness). Our line, its whispering, purring sounds carried by the vowel 'i,' is in love/light where all is calm and joy/*lieto*: *del suo lume fa 'l ciel sempre quieto* (*Paradiso* 1.122): *Veggio negli occhi de la donna mia / un lume pieno di spiriti d'amore / che porta uno piacer novo nel core / sì che vi desta d'allegrezza vita* (Cavalcanti, 26: I saw in the eyes of my lady a light filled with love's spirits that carries a new pleasure into the heart, so that a life of joy lives there).[51] But is love only a way to see? Happiness, only a position of extreme distance? Being, a seeing of the present as the smile of the future/eternal (Boethius)? For those who feel alone (who hasn't?), *peregrino* both reveals and withholds a better question: reveals/what gives the steps of pilgrimage meaning is their direction, refracted in each, but streaming in from the beloved/outside: a person/place that signifies by difference: 'how is this day different from any other day?' In loneliness, that very distance makes us sad. But, (not)filling the emptiness, (in)different fictions smile to console us: 'In Pavia they preserve supposedly Roland's lance, which is none other than the mast of a large barge, armed with a metal tip.'[52] Perhaps all pleasure intersects with feeling that seeing is being: 'I see the unicorn.'[53] **[A]**

MY EYES AND I have a bargain: they say what I cannot speak and I tell them what they cannot see.[54] Being in wonder keeps us busy. So the pilgrim spirit's looking through her splendor is an identical inner relation, an intimate respirating exchange between seeing-as-speaking and speaking-as-seeing that produces silence for profit, the plenitude of sense and medium of all real transaction.[55] 'The soundless gathering call, by which Saying moves the world-relation on its way, we call the ringing of stillness. It is: the language of being.'[56] *La mira* comes here, to the unstopping completion, the quiet saturation from which poetry, or the re-saying of silence, initiates anew 'la gioia che mai non fina.'[57] Gazing on her, *lo peregrino spirito* enters the circumambulation (*tawaf*, *pradakshina*) that is the beginningless beginning and endless end of its wandering desire, 'the pneumatic circle within which the poetic sign, as it arises from the spirit of the heart, can immediately adhere both to the dictation of that 'spiritual motion' that is love, and to its object.'[58] The amorous circulatory system of the sonetto, participating in the trinitarian processions of being it evokes, is inscribed in its subtle self-reflexive numerology, founded on four fives (4+5=9=Beatrice): 'cinque parti,' 5 rhymes, 14 lines (1+4=5), 4 stanzas + 1 poem = 5.[59] So the line groupings (2, 2, 4, 3, 3) place Beatrice (9=2+4+3) at the center. What is the point? In keeping with the conjecture that 'counting was born in the elaboration of a ritual procession re-enacting the Creation,'[60] the sonetto processes its own creation in the breath that speaks it, counting in a circle charted by the two persons (lover and beloved) and their personified relation (*sospiro/pensero/spirito*) so as to arrive, return, and mystically re-arrive at Beatrice. That is easy. A truer question is *where* is the point? That is the place of this line, the place of the gaze to which love ever returns by always never being able to leave. **[N]**

lo peregrino spirito la mira.

Anna Kłosowska & Nicola Masciandaro

ANGEL! If there was a Square that we didn't know, and there, / on an unspeakable carpet, lovers displayed . . . their towers of pleasure, their / ladders, long since standing where there was no ground, only / leaning on each other, trembling. . . before the soundless dead: / Would these, then, throw down their final, forever saved-up, / forever hidden, unknown to us, eternally valid / coins of happiness (Rainer Maria Rilke, *The Duino Elegies*, 'The Fifth')?[61] *Silens*, the dead/silents, giving over their passage fare to the lovers. Happiness as our passage fare out of *this* world: the ghosts who haunt us. . . Trans-substantiation of light in sound: *li fols enfes qui crie / por la bele estoile avoir, / qu'il voit halt el ciel seoir* (Chastelain de Couci: the foolish child that cries to have the beautiful star he sees sitting high in the sky); *Et li dolz son del ruissel sor gravele / que je voi resclaircir / me font resovenir* (CdC: and the sweet sounds of the brook on the sand that I see sparkle, reminds me).[62] Thence, the fountain: a musical instrument that cures madness; a lyric form; a watering can; or, any number of similar things: *chantepleure*, sing-weep, *irrigium,* la chantepleure *gallice vocatum, graece clepsydra*.[63] As the iconic instrument of remembrance,[64] it brings us to time that, like the sigh/t at the same time suspended in splendor and contemplating it, signifies in passing, not as a measure. As the instrument that measures time, *chantepleure*/clepsydra hastens the tellurian union. Measured time's powers of seduction also consist in the insistence of its courtship, its constant repetition-reminder/*mi ridice*; ungrateful, disdainful at first, we misunderstand its splendor as the *locus amoenus* that opens us up so we make love to others, also opened by its splendor. There comes a time, there comes one repetition when we finally understand, and our resistance dissolves, and we fold ourselves into its embrace: 'Earth, my dearest, I will. Oh believe me, you no longer / need your springtimes to win me over—one of them, / ah, even one is already too much' (Rilke, *DE* 9).[65] **[A]**

Vedela tal, che quando 'l mi ridice,

TINIEST DIVINITY: difference & repetition = all I confess I cannot say when I speak *and*. There is what this line says, which is straightforward, and there is what this line is, something that keeps saying it. It keeps saying in a universal sense: 'Man speaks only as he responds to language. Language speaks. Its speaking speaks for us in what has been spoken.'[66] In a general sense: 'Poetry is news that STAYS news.'[67] And in an absolutely *specific* sense which, close as your own breath, is infinitely more important than either. This is not an other or extra or allegorical sense, not a deeper saying hidden underneath the obvious, not something structural or mythic or symbolic. It is a sense living so secretly and openly, so publicly and intimately, that it passes through us visibly unnoticed, incognito. Being seen neither with nor without comprehension, being something apparent but altogether beyond and before surface as such, this sense is exactly what makes all its senses possible, the subtle medium of their presence. Like a face *itself*, an impossible and inevitable silent projection preceding all expression, this can be called the *apophantic* sense, so as to indicate a properly phenomenological meaning-perception of something as it shows itself.[68] Or it can be called the *special* sense, to mean a perception of something's special being, its essential appearance.[69] The A/S sense is tasted by reading two-dimensionally, too close to the page, aperspectivally, floating.[70] The beauty of this sense, its God-proving detail (*whatever* that is), is that it ain't at all abstract, that it is always a *this*. It is, simply, wonderfully, as it appears to be.[71] How does it appear? By being (the sense that appears as) wholly at home with the fact *that* it appears.[72] What does it appear as? As itself, in this case, the rich, ready-to-be-endlessly-glossed idea that the *what* of seeing, its suchness (*Vedela tal*), IS the *when* of its resaying (*quando 'l mi ridice*). That is: 'Habit is the originary synthesis of time, which constitutes the life of the passing present.'[73]**[N]**

CONSUETUDINES, moral habits: 'it is for them that *representatio* is primarily used [because] . . . man does not delight in seeing the mere forms of things existing in nature, but delights in their representations and formation by paints and colors.'[74] Love's crying puts intelligence in the sigh, the sigh reaches its desire (*intentionem*) but pilgrimage between contraries (*spesso/sottile*) continues, circular (*parla al cor che lo fa parlare*). *Sonetto*: music is 'poetry's major part to impress the soul' (*tonus. . . est maior partium ad imprimendum anime et operandum in ipsa*).[75] Averroes/Allemanus deciphering Aristotle call *circulation* and *meaning/significatio* what in Aristotle is reversal/*peripateia* and discovery/*anagnoresis*.[76] Breath *circulates* between the heart and beyond the farthest sphere, a peregrination/*peripateia* between contraries. When the sigh is joined with what it desires (*permutant ad suam intentionem*), it falls/becomes sensuous, *cadens in sensum*. For me, Dante's poem is very unlike the Averroensian tradition that separates poetry from *sha'aria*, divine law.[77] Instead, in Dante as in Aristotle, there is a circular, poetic *cadentia in sensum* unfolded as the circulatory embodiment of the sigh (sigh/t, etc.): sensing/desensing, falling/rising, feeling/not being able to feel. Heart breathes a sigh/t and (not)hears (*no lo intendo. . . 'ntendo ben*), but that does not *end in* recognition. The sonnet (never)ends even as *significatio* proceeds by anagnoresis, in all of the five canonical ways at once: the sigh/t of splendor returns the sigh to the heart (*recordatio*); in that circulation a memory is awakened (*dh-k-r*), a thing forgotten is recalled (*quando 'l mi ridice*); a mark is recognized (mark=the name? *ricorda Beatrice*); a knowledge leads to logical understanding. Intelligence, intention, know[ing] (*so*) only relaunches/releases the *so*spiro and the *so*netto's infinitely complex movement: *e però dico che questo dubbio io lo intendo solvere e dichiarare in questo libello ancora in parte piu dubbiosa* (*VN* 12:17).[78] **[A]**

SUBTLE SPEAKING, language thinner than air, narrower than every whisper. What does a word not pass through? Dante's thought-sigh does a cosmic circuit and comes back talking a language he does not intend. When was it not *logos*? Never other than spoken/speaking, from *sospiro* to *spirito*, it always was and will be *verbum*, the sonic incarnation of inner shining: 'the word which sounds without is a sign of the word that shines within . . . For that which is produced by the mouth of the flesh is the sound of the word, and is itself also called 'word,' because that inner word assumed it in order that it might appear outwardly.'[79] So the poet's 'pensero, nominandolo per lo nome d'alcuno suo effetto' (*VN* 41:3-4), reversely named for its effect, stays word only by ever becoming word, by ceaselessly passing, staying prepositional (*oltre, del, su, per, al, di*). Word transpires, is something breathed and breathing, like a vibrational, lyric touching of the invisible *locutio rerum*, a thing's original, extra-topological in-tention.[80] 'Spiritus ubi vult spirat et vocem eius audis sed non scis unde veniat et quo vadat' (John 3:8).[81]

Listening to the sonetto as logogenetic allegory, bending attention into (in-tendere) its story of becoming-word, this line now talks about the vestigial body of verbal being, the way words travel as traces. Being always windily *between*, essentially whenceless and whitherless, word is known by unknowing its place: 'io non possa intendere là ove lo pensero mi trae' (*VN* 41:8). That is how speaking passes, by being subtle: 'Subtlety takes its name from the power to penetrate.'[82] How verse happens: 'True singing is a different breath, about / nothing. A gust inside the god. A wind.'[83] How love hears: 'Suppose someone hears an unknown sign, like the sound of some word which he does not know the meaning of; he wants to know what it is . . . [this] is not love for the thing he does not know but for something he knows, on account of which he wants to know what he does not know.'[84] **[N]**

io no lo intendo, sì parla sottile

Anna Kłosowska & Nicola Masciandaro

THE CONSTELLATION / of his future love has long / been moving among the stars (Rilke, 'Duration of Childhood').[85] The adequacy of *parla* to *fa parlare*: question to answer, desire to fulfillment. The circulation of tears, sigh/t, and rhyme, 'goddess of secret and ancient coincidences': 'she is very capricious; she comes as happiness comes, hands filled with an achievement that is already in flower' (Rilke).[86] Softly pressing against the margins of burning desire, not refined by the anguish to say everything, filling head and heart with pleasurable things: 'his senses are precipitating out of the clear solution of his soul' (Rilke).[87] The dispersion and recollection choreographed in life continues without it. The self seems less permanent and more intermittent, a retreating wave on the shore of becoming. Self as a wave, a beating heart: not constantly on; rather, constantly on-off. I am a promise of return, *recordatio*, not a presence. What are the limits of identity? To fall in love: as we fall, we trace a signature and a narrative as recognizable as gait, silhouette, voice, its originary events always *present*. How much more alive are we when we are in love. In love, we come to ourselves only by the circular motion of the sigh that offers me to myself having passed through you, the lover offering the beloved to herself. I suppose when one of the lovers dies the sigh, not finding its twin heart near, may well wander far, beyond the largest sphere, and become lost. Or, besotted by the sigh/t, the sigh loses some hearing: the light/splendor dims sound: all my senses are engaged so deeply that I become deaf: I see sound and cannot hear it.[88] I imagine that which the lover hears here as the voices arising when we fall asleep, unmistakable: it's my beloved, my parents, my children. The characteristic fall of a phrase, the color of the content: a story, a quarrel or worry, love, specific words undistinguishable except phatic words or quirks, particular silence-fillers. Writing conserves words, but only magical means conserve sound: jars, crystals, ice, heart. [A]

al cor dolente, che lo fa parlare.

HEART is whom speaking is for. You know this. It does not require commentary. 'I turned away [*detourné*] from philosophy when it became impossible to discover in Kant any human weakness, any authentic accent of melancholy [*tristesse*].'[89] The sigh's sound is the sign of the heart's *turning*. The sorrowing heart's hearing of this sound *is* the sigh's speaking. I.e., heart turns by attending to its sigh and makes (*fa*) sigh talk by hearing it as saying, by letting it be heard as the heart's own voice, at once most intimately for itself and totally exposed.[90] This close but not closed circuit, whereby the *from* (*del*) revolves perfectly into the *to* (*Al*), returns language to breath/spirit by releasing love from the body—a self-restorative movement also called *listening to your heart*, the neither audible nor inaudible exercise of remembering, re*cor*ding one's ancient, deeper will. 'Not of to-day, is my love for Thy musky tress; / Long time 'tis, since that with this cup, like the new moon, intoxicated I was.'[91] Such a sighing one is a whispering tetragrammaton, something on the way to becoming YHWH (I am who I am): '*That's* what I am, after all, at bottom and from the start . . . [one] who not for nothing once told himself: "Become what you are!"'[92] Precisely what Beatrice makes Dante do in Eden after her eyes overcome him: 'Men che dramma / di sangue m'è rimaso che non tremi: / conosco i segni de l'antica fiamma.'[93] Which shows something of the subtle intersection between sighing, confession, and sorrow: how love is a painful secret opening in oneself from and towards another, a word wounding from within that allows you really to speak, to tell all, as if for the first time, even before and beyond there being anything to say: 'And taking him aside from the multitude privately, he put his fingers into his ears, and he spat and touched his tongue; and looking up to heaven, he *sighed*, and said to him, "Eph'phatha," that is, "Be opened." And his ears were opened, his tongue was released, and he spoke plainly' (Mark 7:33-5). [N]

Anna Kłosowska & Nicola Masciandaro

FOR the sake of a single poem, you must . . . know the gesture that small flowers make when they open in the morning (Rilke).[94] As we are nearing the last revolutions of the sonnet, I see this line as an offering, an equivalent of the *envoi*/address in a ballad or a ghazal: 'O Prince!' A devotional gesture, *envoi* as an offering to the Muses recalls the sonnet that opens the first volume of Ronsard's poems: 'with his right hand at your altar he hangs / the humble gift of his immortal book / and at your feet puts his heart, with the other.'[95] In another poem, so well beloved of everyone, Ronsard pleads: 'for obsequies receive my weeping and my tears, / this vase here full of milk, this basket full of flowers / so that, alive or dead, you'll be nothing but roses.'[96] A flower beloved of all: all, become nothing but flowers for the beloved: what is love if not a dedication of all to one aim? And in that dedication, love and poetry resemble each other—an ontological structure that helps me understand the perfection of their fit, their Moebius-like relation: is poetry born of love, or love, of poetry? Nicola's meditations on creation as love resonate with the nouveau baroque *oeuvre* of the Polish Ukrainian poet Eugeniusz Tkaczyszyn-Dycki: 'on a Sunday afternoon, three half-naked soldiers / worked. God did not hide his distraction in their bodies and anew / he created the cosmos the beginning and the end while they / blinded by the sun, rested supine / The Lord burrowed in their bodies surprised by the intimacy of sweat / returned to his sources and became / a drop of dirt without which we would not be ourselves,'[97] a dirty droplet whose twin is a purifying drop of Prince of Denmark's Elixir, from another poem by Dycki: 'Truth too hard to choke out with that lump in your throat? / One drop of the Elixir will cleanse your windpipe.'[98] Language/crutch, a lump of clay 'tormented by inspiration'[99]—or the name that Love puts in the poet's heart, and that takes him, 'astonished, out of himself,' mute, incoherent, like the Delphi oracle.[100] **[A]**

So io che parla di quella gentile,

THAT (*che*), extraordinary magic of whatever happens (see n.74). 'Now I am tempted to say that the right expression in language for the miracle of the existence of the world, though it is not any proposition *in* language, is the existence of language itself.'[101] Whence I, tress-bound–'Fortes tresses, soyez la houle qui m'enlève' [Strong tresses, be the swell that lifts me away][102]—am further tempted to say that *quella gentile* IS language's *that* as the world's miracle, that Dante's 'nuovo miracolo e gentile'[103] is the miracle of language, its witnessed (*So*) aura, not in the shallow sense of a special supplementary happening inside or outside world, but in the only sensible sense of the inexplicable happening of world itself. Knowing *that* the sigh speaks of that blessed one is the word-index of the world as miracle. *Beatrice* =halo of the wor(l)d. I mean this, not (only) in an auto-reductive intellectual way, but in a post-abysmal A.K.-inspired way that knows how to have it both ways, namely, that a Wittgensteinian reading of the poet's beloved only belongs to her being an all-the-more real, live woman. Cf. R. Benigni's gloss on Mary as a maiden God cannot resist being *made* by. 'Quel ch'ella par quando un poco sorride, / non si pò dicer né tenere a mente' [What she seems when she but smiles cannot be said or held in mind].[104] But *that* she appears, this is inevitable: 'the strongest magic of life: it is covered by a veil of beautiful possibilities, woven with threads of gold– promising, resisting, bashful, mocking, compassionate, and seductive. Yes, life is a woman!'[105] *That* is the lovely net we are entangled in, the turning maze which is the way of real guiding: 'Within the curl of Thy tress, went Hāfiz / In the dark night; and God is the guide.'[106] *So io che* . . . curves (*volte*) with the silent power of a sweet conviction, a pure secret surmise that 'between Nirvana and the world there is not the slightest difference,' that in Paradise—the good thief's *today* (Luke 23:43)—'everything will be as it is now, just a little different.'[107] **[N]**

Anna Kłosowska & Nicola Masciandaro

WHAT MOVES US? *Even today a god / could secretly enter this form and not be diminished*: in this passage of 'The Spanish Trilogy,' Rilke is enraptured with a shepherd who 'moves about. . . fixes the hem of his flock where it has grown ragged.'[108] That pastoral vision seems only related to Dante's spheres by Plato's ladder: one body to two, two to all, all to occupations, beautiful occupations to sciences, sciences to one science whose sole object is beauty, and finally beauty in and of itself (*Symposium* 211c). From ladder to gyrating spheres: 'the divine Desire is in itself without end and principle, like a perpetual circle that, thanks to Good, from Good, in the bosom of Good, and with Good in view, traverses a perfect orbit, identical to itself . . . never ceasing to progress and remain stable and return to its first state' (Dionysis, *De nomine*, chap. 4: 13-14).[109] In Augustine, what is worthy of love derives from God, and corresponds to the most lovable part of one's beloved: the part that communes with God:[110] 'the souls of men . . . love rest . . . as, according to its special gravity, a body descends or rises until it reaches a place where it can rest,— oil, for example . . . rising if poured onto water . . . for the feeding and faning of that ardent love, by which, under a law like that of gravitation, we are borne upwards or inwards to rest, the presentation of truth by emblems has great power: for, thus presented, things move and kindle our affection much more than if they were set forth in bald statements, not clothed with sacramental symbols. Why this should be, it is hard to say . . . I believe that the emotions are less easily kindled while the soul is wholly involved in earthly things; but if it be brought to those corporeal things which are emblems of spiritual things, and then taken from these to the spiritual realities which they represent, it gathers strength by the mere act of passing from one to another, and, like a flame of a lighted torch, is made to burn more brightly, and is carried away to rest by a more intensely glowing love.'[111] **[A]**

PAST REASON, FUTURE MEMORY. The sigh's often re-cording of Beatrice is why the *I* knows what its thought is talking about. Where, when is this *why*? The belated explanation of knowing, the memorial giving of its reason, starts to unravel an endless epistemic time-loop–'any point of knowledge can be so multiplied that its instances, far from being few, turn out to extend to infinity'[112]–as if in knowing's moment (*So io*) an infinite series of future statements is already summed (I know that I know that know . . .). Reason (*però che*) re-gives this moment as its past: cause. Memory (*ricorda*) pre-gives this moment as its future: effect. Preparing the way and accelerating the hard-to-recognize arrival of love–'vidi venir da lunghi Amore / allegro sì, che appena il conoscia'[113]–this line properly places reason syntactically after knowledge (*So io . . . però che*) so as to locate memory before it (*ricorda Beatrice*). Thus the explanation intentionally moves, like a trap catching you by setting it, into its own undoing, to the hardly foreseeable point where the end of explanation (*Beatrice*) precludes all reason for it, and more literally, where Dante's thought speaks of Beatrice because he was already remembering her, where knowing is a catching up to memory's future. Knowledge's reason, which makes it seem an effect of something prior, turns out to be a mirror image showing a more real inverse reality wherein knowing precedes its object, where memory is a *forward* projection, where one never hears a name for the first time.[114] This is the space where *spesso* means something incredible: neither past, nor present, nor future. Not instant, not duration. Perhaps a kind of multidimensional repetition, without recurrence. Living here, in the often, a lover is one whose heart always runs ahead, anamnesic map in hand, clearing paths in trackless wilds and voids for trains of thought to run. Credo ut intelligam.[115] 'One in love tastes the glories of life to the full'[116] and always knows what he is (and is not) talking about. **[N]**

però che spesso ricorda Beatrice,

Anna Kłosowska & Nicola Masciandaro

IMPOSSIBLE sea crossing were the beginning of this commentary, and they are now on my mind as we reach the destination of our *peregrinatio/peripateia*: *the experience of sailors, who, when at sea, behold the mountains below them* (Dante, *Quaestio*).[117] If the poem at first seemed self-involved and, in its infinite circular cosmography, self-contained betweeen Love and Lover, now its optic suddenly shifts, allowing for distance, tempting us to see the spheres as a small model astrolabe that a hand can hold, its movement imagined so fully that it 'can be made clear even to women' (*Quaestio*).[118] Perhaps it is this change of optic that invites us, in turn, to descend the ladder and, god-like, secretly enter the form of the shepherd or another form that inspired *this* poem. We will claim and inhabit 'that pure space into which flowers endlessly open' anticipated by Rilke's 'Eighth Elegy.' Rilke thinks elegiacally that the presence of another makes that always-opening space at the same time present and inaccessible, but I feel, instead, that this is an accessible space where lovers take turns moving. Rilke imagines that lovers are close to the always-blooming space/*chora*, that they are almost there: 'if the beloved were not there blocking the view.' He sees the lovers in a continual impasse such that 'neither can move past each other.' I think more happily: that in writing past each other we have been passing behind each other, walking into precisely that space which 'as if by some mistake. . . opens for [the lovers] / behind each other.'[119] 'O shooting star / that fell into my eyes and through my body—: / Not to forget you. Stay!'[120] As in Rilke's 'Archaic Torso of Apollo,' some objects are headless/beheaded but 'still suffused with brilliance from inside,' capable 'from all the borders of itself, / [to] burst like a star,' like Barthes's last unfinished (novel?) project interrupted by his death, like the beginning of a *Vita Nuova*: 'You must change your life.'[121] **[A]**

sì ch'io lo 'ntendo ben, donne mie care.

YES. 'Hectic search for exhilarating experiences should not be mistaken for love. They are the forerunners of grim, relentless penalties and intense suffering. Love from its lowest to its highest expression has its ups and downs. Love suffers the pangs of separation, the stings of jealousy, and all the little pricks that a lover has to endure are the different helpmates in disguise. They stir you up and bring forward to life the most important parts of your nature. Then they no longer maintain their individual life, but merge in one common longing for the Beloved.'[122] Sì. *Sì che . . . io sp[h]ero di dicer di lei quello che mai non fue ditto d'alcuna* (*VN* 42:2) [So that . . . I hope to say of her what was never said of any other woman]. Not running hither and thither to no end. Here. Intent. At play, work. Being beyond the sphere, living and breathing there—understand well my good meaning dear ones—is not somewhere outside of life. Life goes on, more (and more)—'Live more and more in the Present which is ever beautiful and stretches away beyond the limits of the past and the future'[123]— than ever: 'Without life, alive I am. This, esteem no great wonder.'[124] This is being where one *must* be: 'Sāki! come. That wine, that is the soul-cherisher, / Like life, is fit for the shattered heart, / Give, that out from the world, my tent I may pitch; / Above the sphere, my pavilion, may pitch.'[125] Life is a space, a place beyond place, where we breathe in the space that space is within. Getting it, understanding well, drinking deep and tasting the lovely mouth-truth is not turning away. It is entering, being entered into the openness that already infects you: 'The dead god is not a tired, abolished or doomed god but a god with its ultimate weapon of catastrophic devastation. . . . In the process of descending, the dead god rediscovers its . . . corpus as a pestilential but love-saturated communion with the sacred.'[126] Turning (now, forever) to his dear ladies, the poet's sigh spreads the pest.[127] No one can tell me we do not have a fever. *This world or the next, heaven* . . . [128] **[N]**

Anna Kłosowska & Nicola Masciandaro

The text of the sonetto, cited within the circles, is taken from Dante Alighieri, *Vita Nuova*, ed. and trans. Dino S. Cervigni and Edward Vasta (Notre Dame: University of Notre Dame Press, 1995), 142-4. Other references to the *Vita Nuova* (*VN*) use the chapter and division enumeration of this edition.

---

[1] The vast poetic *corpus* that describes lovers tragically separated by sea includes Theseus's return to Aegeus and the tragic mistake of the black sails, reprised in *Tristan and Isolda*; the *Odyssey*; Ovid's *Heroïdes* (ex., 'Phyllis to Demophoon'); lyric poetry (ex. Jaufré Rudel's *amor de lonh*, faraway love).

[2] *La 'Quaestio de aqua et terra' di Dante Alighieri: Edizione principe del 1508 riprodotta in facsimile* . . . ed. G. Bofitto, intro. O. Zanotti-Bianco, trans. G. Bofitto, Prompt, S. P. Thompson and A. Müller (Florence: Olschki, 1905): 60.

[3] Dante Alighieri, *The Divine Comedy*, ed. Charles S. Singleton, (Princeton: Princeton University Press, 1973).

[4] Emmanuel Levinas, *Totality and Infinity: An Essay on Exteriority*, trans. Alphonso Lingis (Pittsburgh: Duquesne University Press, 1969), 62.

[5] Friedrich Nietzsche, *Thus Spoke Zarathustra*, trans. Adrian Del Caro (Cambridge: Cambridge University Press, 2006), 'The Convalescent,' 175.

[6] Augustine, *Confessions* 5.6.11.

[7] Avicenna (d. 1037), *Avicenna Latinus. Liber De Anima seu Sextus de naturalibus,* ed. Simone Van Riet,(Leiden: Brill, 1972), IV, 3, p. 25, quote from Johannes de Rupella (Jean de La Rochelle, d. 1254), *Tractatus de divisione multiplici potentiarum anima*, ed. Pierre Michaud-Quantin (Paris: Vrin, 1964), 77. 'The root of *tadhkir* is *dh-k-r*, a root that means to remember and is regularly used in mystical language. Dhikr (from the same root) refers to remembrance of God, a form of praising and celebrating the nature of God, and remembrance of the *Qur'an*, or reciting the *Qur'an*. The sufi is supposed to spend all his life in *dhikr*. There are more mundane meanings, but this is the obvious one in the context of medieval philosophy' (Karla Mallette, letter of October 21, 2008). The words *dhkir* and *Qur'an* (recitation, reading) are sometimes used interchangeably, because the *Qur'an* serves as a reminder. No doubt, *recordatio* was used because *dh-k-r* and heart are intimately connected: 'of the *Qur'an*'s sixteen instances [of the phrase *ulu 'lalbab*, 'those endowed with hearts,' i.e. understanding], nine are connected with [the root *dh-k-r*]' (Andrew Rippin, *The Blackwell Companion to the* Qur'an [London: Blackwell, 2006] 287). I thank Karla Mallette for her generous help with all things Arabic.

[8] *Mémoires-journeaux de Pierre de l'Estoile*, ed. Madeleine Lazard and Gilbert Schenck (Geneva: Droz, 1996), vol. 2, 188-9, entry for April, 1578.

[9] The famous translator and editor of Aristotle's *Poetics*, Lodovico Castelvetro, was also responsible for the commentary on Petrarca's *Rime*, published in 1582. His annotation of *mia* as *cara* in the sonnet 21 (in his edition, sonnet 19), *Mille fiate o dolce mia guerrera*, has inspired my comment. Another contemporary commentator confirms the importance of Castelvetro's remark: Jacobo Corbinelli, the editor of the Latin original of Dante's *De vulgari eloquentia*. The authorship of *De vulgari*, only circulated in its vernacular version, was suspect–until Corbinelli's edition of the Latin text appeared. Corbinelli left an annotated volume of Castelvetro's Petrarca with a dedication from Giacomo Castelvetro, and in this instance he added two examples from Dante (*molto mio, tutto mio*) to echo and amplify Castelvetro's comment. Casteveltro's Petrarca volume is now part of the collection of Houghton Library, Harvard University: Francesco Petrarca, *Le Rime de Petrarca brevemente sposite per Lodovico Castelvetro* (Basel: Pietro de Sedabonis, 1582), 38.

[10] *The Collected Dialogues of Plato*, eds. Edith Hamilton and Huntingdon Cairns (Princeton: Princeton University Press, 1963), 1178-9.

Anna Kłosowska & Nicola Masciandaro

[11] 'Consider our universe. There is none before it and therefore it is not, itself, in a universe or in any place—what place was there before the universe came to be?—its linked members form and occupy the whole. But Soul is not in the universe, on the contrary the universe is in the Soul; bodily substance is not a place to the Soul; Soul is contained in Intellectual-Principle and is the container of body. The Intellectual-Principle in turn is contained in something else; but that prior principle has nothing in which to be: the First is therefore in nothing, and therefore, nowhere' (Plotinus, *The Enneads*, tr. Stephen MacKenna [Burdett, NY: Larson, 1992], 5.5.9). 'And than our Lord opened my gostly eye and shewid me my soule in middis of my herte. I saw the soule so large as it were an endles world' (Julian of Norwich, *Shewings*, ed. Georgia Ronan Crampton [Kalamazoo, MI: Medieval Institute, 1993], ch.47). 'The synthesis that results [from 'identifying the interior image of Aristotelian phantasmology with the warm breath (the vehicle of the soul and of life) of Stoic-Neoplatonic pneumatology'] is so characteristic that European culture in this period [11th-13th centuries] might justly be defined as a pneumophantasmology, within whose compass—which circumscribes at once a cosmology, a physiology, a psychology, and a soteriology—the breath that animates the universe, circulates in the arteries, and fertilizes the sperm is the same one that, in the brain and in the heart, receives and forms the phantasms of the things we see, imagine, dream, and love' (Giorgio Agamben, *Stanzas: Word and Phantasm in Western Culture*, tr. Ronald L. Martinez [Minneapolis: University of Minnesota Press, 1993], 94). 'The very vibrations of the projection of the divine sub-consciousness of God, through the creation point in the original absolute vacuum, bestirred the divine sound sleep state of God and made manifest the original breath of God, or the original Word—the divine *nad*—together with space, time and the cosmic universe, with all of its paraphernalia of the limited and finite ego, mind, energy and the individual and multiple forms' (Meher Baba, *God Speaks: The Theme of Creation and its Purpose*, 2nd ed. [New York: Dodd, Mead & Co, 1973], 103).

[12] Meher Baba, *Listen, Humanity*, narrated and ed. D.E. Stevens (New York: Harper & Row, 1967), 19. Cf. 'Do not, so that, from my breast, the sigh liver-consuming / May ascend like smoke by way of the window' (Hafiz of Shiraz, *The Divan*, tr. H. Wilberforce Clarke [London: Octagon Press, 1974], 449.5).

[13] As in this opening of Dante's second *canzone* from the *Convivio*.

[14] Dante, *De vulgari*.

[15] In demons, some kinds of intellect (speculative, practical, active, to name a few) are more corruptible than others. The 'practical' intellect affected by free will is corruptible because of the demons' fleshly concupiscence, while their speculative intellect may remain intact, according to Saint Bonaventure, *Commentaria in Quatuor Libros Sententiarum Magistri Petri Lombardi* (Florence: Quaracchi, 1885), vol. 2, p. 191, *Articulus 1. De cognitione daemonum*. Available online at <http://www.franciscan-archive.org/bonaventura/opera/bon02189.html>, accessed on 12/17/2008.

[16] Nothing can be conveyed from one rational mind to another except through a sensible medium.

[17] Gilles Deleuze & Félix Guattari, *What is Philosophy?*, trans. Hugh Tomlinson and Graham Burchell (New York: Columbia University Press, 1994), 85.

[18] 'To be born is both to be born of the world and to be born into the world' (Maurice Merleau-Ponty, *Phenomenology of Perception*, trans, Colin Smith [London: Routledge, 1962], 527).

[19] Giovanni Boccaccio, *Esposizioni sopra la Comedia di Dante*, ed. Giorgio Padoan, vol. 6 of *Tutte le opere di Giovanni Boccaccio*, ed. Vittore Branca (Milano: Mondadori, 1965) <http://dante.dartmouth.edu>; Meher Baba, *God Speaks*, 35.

Anna Kłosowska & Nicola Masciandaro

[20] Much could be said about Catullus 45, an amoebean song (i.e., a dialogue, like ours), widely read since the rediscovery of a Catullus manuscript in Verona in 1314, postdating *Vita Nuova* (1295). Catullus 45 first imposed itself thematically to me because of references to tears, without my knowing at the time that it was relevant in other ways, as a precursor of post-Dante sonnets. The asyndeton *amant amantur* calls forth the too-clever formula *amore, more, ore, re* (love is loving, being a certain way, speaking, and things we do, or give: *verus amicus amore more ore re (re)cognoscitur*), variously attributed (possibly, Vulgar Latin or seventeenth century).

[21] Pierre de Ronsard, *Oeuvres complètes*, ed. Jean Céard, Daniel Ménager and Michel Simonin (Paris: Gallimard, 1994), vol. 2, p. 429, 'The Sonnet on My Lover's Tears,' first published in the 1565 edition.

[22] Guillaume de Machaut, *Poésies lyriques*, 2 vols., ed. V. Chichmaref (Paris: Champion, 1909), 209.

[23] Guillaume de Machaut, *Poésies lyriques*, 2 vols., ed. V. Chichmaref (Paris: Champion, 1909), 206.

[24] The Who, 'Love Reign O'er Me,' *Quadrophenia* (Track Records, 1973).

[25] Guillaume de Lorris and Jean de Meun, *Le Roman de la Rose*, ed. Ernest Langlois (Paris: Firmin-Didot, 1914-24), lines 1571-3.

[26] 'Truly, even though he had attained purity of heart and body, and in some manner was approaching the height of sanctification, he did not cease to cleanse the eyes of his soul with a continuous flood of tears. He longed for the sheer brilliance of the heavenly light and disregarded the loss of his bodily eyes' (Bonaventure, *The Minor Legend of Saint Francis*, 3.3, *Francis of Assisi: Early Documents*, eds. Regis J. Armstrong, J.A. Wayne Hellmann, and William J. Short, 3 vols. [New York: New City Press, 2000], 3.695). Cf. 'Than had sche so meche swetnes and devocyon that sche myth not beryn it, but cryid, wept, and sobbyd ful boitowsly. Sche had many an holy thowt of owr Lordys passyon and behld hym in hir gostly syght as verily as he had ben aforn hir in hir bodily syght' (*The Book of Margery Kempe*, ed. Lynn Stanley [Kalamazoo: Western Michigan University, 1996], ch.78). 'Now if tears *come to the eyes*, if they *well up in them*, and if they can also veil sight, perhaps they reveal, in the very course of this experience, in the coursing of water, an essence of the eye, of man's eye, in any case, the eye understood in the anthropo-theological space of the sacred allegory. Deep down, deep down inside, the eye would be destined to weep. For at the very moment they veil sight, tears would unveil what is proper to the eye' (Jacques Derrida, *Memoirs of the Blind: The Self-Portrait and Other Ruins*, trans. Pascale-Anne Brault and Michael Naas [Chicago: University of Chicago Press, 1993], 126).

[27] '. . . they are addressed to you, you will live from having had the strength to hear them. (In the same way, what do the two lovers, Tristan and Isolde, signify, if considered without their love, in a solitude which leaves them to some commonplace pursuit? Two pale beings, deprived of the marvelous; nothing counts but the love which tears them both apart)' (Georges Bataille, *Inner Experience*, trans. Leslie Anne Boldt [Albany, NY: State University of New York Press, 1988], 94).

[28] Jacques Roubaud, *Quleque chose noir* (Paris: Gallimard, 1986), 131-2: 'Devant ta mort je suis resté complètement silencieux. / . . . / Je ne pouvais plus parler selon ma manière de dire qui est la poésie. / J'avais commencé à parler, en poésie, vingt-deux ans avant./ C'était après une autre mort./ Avant cette autre mort je ne savais comment dire. j'étais comme silencieux. Ainsi, pris entre deux 'bords' de mort.' 'Facing your death I remained completely silent /. . . / I could no longer speak in my way which is poetry. / I have started to talk, in poetry, twenty-two years before. / It was after another death. / Before that other death I didn't know how to say. I was as silent. Thus, caught between two "shores" of death.'

[29] 'Everyone knows . . . different names of the point of cessation, which could be then also called the point of poetry: for one it's death, for another the obscene, for yet another pure meaning, reached by wrenching words

from the sphere of ordinary reference: hermeticism. For others, Mallarmé or Saussure, the point . . . is sound: the sound that must be stripped of all that serves for communication, of all that is distinctive: this is no more a search for the purity of meaning, but for multiple facets of homophony. Astonishingly, the failure is not absolute . . . Sometimes, in 'lalangue' that s/he works upon, one subject leaves its mark and opens the path where the impossible-to-write is written' (Jean-Claude Milner, *L'Amour de la langue* [Paris: Seuil,1978], 38-39. Lalangue is a Lacanian label for an amalgam between language and desire (technically, between libido and signifiers). I have stripped Milner's quote of all the references to Lacan except this one, because my own use of Lacan is eclectic and unfaithful. I use many of his insights, but only as insights, not as binding rules of the only possible economy, including his major concepts (lack, mirror stage). Since essential aspects of Milner's reasoning on extreme poetry echo my own, I think the scission (or my omission) is justified because Lacanian framework was a preconceived notion in Milner's thought, and therefore less interesting for me as I think along with Milner; and, this scission does not seem to make Milner's thought disintegrate. The reason for my interest in Milner's approach is that he looks at poetry from the side of the text, while I am looking at it here from the side of what brings the texts into being within us, and it seems that the two optics result in identical statements, which confirms both what I am trying to say and what Milner says about the way language works, or (to remain closer to his formulation) what the poet works out when s/he works the 'language' understood as a combination of libido and signifiers, *travaille lalangue*. Of course, Milner's Lacanian framework naturally brings his lingustic approach near to, into a compatibility with, an approach like mine. His idea of the 'point of cessation' is particularly interesting to me, because as we have seen with Roubaud or with Dante's sigh, or even his theory of intelligence, this *point of cessation* is limned by similar markers (ex., death, the obscene, hermeticism, sound) whether it is the point of cessation of meaning towards all poetry tends but infinitesimally misses it ('I have started to talk, in poetry, after another death . . . before . . . I was as silent') or cessation of the ability to write ('In the face of your death, I remained completely silent'). Specifically, Milner helped me put into words the intuition that the point of cessation, which is also the 'point of poetry,' is moreover the point where the difference between language and love (or death) becomes negligible. The point of poetry is the point of non-representation (as in: the distance that the word 'representation' implies is infinitesimally small), the point infinitesimally close to pure unmediated meaning (Dante's intelligence).

[30] Love always preserves the presence of those who die or part, and the desire that loss brings out in us to speak of the beloved is as strong as when we first loved. The comical, obsessive desire that turns everything into another story about our lover, and the great pleasure that we take in hearing of him/her, possess us as strongly. The intervals between hearing and speaking of the lover are painful. In this sense, *quand'elli è giunto là dove disira* is the very definition of love.

[31] 'At chorus aequalis Dryadum clamore supremos implerunt montis; flerunt Rhodopeiae arces altaque Pangaea et Rhesi Mauortia tellus atque Getae atque Hebrus et Actias Orithyia. ipse caua solans aegrum testudne amorem te, dulcis coniunx, te solo in litore secum, te ueniente die, te decedente canebat. Taenarias etiam fauces, alta ostia Ditis, et caligantem nigra formidine lucum ingressus, manisque adiit regemque tremendum nesciaque humanis precibus mansuescere corda. at cantu commotae Erebi de sedibus imis umbrae ibant tenues simulacraque luce carentum, quam multa in foliis auium se milia condunt, uesper ubi aut hibernus agit de montibus imber, matres atque uiri defunctaque corpora uita magnanimum heroum, pueri innuptaeque puellae, impositque rogis iuuenes ante ora parentum, quos circum limus niger et deformis harundo Cocyti tardaque palus inamabilis unda alligat et nouies Styx interfusa coercet. quin ipsae stupuere domus atque intima

Leti Tartara caerueosque implexae crinibus anguis Eumenides, tenuitque inhians tria Cerberus ora, atque Ixionii uento rota constitit orbis. imaque pedem referens casus euaserat omnis, redditaque Eurydice superas ueniebat ad auras pone sequens; namque hanc dederat Proserpina legem, cum subita incautum dementia cepit amantem, ignoscenda quidem, scirent si ignoscere manes: restitit, Eurydicemque suam iam luce sub ipsa immemor heu! uictisque animi respexit. ibi omnis effusus labor atque immitis rupta tyranny foedera, terque fragor stagnis auditus Auerni. illa, 'quis et me,' inquit, 'miseram et te perdidit, Orpheu, quis tantus furor? en iterum crudelia retro fata uocant conditque natantia lumina somnus. iamque uale: feror ingenti circumdate nocte inualidasque tibi tendens, heu non tua, palmas.' dixit et ex oculis subito, ceu fumus in auras commixtus tenuis, fugit diuersa, neque illum prensantem nequiquam umbras et multa uolentem dicere praetera uidit; nec portitor Orci amplius obiectam passus transile paludem. quid faceret? quo se rapta bis coniuge ferret? quo fletu manis, quae numina uoce moueret? illa quidem Stygia nabat iam frigida cumba. septem illum totos perhibent ex ordine mensis rupe sub aeria deserti ad Strymonis undam flesse sibi, et gelidis haec euoluisse sub astris, mulcentem tigri et agentem carmine quercus' (Virgil, *Georgics,* Book IV, 453-510).

[32] 'Once, while roaming about and frolicking among hills and dales, the Kasturi-mriga [deer whose navel yields musk] was suddenly aware of an exquisitely beautiful scent, the like of which it had never known. The scent stirred the inner depths of its soul so profoundly that it determined to find its source. So keen was its longing that notwithstanding the severity of cold or the intensity of scorching heat, by day as well as by night, it carried on its desperate search for the source of the sweet scent. It knew no fear or hesitation but undaunted went on its elusive search until, at last, happening to lose its foothold on a cliff, it had a precipitous fall resulting in a fatal injury. While breathing its last the deer found that the scent which had ravished its heart and inspired all these efforts came from its own navel. This last moment of the deer's life was its happiest, and there was on its face inexpressible peace' (Meher Baba, *Discourses*, 6th ed., 3 vols. [San Francisco: Sufism Reoriented, 1967], 2.193).

[33] The 'unfolding of the cosmic time's pure contingency through life and by life is expressed by decay as a dysteleologic process. In this sense, life is the medium for the incommensurable tensions between the contingencies of the cosmic time. And decay is the expression of these incommensurable tensions or contingencies along the infinite involutions of space—a complicity between time's subtractive enmity to belonging and the enthusiasm of the space for dissolution of any ground for individuation, a participation between the cosmic time's pure contingency and the infinite involutions of space from whose traps nothing can escape' ('Memento Tabere: Reflections on Time and Putrefaction,' <http://blog.urbanomic.com/cyclon/archives/2009/03/memento_tabi_re.html>). Note that this commentary participaties in this process: 'It is no accident that hidden writings are associated with collective authors . . . One of the initial symptoms of inauthenticity that Hidden Writing produces is positive disintegration . . . Inauthenticity operates as complicity with anonymous materials' (Reza Negarestani, *Cyclonopedia: Complicity with Anonymous Materials* [Melbourne: re.press, 2008], 62).

[34] Dante Alighieri, *Vita Nuova*, 12:3-4: 'I am like the center of circle, to which all points of the circumference bear the same relation; you, however, are not.'

[35] 'Utopia does not split off from infinite movement: etymologically it stands for absolute deterritorialization but always at the critical point at which it is connected with the present relative milieu, and especially with the forces stifled by this milieu. *Erewhon,* the word used by Samuel Butler, refers not only to no-where but also to

now-here' (Gilles Deleuze and Félix Guattari, *What is Philosophy?*, trans. Hugh Tomlinson and Graham Burchell [New York: Columbia University Press, 1994], 99–100).

[36] Martin Heidegger, *Hölderlin's Hymn 'The Ister'*, trans. William McNeill and Julia Davis (Bloomington: Indiana University Press, 1996), 28.

[37] 'Nulla potest mulier tantum se dicere amatam/ uere, quantum a me Lesbia amata mea est./ Nulla fides ullo fuit umquam foedere tanta,/ quanta in amore tuo ex parte reperta mea est' (Cat. 87): No woman can say she is loved, truly, as much as my Lesbia is loved by me. No faith there ever was in any bond as great as the one that's discovered in loving you, by me.

[38] Disguised as a cleric, Guillaume whispers love to Flamenca each Sunday as he gives her the Psalter to kiss; she whispers back. Through a secret tunnel, he joins her in a bathhouse, and they look at each other all night. In Adrian Clarke's *Supplementary Blues,* the poem that takes our line of Dante's sonnet for its pretext/title, is sensuous (both 'incarnated' and 'ethereal'): 'sidereal drifter / extra / cosmic suspirations,' etc.

[39] 'Questo sonetto ha tre parti: ne la prima comincio a dire a questa donna come lo mio desiderio si volge tutto verso lei; ne la seconda dico come l'anima, cioè la ragione, dice al cuore, cioè a lo appetito; ne la terze dico com'e' le risponde' (38:7).

[40] Pseudo-Dionysius, *The Complete Works*, trans. Colm Luibheid and Paul Rorem (New York: Paulist Press, 1987), 82.

[41] Ronsard, 'Elegie II,' *Oeuvres complètes* 2, 302, ll. 37-70, quote l. 61. Late Ronsard, the distracted, facile Ronsard, and yet revelatory.

[42] Giaccomo Puccini, *Turandot*, 'Nessun dorma.'

[43] Cf. 'The sensual thing itself has a unified and basically ineffable effect on us, one that cannot be reduced to any list of traits. But if such a listing of traits does not sever a thing from its quality, there may be another way for this to happen. . . . The separation between a sensual object and its quality can be termed 'allure.' This term pinpoints the bewitching emotional effect that often accompanies this event for humans, and also suggests the related term 'allusion,' since allure merely alludes to the object without making it its inner life directly present' (Graham Harman, 'On Vicarious Causation,' *Collapse 2* [2007]: 198-9).

[44] Plotinus, *Enneads*, 6.7.35-6.

[45] 'I' mi son un che, quando / Amor mi spira, noto, e a quell modo / ch'e' ditta dentro vo significando' (*Purgatorio* 24.52-4) [I am one who, when Love inspires me, takes note, and goes setting it forth after the fashion which he dictates within me]. Signification itself is a work of love, semiosis an amorous occasionalism. 'Philosophers have long wondered about the nature of causality. Are there true causes at work in the world, and, if so, what makes them the causes they are? How do causes bring things about, and what kind of connection does a cause have to its effect? These questions took on another level of complexity when various religious and theological considerations were brought to bear on these issues. For instance, philosophers came to question how divine causal activity is to be understood, particularly, in relation to the natural causality of creatures. It is from this context, in which questions about the nature of causation intermixed with questions about the relation between divine and natural causality, that occasionalism emerged. Occasionalism attempts to address these questions by presenting as its core thesis the claim that God is the one and only true cause. In the words of the most famous occasionalist of the Western philosophical tradition, Nicolas Malebranche, 'there is only one true cause because there is only one true God; . . . the nature or power of each thing is nothing but the will of God; . . . all natural causes are not *true* causes but only *occasional* causes' [*OCM* II, 312 / *Search* 448]'

Anna Kłosowska & Nicola Masciandaro

('Occasionalism,' *Stanford Encyclopedia of Philosophy* <http://plato.stanford.edu/entries/occasionalism/>). I.e. love is the will, the gravity, that lets things happen, creates the contact of cause and effect.

[46] 'Ove è da sapere che discender la virtude d'una cosa in altra non è altro che ridurre quella in sua similitudine; sì come ne li agenti naturali vedemo manifestamente che, discendendo la loro virtù ne le pazienti cose, recano quelle a loro similitudine tanto quanto possibili sono a venire. Onde vedemo lo sole che, discendendo lo raggio suo qua giù, reduce le cose a sua similitudine di lume, quanto esse per loro disposizione possono da la [sua] virtude lume ricevere. Così dico che Dio questo amore a sua similitudine reduce, quanto esso è possibile a lui assimigliarsi. E ponsi la qualitade de la reduzione, dicendo: Sì come face in angelo che 'l vede. Ove ancora è da sapere che lo primo agente, cioè Dio, pinge la sua virtù in cose per modo di diritto raggio, e in cose per modo di splendore reverberato; onde ne le Intelligenze raggia la divina luce sanza mezzo, ne l'altre si ripercuote da queste Intelligenze prima illuminate. Ma però che qui è fatta menzione di luce e di splendore, a perfetto intendimento mostrerò differenza di questi vocabuli, secondo che Avicenna sente. Dico che l'usanza de' filosofi è di chiamare 'luce' lo lume, in quanto esso è nel suo fontale principio; di chiamare 'raggio', in quanto esso è per lo mezzo, dal principio al primo corpo dove si termina; di chiamare 'splendore', in quanto esso è in altra parte alluminata ripercosso. Dico adunque che la divina virtù sanza mezzo questo amore tragge a sua similitudine' (*Convivio* 3.14, <http://www.greatdante.net/texts/convivio/convivio.html> [Here we must observe that the descent of virtue from one thing into another is nothing but the causing of the latter to take on the likeness of the former; just as in natural agents we clearly see that when their virtue descends into things that are receptive, they cause those things to take on their likeness to the extent that they are capable of attaining to it. Thus we see that the Sun, as its rays descend here below, causes things to take on the likeness of its light to the extent that by their disposition they are capable of receiving light from its virtue. So I say that God causes this love to take on his own likeness to the extent that it is possible for it to resemble him. And the nature of that causation is indicated by saying *As it does into an angel that sees him*. Here we must further know that the first agent, namely God, instills his power into things by means of direct radiance or by means of reflected light. Thus the divine light rays forth into the Intelligences without mediation, and is reflected into the other things by these Intelligences which are first illuminated. But since light and reflected light have been mentioned here, I will, in order to be perfectly clear, clarify the difference between these terms according to the opinion of Avicenna. I say that it is customary for philosophers to call luminosity *light* as it exists in its original source, to call it *radiance* as it exists in the medium between its source and the first body which it strikes, and to call it *reflected light* as it is reflected into another place that becomes illuminated (trans. Richard Lansing, http://dante.ilt.columbia.edu/new/books/convivi/index.html>)].

[47] Giorgio Agamben, *The Coming Community*, trans. Michael Hardt (Minneapolis: University of Minnesota Press, 1993), 2.

[48] 'ché 'n sue belezze son cose vedute / che li occhi li color dov'ella luce / ne Mandan messi al cor pien di desiri, / che prendon aire e diventan sospiri' (*Convivio* 3) [Her pure soul, which receives from him this salvation, For in her beauties are things seen that the eyes of those in whom she shines send messages to the heart full of desires that take air and become sighs].

[49] 'Not for gain of good unto Himself, which cannot be, but that His splendor might, in resplendence, say, '*Subsisto*' . . . the Eternal Love opened into new loves.'

[50] 'Uti est ad intellectum ratiocinatio, ad id quod est id quod gignitur, ad aeternitatem tempus, ad punctum medium circulus: ita est fati series mobilis ad providentiae stabilem securitatem' (Boethius, *De consolatione*

Philosophiae IV.6): as reasoning is to intellect, as that which is coming into being, is to that which is, time to eternity, circle to the median point: so is the moving series of events to the immovable safety of providence—a passage chosen by William P. Ker whose commentary seems worth citing: 'if [Boethius] does not solve Fate and Free-will, he at any rate gives help for the reading of Dante, and his description of the relations between Providence and Fate is a fine example of solemn meditation. It is an expansion of the old passage from the *Timaeus*, about the Divine and the Necessary; Fate is Providence looked at from below. Just as the understanding of man, creeping from point to point, breaks into a long analytical series the unity of Divine reason, so the timeless Providence when it is translated into Time becomes the succession of events that seem to be bound together by the necessity of Fate' (Ker, *The Dark Ages* [New York: Charles Scribner's Sons, 1904], 113-14). But it seems to me that Boethius with his image of the immutably single center point of the innumerable and infinitely mutable *series mobilis*, points of the circle, and Dante with his passing beyond the farthest sphere proffer multiple, not identical consolations (Ker implies the opposite).

[51] Cavalcanti, 22: *quando vide uscire / degli occhi vostri un lume di merzede / che porse dentr' al cor nova dolcezza*: when I saw a light of mercy leave your eyes that carries new sweetness into the heart; see also 25, which echoes Dante's rime *splendor/onore*; and the two sonnets addressed to Dante, 39 and 40. Agamben comments in the *Stanzas*: 'there are not "two loves" . . . but a single "amorous experience" . . . Dante too conceived of love in this way' (Giorgio Agamben, *Stanzas*, 105-07, at 107).

[52] Jean-Louis Bourdillon, *Supplément au poëme de Roncevaux. . . Souvenirs de Roland* (Paris: Tilliard, 1847), 36, citing *Itinéraire d'Italie* (no author, no publisher, Milan, 1810), 147. I thought this was a nice ending because it is the object of a pilgrimage, be it a touristy one; and enchantingly, replaces the fictional weapon with its *cortège* of pain, wounding, war, with a peaceful and very promising barge mast, which at the same time is dollhouse-like out of scale. If we are to dream and not be, why not dream something really nice?

[53] Gilles Deleuze, lecture of March 26, 1973, on 'desire, pleasure, *jouissance*:' Carthesian extraction of the subject from the statement is analogous to the recoiling of pleasure from desire in some theories of love that Deleuze dislikes. 'I think I see the unicorn' is always true, as opposed to 'I see the unicorn'; therefore, for Descartes, 'I think that I see the unicorn' is preferable. The function of 'I think' (and lack) is to preempt shame, to prevent us from 'being wrong' or deceiving ourselves and similarly, in love, bearing the pain of being undeceived, and the shame of having been such idiots. However, once we accept 'I see the unicorn' as a shameless possibility, we don't need to worry about lack. With lack, we'll never be idiots: we'll always already be in pain, we'll have been pre-hurt; the more perfectly we perform that mystification, the more completely we eliminate the probability of shame. So pleasure and shame inhabit different directories; *vide* the *Romance of the Rose* that lists shame as one of the categories inimical to Love, alongside pride, malice/brutality (*vilainie*), despair, and new-thought.

[54] Cf. '*to speak* is in God *to see by thought*, forasmuch as the Word is conceived by the gaze of the divine thought' (Thomas Aquinas, *Summa theologica*, trans. Fathers of the English Dominican Province [New York: Bezinger Brothers, 1947], 1.34.1).

[55]
>In one moment (the only moment) of silence
>Are dying all of my ideas about silence.
>
>As sound beyond sound, beyond hearing, and beyond

Beyond is the densest openness of silence.

There is an endless loveliness in your eyes while
I am trying to say something about silence.

See the past, present, and future of all language
Created, preserved, and destroyed inside silence.

Speak your heart to me, dear one, whoever you are,
In these uncertain moments enclosed by silence.

Word-truth, our rarely achieved alchemy of sense,
Is a sound transmuting silence into silence.

Keep quiet Nicola, failure of what you know,
While we keep listening for answers in silence.

'And Nature, asked why it brings forth works, might answer if it cared to listen and to speak: 'It would have been more becoming to put no question but to learn in silence just as I myself am silent and make no habit of talking. And what is your lesson? This; that whatsoever comes into my being is my vision, seen in my silence, the vision that belongs to my character who, sprung from vision, am vision-loving and create vision by the vision-seeing faculty within me' (Plotinus, *Enneads*, 3.8.4). 'Si cui sileat tumultus carnis, sileant phantasiae terrae et aquarum et aeris, sileant et poli et ipsa sibi anima sileat . . . none hoc est: Intra in gaudium domini tui?' (Augustine, *Confessions*, Loeb Classical Library [Cambridge, MA: Harvard University Press, 1951], 9.10) [If to anyone the tumult of the flesh became silent, silent the images of earth and sea and air, and the heavenly poles and the very soul to itself became silent . . . would this not be: *Enter into the joy of the Lord*?] 'Silence is nothing merely negative; it is not the mere absence of speech. It is a positive, a complete world in itself. Silence has greatness simply because it is. It *is*, and that is its greatness, its pure existence. There is no beginning to silence and no end . . . When silence is present, it is as though nothing but silence had ever existed' (Max Picard, *The World of Silence*, trans. Stanley Godman [Chicago: Regner, 1952], 1. 'He who never says anything cannot keep silent at any given moment. Keeping silent authentically is possible only in genuine discoursing. To be able to keep silent, Dasein must have something to say—that is, it must have at its disposal an authentic and rich disclosedness of itself' (Martin Heidegger, *Being and Time*, trans. John Macquarrie and Edward Robinson [San Francisco: Harper Collins, 1962], 165). 'All prayers ultimately initiate the soul into an ever deepening silence of sweet adoration. . . . That which seeks to reach towards the immeasurable, itself becomes incapable of being measured by any set standards' (Meher Baba, *Beams* [Harper & Row, 1958], 75). 'Things that are real are given and received in silence' (Meher Baba).

[56] Martin Heidegger, 'The Nature of Language,' in *On the Way to Language*, trans. Peter D. Hertz (New York: Harper & Row, 1971), 108.

[57] Guido delle Colonne, 'Gioiosamente canto,' *I poeti della scuola Siciliana: Poeti siculo-toscani*, ed. Rosario Coluccia (Milano: Mondadori, 2008), 67. The opening of Guido's song beautifully gives joy's unendingness in

the form of generative, non-reductive tautology: 'Gioiosamente canto / e vivo in allegranza, / ca per la vostr' amanza, / madonna, gran gioio sento.'

[58] Giorgio Agamben, *Stanzas*, 128.

[59] 'The sonnet could be divided more subtly, and more subtly clarified; but it may pass with this division, and therefore I do not concern myself to divide it any further' (*VN* 41:9). I proceed through some trinitarian passages. 'The same appetite with which one longs open-mouthed to know a thing becomes love of the thing known when it holds and embraces the acceptable offspring, that is knowledge, and joins it to its begetter. And so you have a certain image of the trinity, the mind itself and its knowledge, which is its offspring and its words about itself, and love as the third element, *and these three are one* (1 Jn 5:8) and are one substance' (Augustine, *The Trinity*, trans. Edmund Hill [Hyde Park, NY: New City Press, 1991], 9.3). '[T]he Son proceeds by way of the intellect as Word, and the Holy Ghost by way of the will as Love. Now love must proceed from a word. For we do not love anything unless we apprehend it by a mental conception. Hence also in this way it is manifest that the Holy Ghost proceeds from the son. . . . Therefore in rational creatures, possessing intellect and will, there is found the representation of the Trinity by way of image, inasmuch as there is found in them the word conceived, and the love proceeding' (Aquinas, *Summa theologica*, 1.36.2, 1.45.7). 'The ecstatical unity of temporality—that is, the unity of the "outside-of-itself" in the raptures of the future, of what has been, and of the Present—is the condition for the possibility that there can be an entity which exists as its "there"' (Heidegger, *Being and Time*, 350). 'The fact is, that when the latent infinite trio-nature of God is gradually manifested out of the gradual projection of the finite Nothing, and when it simultaneously protrudes the projection of the finite Nothing as Nothingness manifested *ad infinitum,*this very same infinite trio-nature of God, at this stage of manifestation, becomes enmeshed in the apparent and false infinity of the Nothingness and thus gets itself expressed as the finite triple nature of man with capabilities demonstrated *ad infinitum*. How (1) the mind, (2) the energy and (3) the body, as the triple nature of man, demonstrate their capabilities *ad infinitum* in Illusion is clearly experienced (1) through the inventive mind of a scientist, who finds no end to discoveries and inventions; (2) through the release of nuclear energy in Illusion, which has reached a stage where it threatens with its own force of illusion to destroy the very Nothingness out of which it emerged and evolved into such a terrific force; (3) through the body (typifying happiness) which, now keeping pace with the advanced progress of the evolution of the Nothing, is infinitely urged to seek greater and greater happiness to such an extent that happiness actually becomes the very basis of the life of illusion. The only reason for such infinite demonstration in the field of Nothingness (which is Illusion) is because the basic finite triple nature of man—energy, mind and happiness of Nothingness—is upheld and stretched out *ad infinitum* by the basic infinite trio-nature of God—infinite power, infinite knowledge and infinite bliss of Everything' (Meher Baba, *God Speaks*, 90-1).

[60] T. Koetsier and L. Bergmans, 'Introduction,' *Mathematics and the Divine: An Historical Study* (Amsterdam: Elsevier, 2008), 13.

[61] 'Engel!: Es wäre ein Patz, den wir nicht wissen, und dorten, / auf unsäglichem Teppich, zeigten die Liebenden, die's hier. . . ihre kühnen/ hohen Figuren des Herzschwungs, / ihre Türme aus Lust, ihre / längst, wo Boden nie war, nur an einander / lehnenden Leitern, bebend,—und *könntens*, / vor den Zuschauern rings, unzähligen lautlosen Toten: / Würfen die dann ihre letzten, immer ersparten, / immer verborgenen, die wir nicht kennen, ewig / gültigen Müntzen des Glücks vor das endlich / wahrhaft lächelnde Paar auf gestilltem /

Teppich?': Rainer Maria Rilke, *The Selected Poetry*, ed. and trans. Stephen Mitchell, New York: Vintage International, 1989: 178-181, *Duino Elegies* 5, translation modified.

[62] Chastelain de Couci, *Chansons attribuées au Chastelain de Couci, fin du XIIe-début du XIIIe siècle*, ed. Alain Lerond (Paris: Presses Universitaires de France, 1964).

[63] 'Watering can [*irrigium*], called *chantepleure* in French, clepsydra in Greek.' I thank Jean-Marie Fritz for introducing me to *chantepleure*, the lyric object of his research. The citation is from the title of Jean Coignet's *Penitential irrigium, La Chantepleure gallice vocatum, graece Claepsydra. . .* Paris: Maheu, 1537. Thus, *chantepleure* has here a purgatorial function–perhaps opening the possibility of a pleasant purgatory that we discussed elsewhere: 'But this purgatory would not be purgative, would be the moment of ease' (Dan Remein).

[64] Valentina Visconti adopted a *chantepleure* with the *devise 'plus ne m'est riens'* (nothing is anything for me anymore / there's nothing more for me) after the assassination of her husband Louis d'Orléans by Jean-Sans-Peur, duke of Burgundy (1407).

[65] 'Erde, du liebe, ich will. Oh glaub, es bedürfte / nicht deiner Frühlinge mehr, mich dir zu gewinnen–, *einer*, / ach, ein einziger ist schon dem Blute zu viel.' Rilke, *Selected Poetry*, 202-203, *Duino Elegies*, 5.

[66] Martin Heidegger, 'Language,' *Poetry, Language, Thought*, trans. Albert Hofstadter (New York: Harper & Row, 1971), 210.

[67] Ezra Pound, *The ABC of Reading* (New York: New Directions, 1960), 29.

[68] 'Thus 'phenomenology' means . . . [*apophainesthai ta phainomena*]–to let that which shows itself be seen from itself in the very way in which it shows itself from itself Heidegger' (Heidegger, *Being and Time*, 34).

[69] 'The image is a being whose essence is to be a *species*, a visibility or an appearance. A being is special if its essence coincides with its being given to be seen, with its aspect. Special being is absolutely insubstantial. It does not have a proper place, but occurs in a subject and is in this sense like a *habitus* or a mode of being, like the image in a mirror' (Giorgio Agamben, *Profanations*, trans. Jeff Fort [New York: Zone, 2007], 57).

[70] 'If one form of thinking, rational and horizontal, clamps man to the earth, another, which we may tentatively call meditative, or 'vertical' thinking after Parmenides, may literally raise man into the air. . . Horizontal thinking, we may say as Max Frisch said of technology, is a way of organizing the universe so that man won't have to experience it. Vertical thinking is a way of transcending the horizontal thinking to rejoin the universe. Thus we may say with Heraclitus "The way up and the way down are the same." We might remain satisfied, with the scholars, not to take Parmenides seriously in his vertical description of seeing (flying). This is the same attitude of patronization which art scholars still indulge toward 'flat' Byzantine and Medieval painting and toward the Eastern 'mandala'. These scholars insist that painters lacked the technique for painting in three dimensions; on the contrary, it is we who have lost the capacity to see in two dimensions. . . . Many are the men who have drifted, in dreams, out the door, through the garden, and out into the street. . . . When I was a child my eyes 'flattened' space' (August Plinth, *Principles of Levitation*, 38-42).

[71] Cf. 'He who knows everything displaces nothing. To each one I appear to be what he thinks I am' (Meher Baba, *Life at its Best* [San Franciso: Sufism Reoriented, 1957], 3).

[72] 'Not *how* the world is, is the mystical, but *that* it is' (Ludwig Wittgenstein, *Tractatus Logico-Philosophicus*, tr. C.K. Ogden [Mineola, NY: Dover Publications, 1998], 6.44). 'God or the good or the place does not take place, but is the taking-place of the entities, their innermost exteriority. The being-worm of the worm, the being-stone of the stone, is divine. That the world is, that something can appear and have a face . . . this is the good' Giorgio Agamben, *The Coming Community*, 14).

[73] Gilles Deleuze, *Difference and Repetition*, trans. Paul Patton (New York: Columbia, 1994), 80.

[74] 'Et partes sermonis fabularis secundum quod est representativus due sunt. Omnis enim representatio aut imperat sibi locum per representationem sui contrarii, et post permutatur as suam intentionem (et est modus qui dicitur apud eos circulatio), aut rem ipsam non faciens mentionem aliquam sui contrarii (et hoc est quod ipsi vocabant significationem). . . et pars secunda sunt consuetudines, et est illud in quo primitus usitata est representatio, scilicet est illud quod representatur (et est quidem representatio seu imitatio [in the Arabic text of Averroes's middle commentary, the word used here is 'narrative'--a term used by Averroes for the first time in that part of the treatise, which explains Hermanus's glossing it by two terms in Latin, *representatio seu imitatio*] sustenamentum et fundamentum in hac arte; propterea quod non fit delectatio ex rememoratione rei cuius intenditur rememoratio absque sui representatione) . . . ideoque multotiens non delectatur homo ex aspectu forme ipsius rei existentis in natura et delectatur in eius representatione et formatione per picturas et colores' *Aristoteles latinus* 48-9: 'There are two kinds of mimetic/*representativus* fictional utterance/*sermonis fabularis*: [one,] either mimesis/*representatio* commands a place for herself by representing a contrary and then moves/*permutatur* to intent/*intentionem* (this was called by [the Greeks] *circulation* [*peripateia*]), or the thing itself without any mention of its contrary (what they called signification/*anagnoresis*) . . . two, [moral] habits/*consuetudines*, and it is for them that *represenatio* is primarily used, that is that which is represented, and *representatio* or *imitatio* is the pillar and foundation of that art . . . man does not delight in the seeing of the mere forms of things existing in nature, but delights in their representations and formation by paints and colors.' This and following citations from *Aristoteles latinus: De arte poetica, translatio Guillelmi de Moerbeka . . . accedunt Expositio Media averrois sive 'Poetria' Hermanno Alemanno interprete et specimena translationis Petri Leonii*, ed. Laurent Minio-Paluello (Leiden: E.J. Brill, 1968). The portion cited here is not Aristotle proper, but Hermanus Allemanus's translation/commentary (ca.1256) of Averroes's (1126-1198) 'middle commentary' to Aristotle's Poetics (middle in length--as opposed to the long and the short one). This particular part in Hermanus Allemanus is practically identical with Averroes's Arabic text with which we compared it: Steve Nimis, Greek and medieval Latin, Karla Mallette, medieval Latin and Arabic, and Elizabeth Bergman, medieval and modern Arabic, with Latinists Evan Hayes, Emily Schubeler, and Alex Robbins.

[75] *Aristoteles latinus*, 49: 'and the fifth part [of 'tragedy' or, as Averroes and Hermanus misunderstand it, 'laudatory poetry', poems of praise] . . . is music/*tonus*; and it is the most important part to impress (press on, against) the soul and work in it.'

[76] Plots are divided into complex, with either a *peripateia* or an *anagnoresis*, and simple, without them. Anagnoresis is realized in one of five ways: signs/tokens/marks on the body; arbitrary (*directio*, direct discovery invented by the author); reawakened memory/recall of something forgotten; logic/reasoning; discovery from incidents (probability).

[77] Averroes insists that *cadentia in sensum* is not the essence of tragedy/poetry, but rather 'beauty of the character, praiseworthy actions, and blessed beliefs,' to which Allemanus adds: 'this is not found in the poetry of the Arabs, but in praise poetry concerned with divine law': 'Et partes maiores carminis laudativi sunt consuetudines et credulitates [moral habits and beliefs]. Tragedia etenim non est ars representativa ipsorummet hominum prout sunt individua *cadentia in sensum*, sed est representativa consuetudinum eorum honestarum et actionem laudabilium et credulitatum beatificantium. Et consuetudines comprehendunt actiones et mores. Ideoque ponitur consuetudo una sex partium, et per eius positionem excusatur [supercedes] position actionum et morum in illa divisione. . . Itud vero totum non reperitur in poematibus Arabum, sed reperitur quidem in

Anna Kłosowska & Nicola Masciandaro

sermonibus legalibus [i.e. *sha'aria*]' (*Aristoteles latinus*, 48). One might say that for Averroes, poetry and *sha'aria* were two discrete genres, and Dante makes them back into one ring, as they were among the Greeks (in tragedy, for instance). So, in tracing the readings of Aristotle in the West through Arabic and Latin sources and into the Renaissance, we are looking at the ebb and flow of genres (poetry, philosophy) reconstituting themselves, sometimes discrete, sometimes intertwined. I keep in mind that Dante names his poem 'comedy,' not tragedy: as if he aimed not to praise. Cf. the distinction between praise and vituperative poetry (corresponding to Aristotelian distinction between tragedy and comedy) in Averroes and Allemanus.

[78] 'And that's why I say that I intend to solve and declare/remove this doubt in this little book in an even more doubtful part.'

[79] Augustine, *On the Trinity*, trans. Stephen McKenna (Washington: Catholic University of America Press, 1970), 15.11.20. '[V]erbum quod foris sonat, signum est verbi quod intus lucet, cui magis verbi competit nomen. Nam illud quod profertur carnis ore, vox verbi est: verbumque et ipsum dicitur, propter illud a quo ut foris appareret assumptum est' (PL 42:1071). 'I can remember when I was a little boy, my grandmother and I could hold conversations entirely without ever opening our mouths. She called it shining' (*The Shining*, directed by Stanley Kubrick [Warner Bros., 1980], Halloran speaking to Danny).

[80] '[A]lthough it is clear that the beings that were created were nothing before their creation . . . yet they were not nothing, so far as the creator's thought is concerned, through which, and according to which, they were created. This thought is a kind of expression of the objects created (*locutio rerum*), like the expression which an artisan forms in his mind for what he intends to make [*sicut faber dicit prius apud se quod facturus est*]' (Anselm, *Monologium*, trans. Sidney Norton Deane [Chicago: Open Court, 1903], chapters 9-10). Anselm goes on to compare and identify this thought with the universal *verba mentis*: 'all other words owe their invention to these, where these are, no other word is necessary for the recognition of an object, and where they cannot be, no other word is of any use for the description of an object. . . . This . . . then, should be called the especially proper and primary *word*, corresponding to the thing. Hence, if no expression of any object whatsoever so nearly approaches the object as that expression which consists of this sort of *words*, nor can there be in the thought of any other word so like the object, whether destined to be, or already existing, not without reason it may be thought that such an expression of objects existed with (*apud*) the supreme Substance before the creation, that they might be created; and exists, now that they have been created, that they might be known through it' (ch.10).

[81] 'Spirit blows where it wants and you hear its voice but know not whence it comes or where it goes.'

[82] *Summa theologica*, Supplement.83.1.

[83] 'In Wahrheit singen, ist ein andrer Hauch. / Ein Hauch um nichts. Ein When im Gott. Ein Wind' (Ranier Maria Rilke, *Sonnets to Orpheus*, 1.3, in *The Selected Poetry of Rainer Maria Rilke*, ed. and trans. Stephen Mitchell [New York: Vintage, 1989], 231).

[84] Augustine, *The Trinity*, trans. J. E. Rotelle (New York: New City Press, 1997), 10.1.2-3.

[85] 'Und das Gestirn seiner künftigen Liebe/ geht doch schon längst unter Sternen,/ gültig.' Rilke, *Selected Poetry*, 264-5.

[86] Rilke, *Selected Poetry*, 297.

[87] From *The Notebooks of Malte Laurids Brigge*: 'Und schon schlagen sich seine Sinne nieder aus der hellen Lösung seiner Selle.' Rilke, *Selected Poetry*, 104-5.

⁸⁸ Rilke's description of 'primal sound,' a sound that would be generated if the coronal suture (the line between skull bones that, separate at birth, fuse later) was read by a phonograph's needle, devolves to his description of Arabic poetry that uses all five senses (as opposed to the Western poetry centered on sight): 'a lady, to whom this was mentioned in conversation, exclaimed that this wonderful and simultaneous capacity and achievement of all the senses was surely nothing but the presence of mind and grace of love–incidentally she thereby bore her own witness to the sublime reality of the poem. But the lover is in such splendid danger just because he must depend upon the co-ordination of his senses, for he knows that they must meet in that unique and risky centre, in which, renouncing all extension, they come together and have no permanence. As I write this, I have before me the diagram that I have always used as a ready help whenever ideas of this kind have demanded attention. If the world's whole field of experience, including those spheres which are beyond our knowledge, be represented by a complete circle, it will be immediately evident that, when the black sectors, denoting that which we are incapable of experiencing, are measured against the lesser, light sections, corresponding to what is illuminated by the senses, the former are very much greater. Now the position of the lover is this, that he feels himself unexpectedly placed in the centre of the circle, that is to say, at the point where the known and the incomprehensible, coming forcibly together at one single point, become complete and simply a possession, losing thereby, it is true, all individual character. This position would not serve the poet, for individual variety must be constantly present for him, he is compelled to use the sense sectors to their full extent, as it must also be his aim to extend each of them as far as possible, so that his lively delight, girt for the attempt, may be able to pass through the five gardens in one leap. As the lover's danger consists in the non-spatial character of his standpoint, so the poet's lies in his awareness of the abysses which divide the one order of sense experience from the other: in truth they are sufficiently wide and engulfing to sweep away from before us the greater part of the world–who knows how many worlds?' (Soglio, Assumption of the Virgin, 1919).

⁸⁹ E. M. Cioran, *A Short History of Decay*, trans. Richard Howard (New York: Arcade, 1949), 47. Dante's likewise turns/is turned away weeping from the *itinerarium mentis* of 'il dilettoso monte' (*Inferno* 1.77) [the delectable mountain], corresponding to the unfinishable philosophical project of the *Convivio*: '"A te convien tenere altro vïaggio," / rispuose, poi che lagrimar mi vide, / "se vuo' camper d'esto loco selvaggio"' (*Inferno* 1.91-3).

⁹⁰ For a footnote, imagine here a long posthumous essay by a philosopher on the subject of the sigh beginning *I sigh. For whom is a sigh?* with this as epigraph: 'And surely I am not giving myself a report. It may be a sigh; but it need not' (Ludwig Wittgenstein, *Philosophical Investigations*, trans. G. E. M. Anscombe [New York: Macmillan, 1958], I.585).

⁹¹ Hāfiz, *Divan*, 397.2.

⁹² Friedrich Nietzsche, *Thus Spoke Zarathustra*, 'The Honey Sacrifice,' 192.

⁹³ *Purgatorio*, 30.48 [Not a drop of blood is left in me that does not tremble: I know the tokens of the ancient flame].

⁹⁴ From *The Notebooks of Malte Laurids Brigge*: 'Um eines Verses willen muss man. . . die Gebärde wissen, mit welcher die kleinen Blumen sich auftun am Morgen.' Rilke, *Selected Poetry*, 90-1.

⁹⁵ Ronsard, *Oeuvres complètes*, vol.1, p. 18: de la main dextre apand a vostre autel / l'humble present de son livre immortel / son coeur de l'autre aux pieds de cette image.

⁹⁶ Ronsard, *Oeuvres complètes*, vol. 1, p. 254-5, *Le Second Livre des Amours*, 2, sonnet 4: Comme on voit sur la branche au mois de May la rose / En sa belle jeunesse, en sa première fleur . . . Pour obsèques reçoy mes

larmes et mes pleurs, / Ce vase plein de laict, ce panier plein de fleurs, / Afin que vif et mort ton corps ne soit que roses.

[97] *Nenia*, XXXI. The most recent bilingual (Polish-English) edition of Tkaczyszyn-Dycki is *Periegrinary*, transl. Bill Johnston (Brookline, MA: Zephyr Press, 2008). Eugeniusz Tkaczyszyn-Dycki, *Nenia i inne wiersze* [Nenia and Other Poems] (Lublin: Lublin: Zwiazek Literatow Polskich, 1990), cited by Przemyslaw Pilarski, 'Obsesje Dyckiego. Homoseksualnosc na tle pozostalych problemow tozsamosciowych bohatera wierszy autora *Przewodnika dla bezdomnych*. . .,' in Tomasz Basiuk, Dominika Ferens, and Tomasz Sikora, *Parametry Pozadania: kultura odmiencow wobec homofobii* (Krakow: TAiWPN Universitas, 2006), 251-61, at 260.

[98] Eugeniusz Tkaczyszyn-Dycki, 'Piosenka o kroplach krola dunskiego (Bulat Okudzawa) [The Song of the Danish King's Elixir (Bulat Okudzhava)], author's recording online at http://www.biuroliterackie.pl/przystan/content/media/m_010/Dycki__Piosenka_o_kroplach_krola_dunskiego.mp3, accessed on August 16, 2009. Bulat Okudzhava is a famous Russian singer-songwriter of Georgian, Armenian and Azerbaijani descent. Perhaps the reference is to his reciting Boris Pasternak's poem 'Hamlet,' with guitar accompaniment. Pasternak Translated Hamlet in 1940; the poem (1946) was often set to music; it describes Hamlet as poised at the threshold of the stage, his destiny before him; the last line reads, 'to live through a life is no walk through a field.'

[99] 'With language, you have to be firm / it is what it is a piece / of wood we use as a prop / and an aid on the way / but not always luckily / it is what it is and there is / not a shadow of a doubt that it's clay / tormented by inspiration/ of the Lord and each one / of us, when we're breathless' (Eugeniusz Tkaczyszyn-Dycki, 'X.,' *Piosenka o zaleznosciach i uzaleznieniach* [The Song of Relations and Dependences] [Wroclaw: Biuro Literackie, 2008], <http://biuroliterackie.pl/przystan/czytaj.php?site=100&co=txt_1959>, accessed August 16, 2009).

[100] 'Car son beau nom qui l'esprit me martyre / Hors de moymesme estonné me retire /. . . Je suis semblable à la Prestresse folle, / Qui bégue perd la voix et la parolle, / Dessous le Dieu qui lui brouille le sain': for this beautiful name that torments my wit draws me, astonished, out of myself. . . I am like the mad Priestess who, lisping, loses voice and speech under the God who muddles her heart: Ronsard, *Oeuvres complètes* 1:38, *Le premier livre des Amours*, sonnet XXVII.

[101] Ludwig Wittgenstein, 'A Lecture on Ethics,' *Philosophical Review* 74 (1965), 11.

[102] Charles Baudelaire, *The Flowers of Evil* (New York: Oxford, 1993), 'La Chevelure,' line 13.

[103] *Vita Nuova*, 21:4.

[104] *Vita Nuova*, 21:4.

[105] Friedrich Nietzsche, *The Gay Science*, trans. Josefine Nauckhoff (Cambridge: Cambridge University Press, 2001), 4.339.

[106] Hafiz, *Divan*, 572.8.

[107] Agamben, *The Coming Community*, 52, citing Nagarjuna and Ernst Bloch (citing Walter Benjamin citing Gershom Scholem citing a well-known Hasidic parable), respectively. In other words, the indifferent difference between the world and paradise is identical with the space of the *that*.

[108] 'seine Herde besäumt, wo sie sich ausfranst. / . . Noch immer dürfte ein Gott / heimlich in diese Gestalt und würde nicht minder' (Rilke, *The Selected Poetry* 120-121, 'The Spanish Trilogy,' *Uncollected Poems*).

[109] Passage cited in Ruedi Imbach and Iñigo Atucha, *Amours plurielles: Doctrines médiévales du rapport amoureux de Bernard de Clairvaux à Boccace* (Paris: Seuil, 2006), 267.

Anna Kłosowska & Nicola Masciandaro

[110] Augustine, *On Christian Doctrine* I, chap. XXVII, 28, passage cited in Imbach and Atucha, *Amours plurielles*, 264: 'we should thus love others more than our body, because we must love all in relation to God and that the beloved is called upon to enjoy with us the proximity of this sovereign Being: a privilege that does not belong to the body, since it is only alive through our soul, that alone makes us enjoy God.'

[111] Augustine, Letter to Januarius 55 chapter 10:18 and chapter 11:21. *A Select Library of Nicene and Post-Nicene Fathers of the Christian Church*, Saint Augustine of Hippo, Saint John Chrysostom (New York: Christian Literature co., 1886, repr. Grand Rapids, Mich.: W. B. Eedermans, 1956), vol. 1: The Confessions and Letters of Saint Augustine, 309-10.

[112] The passage continues, '. . . thus the man who says 'I know I am alive' says he knows one thing; but if he says 'I know that I know I am alive,' there are two things. The fact that he knows these two things makes a third knowing; and in this way he can add a fourth and a fifth and a countless number more, if he has the time. But because he cannot either comprehend an innumerable number by adding up single ones or give it innumerable expression, what he certainly does comprehend is both that this is true, and that it is so innumerable that he cannot comprehend or express the infinite number of its word' (Augustine, *The Trinity*, 15.4).

[113] [I saw, approaching from afar, Love / so joyous that I hardly recognized him] (*VN* 24:7).

[114]

> Memory, my peephole to eternity, wanders
> Forward in recognition, finds you in wonder.
>
> So busy falling into being, there is no time
> Not to see you in the corridors we wander.
>
> A little child running ahead of me, playing.
> Who is following or leading whom, I wonder?
>
> I am talking about something never, always
> Known: a friend returning where I do not wander.
>
> A new name so familiar it cannot be heard
> Slipping within the secret chambers of wonder.
>
> Happening does not happen the way other things
> Happen, stumbling along a path that wanders.
>
> Event's always-forgotten event of itself.
> Why, how this goes for granted, Nicola wonders.

[115] 'The intellect of most persons is harnessed by innumerable wants. From the spiritual point of view, such a life is the lowest type of human existence. The highest type of human existence is free from all wants and is characterised by sufficiency or contentment. . . . complete non-wanting is unattainable as long as life is mind-

ridden. It is possible only in supra-mental existence. One has to go beyond the mind to experience the spiritual bliss of desirelessness. Between the two extremes of a life harassed by wants and a life which is completely free from wants, it is possible to arrive at a mode of practical life in which there is harmony between the mind and the heart. When there is such harmony the mind does not dictate the ends of life, but only helps to realise those ends which are given by the heart. It does not lay down any conditions to be fulfilled before any utterance of the heart is adopted for translation into practical life. In other words it *surrenders its role of judge*, which it is accustomed to play in its intellectual queries concerning the nature of the universe, and accepts unquestioningly the dictates of the heart. . . . It is futile to try to glean knowledge of true values by exercise of the mind alone. Mind cannot tell you which things are worth having, it can only tell you how to achieve the ends accepted from non-intellectual sources. In most persons the mind accepts ends from the promptings of wants, but this means denial of the life of the spirit. Only when the mind accepts its ends and values from the deepest promptings of the heart does it contribute to the life of the spirit. . . . Spiritual understanding is born of harmony between mind and heart. This harmony of mind and heart does not require the mixing up of their functions. *It does not imply cross-functioning, but co-operative functioning.* Their functions are neither identical nor co-ordinate. Mind and heart must of course be balanced but this balance cannot be secured by pitching the mind against the heart or by pitching the heart against the mind. It can be attained *not through mechanical tension, but through intelligent adjustment*' (*Discourses*, I.139-41).

[116] Meher Baba, cited from Kitty Davy, *Love Alone Prevails* (North Myrtle Beach, SC: Sheriar Press, 1981), 165.

[117] Dante 1905: 62.

[118] Dante 1905: 77.

[119] 'Liebende, wäre nicht der andre, der / sie Sicht verstellt, sind nah daran und staunen . . . / Wie aus Versehn ist ihnen aufgetan / hinter dem andern. . . Aber über ihm / kommt keiner fort, und wieder wird ihm Welt' (Rilke, 'The Eighth Elegy,' *Duino Elegies, The Selected Poetry*, 192-3).

[120] 'O Sternenfall, / von einer Brücke einmal eingesehn–: / Dich nicht vergessen. Stehn!' (Rilke, 'Death,' *Uncollected Poems, The Selected Poetry,* 144-5).

[121] 'Aber / sein Torso glüht noch wie ein Kandelaber, / in dem sein Schauen, nur zurückgeschraubt, / sich hält und glänzt. . . . und bräche nicht aus allen seinen Rändern / aus wie ein Stern: denn da ist keine Stelle, / die dich nicht sieht. Du musst dein Leben ändern.' Rilke, 'Archaic Torso of Apollo,' *New Poems, The Selected Poetry*, 60-1.

[122] *Love Alone Prevails*, 165.

[123] Meher Baba, *The Everything and the Nothing* [Beacon Hill, Australia: Meher House Publication, 1963], no. 37.

[124] Hafiz, *Divan*, 288.4.

[125] Hafiz, *Divan*, 686.23-4

[126] Reza Negarestani, *Cyclonopedia*, 204-5.

[127] In fulfillment of the causal chain set in motion by the *virtù*–'mi salute molto virtuosamente' (*VN* 3:1)–of Beatrice's saluation: sweet greeting (*dolcissimo salutare*)→intoxication (*come inebriate*)→solitude (*solingo luogo*)→thinking (*pensare*)→sweet sleep (*soave sonno*)→marvelous vision (*maravigliosa vision*)→anguish (*angoscia*)→waking (*disvegliato*)→thinking (*pensare*)→sonnet (*sonetto*)→friendship (*amista*)→frailty and weakness (*faile e debole condizione*) . . . (*VN* 3:2-4:1). In other words, love is dis-locating (Cf. Anna Kłosowska and Nicola

Masciandaro, 'Between Angela and Actaeon: Dislocation,' forthcoming in *L'Esprit Créateur*). So Averroes's commentary on the immobility of Aristotelian place (place as unmovable vessel) suggests an originary relation to desire: 'place is that towards which something moves or in which something rests. If something were to move toward a term which is itself in movement, the thing would be moving in vain' (Averrois Cordubensis, *Commentaria magna in octo libro Aristotelis de physico auditu*, lib. IV, summa prima: De loco, cap. VIII, comm.41, cited from Pierre Duhem, *Medieval Cosmology: Theories of Infinity, Place, Time, Void, and the Plurality of Worlds*, trans. Roger Ariew [Chicago: University of Chicago Press, 1985], 142.) Never possessing it, never lacking it, we desire place as an inevitable impossibility, whether negatively as what is beyond body (nowhere, void, utopia,) or positively as what incorporates all bodies, their infinite sum (self, body, world, cosmos, everything). Either way the desire for place moves *from* the body, the boundary between self and cosmos which is the place of place, towards what would give or return place to the self. Eros, love that demands the presence and possession of the loved, is the vain movement of Averroes (fr. *habere ereos*!) towards something that is itself in movement, a desire for another boundary, another body, a place for our place. That two bodies cannot occupy the same place is the eros's sorrow, sigh.

[128] '. . . or hell, we no longer bother about; / . . . What has value and importance for us now is to live in the active present. / . . . Let despair and disappointment ravage and destroy the garden (of your life); / Beautify it once again by the seedlings of contentment and self-sufficiency. / Even if your heart is cut to bits, let a smile be on your lips. / For us . . . it is only hopelessness and helplessness. / How else should I tell you what our New Life is?' (Dr. Abdul Ghani Munsiff, 'Song of the New Life,' *The Awakener* 6 (1959): 16-8).

TINTERN ABBEY, ONCE AGAIN
J. H. Prynne

Much has been written about this central composition of Wordsworth's most germinal phase in the ordering of his inward and outward modes of experience. Many features of its rhetorical and incremental structure have been analysed, in convincing fine detail; as also the circumstances of its composition, its place in the mutations of meditative georgic pastoral, and its supposed literary and other sources. Also there has been much discussion of the prominent thematic omissions from this poem, at least on a surface level: the absence for example of the Revolution in France and of Tintern Abbey itself, and the by some presumed anxiety of these omissions. These comments here have the more local purpose initially of drawing attention to a feature of the opening verse paragraph, as it 'sets the scene', or rather two scenes, for the thoughts which are to ensue. The double setting has been often remarked; Wordsworth has a remembered prospect lodged deep in recollection's inward eye, while his present gaze scans the visible outlook for the prompt of matching forms: nourishing, sustaining, confirming.

> Five years have passed; five summers, with the length
> Of five long winters! and again I hear
> These waters, rolling from their mountain-springs
> With a soft inland murmur.*–Once again
> Do I behold these steep and lofty cliffs,
> Which on a wild secluded scene impress
> Thoughts of more deep seclusion; and connect
> The landscape with the quiet of the sky.
>
> * The river is not affected by the tides a few miles

A specific technical aspect of this doubling is the repetition of vocabulary forms, words that interweave a dense pattern of recurrence within and through this section of the poem and figure thereafter as more intermittent threads through the sections which follow. There are prominent markers for the start of these overlays: the 'five years' which split into 'five summers' and their five long counterpart winters. The present visit is made 'again' after this double interval, part-clement and part-forbidding, and 'again' is a marker word which is itself repeated, so that these linked doublings establish a rhythm not dissimilar to the rhetorical patterns of the renaissance handbooks, or the looping journeys of a tour of visitations. By like token, what is first wildly green is later how the green runs wild, over-running the order whose boundaries it marks, and the trees and copses which are of this simple green hue are then inclusively part of a more extended green landscape, seen initially from within the leafy shade of a darker tree closer by.

Hidden repeats confirm these echoes; the vagrants who do not have settled resources to harvest and seasoned wood for burning must make fire from green boughs and thus produce the visible tributary smoke which in likelihood marks out their transient sites; or if the smoke comes in fact from the hermit's fire then this smoke too will be of human but undomesticated origin. Likewise the orchard trees which, past blossom and before the colour of ripening fruit (we are after all in mid-July), shew the same overall green hue as the rest of the woodland cover, repeated in the sportive woods of hedgerows, themselves repeated as not quite what they seem, running in lines back and forth as the lines announced initially in the opening title to the poem. The observing eye could not at this distance know a fruiting tree from its 'wild' counterpart, unless a previous visit at a different season had discerned and registered the difference. The landscape, its variations of nature and nurture, is thus read as well as seen.

Yet more latently the sound of mountain springs, not directly audible from this somewhat lower and lusher valley scene, has already broadened into a rolling motion within the mind's ear, described as specifically inland because the rollers suggest a more distant and mighty sea towards which these flows, soon to become tidal, have their convergent tendency, as indeed they explicitly do in the ninth section of the 'Immortality Ode'; a not unrelated motion, shifted into the domain of spirit, will later in the Tintern Abbey poem impel and roll through the totality of all things. By comparable latency, 'murmur' contains its own repeat within the duplication of its word-form, and when actually repeated its later hint of diminished presence is adjusted by gifted recompense; the promise in 'murmur' is not distinct, and so shortfall may be made up by transferred powers of presence, less direct but more abundant and profound.

A related overlay of large and small scales is announced in the miniature 'tufts', their remoteness forming part of the deeper connection between visible landscape and the quiet of the sky; they represent the inferred reality of full-grown trees but, seen from a distant eminence some fair way above the scene itself, reduce playfully to toy-like forms, as the hedge-rows also play at being woods with their imitation of grown-up trees allowed their sweet liberty; the orchard-tufts and hedges present their own parallel flushes of childhood, all of these forms of growth performing for the observer an inferred return to his own youth now already a good way behind him. We may recall a similar implicative richness in Coleridge's 'Frost at Midnight', composed five months earlier, in which the 'tufts of snow' of the apple-tree's bare wintry branch lodged themselves upon the puckerings of bark around the dormant leaf-buds, and portended by miniature snowy imitation what would later be the vernal green foliage to sprout from just those same germinal nubs. The pattern of insistent, passionate repetition is present in both Wordsworth's and Coleridge's poems, as instanced in the iterative formula 'how oft…how oft', with the lapping sound-plays across 'oft/soft/tuft' and the dispersed presence of 'oft' and 'soft' within the letters of 'frost' itself.

> These hedge-rows, hardly hedge-rows, little lines
> Of sportive wood run wild; these pastoral farms
> Green to the very door; and wreathes of smoke
> Sent up, in silence, from among the trees,
> With some uncertain notice, as might seem,
> Of vagrant dwellers in the houseless woods,
> Or of some hermit's cave, where by his fire
> The hermit sits alone.

This quiet of the sky above Tintern is outwardly the consequence of the distance of the scene from the observer, too far for busy sound to travel, which also accounts for the silence of the smoke rising from the unseen fires of the vagrants or of the solitary hermit; but inwardly the human emptiness of the sky canopy absorbs and locates this silence as of consciousness itself, so that only the soft inland murmur crosses the divide, as if directly counterpart to the fluent susurrus of feeling and reflection within the mind. Even the hermit figure, a more solemn variant of the vagrants (gypsies, we may suppose), who provides station within the prospect for these contemplative thoughts which fathom its deeper seclusion, is twice named, as the owner of his own cave. Descriptively he is no more than fancied presence, but his cave, like Plato's, holds the implicit focus for crossings between nature and spirit, the objects of perception and images of memory and love. The abbey at Tintern must in a more devout age have served to express and celebrate such a focus; its absence from the scene here except as an inferred and half-ruined landmark may betoken the general omission of any formal shrine, in contrast to the more ecclesiastical *habitus* of Wordsworth's later work. This absence maybe also raises a more profoundly unspoken question, which is the relation of a living spiritual presence, paired within nature and the human mind, to the specific providential direction a of a Godhead not reducible to a pantheistic sublime: which Coleridge in 1795-7 had somewhat recklessly called 'the one life, within us and abroad, / Which meets all motion, and becomes its soul' ('The Eolian Harp'). Meanwhile untroubled by theological dilemmas, each of these cottage-plots and pastoral farms comprises instead a mute stationing of hearth and domestic occupation, their own more modest blend of nature and spirit in human presence. The purposeful reclusion of the hermit, separated like the poet from this domesticity all around him even as seeking to divine its higher spirit, also prompts acknowledgment of a difference between a visit (which might be partly the accident of its occasion, as in gypsy wanderings) and a *re-*visit (which bears the mark of full deliberateness).

For twenty three lines all of this opening section displays a marked frequency of significant word-repeats, made notable by the many ways in which these usages slip back and forth between inner and outer, between seeing and recognising, apprehending a known form through the prompting cue of its recurrence. The 'wild green landscape' in particular is made up of three descriptor words which are, all three, items in the list of repeats; the mind notices the wildness of natural disorder as containing the latent fruits of patient nurture, running to wildness as up to the very door and threshold of purposeful indwelling; even the houseless vagrants mimic this settlement by their temporary encampments. The view of 'these' hedge-rows runs with the general greenness to connect directly with 'these' pastoral farms, made pastoral by the greenness which nourishes their purpose to nourish into cultivation the fruitfulness of natural growth. 'The day is come' announces the appointed due moment as if by almost biblical fulfillment of a tryst or prophecy; all the eight pointing gestures with 'these' and 'this' confirm by their incremental cadences, as proxy for the reader, the focus of viewpoint and visible scene: the steadily intensified here and now of where we are.

> The day is come when I again repose
> Here, under this dark sycamore, and view
> These plots of cottage-ground, these orchard tufts,
> Which, at this season, with their unripe fruits,
> Among the woods and copses lose themselves,
> Nor, with their green and simple hue, disturb
> The wild green landscape. Once again I see

Such variability within the landscape, however, could threaten to unsettle by erosion or encroachment of forms, leading to loss of continuity in the life of remembrance; the pleasures of instant diversity were what characterised, and weakened, the prospect-poem of earlier tradition. But the latent threads of connection here, across the contrasts of 'uncertain notice', hold the links in place: 'wild green landscape' will not be disturbed by these interplays, since its component lexical markers are each stabilised in close proximity elsewhere; or if indeed disturbed, then brought thus to record feelings and perceptions reconnected in due time as with the joy of elevated thoughts. Nothing slips into a mere margin of attention. In such ways, reciprocal passage is possible between the old and the new, the wild and the stable, and this passage becomes itself nourishing to consciousness. The underlying theme of continued identity is performed, I suggest, by the repeats of identical words, making a cognate vocabulary out of memory that shall be a vocabulary for acts of remembering, leading (in other words and the same words too) into cumulative instances of recognition. To recognise is to confirm by second looks, and to experience why such recognition may move the soul is to feel each just pleasure in confirming a hunger for acknowledgment which, until thus confirmed, might have never been admitted or even registered.

The central field of strangeness, become familiar while still playfully distinct, gives a delicate blissful sport across the surface of this opening narrative, such as can mask the sensible reserve of emotion while following out the meaning of what this sport covers and thus reveals. Each contour is deepened by revisiting echo and acknowledgment, by the words which strike and open their chords. The effect is too delicate to be constructed, too rich to be accidental.

The afterlife of the 'wild green landscape' within the poem's ensuing later sections is transferred through subsequent recurrence from sensation to emotion, not without danger from fear and grief, and thereby to stabilizing constancy in recognition and in love. The shifts in reference of 'deep' through the whole sequence map out these exemplary powers of transfer: deep seclusion, deep power of joy, deep rivers, the deep and gloomy wood, something far more deeply interfused, deeper zeal; the natural feeds the emotional and metaphysical with the perspectives of focus and cumulative intensity, just as the metaphysical donates to the natural its reciprocating ardency of regard for natural occasions and their perceptible forms of local being. These interchanges were acknowledged by Wordsworth himself: in the Preface to *Lyrical Ballads* (in a passage added in 1850) he speaks of 'the general passions and thoughts and feelings of men' as the poet describes them, and their connections 'with our moral sentiments and animal sensations, and with the causes which excite these; with the operations of the elements, and the appearances of the visible universe; with storm and sunshine, with cold and heat, with loss of friends and kindred, with injuries and resentments, gratitude and hope, with fear and sorrow.' What is general in passion, as well as specific, is mediated by the recognition of transfer and the truth in likeness; essentially, the understanding through recurrence of recurrence itself.

The wildness of errant natural forms is thus found reflected by anticipation and recovery in the wild eyes of the narrator's sister and dearest friend, and in her wild moments of solitude; the gleams in later years from the sparks of memory in these eyes shall serve as storehouse of a conserved community of spirit. Former pleasures are formative of their successor insights, just as the greenness of woods and copses records the point of earliest entry into cherishment and gratitude felt towards the entire green earth of natural life. The landscape composed of memory still green and the greenness of the summer season likewise mark the connection between seasons of dearth and their subsequent regreening, the sweet inland murmur echoed in the comparable sweetness of restored sensation passing from blood to heart and heart to mind: a present pleasure as from a presence that self-construes upon reflection into the grandeur of fulfilled sublimity. These are 'the transitions and the impassioned music of the versification' which in his later note Wordsworth hoped might cause his poem to be recognised as an ode in all but name.

By such power of transformation the paradoxical vagrancy of local dwelling where no door-entrance offers a threshold between inner and outer space, natural unhoused wandering and its mimicry by the traveller on tour, enlarges into a mighty horizon of human remembrance hinting at closure, the light of setting suns; itself the dwelling or hermitage of vagrant being and presence beyond all simple locality, where the narrative of any one single sunset is subsumed into their constancy of recurrence. What separates at the outset is the apparently divisive effect of years of absence; but just as five years can be mended through echoes marked by repetition, guiding and guarding the genial spirits, so too the intermissions of a lifetime can enhance the vehemence of feeling into the marks of connection restored and held dear. Even the culminations of seasonal cycles, of diurnal rounds and many passing years, intimating a tacit final separation at the close of mortal life, strike no ultimate terrors for the holiness of the heart's affections, the prospect of a motion and a spirit that, not quite within the boundaries of a traditional theology, shape the oncoming form of a completed life.

J. H. Prynne
Cambridge, August 2001

NOTES

WILLIAM WORDSWORTH, 'Lines Written a Few Miles above Tintern Abbey, On Revisiting the Banks of the Wye during a Tour, July 13, 1798', in [William Wordsworth and S.T. Coleridge], *Lyrical Ballads, with a Few Other Poems* (London, 1798), pp. 201-210 [the final poem]. This book was conceived as a jointly-authored project in the spring of 1798 and published anonymously in September of that year; the Tintern Abbey poem was composed probably in the second week of July, when the book was already in press, and just in time to be included (which may, or may not, account for its final position). From 1815 it was included among 'Poems of the Imagination'. For detailed textual history and extensive secondary bibliography consult James Butler and Karen Green (eds), *'Lyrical Ballads' and Other Poems, 1797-1800* (The Cornell Wordsworth; Ithaca and London, 1992), pp. 116-120 (reading text); 357-359 (notes); 372-3 (nonverbal variants). To the second edition of *Lyrical Ballads* Wordsworth added this: 'Note to the Poem on Revisiting the Wye, p. 201.– I have not ventured to call this Poem an Ode; but it was written with a hope that in the transitions, and the impassioned music of the versification would be found the principal requisites of that species of composition' (William Wordsworth, *Lyrical Ballads, with Other Poems. In Two Volumes* [2nd ed., London, 1800], Vol. I, p. [215]; Wordsworth later inserted the missing comma after 'versification').

On 10th July 1798 William and Dorothy Wordsworth set out from Bristol (the 'tour' of the poem's title) and walked to Tintern, then on 11th July onwards to Goodrich, then (12th July) back to Tintern, returning to Bristol on the 13th. William was 28, Dorothy 27. Wordsworth's first visit to Tintern Abbey in the summer of 1793, age 23, alone and in very different mood, coincided with the height of revolutionary turmoil in France, and followed on from his journey across Salisbury Plain and thence from Bristol to Tintern. For his mood in 1793 compare *The Prelude* (1805-6), X, 757-90; *The Thirteen-Book Prelude*, ed. Mark L. Reed (3 vols, Ithaca and London, 1991), Vol. I, pp. 287-8.

Butler and Green cite in full the Fenwick Note, thus: 'July 1798. No poem of mine was composed under circumstances more pleasant for me to remember than this. I began it upon leaving Tintern, after crossing the Wye, and concluded it just as I was entering Bristol in the evening, after a ramble of 4 or 5 days, with my sister. Not a line of it was altered, and not any part of it written down till I reached Bristol. It was published almost immediately after in the little volume of which so much has been said in these notes (The Lyrical Ballads, as first published at Bristol by Cottle)' (p. 357).

For the (absent) abbey itself consult e.g. Arthur Edward Henderson, *Tintern Abbey; Then and Now* (2nd ed., London, 1937); David M. Robinson, *Tintern Abbey* (Welsh Historic Monuments; 4th rev. ed., Cardiff, 2002), also his *William Wordsworth's Tintern* (5th ed., Cardiff, 2002); for the question of contemporary touristic 'interest' in Tintern Abbey see John Rieder, *Wordsworth's Counterrevolutionary Turn; Community, Virtue, and Vision in the 1790s* [Newark, Del., 1997], pp. 202-220.

ISSN 1942-3381

J. H. Prynne

'Double-setting':

> A tranquillizing spirit presses now
> On my corporeal frame so wide appears
> The vacancy between me & those days
> Which yet have such self presence in my heart
> That some times when I think of them I seem
> Two consciousnesses, conscious of myself
> And of some other being.

From the 1799 draft for Part Two of *The Prelude*, first recorded in MS RV (fol. 1ʳ) and transcribed in Stephen Parrish (ed.), *The Prelude, 1798-1799* (Ithaca and Hassocks, 1977), p. 169 (see also p. 55). This passage survives practically unaltered into the 1805-6 text (II, lines 27-33) and thence into the final version of 1850; see Jack Stillinger, 'Multiple "Consciousnesses" in Wordsworth's *Prelude*', in his *Multiple Authorship and the Myth of Solitary Genius* (New York, 1991), Chap. 4 (pp. 69-95), p. 73; also, M.H. Abrams, *Natural Supernaturalism; Tradition and Revolution in Romantic Literature* (New York, 1971), p. 75; and (briefly also) Alan Richardson, *Literature, Education, and Romanticism; Reading as Social Practice, 1780-1832* (Cambridge, 1994), p. 18.

'The general passions and thoughts and feelings of men': 'Preface' to *Lyrical Ballads*, in a passage added in the 1850 edition; see *The Prose Works of William Wordsworth*, ed. W.J.B. Owen and Jane Worthington Smyser (3 vols, Oxford, 1974), Vol. I, p. 142.

'Immortality Ode': 'Ode. Intimations of Immortality from Recollections of Early childhood' (1802-4), best reading text: *Poems, in Two Volumes, and Other Poems, 1800-1807*, ed. Jared Curtis (Ithaca, N.Y., 1983), pp. 269-77 (reading text), 428-430 (notes). The 'mighty waters rolling evermore' of line 168 in the *Ode* are not unrelated to the 'sense sublime' that in 'Tintern Abbey' 'rolls through all things' (line 103); these wave-motions constantly recapitulate their own recurrent forms, both transient and abiding—as also for Wordsworth does the measured recurrency of his blank verse composition and paragraphing, taking its cue from the spacious phrasing of the extended title.

'"murmur" contains its own repeat': compare J.H. Prynne, *Field Notes: 'The Solitary Reaper' and Others* (Cambridge, 2007), pp. 43, 75; 'Wild eyes': *ibid.*, p. 85. 'Tin/tern' is likewise near-reduplicative.

'From blood to heart and heart to mind':

> sensations sweet,
> Felt in the blood, and felt along the heart,
> And passing even into my purer mind
> With tranquil restoration.

'Tintern Abbey', lines 28-31; Butler and Green (eds), *'Lyrical Ballads' and Other Poems*, p. 117; 'along' is characteristically puzzling here, compare *The Prelude* (1805-6), I, 277 ('flow'd along my dreams'). For background to the contemporary arguments concerning body function and vital principle see e.g. June Goodfield-Toulmin, 'Some Aspects of English Physiology: 1780-1840', *Journal of the History of Biology*, 2 (1969),

p. 283-320; also Duncan Wu, *Wordsworth; An Inner Life* (Oxford, 2002), p. 40-2. Butler and Green cite Milton Wilson, 'Bodies in Motion: Wordsworth's Myths of Natural Philosophy' in *Centre and Labyrinth: Essays in Honour of Northrop Frye*, ed. Eleanor Cook *et al.* (Toronto, 1983), pp. 206-209.

'Tufts of snow': 'Frost at Midnight' (Feb 1798), best reading text: *The Collected Works of Samuel Taylor Coleridge*, ed. J.C.C. Mays (6 vols, Princeton, N.J., 2001), Vol. I.1: *Poems (Reading Text: Part 1)*, pp. 452-7 (line 68).

'The prospect-poem': see e.g. Rachel Crawford, *Poetry, Enclosure, and the Vernacular Landscape, 1700-1830* (Cambridge, 2002), Chap. 6: 'Jago's *Edge-Hill*: Simulation and Representation' (pp. 138-165); also C.V. Deane, 'The Prospect Poem', in J.R. Watson (ed.), *Pre-Romanticism in English Poetry of the Eighteenth Century; The Poetic Art and Significance of Thomson, Gray, Collins, Goldsmith, Cowper & Crabbe* (Houndmills, 1989), pp. 125-33.

'The one life': 'The Eolian Harp: Composed at Clevedon, Somersetshire' (Aug-Oct 1795, also Feb? 1796); *Collected Works*, Vol. I.1, pp. 231-5 (lines 26-7).

'Diurnal round': 'A slumber did my spirit seal' (1800); Butler and Green (eds), *'Lyrical Ballads' and Other Poems*, pp. 164 (reading text), 384 (notes); also *The Prelude* (1805-6), I, 485-7; *The Thirteen-Book Prelude*, Vol. I, p. 120; compare also Shelley, 'With a Guitar. To Jane' (1822), 'driven on its diurnal round' (line 76).

'The holiness of the Heart's affections': letter to Benjamin Bailey of 22 November 1817; *The Letters of John Keats*, ed. Hyder Edward Rollins (2 vols, Cambridge, 1958), Vol. I, p. 184.

'A motion and a spirit': 'Tintern Abbey', line 101; Butler and Green (eds), *'Lyrical Ballads' and Other Poems*, p. 119.

NEW WORK: A PROSIMETRUM
Daniel C. Remein

This work consists of new poems and commentary in the tradition of Dante's prosimetric self-commentary. It aims to explore the shared ground of poetry and commentary, and the potential symbiotic and generative relationships between the two modes. The work proposes the elaboration of at least three particular formal poetic structures—which it names the 'riddle,' the 'missive,' and the 'miniature romance'—, cites moments from a broad range of medieval, modern, and contemporary literary history, and attempts to provoke a poetics of both poem and commentary that might help generate a more politically salient concept of literary community.

> ... *what should be the primary insight of all historically aware, destructive criticism: poems do violence to their interpreters and potentially destroy methods of criticism which are used to "illuminate" them.*—Paul A. Bové, *Destructive Poetics: Heidegger and Modern American Poetry*[1]

1

> *In the first part I encountered Love and how he looked; in the second I relate what he told me—only in part, however, for fear of revealing my secret*—Dante Alighieri, *Vita Nuova*, IX[2]

These verses could not have been written until I wrote **here begins a book of the poets** on a sheet of a paper originally intended to be a page in a book manuscript. Only then could I find these poems beginning. Of course, I could not be sure this work was indeed beginning until I found another sheet and then wrote on it ***incipit***. The commentary on these poems will begin the work of writing these poems, and undoing them as a book of poems. But, before any poem or comment on any poem, I would ask what *new work* could be set in motion by such poems which, though I could not find them beginning until I wrote the word *book*, form in fact no book and do not begin their work without their commentary? And how can one comment on the work that cannot begin until its commentary begins to work? I would not, for instance, attempt to *account for* the beginnings of the works with a narrative, or explain away the anticipated work with such a narrative as explaining (away). Nor can I in my comments tell the truth about the poems, or provide *information* concerning them beyond what is necessary to set them to work. Yet, I would not render the work of these poems as such a secret that they would demand an informative commentary.

Does the new work begin with poem or commentary? The American nineteenth-century writer of fiction Nathaniel Hawthorne described, with all that cagey tone proper to the voice of a fictional narrator, his poetics and their workings in his fictional preface to *The Blithedale Romance* in such a way as to make wonderfully

---

With a project of this size, I owe great thanks to *Glossator*'s editors and anonymous readers, whose commitment to the project of this new work has been sustained and immense. Additionally this project could not have been completed without those whose lives and work have become increasingly necessary for me to think and write, and whose specific projects, instruction, or commitment has explicitly enabled this project. I list them here: the Pittsburgh poets (Sten Carlson, Emily Gropp, Robin Clarke, Joshua Zelesnick, Sarah Bagley, Blaire Zeiders), the BABEL working group, my collaborator in another (to my mind related) project Anna Kłosowska, and those who commented on early drafts of this material on my blog including Eileen A. Joy.

[1] Paul A. Bové, *Destructive Poetics: Heidegger and Modern American Poetry* (New York: Columbia University Press, 1980), 221-222.

[2] Dante Alighieri, *Vita Nuova*, in *The Portable Dante*, ed. and trans. by Mark Musa (New York: Penguin, 1995), 598-599.

problematic the reading of his fictional 'Romance' as a commentary on a particular experience which readers may be tempted to invoke to explain away the genesis of the work. He writes anticipating that "In the 'Blithedale' of this volume many readers will probably suspect a faint and not very faithful shadowing of Brook Farm," that, as Hawthorne puts it, failed "Socialist Community" of which he took part.[3] And the relation of the poetics to this occasion of the work of the book is indeed 'shadowy,' but not, I would argue, for purposes of what we now call 'escapism,' or what might be denounced as a religious flight from the world; but, rather, to allow a certain effect of the poetics of the book to come to the fore, having seen rightly the time at Brook Farm as "essentially"[4] a day dream and yet a fact—and thus offering an available foothold between fiction and reality. The poems of a *new work* would have function as such a foothold between their commentary and the world. The proper effect of a commentary's romance appears in an entry into the world by means of a thinning of what stands between the regions of poem and commentary, production of and accounting for the poem—of a strange and hard to picture fading away of the solidity of this foothold. For, this foothold, even if it is the point of commerce between the two, being solid enough to act as a foothold, is also solid enough to provide an excuse for the kind of interpretation that would use its very solidity to deploy it as a barrier to keep separate, or as an arbitrary barrier to hermeneutically penetrate so as to produce (bogus) meaning. I do not mean a negation of everything or a negative-theological or skeptical denial of the real either (or, again, that flight from responsibility to dream) but the thinning away of the very *opaqueness* or *interpretability* of this foothold as a block, a veil to be eliminated (as well as the possibility of a 'real' history or a psychologizing *narrative* that would explain (away) the commentary and its poems) as the act of interpretation common to the history of what remains a bad-faith enemy of the literary in the practice of interpretation as the production of distinction, of returning dream to dream and reality to reality, of putting poem and commentary in their (proper) places as the very production of the proper. Here we are, after all, in a problem not dissimilar to Jacques Derrida's temporalization of representation and the sign, where the sign as always already a *re*-ference, a *re*-pointing in which "one must think of writing as a game within language . . . This *play* . . . is not a play *in the world*, as it has been defined, for purposes of *containing* it."[5] How to get in the world without containing the play of writing, from within the writing itself? Thus in Derrida's chapter on Rousseau in the same volume as the above quote we read that "what opens meaning and language is writing as the disappearance of natural presences."[6] How to find, or to produce, or to wear through the structures of the foothold so as to leave behind what Derrida calls the "hinge [*brisure*]"[7]—here between poem and gloss? Admit first that we are in language, and then consider how to get into the world without unproductively explaining (away) its relation to language. What will begin this work of perversely cultivating—I am not sure poets or commentators have begun or recognized that they have begun this work yet, even though some of their texts are already *at work* on it—the "*dead time* within the presence of the living present,"[8] while all the time rigorously affirming a *joyous* or *wonderful* worldliness: the modernist abysmal as optimism par excellence at the beginning of the work between a poem and its

---

[3] Nathaniel Hawthorne, *The Blithedale Romance*, Preface (New York: Penguin, 1986), 1.

[4] Ibid., 2

[5] Jacques Derrida, *Of Grammatology*, trans. Gayatri Chakravorty Spivak (Baltimore: Johns Hopkins University Press, 1976, corrected edition 1997), 50.

[6] Ibid., 158.

[7] Ibid., 69.

[8] Ibid., 68.

commentary.[9] The foothold between poem and commentary, reality and dream (all the terms can here be moved around) stands to be worn down so there is an incalculable commerce and indeed substantial mixing between the two regions of writing. The foothold will have to remain as a ruin of itself, to be a marvel even in what must become its wispy state.

Thus this text *is beginning* a new work that will work to wear down its secrecy in a manner secret even to itself so that the secret of the work of a poem or a commentary be entirely apparent without either ceasing to function as a site of wonder. So I would address critics, even against their wills, as poets; and, I would address poets, against their wills as critics—and I would offer this work not for a tiny public, however tiny its public may inevitably be. Also, I should note that while the nature of this writing works to confound that foothold that would allow a narrative of 'lived experience' to explain (away) the poems, and that while this work does not attempt either to work as a chronicle of 'the times,it would still work at being a work of history (at least for itself) in the spirit of the vocal commentary during the final flourish of Jean-Luc Godard's *Tout Va Bien* ('All Is Well'), which wishes, "May each be his own historian" [*Puis chacun être son propre historien*].[10]

So, as to the question of when this work will begin to work, with the poems or with the commentary, we remember of Derrida's 'writing' that "We must begin *wherever we are* and the thought of the trace . . . has already taught that it was impossible to justify a point of departure absolutely."[11] Already these words are the text of the poems and the work of their commentary.

§

And, *what* work does this begin? *The commentary on these poems will begin the work of writing these poems, and undoing them as a book of poems.* How should we name the form of this work, this 'prosimetrum' in such unregulated meters of 'free verse'? Jacques Derrida opened a book in 1972 with a similar question, writing: "La question s'y agite précisément de la présentation. Si la forme du livre est désormais soumise, comme on sait, à une turbulence générale, si elle paraît moins naturelle, et son histoire moins transparente que jamais, si l'on ne peut y toucher sans toucher à tout, elle ne saurait plus régler—ici par exemple—tels procès d'écriture qui, l'interroget *pratiquement*, doivent aussi la démonter" [The question which stirs itself here, precisely, is presentation. If the form of the book henceforth must submit to a period of general upheaval, and that form appears less natural, and its history less transparent than ever, if one cannot touch on it/disturb it with it without touching on

---

[9] That Derrida is commonly called *postmodern* does not trouble here. The movements of his readings in *Of Grammatology* remain devoted to literary and philosophical modernism (Malarmé, Heidegger, Lévi Strauss) or more generally 'modern' humanism (Rousseau) and his deconstruction of these discourses is not a break from them as a moving on, a leaving behind, but an exhaustion of them as a result of a commentarial devotion to them from the inside, cf. p. 24, "The movements of deconstruction do not destroy structures from the outside. They are not possible and effective, not can they take accurate aim, except by inhabiting those structures. Inhabiting them *in a certain way*, because one always inhabits, and all the more when one does not suspect it."

[10] Voiceover in final moments of Jean-Luc Godard's *Tout Va Bien* (1972, Gaumont; Criterion Collection DVD reissue 2005) circa 1:33:48 and 1:35:24.

[11] Derrida, *Of Grammatology*, 162.

everything, then it alone can no longer determine—here for example—such processes of writing which, in *practically* interrogating that form, must also dismantle it].[12] To touch on everything would require that "pluri-dimensional" thought around which Derrida earlier announced "The End of the Book and the Beginning of Writing"[13] along with the end of "linear writing" as the end of the book.[14] Additionally, since when "beginning to write without the line, one begins also to reread past writing according to a different organization of space," my commentary will place certain pasts and certain histories in the same space, leaving certain gaps and folding the shape of the page across centuries and continents. What is needed is a textural arrangement—writing which is fixed in its written-ness and historicity, but already suggesting a certain unaccountable movement—as Eve Kofosky Sedgwick wrote analogously of texture that "Texture, in short, comprises an array of perceptual data that includes repetition [and thus paradoxically, movement in stasis], but whose degree of organization hovers just below the level of shape or structure."[15] So the forms of these poems and their commentary are like various revolutions around nothing like a sphere brought forth in the possibility of work that works: work quick enough to be working so as to be equidistant from all points in an area nothing like a circle, flitting and folding back through time when necessary. What I work into this little work is but the rhythm of what I hope will become a provocative texture, which being bound even to a digital page would always already be at work towards the movements of such folds.

§

Plato famously asserted that poetry is only a copy of a copy. It was thus of rather low rank within his cosmology, banned from his *Republic*.[16] According to Erich Auerbach, Plato's demeaning of poetry

---

[12] Jacques Derrida, *Dissemination* (Paris: Éditions du Seuil, 1972), 9. translation, mine. Quotation in French here serves, I hope, to outline the syntactic dismantling (or as Rimbaud would say, the *dérèglement*) of form in Derrida's prose, as well as its effect when allowed to effect English, hence my own particular translation.

[13] Cf. Chapter one of Part One of *Of Grammatology*, 6-26.

[14] Ibid., 86-87. "The end of linear writing is indeed the end of the book, even if, even today, it is within the form of a book that new writings—literary or theoretical—allow themselves to be, for better or for worse, encased. It is less a question of confiding new writings to the envelope of a book than of finally reading what wrote itself between the lines in the volumes. That is why, beginning to write without the lines, one begins also to reread past writing according to a different organization of space. If today the problem of reading occupies the forefront of science, it is because of this suspense between two ages of writing. Because we are beginning to write, to write differently, we must reread differently." It is worth noting that *today* not all new writings, literary or theoretical, confine themselves to the traditional book and this piece in particular is already being written for a so-called 'online' journal. One could still print out pages and construct a codex with which to read this, but one could just as easily read non-linearly with the help of the basic scrolling function of 'today's' internet 'browsers.' As well I should note the short, the aphoristic form of these poems, as sympathetic with such a resistance to the linear book of poems, the *short form* as a raid on the linear model as the long "*epic model*" (Ibid., 87).

[15] Eve Kofosky Sedgwick, *Touching Feeling* (Durham: Duke University Press, 2003), 16.

[16] See Most especially Book X of Plato's *Republic*, trans. G.M.A. Grube, rev. C.D.C. Reeve (Indianapolis: Hackett, 1992).

inadvertently "bridged the gap between poetry and philosophy" because it "set poets the task of writing philosophically."[17] That is, poets, finding their discourse denied the seriousness of philosophy (the ability, colloquially, *to matter*) were, contrary to Plato's will, making sure that they took on this very task—and this is not to say that before Plato what was philosophy was not, by appearances, in meter and thus 'poetry' as in Parmenides, or Heracleitus;[18] or, that after Plato the same did not happen, as in Boethius.[19] What I mean to assert here, even if Auerbach's observation is limited in a certain way, is simply a very old capacity of a *poetics* to do the work of philosophy (beyond the sense of simply regularly metered writing). Poets taking this seriously may fear that while such poems labor among friends, they rarely do so for a larger public? For such a circumstance I would suggest that poems be written in the form of a missive like the one below that begins *as far as counting*. Perfect as a practice of philosophy so nourished by aphoristic care for 'the good life,'[20] a missive is abrupt and productive to chain together into a longer work in between other poems of the same or of diverse forms, not unlike the 'lustrum' of Ezra Pound in length and meter. The missive moves along a deictic vector: a tactile index of cosmos, a line of flight from one friend to many other unknown ones.

> as far as counting,
> these days we only
> count what we believe:
>
> a lampshade stained
> with the juice
>
> of a peach
> at lunchtime,
>
> a chair my father gave you.

This poem appears to be a single sentence reading smoothly but somehow elegaically over its line-breaks. After the first stanza, the poem consists primarily of a list. As far as the referents that constitute this list (*a lampshade stained . . .* and *a chair my father gave you*) as well as the *you* of the last line—not to mention the *we* of the third line—

---

[17] Erich Auerbach, *Dante: Poet of the Secular World*, trans. Ralph Manheim (New York: New York Review of Books, 2001), 5.

[18] See *A Presocratics Reader: Selected Fragments and Testimonia*, trans. Richard D. McKirahan (Indianapolis: Hackett, 1995).

[19] See Anicius Boethius, *The Consolation of Philosophy*, trans. Victor Watts (London: Penguin, 1966, revised 1999).

[20] Theodore Adorno advocated for the return of philosophy to the 'good life' in his *Minima Moralia: Reflections on a Damaged Life*, trans. E.F.N. Jephcott (London: Verso, 2005); Adorno writes, in his Dedication to Max Horkheimer, "The melancholy science from which I make this offering to my friend relates to a region that from time immemorial was regarded as the true field of philosophy, but which, since the latter's conversion into method, has lapsed into intellectual neglect, sententious whimsy and finally oblivion: the teaching of the good life," 15.

ISSN 1942-3381   Daniel C. Remein

all these must remain vague for the reader, who must invent first the *we* and then the subsequent crib-guide for the rest of what these referents refer to, hopefully putting herself in that *we* as well and inventing an I who is another to be the *you* who received a chair from the father of the poem's speaker, who is not *me*. Or, this *we* can be understood as the public to whom these poems are addressed, and thus as a missive *to* the public which as of yet is *not* but, in receiving a missive, might perhaps *appear*.

as far as counting: this missive is pluri-directional; this poem has antlers which sprout so quickly and bountifully that they are unaccountable. **what we believe**: perhaps what we believe is counted "these days," but it too is unaccountable. What we believe amounts to the list which follows the colon. **a lampshade stained**: "Is a lamp brought in to be put under the bushel basket, or under the bed, and not on the lampstand? For there is nothing hidden, except to be disclosed; nor is anything secret, except to come to light"[21] The stain of the lampshade by juice as the *waste* product of poetry and consuming the (transgressive, edenic) primordial poem enhances the translucency of the shade, the hinge between mediated and unmediated radiance. This antler of the poem grows out and up in radiance. **a peach / at lunchtime**: as with one of Pound's *lustrum* poems "Coitus," of sex as failed redemption, where "The gilded phalloi of the crocuses are thrusting at the spring air," here too, in this Poundian image "there is naught of dead gods / But a procession of festival."[22] **a chair**: "My eighteen-inch deep study of you / is like a chair carried out into the garden,/ And back again because the grass is wet,"[23] as far as this chair relates to the *you*. But also, if the *you* is so ontologically separate from the speaker, "In a day or two the chairs will fall to pieces: / Those who were once lovers need the minimum / Of furniture."[24] This one is a three-legged chair, of difficult balance, and a tepee-shaped back. It was made well and painted quietly. The father of the speaker once sat in the chair for a long time while listening to a friend discourse on a garden whose discourse of sleep was so public that the gardeners were referred to as court poets and philosophers.

§

There is no hidden knowledge to be gained, by cunning guesswork, in the poems I will write. They are working at something else. Close friends are at no advantage. Yet, too often, it is only among friends that such a poem can circulate. I phoned one of these good friends. She said, "when a black man is running for president we need to keep him from getting shot." In the spirit of this phone call I composed the following hymn which begins *only in romance*: a song that is not about any politician or election, but the radiant circuitries of wonder.

> only in romance
> is the state glued,
> each thread
> of fish is added to your hair

---

[21] Mark 4:21-22 (NRSV)

[22] Ezra Pound, "Coitus" from *Lustra* in *Personae: The Shorter Poems of Ezra Pound*, Revised by Lea Baechler and A. Walton Litz (New York: New Directions, 1990), 113.

[23] Medbh McGuckian, "What Does 'Early' Mean?" in *On Ballycastle Beach* (Winston-Salem: Wake Forest University Press, 2003), 12.

[24] Ibid., "Little House, Big House," 33.

>   just before the last one
>   dissolves: a fortunate
>
>   arrangement for the president.
>
>   beatrice will swallow
>   no more
>
>   wrath drives
>   a little
>
>   a deer, a cell-phone,
>   a marvel.

The poem is punctuated as if it consists of two sentences, but what would be the second sentence seems to break apart, or allow for the possibility that something was not properly transposed from the initial typescript (or perhaps maliciously, carelessly, or for some strange design, omitted from that same typescript), so that one cannot tell how closely to attempt to relate the grammar of each couplet, beginning with the reference to the object of Dante Alighieri's Love and Poetry, *beatrice*.

thread / of fish: the image evokes the great cords of braided animals that will be used to hoist the Washington Monument after the next raid by the Centaurs. Chiron can no longer stop them, and they carry the teeth they lose in battle braided into their hair just like those remaining in the capital will braid themselves amidst any other remaining living mortal animal as a sign of their devotion to romance and fiction over and against that of their adversaries' mythologizing. ***arrangement***: "The hand, fastidious and bold, which selected and placed–it was that which made the difference. In Nature there is not selection."[25] It is, whether the case of a poem or a comment on a poem, or a political ruse about one who was or was not successfully elected president, the selection and arrangement that matters in the effort to dim or wear away any natural presence (see above, quotation from Derrida, *Of Grammatology*, 158). ***beatrice will swallow no more***: beatrice refuses to swallow not only wrath, as once might surmise, despite punctuation or clear grammatical relation, from the next stanza. She also refuses to swallow *more* itself, as a substantive noun. *More* here of course refers to the very condition of making harder and firmer, making more 'real' each and every thing and thus reinforcing it as proper. See Leo Bersani's argument that "Lessness is the condition of allness."[26] This is Beatrice's secret rebellion even while within her proper sphere and her Aristotelian-Thomist lessons to Dante about 'everything in its right place': that she knows that every other orbit, even if entirely *other*, also secretly mixes with each other–by riding hard through the turn long enough you can wear through the One's foothold needed to keep the gravitational pulls in place. ***wrath***: wrath here is what can consume while remaining consumable, which moves anger into the

---

[25] Willa Cather, *The Professor's House* (First Published New York: Knopf, 1925, New York: Vintage, 1990), 61.

[26] Leo Bersani and Ulysse Dutiot, *Forms of Being: Cinema, Aesthetics, Subjectivity* (London: British Film Insititute, 2004), 165.

realm of an impossible by moving it into a just-ness beyond ethics that becomes murderous and can destroy friendship. See Anne Carson's "Book of Isaiah." For example, "Isaiah awoke angry. / Lapping at Isaiah's ears black birdsong no it was anger. / God had filled Isaiah's ears with stingers. / Once God an Isaiah were friends."[27] ***a cell-phone, / a marvel***: like the display of wonder in the intricacies of medieval poetic accounts of courtly carvings of deer, the cell phone might shine brightly in the modern poem. Cell-phones, for good or for ill, whether intentional on any level of their production or not, represent the fruition of the flip-open shaped device for wireless voice communication—often relying literally on 'space/space-age' technology—which once was the sole province of the "communicator" props in the original *Star Trek* television series. May a hymn to wonder, or a radiant poetic missive, shine as a cell-phone with an alluring curve, glowing in the night.

Apart from these notably specific references, the poem contains no arguments or dilemmas and it is otherwise very clear.

§

It has been determined by certain experts that there is a ghost at work in this new work—in the poems or in the commentary? W.H. Auden's poem "Family Ghosts" ends with the lines "and all emotions to expression come, / Recovering the archaic imagery: / This longing for assurance takes the form / Of a hawk's vertical stooping from the sky."[28] In each movement to recover the work to come, to imagine the recovery of it, one who is on the ground might feel a gravitational pull from elsewhere arriving at, or emitting from, the writing body. A text may likewise be haunted.[29] Such moments turn us again to the origin of these poems and when they work as

---

[27] Anne Carson, "Book of Isaiah" in *Glass, Irony, and God* (New York: New Directions, 1995), 107.

[28] W.H. Auden, "Family Ghosts," in *Collected Poems*, ed. Edward Mendelson (New York: Modern Library, 2007), 41.

[29] I am referring here to Jacques Derrida's *Specters of Marx*, trans. Peggy Kamuf (New York: Routeledge, 1994), yet (re?)focusing the possibility of a hauntology not only on 'the times' or a particular individual and his relation to a past or a tradition (such as Derrida and the inheritance of 'Marxism'), but additionally as a secular way to talk about the multiple non-human agencies and relations between texts—further obliterating the role of the poet in actually writing the poem—or the responsibility of the single mind (as genius) for a given work—as what *works* in the space that disarticulates the opposition between all oppositions, past/present, literary-history/literary-present, and for this, writer/reader, poem/commentary. What is working here is the work and what is haunted is the work by work. From this point we can begin to try to think about how the work will get us into the world, rather than beginning with assumptions of facile relations between work and world (including that of work and poet or work and reader). For Derrida, the ghosts related to the anachrony of our readings and our inheritances of readings is exactly one path into the world, as "If it—learning to live—remains to be done, it can happen only between life and death. Neither in life nor in death *alone*. What happens between the two, and between all the 'two's' one likes, such as between life and death, can only *maintain itself* with some ghost, can only *talk with or about* some ghost. So it would be necessary to learn spirits. Even and especially if this, the spectral, is *not* . . . to learn to live *with* ghosts, in the upkeep, the conversation, the company, or the companionship, in the commerce without commerce of ghosts. To learn to live otherwise, and better. no, not better, but more justly. But *with them*" (xvii-xviii).

ISSN 1942-3381   Daniel C. Remein

either lacking agency in time and space, or as multiple in their agencies. Nevertheless, some attendance to or cultivation of the text might better invite the ghosts to, felicitously, further compromise the agencies of these texts that are already not mine.[30] There must be a work of conjuring, some ritual (and yet one proper to the writing of poems and commentaries and not to religions!) Thus, Auden would later write of Iceland: "Europe is absent: this is an island and should be a refuge, where the affections of its dead can be bought / by those whose dreams accuse them of being spitefully alive."[31] Here the practice of spectral relation would seem to consist of accusations put to those who are dead. This is particularly a notable line, because it appears in this 'final' form perhaps for the first time in Auden's typescript of the poem in preparing his *Collected Shorter Poems 1927-1957*, as it will appear in that volume and later in the *Collected Poems* edited by Edward Mendelson.[32] Initially, the line appears in 1937 in *Letters from Iceland* (the book co-written with Louis MacNiece, as "Islands are places apart where Europe is absent. / Are they? The World still is, the present, the lie, / And the narrow bridge over a torrent . . ."[33] Here, the lines seem only concerned debunking the desire to have *place* apart from Europe with the clumsy "Are They?" But, more was at work in these lines on the absence of Europe and condition of Island, as it relates to the production of poems (the poem ends with "again some writer runs howling to his art").[34] Already the tone of the poem more confidently drives Europe from Iceland (perhaps a growing political stance of Auden in desiring to fend off British hegemony from a place he saw in a creatively productive relation to European literature and history—right on the edge) in the 1938 *Collected Poems*: "For Europe is absent. This is an island and therefore / Unreal. And the steadfast affections of its dead may be bought / By those whose dreams accuse them of being spitefully alive."[35] Moreover, this major revision brings into the poem what is truly distinctive about the place apart from Europe: the economy of spectral relations—its market for the affections of the dead. The version of the poem in the 1945 Random House *Collected Poetry of W.H. Auden* thus marks a transition to the 'final' form from the *Collected Shorter Poems* quoted above, as "This is

---

[30] For Derrida, the relation to the ghost as inheritance "is never a given. It is always a task. It remains before us just as unquestionably as we are heirs of Marxism, even before wanting or refusing to be, and, like all inheritors, we are in mourning. In mourning in particular for what is called Marxism" (*Specters of Marx*, 67).

[31] W. H. Auden, "Journey to Iceland," cited from the typescript of the poem for the *Collected Shorter Poems 1927-1957*, New York, Columbia University Rare Book and Manuscript Library, Special MS Collection Auden.

[32] See W.H. Auden, "Journey to Iceland," in *Collected Shorter Poems 1927-1957* (London: Faber and Faber, 1966), 100; and the same poem in *Collected Poems*, ed. Edward Mendelson (London: Faber and Faber, 1976, revised 1991, 2007), 150. The current edition has the poem on page 150, and Mendelson's preserves Auden's 'final' revision for the *Collected Shorter Poems* in all revisions.

[33] W.H. Auden and Louis MacNiece, "Journey to Iceland," *Letters from Iceland* (New York: Random House, 1969), 24.

[34] Auden, "Journey to Iceland," *Collected Shorter Poems 1927-1957*, 101.

[35] W.H. Auden, "Journey to Iceland," in *Collected Poems* (London: Faber and Faber, 1938), 123. This Revision is preserved in Edward Mendelson's *The English Auden: Poems, Essays, and Dramatic Writings 1927-1939* (London: Faber and Faber, 1977), 203–perhaps as a record of the poem's original appearance from the 'English period'; and also, to this day, as if the final version of the poem, in Mendelson's *Selected Poems: Expanded Edition* (New York: Vintage, 2007) 49.

an Island and therefore / A refuge."[36] What is important about these revisions is the move first to the concern with the economy of spectral relations, and then towards the idea that such relations are proper not so much to unreality, but rather, to the refuge from Europe of the Island or the poem. Finally, Auden tempers the hope of this sense by revising the logical and complete force of the *therefore* to the uncertain modal *should be*, emphasizing that even if the affections of the dead are to be bought, that they are in fact dead, and that the practice of accusing them of being spitefully alive is only possible, perversely, in dreams—thus the unreality from the 1937 version. The revisions suggest the line is not only of great importance to the poem, but that, given the desire it suggests for spectral relations, that the agency at work on this poem is multiple and temporally heterogeneous. Moreover the modal 'should be' is ambiguous enough to allow us to wonder if the Island *should be a refuge* but in fact is not, if it has the capacity to be so and is prevented by something beyond control, or if in fact there is some practice which would allow it to function as it should. Friends arrive to work on a book from various times. We hide nothing from each other. We un-hide each other. We resolve to write a series of warnings. This poem, which begins *all 500 breastplates*, is a riddle caught up in the work of spectral un-hidings.

> all 500 breastplates
> off-kilter and combat
>
> distillery run amock
> no help my netizen,
>
> a passbook of
> free greetings
>
> no levers left anymore.

The various fragments appear to consist of at least five different utterances, perhaps from difference speakers. Or, there is no need to construct a narrative or a speaker, and the words are not spoken, but just jumble themselves on the page or the screen. The poem is in four stanzas. Consider this the best way to divide the utterances, or don't.

breastplates: the radiant armor of a minor hope when all of the bloodlines are cut and a language is dulled by an infusion of combat readiness. Such was the trouble of a young Perceval in Chrétien de Troye's poem by the same name, when the young boy mistakes *Chevaliers* for Angels.[37] **distillery**: see Samuel Beckett on Dante: "His conclusion is that the corruption common to all the dialects makes it impossible to select one rather than another as an adequate literary form, and that he who would write in the vulgar must assemble the purest

---

[36] W.H. Auden, "Journal to Iceland," in *The Collected Poetry of W.H. Auden* (New York: Random House, 1945), 8.

[37] See *Perceval ou le Conte du Graal*, Ed. Charles Méla, in *Chrétien de Troyes: Romans* (Paris: La Pochotèque, 1994), lines 121-169; or, in translation, see *Perceval: the Story of the Grail*, in *Chrétien de Troyes: Arthurian Romances*, trans. D. D. R. Owen (London: Everyman, 1993), lines 111-185.

elements from each dialect and construct a synthetic language that would at least possess more than a circumscribed local interest."[38] But is a distillation necessary to get to the message of a missive as the solution to the riddle? Or, if it is "distillery run amock," then is the problem of distillation one which cannot help eliminate the need for breastplates? Such distillery would need to occur in a transparent caldron, of a flame pleasurably bright. The help for the netizen (see next comment) in language must burn just as brightly as the radiant screens plotting drone attacks on Afghanis from Nevada, while where we still find ourselves in terms of purgatorial distillation is that peculiar modern condition which Beckett found in Joyce: "neither prize nor penalty, simply a series of stimulants to enable the kitten to catch its tail. And the partially purgatorial agent? The partially purged."[39] Distillation as purgative in the modern world, as refining and purifying heat, is thus akin to the failed attempts of alchemy. And even there, so often the search for the stone is more important than the transmutation it would produce. **netizen**: this word is advertised on the back of the dust jacket of the *Merriam-Websters Collegiate Dictionary* 10th Edition, in 1999, along with *netiquette, spammer, face time, echinacea, fusion cuisine, feng sui,* and *velociraptor*.[40] Thus the word registers as among a group which, when taken together, collect the bright hive of the internet as the radiantly new along with—among others—a notably ancient reptile so that what is caught in between are the mundane practices of human communication and food as their own luminousities. This is important to the study of the work of this poem if one is to present the proper passbook and take her place among the shinning radiant breastplates of the first stanza. These breastplates are hanging from the sprouting antlers of this poem and most of the others in this work. **free greetings**: do not mistake greetings for transparent communication. The greeting of this poem is only the entrance into its commentary, which, though 'below' the poem as you now read it, might be just as well taking place into the unhinging between the paratactic syntax of *free greetings* with all its plenitude and the assertion(?) *no levers left anymore* with is announcement of privation. This is the roomy dwelling space for our friendship in this poem—the space in which you or a literary ghost may be invited to take up an abode, such as a speechmaking *Beowulf* beginning to send a missive to his own friend, Hrothgar, in wearing perhaps not a breastplate but a *byrne* (mail-coat) such that it is well-displayed as a smith's work.[41] Such a space, like Beowulf's missive, is in this riddle itself and the room bounded off by its syntactic turns and gaps, radiant as the armor of its speaker, fearful or courageous. **no levers**: here the lever is not a phallus, nor is it to be related to the phallic elevator lever about which the elevator operator has to complain in *The Great Gatsby* to Mr. McKee to "keep your hands off the lever"—to which McKee replies, "I didn't know I was touching it."[42] We lament, with the rise of the digital, the loss of the mechanical in our dwelling spaces, and would attempt to re-insert the mechanical into the secret of a poem's radiance so as to not lose its memory. Without a lever to pull, how can we unlock the mechanics of any riddle? Even if a digital inscription on the passbook of free greetings implores you *say what I am called.*

§

---

[38] Samuel Beckett, "Dante . . . Bruno . . . Vico . . . Joyce," in *Samuel Beckett: The Grove Centenary Edition Vol. 4: Poems, Short Fiction, Critcism* (New York: Grove Press, 2006), 507.

[39] Ibid., 510.

[40] *Merriam-Webster's Collegiate Dictionary*, 10th ed., (Springfield, Mass: Merriam-Webster, 1999).

[41] See *Beowulf* in *Beowulf and the Fight at Finnsburgh,* Ed. Fr. Klaeber 3rd ed. (Boston: D.C. Heath and Company, 1950), lines 405-406.

[42] F. Scott Fitzgerald, *The Great Gatsby* (New York: Collier, 1992), 42.

These systems of sublimating the riddles and absurd elements of linguistic happenings into the intricate flowers of textual kissing–the dreaming up of the vain *eidos* to enrich the texture of *cosmos*–these things are strange reversals of what our masters taught us in the Occitane masterpieces. So we poets now should guard no new style. The short-lived colony of some poets should run itself into a whirring hive of production, a burning festal collective. Being so festal, we would refute all confessions and embrace riddles as the vector for our missives. Here is another riddle, beginning *output is.*

> output is
> they elect
>
> a terrorist
> the antlered
>
> wall won't hold
> any more foetuses
>
> holy or otherwise.

There are three couplets, and a final line, forming a single sentence–though one enforcing a strange punctuation.

output: the term is not used with reference to the operations of a computer, though the word is certainly taken from there. More as the mechanization of the movements of Walt Whitman's grass, as "the beautiful uncut hair of graves."[43] I saw a strange beard with great output. It moved in time with the foot of the line Emily Dickinson breathed when dying. Say what I am called. ***they elect***: the idea of a *they* electing must either refer to a republic, democratic, or semi-democratic body (perhaps of a state), or, alternately, as an insistence on a heterodox revision of John Calvin's immutably sovereign God who elects the saved and damned as a plurality and thus a *they*. Of course, the Christian doctrine of the trinity has always had to attempt to disambiguate its orthodox stance of three in one and one in three from a polytheism.[44] ***a terrorist***: to solve the riddle, one must

---

[43] Walt Whitman, "Song of Myself" in *Leave of Grass: The First (1855) Edition*, Ed. Malcom Cowley (New York: Viking, 1959), line 101.

[44] See Jaroslav Pelikan, *The Christian Tradition: A History of the Development of Doctrine, Vol. 1 The Emergence of the Catholic Tradition (100-600)* (Chicago: University of Chicago Press, 1971). Even more than the apologetic disambiguation of orthodox from gnostic dotrine, Pelikan refers to the dogma of the Trinity as "The climax of the doctrinal development of the early church" (172). Thus the Arian practice of "baptizing in the name not only of the Father, but also of the Son and of the Holy Spirit"–which would eventually become orthodox (Pelikan indeed suggests that the Arians, in the long term, made a significant contribution for the good to Christian doctrine, despite their heretical status, cf. 200)–attracted accusations of polytheism that may confuse students now because it was part of a process of strange disambiguation: "It was an acknowledgement of this relation between what was believed, taught, and confessed when the opponents of Ariaism, from Athanasius

ask perhaps not only why *they* would elect a terrorist, but as well, to what position? If there is to be a festal collective of poets, would such a hive of riddles allow for the possibility of an 'election?' **the antlered**: a plea, really—for this and other poems indeed to sprout such multiplying outgrowths. That the 'wall' might be what is antlered presents little trouble to this, beyond the mistake of imagining a set of mounted hunting trophies. What is meant are poems. **wall won't hold**: because it is either already the wall of an old crypt or the wall attempting to hold off invading death. Such is the possibility of a wall of fetuses which may even be hanging by the poems, unless all of this takes place either a) impossibly within a womb or other incubator, or b) as an image suggesting the entry of death into the governing position of the economy of 'life' already from before birth. This returns us again to the problem of *wearing out* or dimming to get back into the world, and all such activities bring along:

> The flower dies down
> and rots away .
> But there is a hole
> in the bottom of the bag.
> It is the imagination
> which cannot be fathomed.
> It is through this hole we escape.[45]

The solution to the riddle is *cryptology*, or *biopolitical mystery religions*.

§

The poem beginning *you will understand* is—oddly enough—at once a missive to both T. S. Eliot and Walter Benjamin.

> you will understand
> *ashes* when the firewall
> slips your skin

---

and Hilary through Marcellus of Ancyra and Boethius, accused it of being polytheistic despite its rigid monotheism; for by worshipping as divine one whom they refused to call divine, they would 'certainly be going on to more god' and would 'lead into a plurality' of divine beings" (199-100). Pelikan's claim is that by continuing to use the name of Christ as divine even when the Arian's theologically questioned his divinity was to set one's self up for a slippery slope of objects of worship, and that thus the Arians understood the Trinitarian debate better than anyone else in making their contribution: "As the official doctrine of the church proceeded to settle the question of the relation of Christ to God by means of the formula 'homoousios,' it was Arianism that helped, through its demand for precision, to rescue that formula from the heretical, Gnostic incubus that afflicted it" (200). Especially in the language of Baptism there was an anxiety about reflecting that "to be Christian meant to be set free from worship of creatures and to be baptized into the one Godhead of the Trinity, 'not into a polytheistic plurality'" (217).

[45] William Carlos Williams, *Patterson* (New York: New Directions, 1992), 210.

> like lobsters &
> gin unlinks
>
> did you learn
> *to remember* is
>
> an acrylic growth
> in the chapel
>
> i don't have claws

The missive begins explaining the manner of an understanding's projection onto a *there* of meaning proper to certain Beings and then shifts at *did you learn* to a chain of words both asking of and explaining to the receivers of the missive the ontology of *to remember*, which, with *an acrylic growth*, begins to be explained.

you will understand / ashes when: that is, you will *begin* to understand at some point which will arrive in the future. Here, what one is to understand, is the secret to the riddle of this and every missive. And yet, if this is the case, if the understanding must begin then it must be that you already understand, or perhaps that you cannot begin to understand. To return to the discussion of beginning, recall Derrida's assertion that "Everything begins by referring back [*par le renvoi*], that is to say, does not begin; and once this breaking open or this partition divides, from the very start, every *renvoi*, there is not a single *renvoi* but from then on, always, a multiplicity of *renvois*, so many different traces referring back to other traces, and to traces of others."[46] Thus the comparison of a certain motion in this poem to the manner in which lobsters and gin *unlink* should unlink for you (as Dante might say *untie the knot*) the path the un-original unlinking of the missive as a riddle. **did you learn / to remember**: the question without the punctuation of the question mark asks whether or not it is in fact a question, especially since subordinated to the copula *is*. To ask about a learning 'to remember' in this way is to ask about the impossibility of beginning to unlock the riddle of the missive, which you must, at the same time, have always already begun to unlock. Here, unlike the learning proper to the Platonic soul,

> Memory is a kind
> of accomplishment
> a sort of renewal
> even
> an initiation, since the spaces it opens are new
> places
> inhabited by hordes
> heretofore unrealized.[47]

---

[46] Jacques Derrida, "On Representation," trans. Peter and Mary Ann Caws in *Transforming the Hermeneutic Context,* ed. Gayle L Ormiston and Alan D. Schrift (Albany: State University of New York Press, 1990), 136.

[47] William Carlos Williams, *Patterson*, 78.

The riddle, though language on a page or a screen, glows in your hands like the radiance of ***an acrylic growth***: this growth is without question the sprouting of unnatural antlers which will scratch at and wear down the veils in the windows of the chapel so as to let more light into the poem to the extent that it can capture that light (like a black hole) and hold within its missive-nature an unseen radiance as a riddle. ***i don't have claws***: the assertion might additionally be read as an admission that the poem gives itself over to the growth of multiple unnatural antlers as and from its (un)original space of division between the time of its beginning and its assertions of what you will do (remember, etc.) again, even if you have not already begun. Alternately, the poem might be attempting to ask an overwhelming question, swelling, with its non-claw outward growths, or flashes in an empty chapel—a small creature trying to speak over the voice of the thunder and being told to "make up yr. mind you Tiresias if yo know damn well or else you dont."[48]

§

> some hagiography is
> glued & additive. beatrice
> was forged.
>
> an eyelid dips
> a fish into a pool. this is the real
> part. belief has substance
> when heated. an elect lends
> a helping hand.
>
> families link
> this or the next &
> a synthetic bone is
> placed gently into
> each child's hairshirt
>
> to remind us, watch the video
> with only the greatest
> of care.

This poem is a missive, divided into four sections.

glued and additive: such a hagiography would be in the mode of *bricolage*, from parts of the saint's life and parts of what is available at a given time as holy. Yet, such *bricolage*, however attractive to the contemporary

---

[48] Ezra Pound, comment in pen on the typescript of "The Waste Land" by T.S. Eliot in *The Waste Land: A Facsimile and Transcript of the Orignal Drafts Including The Annotations of Ezra Pound*, Ed. Valerie Eliot (San Diego: Harcourt, 1971), 47.

poet, theorist, or historian, would maintain the boundaries of the edges of each moment or part. There would be no flash of brilliance, no anachronistic simultaneity as with the forging of the next line. However, a certain distinction must be made here, between the sort of flash of heat and radiance proper to the purgatory of the abysmal painful threshold (alchemical transformation or the transformation of metal at the hands of the more conventional blacksmith as purgatorial 'refining by fire') as spiritual purgatorial process and the flash of a worldly radiance that while remaining finite, can disarticulate certain temporal or semantic (holy vs. profane) distinctions in the life of the saint as an alluring moment of poetic luminosity. Thus we must look not—however alluringly it rolls off the tongue—to Eliot's

> The dove descending breaks the air
> With flame of incandescent terror
> Of which the tongues declare
> The one discharge from sin and error
> The only hope, or else despair
>   Lies in the choice of pyre or pyre—
>   To be redeemed from fire by fire[49]

nor can we look to Yeats's "O sages standing in God's holy fire/ As in the gold mosaic of a wall,/ Come from the holy fire, perne in a gyre,/ And be the singing-masters of my soul."[50] Instead here is the trouble of how to think the exhilaration of the fire and the intensity of its radiance without either the need for purgation or redemption in the first place, or redemption as the result—and to think the exhilaration without the terror—the radiant allure without the flame. Yeats's Magi, "In their stiff, painted clothes, the pale unsatisfied ones," these perhaps, with "all their eyes still fixed, hoping to find once more,/ being by calvary's turbulence unsatisfied, / The uncontrollable mystery on the bestial floor," offer an alternative.[51] Though Whitman's "I sing the body electric" is easier.[52] **an eyelid dips / a fish into a pool. this is the real / part**: This idea of dipping into the real should be considered in relation to Pier Paola Pasolini's *Heretical Empiricism*—and in terms of a debate with Jean-Luc Godard about realism, cinema, and revolution.[53] Pasolini postulated that *"reality is, in the final analysis, nothing*

---

[49] T. S. Eliot, "Little Gidding," in *Collected Poems 1909-1962* (New York: Harcourt, 1968), 207.

[50] W.B. Yeats, 'Sailing to Byzantium,' from *The Tower*, in *The Collected Poems of W.B. Yeats* (New York: Macmillan, 1956), 191.

[51] Yeats, "The Magi," from *Responsibilities*, in *The Collected Poems of W.B. Yeats*, 124.

[52] Walt Whitman, "I Sing the Body Electric," in *Leaves of Grass: The First (1855) Edition* Ed. Malcolm Cowley (New York: Viking, 1969), 116-123.)

[53] Pier Paolo Pasolini, *Heretical Empiricism* (Bloomington: Indiana University Press, 1988). As will be hinted, Pasolini found that the world was already audio-visual technique, in the form of action—thus, *"Human action in reality*, in other words, as first and foremost language of mankind" (198)—and that film only needed to take it up into itself. For Godard, one might generalize that the world was constructed by our filming ourselves—the concern would have been more for history than the world and language [Godard for instance suggests in an interview that a 'political film' occurs when a worker takes an instamatic movie camera on vacation with him (in an interview on the *Tout Va Bien* Criterion DVD)]. Thus Pasolini points out "how much such a philosophy, produced by a semiological description, would have in common with phenomenology: with Husserl's method,

more than cinema in nature"[54] and that as one result "the graph of the grammatical modes of film language could be a *vertical line*: a line, that is, that *fishes* in the Significando, continuously takes it upon itself, incorporating it in itself through its immanence in the mechanical audiovisual reproduction."[55] Perhaps it is time for a poem to be a film. But additionally, such a *fishing* would imply contact that is fluid. So no real here would be distinct from the unreal, but would freely and unnaturally mix. What if Beatice is so happy because in the moment she is forged, she dips into the real? **an elect**: does an antler elect to grow or is it instead *elected*? And who would be the elector? Us, me, you? **this or the next**: meaning, either this poem or the next the dwelling of the commentary, while in discontinuous units, will sprout some metamorphosing antler to enable travel; but this will be unintelligible to the families because, very simply, of the strangeness of feeling and knowing a pluridirectional plurality of agencies, or, alternately a secret agency, as in:

> The back-swell now smooth in the rudder-chains,
> Black snout of a porpoise
>   where Lycabs had been,
> Fish scales on the oarsman.
>   And I worship.
> I have seen what I have seen.
>   When they brought the boy I said:
> 'he has a god in him,
>   though I do not know which god.'[56]

synthetic bone: how is the bright bone grown? How does it spout from the living? Is this a question of the relic produced in advance of death, of the circulation of one's own body for the holiness of others? This is the reverse operation from Eliot's shirt of flame, or alternately, **a child's hairshirt**: the hairshirt being threaded with disappearing fish in the poem *only in romance*. To continue with the problems of purgatorial processes above, recall the devasting "Who then devised the torment? Love. / Love is the unfamiliar Name / Behind the hands that wove / The intolerable shirt of flame / Which human power cannot remove. / We only live, only suspire / by either fire or fire."[57] **watch the video**: a viewing of bright carefulness possible only in a commentarial space of dream and reality mixing in language to wear language out and into the world. This video must be watched because it is a film/dream/poem transcript, having nothing to do with childhood or a screen memory (though I would not exclude all of semiotic analysis—I leave this up to you if you ever make

---

perhaps following Sartre's existential approach" (199). It would seem to me that the desire if both approaches has to do with the intersection of language and historicity with the concept of reality in cinema, but that Godard would insist no human action as audiovisual technique could be naturally taken into the *Significando* so naturally as by dipping in a fishing line, would be necessarily contingent and arbitrary, and interesting only to the extent it was historical. I am attracted to both approaches, and would like to believe they can be demonstrated to be working at the same thing, but fear this is not the case.

[54] Ibid., 198.
[55] Ibid., 206.
[56] Ezra Pound, *Canto II*, in *The Cantos of Ezra Pound* (New York: New Directions, 1996), 9.
[57] Eliot, "Little Gidding," 207.

and see this video!) I dreamed we were kissing: the one reading this and the one writing this, even knowing that "l'agencement de ces textes est un autre" [the agency of these texts is an other].[58] More and more that dream is work. I would have shared a poem about this dream with a colleague in the hopes of provoking the same dream, but we forgot to wear the bright clothing, so there would be no kissing. We forgot to pack the list and the manuals when we flew to the conference in the hopes of getting interrogated. We couldn't even get exiled. It becomes so difficult if everyone's already been touched. ***the greatest / of care***: such care is necessary because of the sensitive nature of any coded information in a missive which aims at a vector of importance in the world. The tradition of poetry written in a code, or, rather, a dialect or an allegorical system full of specialized forms and complexities among a group of elites or a specific intellectual circle, came perhaps to its fullest fruition in the work of the troubadours. Auerbach, whose writings so consistently register as a chronicle of the human in literature, teaches of the troubadours: "Here again we have allegory; but the riddles are not interpreted, and perhaps they do not even contain any intelligible general idea that can be interpreted for all. In a defensive, esoteric form, as though behind high walls, they hold the endangered secret of the soul . . . "[59] Let missives be sent regularly to certain friends who have been co-conspirators in the drafting of riddles to confound not our readers but ourselves, in the hope that both us and the work will open to our readers whatever might shelter that which carries the excitement of the secret in its movement, but without the mistrust proper to the secret itself.

2

This sonnet was answered by many, who offered a variety of interpretations; among those who answered was the one I call my best friend, who responded with a sonnet beginning: Think that you beheld all worth. *This exchange of sonnets marked the beginning of our friendship. The true meaning of the dream I described was not perceived by anyone then, but now it is completely clear even to the least sophisticated.*–Dante Alighieri, *Vita Nuova*, III[60]

§

Someday, one of my dear friends will ask me if writing or reading a poem is anything like friendship. I think I will want to say yes. But I fear that, by then, I will only have wit enough to offer a warning. Occupying, as they so often do, the foothold between dream and reality, like a friend, a poem exerts a gravitational pull on any given set of relations within a World, and allows a new potential beginning to arise in front of where a reader finds herself thrown, altering in turn all the relations within the totality of that World. Is the space of this set of alterations within some 'real' world, or the world of the poem's commentary? How can the commentary wear down the poem while the poem wears down the commentary? I constructed a reader for myself, imagining myself having a dream-vision of my dear friend who will ask me the above question, and wrote the missive that begins *remember your*.

---

[58] Jacques Derrida, *Dissemination*, 9.
[59] Erich Auerbach, *Dante: Poet of the Secular World*, 22-23.
[60] Dante, *Vita Nuova*, 592.

> remember your
> abruptness,
>
> it sings out
> help, anecdote
>
> of belief,
> a sleep-offering.

I am still awaiting a reply to this missive. Perhaps one of my good friends will reply, or perhaps some reader that I have not yet met will reply. This poem is in three couplets. The poem begins with an exhortation to the reader to remember a certain quality of herself, and proceeds to explain what that quality does.

remember your / abruptness: "write carelessly so that nothing that is not green will survive."[61] This is an important practice when considering the future of a poem in a friendship, especially if the poem is a particularly riddling missive. ***anecdote***: one needing help. An anecdote, inherently narrative, might need help for this reason alone, thus the difficulty of writing about friends in poems. Thus the *sleep-offering* (see final note) becomes important as well as the form of the riddle itself, to confound the troubling ways of narrative. And still, this particular anecdote as an anecdote *of belief* renders it perhaps even more troubling (as a question of religion?), and leads us to wonder if the anecdote concerns a belief in the yet uncertain or unarrived (perhaps thus pertaining to the future, to the secret and the very substance of the riddle), and thus perhaps must function as an anecdote in a riddling manner, one which accommodates not the narrative tendency of anecdotes, but rather that spectral capacity of the future's (or the past's) secrets. So, if a missive is to reference an anecdote of belief that might in fact constitute a *sleep-offering* (again, see below), it should heed the reminder to

> Look at
> what passes for the new.
> You will not find it there but in
> despised poems.
> It is difficult
> to get the news from poems
> yet men die miserably every day
> for lack
> of what is found there.[62]

sleep-offering: "I never loved you more / Than when I let you sleep another hour, / As if you intended to make such a gate of time / your home. Speechless as night animals, / The breeze and I breakfasted / With the pure

---

[61] William Carlos Williams, *Patterson*, 129.

[62] William Carlos Williams, "Asphodel, That Greeny Flower, Book I," in *The William Carlos Williams Reader*, Ed. M.L. Rosenthal (New York: New Directions, 1965), 73-74.

desire of speech."[63] Additionally, and as long as this missive insists on speaking in riddles (do we accuse all those who speak in riddles as speaking as the Christ himself?), "Sleep for you is a trick / of the front, a light green room in a French house." So finally, one must offer for sleep a cover, a blanket (here, you will see, of snow), to cover what is hidden just as a riddle too dissimulates—so if sleep is itself a riddle, and an offering of sleep a double riddle, one also needs paradoxically to first produce the riddle for its secret sleep to arise: "Sky of blue water, blue-water sky, / I sleep with the dubious kiss / of my sky-blue portfolio. / Under or over the wind, / In soft and independent clothes, / I begin each dawn-coloured picture / Deep in your snow."

§

I should like to invent a new form which would function like a well-set trap: the mode of Romance, but *miniaturized*. We might take *Romance* as poetry written in *romanz* as opposed to Latin, and coming to be known as poetry of a certain perfection in long poems with opaque characters of unknowable motivations and narratives which turn and break off by some unknowable generative device. And yet, this literary epithet also found a more recent application in the work of American fiction writers, as that which offers a convincing confounding of mimetic reading strategies.[64] How, when I write these poems, I will wish to cathect at least two moments of literary theory and composition not my own! When I succeed at writing a poem theorizing historiographies pertaining to Dante Alighieri and Snorri Sturluson, I will so name poems *miniature romances*. This poem, beginning, *bring your flute*, was written in the hope of provoking such a miniaturized Romance. I should say it owes a debt to Nathaniel Hawthorne's novels, which teach a most difficult and excellent poetics of disarticulating mimetic reading.

> bring your flute, young
> & come to me st.
> edmund your head
> between my
>
> wolf teeth
>
> space in the unclasped
> head gear helps only so
>
> flight attendant
> forgot tribute
>
> safe between my teeth
> speaking but write it down and

---

[63] This and all other quotations in this note on *sleep-offering* from Medbh McGuckian, "Minus 18 Street," in *On Ballycastle Beech*, 19.

[64] See Jonathan Arac, "Reading the Letter" (Review), *Diacritics* 9:2 (1979): 42-52. "Hawthorne's special virtue for criticism is that he frustrates mimetic reading" (42).

ISSN 1942-3381   Daniel C. Remein

>   write it down and don't
>
>   is this a translation
>   or a warning?

This poem is longer than some of the others in this new work.

bring your flute: the flute here is the flute of a sylvan creature designed to intoxicate or call away with the strains of a music that, being metrical and poetic, exemplifies a certain deadly art of technique and unnaturalness. In Hawthorne's *The Marble Faun*, the Tuscan Donatello who goes amongst a group of English-speaking expatriates, "is not supernatural, but just on the verge of nature, and yet within it. What is the nameless charm of this idea . . . ?"[65] Such is the nature of the call as a call, calling into nearness, drawing or alluring near with a music that, being so unnatural, convinces us deceitfully that there is such a thing as *physis* and draws us towards what we think is a source but will prove nothing other than a gap and an always already unnatural technique (the space of the flute through which the wind blows is not the flute's presence of course but its absence, just as the meter of the poem is determined by spacing that marks the limit of breath and non-presence).[66] Further then, the call to *bring your flute* is actually a call to begin calling, to begin the technique of bringing near, always necessarily by some economy of allure (which is or must be a sort of deceit, or no?)—a call to begin the work of Romances. And, this holds true equally, I should think, for Romance as medieval genre (discussed briefly above), romance as Hawthorne deploys it in an act of (knowing or unknowing) medievalism, and even poems today which might thwart mimetic reading because they, rather than represent to the reader, seek to directly effect the reader and reality as such. Thus, I do not think that Hawthorne's narrator is correct in claiming, in the preface to *The Marble Faun* (which defends Italy as a setting for 'his' book in the third person), that: "Italy, as the site of his Romance, was chiefly valuable to him as affording a sort of poetic or fairy precinct, where actualities would not be so terribly insisted upon, as they are, and must needs be, in America. No author, without a trial, can conceive of the difficulty of writing a Romance about a country where there is no shadow, no antiquity, no mystery . . . It will be very long, I trust, before romance-writers may find congenial and easily handled themes either in the annals of our stalwart Republic, or in any characteristic and probable events of our individual lives. Romance and poetry, like ivy, lichens, and wall-

---

[65] Nathaniel Hawthone, *The Marble Faun or the Romance of Monte Beni*, The Centenary Edition of the Works of Nathaniel Hawthorne Vol. IV (Columbus: Ohio State University Press, 1971), 13.

[66] Derrida, *Of Grammatology*, "*Spacing* (notice that this word speaks the articulation of space and time, the becoming-space of time and the becoming-time of space) is always the unpercieved, the nonpresent, and the nonconscious . . . Arche-writing as spacing cannot occur *as such* within the phenomenological experience of a *presence*. It marks the *dead time* within the presence of the living present, within the general form of all presence. The dead time is at work" (68); "What writing itself, in its nonphonetic moment, betrays, is life. It menaces at once the breath, the spirit, and history as the spirit's relationship with itself. It is their end, their finitude, their paralysis. Cutting breath short, sterilizing or immobilizing spiritual creation in the repetition of the letter, in the commentary or the *exegesis*, confined in a narrow space, reserved for a minority, it is the principle of death and of difference in the becoming of being" (25).

flowers, need Ruin to make them grow."[67] At the risk of an imbalance I would then keep on with this note, because it would seem that rather that Romance *requiring* ruin, it is rather perhaps an alluring *practice of ruin*. Hawthorne's comment, after all, can only be tongue in cheek on the heels of his success of having applied the epithet of *Romance* to both *The Scarlet Letter* and *The House of the Seven Gables* as particularly *American* stories which relied perhaps more on the poetics of the text to *produce* New England as *always already* an alluring if dangerous ruin than having found it so in the first place (Hawthorne is thus subtly congratulating himself for doing the impossible, knowing full well that he has been asking us to bring our flutes all along). Romance here thus sings a contagious practice of ruin-izing reality, of rendering reality quite *improbable* rather than assuming with realism that novels should first assume reality as probable and set out to the task of reliably representing it. See the discussion above of the dimming of the foothold between dream and reality. The call to bring your flute is then equally an attempt to realize the theoretically and politically anarchic latencies within that strain of 18th-century writing traditionally forsaken by the left for the representation of social relations in Balzac et al., as well as an attempt to produce a non-escapist poetics of Romance as temporally durable genre–while at the same time, connecting a modern poetics more intimately with the Middle Ages. More on this in relation to *Sir Gawain and the Green Knight* below. ***st. edmund***: St. Edmund was killed by Vikings on 20 November, 869. According to hagiography on the subject, after the killing, his body proceeded to produce miracles and signs of sanctity, before and after burial. I number among the most striking yet still conventional elements of the hagiography that a wolf protects Edmund's severed dead head from all the other beasts while the head calls out to be found. My own source is the Old English version, from Aelfric, who identifies his source as a Latin text, by Abbo of Fleury. Thus, from English through Latin and back to English, and now in Modern English, an English King's dead head, from whatever impossibility moves it to speech, calls, just like a romance, to *bring your flute* and attend on it, calling "Here, here, here." The severed head (see also below on *the unclasped/ head*) thus also forms the figure not of the miracle in a hagiography, but of a more multi-temporal poetics of Romance, calling us to attend to the making dim of, or the ruin-izing of, or the dimming of (the difference between dream and) reality–but only because cradled by the jaws and paws of the reader, alone or in a pack, as with the reference to ***wolf teeth***: *A wolf attacks, a wolf travels in packs*. Yet this is the lone single wolf of the reader who now must tend to the romance tucked within this historiography.[68] The wolf teeth that hold the head of St. Edmund can thus only be you, dear reader, since the original wolf is long gone. You must be, in reading this poem, a friend to the head of the dead saint, a friend to the technique of allure which calls you to bring your flute and join the festal collective cited above in part 1. ***space in the unclasped / head***: this could of course refer to the unclasped head of St. Edmund, and the strange space inside which animated the mouth and voice without a body, proving that the head still functions just as it did before the beheading, except now as recognized as a head and not just an appendage. Now is it not the saint who speaks, but the saint's head. Yet the unclasping of a head, and its miraculous continuation of speech should not be considered a trope of hagiography so much as of

---

[67] Hawthorne, *The Marble Faun*, 3.

[68] For this thinking about the link between Old English Haigiography and later vernacular Romance in England, I owe a debt to recent thought and speculation in the line of literary history by Haruko Momma, who reads the conventions of Old English hagiography as not so much as an old style 'source' as the trope of English romance itself–as its genealogical prehistory–with its own thinking of wondrous deeds, sexual conducts, and relations to an Other World (here, of course, heaven). Momma's work relies on a revision of Bakhtin's thought on romance. From private correspondence and unpublished work.

Romance (and here I reference the above note on Hawthorne, and would gesture towards linking the medievalism of Hawthorne's genre anachronistically as part of if not prior to the medieval genre itself, finding romance a category available through a deeper sense of literary-historical time–not in a particular narrative convention but a poetic-philosophical effect on reality itself). Because my notes here speak so much of Romance, whether or not it is in the poem at all, the commentary produces this point of the poem as possibly also alluding to (at least in the similarity of images if not explicitly) the head of Bertilak as the Green Knight in the medieval romance *Sir Gawain and the Green Knight*, written in alliterative Middle English verse. Compared to the Old English King Edmund and its language, the poem is of a much later Middle Ages, and thus depends on producing England as the ruin of an Old Arthurian splendor just as Hawthorne would produce certain of his settings as ruins as a condition of operation of the genre. Thus, in the splendid but decadent Arthurian court, Gawain, for the King, cuts off the head of an intruder at New Years who is entirely green, the head of which subsequently demands that Gawain find him at the same time the next year to receive his own blow in return before being picked up by the body which rides off: "For the hede in his honde he haldez up even, / Toward the derrest on the dece he dressez the face, / And his lyfte up the yye-lyddez and loked ful brode, / And meled thus much with his muthe, as ye may now here: / 'Loke, Gawan, thou be graythe to go as thou hettez, / And layete as lelly til thou me, lude, fynde.'"[69] Thus, the poet uses, like Hawthorne, a certain anachronism (of England's ruined Arthurian–though here Christian–past) to cite a speaking beheaded head held up not as an escape from a present into a fairy land, but to produce England now as a fairy land (since the alliterative meter of the poem produces a certain allure to the language, making it an object of desire for the present itself not as escapism but as transformative in its poetic pull, a linguistically ornamented jewel) and to produce reality as the space in the unclasped head of the Green Knight, to steal it back, call it back, from the clutches of reality as the metaphysical ordering of the proper (everything in its place where nothing mixes or is fluid, the closed circle)[70] where the world is outside the head and the head must rest on the body to seal off what is clasped inside of it. Reality inside the space of the unclasped head calls us to go find it: this is the work of commentary on Romance and Romance as a commentary. ***write it down and / write it down and don't***: each imperative verb is a sprouting antler of the poem's desire to rend reality as improbable, to render dim what keeps the proper in its place. Thus there are here multiple kinds of writing which are all equally literary

---

[69] *Sir Gawain and the Green Knight*, Ed. J.R.R. Tolkien and E.V. Gordon, 2nd Ed. Edited by Norman Davis (Oxford: Clarendon, 1979), lines 444-449. I have altered the orthography of the Tolkien-Gordon-Davis edition to modern conventions for the sake of a hopefully diverse readership.

[70] On this subject, see Luce Irigaray's *The Forgetting of Air in Martin Heidegger* trans. Mary Beth Mader (Austin: University of Texas Press, 1997). Irigaray sees the production of space and the circle as requiring the assimilation of the female one (in which there is air, fluid movement and mixing, no distinctions of the *proper* which belong to the metaphysics of the male one) as a way of producing the limits and boundaries of thought and language, to ensure that man can think *as* the returning of everything to the same. The assimilation of the female one produces the space between things to make them distinct and proper to themselves and their places. Irigary of course sees this process as undesirable. I should note the affinity between Irigray's distaste for the proper and return to the Same with Kierkegaard's preference of the radical risk of repetition to 'recollection' as returning to the Same, and its more contemporary treatment by John D. Caputo in *Radical Hermeneutics: Repetition, Deconstruction, and the Hermeneutic Project* (Bloomington: Indiana University Press, 1987). This entire work owes a debt to Irigaray's book as a pervasive undercurrent, but in such a way as to evade direct citation.

ISSN 1942-3381   Daniel C. Remein

writing. The impulse here is the same as that of Jonathan Arac, writing in search of a new literary history in the late nineteen-eighties with the notion that for this search to succeed, both history-writing and criticism must admit the extent to which they function as literary writing (thus, 'theory' forms a genre with its own conventions just like 'poetry' or 'short fiction'), for Derrida or Matthew Arnold have been read and can be read as literature (as in, like Hawthorne), only "literary writing that begins from previous literary writing."[71] This can be seen to put criticism in a supplementary relation to literature, or we can take such a possibility as a way of understanding the shared ground of literary and critical writing. Such is the romance of commentary.

§

Occasionally poems by me or one of my colleagues appear like a single sorrowing animal; exposed, a little confident, but left alone and never found, layered under so many other vibrations and seductions, hidden in their format of weblog or little online literary journal. Such labor has its own economies of fame, which do not necessarily threaten gifts of friendship, but strangely, unlike the difficult and always hegemonic exchanges of other economic systems, allows its own investment patterns to be deconstructed to make way for such a gift. I am still trying to invent the secrets of this text so that they might be taken as a gift to the kiss of a reader's understanding. There is nothing to guess, there are only more guesses to make. The poems that begin *your news-ticker*, and *your haircut is like*, both missives, are, neither of them, enigmas.

> your news-ticker
> finger, unravels
>
> points out
> the antlers,
>
> odor of sanctity,
>
> don't wash his clothes,
>
> key in the final codes
> for inscription.

For fear that antlers will spring up in books let this not be part of a book—a form already sufficiently sharp and multi-pronged.

your news-ticker / finger, unravels: This is the death of barriers in air, "Or as if a writ sputtered white noise in a blackout and slammed wiring / into a sink to sink a sink in a blackout bitter white: the text that was one the

---

[71] Jonathan Arac, *Critical Genealogies: Historical Situations for Postmodern Literary Studies* (New York: Columbia University Press, 1987), 7.

writ / might have been vapor."⁷² ***antlers***: here the antlers, sprouting forth from the poems, are pointed out by the agency which is of the poems themselves—the one of the unraveling deictic manicule above. Thus, the new work of the poems must also consist of their commentary, cannot indeed begin until their commentary begins to work—to point back to them or ahead to them while expending itself and its secrets at the same time of its exhaustion of the poems, and exposure of itself as the secret of the poem's ***odor of sanctity***: not the scent of the saint at death but the radiant jewel of the poem which, shinning, proclaims the joyous disarticulation of the two in the same moment that its shine disarticulates the possibility of marking off what is proper to the gleaming of the jewel and the polishing of its commentary. The nimbus of the poem's burning mixes with any in proximity, also concerning the proper as such. That it is the fragrance of a poem as a jewel is demonstrated in the following account by the poet H. D.: "'What is the jewel colour?' / greenwhite, opalescent, / with under-lyer of changing blue, / with rose-vein; a white agate / with a pule uncooled that beats yet, / faint blue-violet; / it lives, it breathes, / it gives off—fragrance? / I do not know what it gives, / a vibration that we can not name / for there is no name for it; my patron said, 'name it'; / I said, I can not name it, / there is no name; / he said, / 'invent it.'"⁷³ We must ask, is the patron here a friend? and will s/he be able to un-code the name, and who will make it known to anyone else? ***the final codes / for inscription***: that is, the etching of the name, or at least a single verse, by the poet, into some rock or plaque so as to commemorate, paradoxically, the moment of the unraveling of a barrier. There must be some means by which to convey the missive to a friend and await the friend's response. Must I receive this response for it to 'count,' and how could such responses be accounted for? How could the code of such an inscription ever be *final*? And, would it not have to unravel itself along with the deictic finger that opened the poem? Antlers, which are poems, sprout. Fingers, which are codes, unravel. This is why atomic weapons have codes, and one pushes 'the button' with a finger. Antlers sprout up in romance of the commentary radiating, not in the code of a so-called poem inscribing itself as the frozen hagiography. A hagiography must point at the correct thing, must endlessly refine itself as holy and assure the holiness of that to which it points, must never wash the clothes. In criticizing a particular strand of poststructuralist critique that ran into a dead-end, Jonathan Arac (who otherwise prizes this tradition) points out how certain of the Yale school became "less modest, no longer so historical, but even more rigorous" as a way of legitimizing their work, fearing any concession against rigour that would be perceived as a romantic flight of 'unmanly' weakness. But Arac rightly points out as well that the very term *rigor* (by which, here, the pointing finger in the romance of a commentary must unravel itself as it shares in the poem's radiance (to which it is of course always already a part of, as a Derridean supplement) must not fear pointing to the wrong thing, must not be so concerned with being correct or incorrect and fall into the fears of the hagiography) "in Latin means 'numbness, stiffness,' and its OED senses include 'harshness', 'hardness of heart', 'puritanic severity', as well as 'propriety' and 'severe exactitude'."⁷⁴ For Arac this is simply too bad, since criticism has an inherent capacity to be much more expansive than a literally dead exercise in being correct about the text as an exercise. Rather, according to the romantic poet Shelley, "For poetry itself proves secondary and thus crosses over to the side of life: it is an 'expression of the imagination' [qtd. from Shelley]. The defense of poetry,

---

[72] Marjorie Welish, "Clans, Moieties, and Other," *Word Group: Poems* (Minneapolis: Coffee House Press, 2004), 63.

[73] H. D., *Tribute to the Angels* no. 13, in *H.D.: Collected Poems, 1912-1944* (New York: New Directions, 1986), 554-555.

[74] Jonathan Arac, *Critical Genealogies*, 104.

therefore, necessitates praise of the secondary."[75] So Arac would recognize the need to retain the fragments of the Arnoldian impulse which would maintain an expansive sense of criticism against the kind of criticism which Arac [With Said and Gerald Graff] saw in 1987 as having "lost its social bearing in pursuit of endless refinement."[76] One would have to oppose criticism–expansive in its commentary on poetry, unafraid to unravel into the world–to the endless refinement of "scholarship."[77] The comment must not worry too much about getting its final codes right if it is going to participate in the poem, if it is going to always already be the radiance that is the romance of the poem–the sprouting antler sprouting more in the shape of an infinity of codes. To merely point at the right thing at the right time is to hold it dumbly holy and render the text as hagiography and not as romance. Here, with this gem fertile for antler-growth, the inscription is the poem and the radiant jewel in which it is inscribed was its commentary from the start.

> your haircut is like
> a story i hear election night
>
> before beatrice's ¼ revolution.
> musn't have any
> at all if to win.
> & for belief
>
> only if without
> to know

It can be important for poems like these, attempting to confound the mechanism of narrative, to also confound the mechanism of knowing. To this end, in addition to the hint in the last stanza, *only if without / to know*, this poem also *seems* to break down syntactically, but only after a rather clear simile, and reference to a way of referring artfully to the passing of time used often by Dante in accordance with his cosmology.

your haircut is like / a story: alternately, "her Hitler hairdo / is making me feel ill."[78] Such is the simile of a fashion element to a narrative, a static bit of humanly sculpted material to all the inhumanity of the narrative, the inevitable arc and its politics. It will break in clumps and gaps and only a particular sort of randomness of the commentator intoxicated by his own radiance can break up the clumps, burst the arc, ruffle the hair or the feathers and strip off that moustache. The trouble is the status of the simile as part of the missive. To whom? If to the reader as a friend, such an indictment might not seem so friendly. ***musn't have any / at all if to win***: *any* here operated as a substantive, the dangerous pluridirectional space-time of a nothing as a positively defined *thing*. This is the logic of the romance or the poem set against that of the narrative, and indeed the logic of the friendship and the space of the friendship that would open in a commentary. Not in a plenitude of the words themselves, but in the more than ample opportunities for gaps between the comment and the poem. This is, of

---

[75] Ibid., 103.
[76] Ibid., 122.
[77] Ibid., 82.
[78] Radiohead, "Karma Police," on *OK Computer* (Capitol Records, 1997).

course, that same spot of the foothold between dream and reality, poem and commentary, friend and friend, the space the poem and the commentary must wear out by wearing out their own secrets, expending until only their *any* is left. **to win**: the English word comes from its earlier English and Germanic source of *win* for *struggle* and the verbal form of *winnan* (infinitive) for *to struggle, to fight*.[79] Winning in its modern sense only emerges as the end result or culmination of a struggle, and thus was indicated verbally by the common (intensifier) prefix *ge-* in *ge-winnan*. Thus the struggle inherent to having an *any* is revealed simply by the possibility of its leading to a situation in which one might *win*. Of what would this struggle consist? Since the poem's reference to time is that of the orbit of the spheres as blessed souls, as Dante's *Commedia* would have it—and specifically a reference to *before* a particular span of time so-measured elapses—perhaps it is the struggle of turning within the bounds of time at all, and actually, the very ease of this. The struggle is in the ease and repose of circling around according to one's proper place, in accordance with how much one is moved by the holy gravitons of the cosmos. The struggle is then the limit of time set on its missive itself: how long the missive has to reach its receiver, as well as the limited currency of its secret idiom. **only**: as in, the diction of street-signs; trucks only, caravans only, convoys only. No envoys. The missive, from Latin *mitteo, mitere* (to send), is sent, but from whom and to whom, and along what lines? A single sorrowing animal sniffs out its track, leaves little or no trace, and follows—not the secret scent like insects—but the open paths of ease, even in the hastiest of moments. Belief demanded without the inflected infinitive *to know* is an anti-gnostic demand for any poem, a desire that a missive or a riddle have nothing to do with knowledge and yet maintain themselves as missives and riddles.

§

I hope, eventually, to avoid entirely the construction of a narrative around, before, or behind my poems. The commentary will grow up, an apparatus around them, well before the poems themselves are written, spreading like a system always equidistant from every point in the writing, but shaped nothing like a sphere or a circle [much like the expansion of the cosmos/universe]; accompanied by and producing theories connecting writing to everything. Tomorrow I *will have written* the poem beginning *a secret most marvelous*, a riddle.

> a secret most marvelous:
> candidate reports
>
> teeth and claws
> most humane mode
>
> of being drawn towards
> un-rest. & as for
>
> counting the faces

---

[79] See Bosworth and Toller, *A Dictionary of Old English*, s.vv. *winnan* and *gewinnan*. In Old English, in its most pedestrian senses, the word only means to labor, toil, work, or fight (it is used as a verb for combat) (Bosworth-Toller *A Dictionary of Old English*, s.v. *winnan*); in Old High German the word meant 'to suffer, to struggle', see Joseph Wright, *Grammar of the Gothic Language* (1910), s.v. *winnan*.

of the screened . . .

The poem is in four stanzas, with a good deal of enjambment. There are two sentences, the second of which does not complete its course before an ellipsis. The first sentence is an announcement of a most marvelous secret, and the second consists of a digression.

secret: "What is the interpreter to make of secrecy considered as a property of all narrative, provided it is suitably attended to?"[80] What are we to make of secrecy or the secret as something which *is* not but rather is generated. What indeed if secrecy appears not in narrative, but in a radiance which resists narrativization? Or, rather, is there any hope for such resistance? For, "there has to be trickery."[81] Frank Kermode may speak of the "radiant obscurity of narratives,"[82] but is there not some hope not only in the seeking of the "divined glimmer" that one *perceives* as 'behind' the fabric of the text, but rather in the manufacturing of a secret which radiates as it undoes itself as a secret? Then, even if "Hot for secrets, our only conversation may be with guardians who know less and see less than we can, and our sole hope and pleasure is in the perception of a momentary radiance, before the door of disappointment is finally shut on us,"[83] and even if that the momentary radiance is a fiction anyway–none of this threatens the optimism of the riddle. ***most marvelous***: the marvelous here radiates as the expenditure of its secret, not as the intentional concealment thereof so as to effect a flight from the world. The marvel of the riddle is to pull one into the text in such a way that the text wears a hole in itself and one winds up back in the world *because* of following a marvelous radiance. And the marvel? There was nothing there to begin with. ***teeth and claws/ most humane mode***: perhaps an addendum to Frye's *modes* as an (Aristotelian) category of literature. The teeth and claws of the riddle that bites back, of the claws scuttling at the bottom of silent seas which occasionally beat out a rhythm that churns into a maelstrom without intending any such thing. These are the teeth and claws of the 'creatures' of high modernism with a certain "image-breaking enterprise,"[84] associated with a lineage of certain of Eliot's poems, Samuel Beckett, Dostoevsky, Kafka, the late Pound and the late H. D., and even certain of the L=A=N=G=U=A=G=E poets and others usually seen as so serious and abysmal, as provoking primordial anxieties. But, equally, these teeth and claws are for pleasure and delight. And such a modernist poetics, in tune with the radiantly medieval texture of the work by the poet and theorist Dante (whose quotations provide epigraphs for this new work), also, and first, could be re-understood as turning to expose the human to a more intense and radiant pleasure: scratching nether-regions and biting exquisitely–clawing away at the image not just to pull back and expose an abyss, but also to kindle the ruin of the image into a burning radiance. ***drawn towards / un-rest***: "Our time calls for an existence-Art, one which, by refusing to resolve discords into the satisfying concordances of a *telos*, constitutes an assault against an *art*-ificialized Nature in behalf of the recovery of its primordial terrors. The most immediate task, therefore, in which the contemporary writer must engage himself–it is, to borrow a

---

[80] Frank Kermode, *The Genesis of Secrecy: On the Interpretation of Narrative* (Cambridge: Harvard University Press, 1979), 144.

[81] Ibid., 145.

[82] Ibid., 47.

[83] Ibid., 144.

[84] William V. Spanos, "The Detective and the Boundary," in *Early Postmodernism: Foundational Essays*, ed. Paul A. Bové (Durham: Duke University Press, 1995), 39.

phrase ungratefully from Yeats, the most difficult task not impossible—is that of undermining the detective-like expectation of the positivistic mind, of unhoming Western man, by evoking rather than purging pity and terror—anxiety . . . to drive him out of the fictitious well-made world, not to be gathered into the 'artifice of eternity,' but to be exposed to the existential real of history, where Nothing is certain."[85] Such is the riddle for which the only solution is its own burning-up. The addition of *pleasure* and radiance to this formulation of William Spanos is perhaps necessary after the years in the interim between when this work appeared as a beginning of the moment which would assess and praise a disruptive modernism following the rationale that "The Western structure of consciousness is bent, however inadvertently, on unleashing chaos in the name of the order of a well-made world"[86] (suggesting that the cost of a resolving well made anything is simply too high). Because, crudely put, a well-made thing and things done in the name of the well-made, the resolved, the solvable, comfort the western positivistic mind, Spanos calls for the anxiety-evoking.[87] The riddle is, the wonder would be, to take pleasure in and make pleasurable the production and experience of an art that un-homes the human with ease—that infinitely frustrates the detective without losing a certain radiance. The trouble with being entirely 'post'-abysmal is that the "*Urgrund*, the primordial not-at-home" is "where dread, as Kierkegaard and Heidegger and Sartre and Tillich tell us, becomes not just the agency of despair but also and simultaneously of hope, that is, of freedom and infinite possibility."[88] And the problem of being purely negative and abysmal: the pleasure of falling, the ability of some to experience the riddle whose answer is at once everything and yet does not exist as a radiance all its own. **the faces of the screened**: me, us, you, we, them, she, he, us, you, me, we. Totally unaccountable, various answers to the riddle. Various subjects on which any *candidate* as solution to the riddle *reports*.

---

[85] Ibid.

[86] Ibid., 38.

[87] For Spanos, in the moment of his work on this essay, the modern mind produces certain expectations and "these expectations demand the kind of fiction and drama that achieves its absolute fulfillment in the utterly formularized clockwork certainties of plot in the innumerable detective drama series—*Perry Mason, The FBI, Hawaii 5-0, Mannix, Mission Impossible,* etc.—which use up, or rather, 'kill,' prime television time [that these shows are dated at the drafting of this essay is not a problem—the situation has changed little beyond expanding the 'stakes' and the terms of the detective show from Cold War conflicts to that of 'global terror' in shows like *24, The Fringe, CSI, and The Wire*, while perhaps adding a new element of biopolitics in shows where the solution is medical but no less detective-style detectable in *House* or *Bones*—the point is that there is a resurgence of shows where there are resolved detectable answers, rendered unsecret by positivistic science and technology, for the sake of a well-made capitalist state]. Ultimately they also demand the kind of social and political organization that finds its fulfillment in the imposed certainties of the well-made world of the totalitarian state, where investigation or inquisition on behalf of the achievement of a total, that is, preordained or teleologically determined structure—'a final solution'—is the defining activity. It is therefore no accident that the paradigmatic archetype of the postmodern literary imagination is the anti-detective story . . . the formal purpose of which is to evoke the impulse to 'detect' and/or psychoanalyze in order to violently frustrate it by refusing the solve the crime . . . I am referring, for example, to works like Kafka's *The Trial*, T.S. Eliot's *Sweeney Agonistes* . . . Beckett's *Watt* and *Molloy* . . . Robbe-Grillet's *The Erasers* . . . " (25).

[88] Ibid., 27.

§

Paths to the radiant abyss: Tomaž Šalamun almost ends one of his poems with the simple line "My hands shine."[89] Another such jewel arises from a poem which, being very brief, is easily quoted in full: "A book of photographs: / A tale of the perfect lover. / Learn from the eye of others. / God is my reader."[90] Thus the poet makes friends with readers of his poems. I would offer this next poem, beginning *but if i offer you*, a missive, in the spirit of such work which would allow a re-thinking of the ground of connection and time:

> but if i offer you
> any
> make for the little seam
>
> & it's true,
> if only because
> a flag of your blood
> on your palm
>
> says,
> i heed you
>
> famously, beatrice,
>
> with a feather, on
> the hunt.

any: *any* is a queer creature of two-syllables and the substantizing again of *any* is commensurate with a certain evasion of description proper to the transfer of energy that the missive must entail, and the particular efficiency of this two-syllable word, bright as a small flag of blood itself and pluridrectional in its potential travel down the lip of the poet. As something *offerable*, the energy of two tiny syllables is potentially immense, for "It would do no harm, as an act of correction to both prose and verse as now written, if both rime and mater, and, in the quantity of words, both sense and sound, were less in the forefront of the mind than the syllable, if the syllable, that fine creature, were more allowed to lead the harmony on. With this warning, to those who would try: to step back here to this place of the elements of and minims of language, is to engage speech where it is least careless—and least logical."[91] For Charles Olson, the syllable is the product of the incest of the brother mind and sister ear.[92] *any, any, any;* brother or sister; breath listening *any* as offered; the thing itself issues from **the**

---

[89] Tomaž Šalamun, "a ballad for metka krašovec," in *A Ballad for Metka Krašovec*, trans. Michael Biggins (Prague: Twisted Spoon Press, 2001), 65.

[90] Ibid., 66.

[91] Charles Olson, "Projective Verse," in *Postmodern American Poetry: a Norton Anthology*, ed. Paul Hoover (New York: Norton, 1994), 615.

[92] Ibid.

little seam: as the very tiniest beginnings of the abyss—the seam or split in the fabric—perhaps here even still stitched together so close, so there it is. The little seam a little leverage here for the horns growing in the breast of the human, ready to take on the cosmos as unmixing with h/er/is *proper* person, as confined into the correct syntactic slot and the slip where those creatures—yes, even creatures consigned to hell in Dante's *Commedia*—appear and verify urgency of the missive: "How uncertain when I said unwind the winding, Chiron, / Cross of Two Orders! Grammarian! from your side the never / healing! / Undo the bindings of immutable syntax! / The eyes that are horns of the moon feast on the leaves of trampled sentences."[93] *& **it's true***: "The process of definition is the intent of the poem" and yet "A poetry denies its end in any *descriptive* act."[94] As a result, "One breaks the line of aesthetics, or that outcrop of a general division of knowledge. A sense of the KINETIC impels recognition of force. Force is, and therefore stays."[95] So the poem appears a place, or place appears as a *practice* of poetics, a tekné ("to build out of sound/ the wall of a city")[96] and marks itself in its force with ***a flag of your blood***: "It's that when I see you / I bleed a little, / into the teacup and into the wren's nest."[97] This is what you might say when the energy of the syllable bursts up through the tiniest seam, when a tiny bit of a medieval poem bursts into your own present through the cracks in the surface of the syntax. It is thus as this flag-blood that famously, Beatrice can speak as her own missive or signal within the poem such that the speaker might heed her famously. ***beatrice***: as for Dante, a warning as if a storm warning indicator flag, poking up through the seam through the centuries. A little flag of a syllable beats out its queer warning. Olson teaches:

> I say the syllable, king, and that it is spontaneous, this way: the ear, the ear which has collected, which has listened, the ear, which is so close to the mind that it is the mind's, that it has the mind's speed . . .
> it is close, another way: the mind is brother to this sister and it, because it is so close, is the drying force, the incest, the sharpener . . .
> it is from the union of the mind and the ear that the syllable is born.[98]

Thus, *be-a-tri-ce,* four syllables, compacted by the mind and pushed out from the heart into the breath of the projecting line, at just the right moment, from the past, makes for the queer warning to any Dante of the 21st century, flagging down the ear with the single syllable *blood,* and then the single syllable *heed.* The mind, getting medieval, becoming syllabic, hearing its own incest with the past to crack the surface of a syntax and allow the *effects* of the line to arise, wherein "the descriptive functions generally have to be watched, every second . . . because of their easiness, and thus their drain on the energy which composition by field allows into the poem. *Any* [and there is that word again] slackness takes off attention, that crucial thing, from the job in hand, from

---

[93] Robert Duncan, "The Structure of Rime VIII," in *The Opening of the Field* (New York: New Directions, 1960), 70.
[94] Robert Creeley, "To Define," in *A Quick Graph,* ed. Donald Allen (San Francisco: Four Seasons, 1970), 23.
[95] Ibid.
[96] Charles Olson, *Maximus Poems,* qtd. in *Causal Mythology* [Transcript of a Lecture] (San Francisco: Four Seasons, 1969), 3
[97] Thomas Kane, "Suppose What Is Left Behind," *McSweeney's* 22, Book 3 *The Poetry chains of Cominic Luxford,* 48.
[98] Olson, "Projective Verse," 615.

the *push* of the line under hand at the moment."[99] **On / the hunt**: beatrice is on the hunt after the boar, like Bertilak in *Sir Gawain and the Green Knight*. Beatrice here is unlike Bertilak's lady, who hunts the knight Gawain. The push of Beatrice's line follows with the energy of Bertilak's dog's, pushing up enough air for breath that in her wake (for, consider the syllables at play in such a line as this: "The howndez that it herde hastid thider swythe" [the hounds that heard it hurried there forcefully])[100] that here, now, we might, we, alternately, in the space of the commentary on her bright and forceful flag, "much speche" here "expoun/ of druyes greme and grace."[101]

§

The moment of transition from one temporality to the next in poems, whether between the medieval and the modern, or one moment to the next. How does a poem move between two moments, two syllables? On what grounds? Such a dilemma can be likened to a certain dilemma common to the thought of the so-called Pre-Socratic philosophers. To simplify the problem a little bit too much: *is everything the same or is everything different?* Similarly, *is change possible? How can we tell where things, be they 'objects' or 'phenomena,' begin or end?* An epigram is attributed to Heraclitus consists of simply "changing, it rests,"[102] while Parmenides claimed that "For if it came into being, it is not, nor if it is ever going to be."[103] The Pluralists, such as Anaxagoras and Empedocles on the other hand, took a different tact, suggesting that "The Greeks are wrong to accept coming to be and perishing, for no thing comes to be, nor does it perish, but they are mixed together from things that are and they are separated apart."[104] These dilemmas illustrate a problem taken up again by Martin Heidegger in *Being and Time*, who suggests giving into the circular structure of interpretation, following the claim that "Interpretation is not the acknowledgement of what has been understood, but rather the development of possibilities projected in understanding."[105] For interpretation of a thing to happen there must already be an understanding projected onto that thing. For Heidegger, "In interpretation understanding does not become something different, but rather itself."[106] All of this can be understood in part as a problem of the sameness and difference of All, or, alternately, a problem of starting and stopping. For two modernists, from differing temporal ends of a radical literary modernism (Gertrude Stein and Samuel Beckett) the beginning and ending of moments of consciousness presented itself as a question. Both writers write the texture of what such questions feel like. Stein puts these sentences near the end of her *Three Lives,* about a main character's fatal pregnancy: "When the baby was come out at last, it was like its mother lifeless. While it was coming, Lena had grown very pale and sicker. When it was all over Lena had died, too, and nobody knew just how it had happened to her."[107] Such is

---

[99] Ibid., 616.

[100] *Sir Gawain and the Green Knight,* line 1424.

[101] Ibid., lines 1506-1507.

[102] *A Presocratics Reader*, 37.

[103] Ibid., 47.

[104] Ibid., 58.

[105] Heidegger, *Being and Time*, trans. Joan Stambaugh (Albany: State University of New York Press, 1996), 139.

[106] Ibid.

[107] Gertrude Stein, *Three Lives* (New York: Vintage, 1936), 279.

ISSN 1942-3381   Daniel C. Remein

the riddle of how to move from one moment to the next, from one syllable to the next, held within the field of a poem that is open and would remain so even when crowded by commentary, as if it could open further by being surrounded, extend what syllables it holds in its sway far beyond where it begins and ends as a 'poem' because of its tiny economy and the strength of each syllable—a poem which would admit its commentary even unto its own The riddle which begins *few friends left,* in its sorrowful thinking of the problem of where moments in space-time start and stop, would want exactly this.

> few friends left
> to stray past
>
> the silt beds.
> but the shield
>
> was justified
> if only to allegorize
>
> and shelter out
> peaceful inclinations.

few friends left: as Robert Duncan introduced his friend Charles Olson as a Lecture of Olson's: "There were—now that Williams is dead, and H. D. dead, there *are* five poets left that I study. I know I must study them because at every turn I am back at those texts in order to get at the information I need, to find something that is not a matter of literature but of my own inner reality of life. These five were very clearly, three I feel superiors, for I find in their mastery of the craft and their depth of thought and feeling challenge beyond my own craft and depths: Ezra Pound, Louis Zukofky, Charles Olson; and then two I feel are peers and companions, for in their craft and their depth they have increased my share: Robert Creeley and Denise Levertov."[108] And how to move a poem between them? "As Aristotle is the exemplary structuralist, the great critic of the moment is Longinus on the sublime. Against structural unity, we have noted that the sublime is a 'flash of lightening' that 'scatters all before it.' Longinus' discontinuous theory of influence—as the agonistic relation between two literary consciousnesses across a wide span of time, like that of Plato to Homer—offers the nearest precedent to Harold Bloom's 'revisionary' theory of poetry."[109] The sublimity of a feathery poem. The possibility that all with a single feather have many, of discontinuous strips velcro-ing to each other and that in a moment of feathery bliss, one can leap from one to another, held within the same field of sublimity. So, friends can also be taken as syllables. ***silt***: fertile death, held in the sway of a river, a discontinuous sludge made up, upon close inspection, of discontinuous moments of matter. Each particle falls in its bed and ready to sprout new poems, filtering in to fill up the gaps between the tiny poems and the shoreline of commentary. Silt is small but still it punctuates! Careful near the river, it is easy to cut your feet! But get the adjectives out of it anyway! ***the shield / was justified***: "Encounter *is* separation. Such a proposition, which contradicts 'logic,' breaks the unity of being—which resides in the fragile link of the 'is'—by welcoming the other and difference into the

---

[108] Robert Duncan, qtd. in Charles Olson, *Causal Mythology*, 1.
[109] Jonathan Arac, *Critical Genealogies*, 172.

source of meaning."[110] The justification of a shield as the principle of separation is a principle of shelter as much as a principle of filtration, and thus, in a reverse sense, purgation. The same problems as above in terms of how to effect a connection between two moments of poësis, or between two beings in time. If encounter separates, can the inverse operate as well–separation fostering encounters?–in which case, the question of the impossibility of removing the syllable from the hold of the line once it has been uttered will perhaps arise. ***if only***: and yet no antler will sprout alone and not sprout further again from itself, stretching into the heavens from this edge of the poem's commentary. What work would *only* do *if only* only was alone. But *only*, unlike *any* is left here without form or substance, only the sap and not the wood. ***allegorize***: essential work of bucking the divisions of mimesis. Where does the allegorical figure begin and the actual figure end? The virtuous allegory will dim this distinction, not in the fantastic flights of an escapist book, but in a work it sets to work on the very realities of the reader. For, "The word 'dream' is technical and means nothing / so we can use it whenever we want."[111] So I have left nothing to vagueness, and made all plain so that the reader will be given to allegorize. ***shelter out***: the poem insists on this even with few friends left. The riddle of what is implied by these 'few friends' comes to better light when held together within the concept of 'sheltering out,' as exposure to the sorrow of the poem whose riddle begins to work only when the riddle can exhaust itself as riddle, can be a riddle and make its solution both impossible and superfluous–not by sheltering, concealing, its solution, but by exposing it, wearing it out for all to see, an invitation for friends, for commentary. ***inclinations***: here, like phenomena: mine, ours, yours, his, hers, mine yours ours; "All phenomena are [ultimately] selfless, empty, and free from conceptual elaboration. / In their dynamic they resemble an illusion, mirage, dream, or reflected image, / A celestial city, and echo, a reflection of the moon in water, a bubble, an optical illusion, or an intangible emanation. / You should know that all things of cyclical existence and nirvana / Accord [in nature] with these ten similes of illusory phenomena."[112]

The opening sentences of Samuel Beckett's novel *Molloy*–"I am in my mother's room. It's I who live here now. I don't know how I got there"[113]–serve as introduction to the riddle beginning *few lamps left*.

> few lamps left
> and seams
>
> left to blame.
> without a courier

---

[110] Jacques Derrida, "Edmund Jabès and the Question of the Book," in *Writing and Difference*, trans. Alan Bass (Chicago: University of Chicago Press, 1978), 74.

[111] Michael Palmer, "View from an Apartment" from *First Figure* in *Codes Appearing: poems 1979-1988* (New York: New Directions, 1988), 154.

[112] "Natural Liberation of Nature of Mind: The Four-Session Yoga of the Preliminary Practice," in *The Tibetan Book of the Dead First Complete Translation [English Title]: The Great Liberation by Hearing in the Intermediate States [Tibettan Title]*, trans. Gyurme Dorje (New York: Penguin, 2005), 9.

[113] Samuel Beckett, *Molloy,* in *Samuel Beckett: The Grove Centenary Edition*, ed. Paul Auster (New York: Grove, 2006), 3.

ISSN 1942-3381   Daniel C. Remein

> no visions until
> so resolve to keep quiet.
>
> the squint
> of your hair
>
> explains this
> particular arrangement
>
> of bones.

The poem is in six stanzas. The person to whom the statement about *the squint of your hair* is addressed, is unknown. Perhaps she or he does not yet exist. The third stanza is quite important, and in fact this entire work could have ended with the line *so resolve to keep quiet*. Other poets end new labors on a resolution to cease until a more suitable form or more refined skill has been obtained with respect to their topic. But, when the work of this poem has begun I will immediately write another comment in the hopes of generating another poem that will itself begin seeking a more suitable form for itself.

few lamps left: the fewer the lamps the more radiant the poem and so only hope for the future forms of the riddle. Thus, in a poem, Michael Palmer writes: "Truth to tell the inventor of the code weeps and lays the text aside. Here and there calendars and walls remind him that it's night, a sleeping lion is curled up in one corner, a voice can be heard behind a door, and Plato told us of the law, Plato warned us about the poem. The dead mayor wonders if the king of France is bald," and that "Plato warned us of the shadows of the poem, of the words cast against the wall, and Plato warns against the song. / The tree's green explains what a name means apart from memory, flickers of light in the darkened room, our eyes fixed on the screen on the figures of nothing. / The inventor of the code hears each note and swallows his tongue, frightened by shadows. The lion red as a lobster is green sleeps in one corner dreaming of the hours' numbers and names, a river flowing at his feet. 'Shuffle Montgomery' was the song."[114] Here is the reader, in the dark, few friends and few lamps, who has already written this riddle by the time the riddle is read, has already re-written it in beginning the work of commentary on it. Here is the riddler who will keep quiet and invent the newer codes for riddles. ***without a courier***: you, me, them, us, we. Taken by glowing owls last night, specially directed hearing and a line of green missives chained one to the other to link mountain and syntax and knit them into the shoreline of the riddle. With friends, the riddle will maneuver the missive and the code will appear held by the in-suck of silence between each breath. I would explain further, but the instructions were not explicit. We dry them like silt which cakes into dust and opens the seams of the earth, the portal to the world. With the owl-feathers bursting from each antler as needles we stitch together the festal parts of beaches to which we call new couriers. ***no visions until / so resolve to keep quiet***: unlike Dante, who claims at the end of his *Vita Nuova*: "After I wrote this sonnet there came to me a miraculous vision in which I saw things that it made me resolve to say no more about this blessèd one until I would be capable of writing about her in a nobler way."[115] This new work, as it

---

[114] Michael Palmer, "Notes for Echo Lake 5," from *Notes for Echo Lake*, in *Codes Appearing*, 27-28.

[115] Dante, "Vita Nuova," in *The Portable Dante*, XLII, p. 649.

draws to one of its material ends, cannot afford to cease at working until a new style is developed or a better vision is to be had. If the poem, or the romance, or the lyric, or the necessary missive, is impossible, the new work must work, like a mourning Egil, from the Icelandic Sagas, who makes verses even when all the techniques of verse seem unavailable or impossible: "My tongue is sluggish / for me to move, / my poem's scales / ponderous to raise. / The god's prize / is beyond my grasp, / tough to drag out / from my mind's haunts. / Since heavy sobbing / is the cause– / how hard to pour forth from the mind's root the prize that Frigg's progeny found / borne of old / from the world of giants."[116] Egil, whose verses may or may not have been entirely fictionally attributed to a living person other than the writer of his prose Saga (attributed to the medieval Icelandic historial, prose-writer, poet, and theorist of poetics Snorri Sturluson), thus sprouts multiple antlers of missives with which these missives would entangle themselves at least partially (for Egil's violence is another story): "My stock / stands on the brink, / pounded as plane-trees / on the forest's rim, / no man is glad / who carries the bones / of his dead kinsman / out of the bed. / Yet I will first recount my father's death / and mother's loss, / carry from my word-shrine / the timber that I build / my poem from, / leafed with language."[117] The figure of Egil and Snorri perhaps provides an alternative—with his short riddles and missives—to Dante as a literary history—as a beginning—of the work at work in this prosimetrum. And, "we believe that when politics is inescapable, the alternatives of imagination are necessary. In this arena, too, literary history may do some slow good."[118] This would result from an unresolved juxtaposition of Snorri/Egil with the new work's obvious debt to and reliance upon Dante's forms of visionary prosimetrum and visionary philosophical poem that also acts as dimming the boundary between the medieval and the modern. ***this particular arrangement***: a loose skein to cover the knees of the dead, the particular arrangement of which is selected by the hand of a weak and slowing Mercury. As Olson puts it, "what I there call history. And I'm happy to use the word [history] to stand for city."[119]

§

The mechanism of *immoderation,* so important to understand writing and friendship, comes to this work from a pedagogical text on spiritual contemplation from the Middle Ages, *The Cloud of Unknowing*. This text teaches, with respect to the approaches to contemplation outlined in the book (involving entering into a cloud of unknowing, that which is always between the contemplative and God):

> And forthermore, yif thou aske me what discrecion thou shalt have in this werk, than I answere thee and sey: "Ryght none!" For in alle thin other doynges thou shalt have discrecion . . . Bot in this weke shalt thou holde no mesure; for I wolde that thou shuldest never seese of this werk the whiles thou levyst.[120]

---

[116] *Egil's Saga*, trans. Bernard Scutter, in *The Sagas of Icelanders: a Selection* (New York: Penguin, 2000), 152.
[117] Ibid., 153.
[118] Jonathan Arac, "What Good Can Literary History Do?," *American Literary History* 20:2 (2008), 11.
[119] Olson, *Causal Mythology*, 19.
[120] *The Cloud of Unknowing*, ed. Patrick J. Gallacher (Kalamazoo, MI: Medieval Institute Publication, 1997), 1479-1485.

The structure of immoderation theorized a little by this poem that begins *i made the bed* partakes in the hope of time and action that *holde no mesure*. Even while I do not implore the reader to engage in a spiritual exercise, a reader might nonetheless *holde no mesure* without ignoring the world—while being abandoned or handed over (writing, writer, friendship, and reader) to the World, and all the risk which might arise from the *there* found therein. After I write the poem that begins *i made the bed*, a love-poem, I will or will not rest. I will or will not have any visions that illuminate the poems included in this work. I will or I will not consider God as my reader. I will or I will not include more poems or revisions of poems or comments in this work. If I write a poem about constructing a dream-vision, a friend will be commenting on my poems, she will kiss them and I will wonder if that is anything like *hope*, and she will say *a comment is always already shot through with poetic time*.

        i made the bed
        with the wolf you left
        when you left

        milk out
        when you

        we no longer
        believe in rest.

made: yes, there is nothing incorrect about this. **the wolf you left**: "they are right, the poet mother / carries the wolf in her heart, / wailing at pain yet suckling it like / romulus and remus. this now. / how will I forgive myself / for trying to bear the weight of this / and trying to bear the weight also / of writing the poem / about this?"[121] Nobody's grandmother but your own. It is the dramatics of beginning of the end of a new work left with a hunger, because "The entire momentum of the book resembles the implosion of a giant crater. Because nature and childhood are absent, humanity can be arrived at only via a catastrophic process of self-destruction."[122] Walter Benjamin here speaks of Dostoevsky's *The Idiot*, but the momentum of the quote would present itself in high density in the tiniest of poems, if this poem would only invite in all the wolves which raised it. **you left**: and someone blames. **milk**: one part fern and one part electric bulb. "That it is justifiable to call desire *heart* and reason *soul* is certainly clear to those persons that I wish my procedure to be clear to."[123] **you**: ". . . so many of you are the one's that I've lived mostly for, and with, and by, myself, and care the most for in the world."[124] **we**: various riddles apply, *you, me, them, us, we, us, me, you, us, this, we, this*. **believe**: as in, Robert Creeley's "The Revelation": "I thought that if I were broken enough / I would see the light like at the end of a small tube, but approachable. / I thought chickens laid eggs / for a purpose. / for the reason expected,

---

[121] Lucille Clifton, "Children," in *Mercy* (Rochester: BOA Editions, 2004), 18.
[122] Walter Benjamin, "Dostoevsky's *The Idiot*," in *Walter Benjamin: Selected Writings Vol. 1 1913-1926*, ed. Marcus Bullock and Michael W. Jennings (Cambridge, Mass: Harvard University Press, 2004), 81.
[123] Dante, "Vita Nuova," in *The Portable Dante*, XXXVIII, p. 644
[124] Olson, *Causal Mythology*, 2.

a form occurred more / blatant and impossible / to stop me."[125] Yet, as with ***rest***: "I will go on talking forever."[126] A wolf runs the length of the riddle, twice. At each end is a green bedpost, where the word 'green' is code for 'antler'. Once finished, the wolf carries in her mouth a scroll on which is written the results of the election, though she did not have it when she began and has never left your sight since beginning to run the length of the riddle. Her paws are smoking, her eyes are analog radio dials. No wolf's tongue—not the one which brought the king's last command concerning the poets, nor the one which infiltrates our allegory on a yearly basis—was ever a brighter ruby than this one. As her mouth opens to give you the scroll and then to eat you up, she howls, and her teeth are various letters of the Latin alphabet. They are in the order of a particular message and the wolf is laboring to open her mouth as wide as she can, as if she would turn inside out, as if to give over to you her very teeth, to be rid of the burden of the missive. And yet, for a wolf, this creature is very small. So say what it is called. The wolf will not rest until you can decipher this.

---

[125] Robert Creeley, "The Revelation," from *The Charm*, in *The Collected Poems of Robert Creeley: 1945-1975* (Berkley: University of California Press, 2006), 58.

[126] Creeley, "The Door," in *For Love*, in *The Collected Poems of Robert Creeley*, 201.

ISSN 1942-3381   Daniel C. Remein

PRELUDE TO A READING OF ARISTOTLE'S *METAPHYSICS*: BETA 1, PARAGRAPH ONE

Adam Rosen

With regard to the science which is the subject of our inquiry, we must first state the problems which should be discussed first. (995a24-25)

Opening treatise Beta, we are opened onto that which remains concealed as a result of our regimes of relevance, our steadfast concerns, our habits of inquiry. "With [the] regard [that opens us] to the science which is the subject of our inquiry," that is, with the regard that opens beyond our regional concerns onto the science of wisdom, we are opened at once beyond ourselves and onto ourselves; for, it is the broadening of the scope of our concern that enframes our more habitual inquiries and interests in such a way that they become available in their narrowness. We are both ek-statically projected beyond our habitual limits and returned to what is most proximate. "With regard[1] to the science which is the subject of our inquiry," we will learn that it is precisely the modes of our concern with the beings that proximally and for the most part concern us that conceals "the problems which should be discussed first" if we desire to know in the highest degree, if we seek the ultimate telos (the good without qualification), if we seek the science of wisdom. The problems that regularly organize our methods of inquiry and the interests they express, then, are themselves rendered problematic, even uncanny, by this regard, this unsettling gaze attuned to the science of wisdom.

That through which we become aware that "we must first state the problems which should be discussed first" is the regard responding to and organized by "the science which is the subject of our inquiry." "With regard to the science which is the subject of our inquiry," with a broadly circumspective regard, with a gaze expansive enough to encompass previous modes of concern and in this encompassing redirect attention toward the science of wisdom such that we can hope to discern the order of that science (the order that allows one to "first state the problems which should be discussed first"), the order of the *cosmos* that science discloses, and the situatedness, relationality, or positioning of ourselves as inquiring beings within that *cosmos* (whereby our gaze turns back upon and envelops us), we surely are attuned elsewhere and otherwise, but that does not mean that we become oblivious to or ignore our various regional concerns. Rather, acceding proleptically to the science of wisdom and thus attending to these habitual concerns in their regionality, in their inability to disclose the *why* of beings to the highest degree, we are afforded the opportunity to investigate other modalities

---

[1] Here it may be useful to heed the resonance of *pros* (with regard) in its configurations as *pros-agoreuo* (to address), *pros-erkomai* (to approach), *pros-eko* (to attend, to heed).

of emergence of the beings we find ourselves concerned with in our habitual modes of inquiry and to investigate ourselves as prone to concern ourselves with beings in the manners that have become habitual. Attending to that which exceeds and contains the human and its regional concerns, we are offered anew that which is most intimate: both the objects of our concerns and ourselves as concerned beings. Spanning beyond and rounding back, the regard that opens us onto the science of wisdom is both unsettling and itself unsettled, a kinetic force, as if a matter of *physis*.

Gathering and consolidating our focus into the "regard [directed toward] . . . the science which is the subject of our inquiry," it seems as if Aristotle paradoxically opens our inquiry into the science of wisdom by declaring the necessity [*anagke*] of having already undertaken such an inquiry. For it seems that only a retrospective gaze, an experienced gaze already aware of what problems should be stated and discussed first, can "regard . . . the science which is the subject of our inquiry . . . [and] first state the problems which should be discussed first." As if returning from the end of an inquiry into "the science which is the subject of our inquiry," Aristotle enticingly yet vexingly inveighs us to "state the problems [*aporias*] that should be discussed first," thereby posturing as if he is already able to discern such an order, as if he had already stated certain problems (perhaps those which we will state and discuss in the ensuing paragraphs, perhaps others), inquired into them to the greatest possible degree, determined which are the most fecund and which lead astray, and is thus in a position to tell us which problems (*aporias*) must be stated and discussed first.[2] In the name of the science of wisdom,[3] Aristotle, speaking as a privileged representative of this science, as if initiated and thus able to direct us, perhaps so well initiated as to direct us through the process(es) *necessitated* by the science we are opening onto, conveys its injunction (thus, in an extremely complicated gesture, assimilating its authority) that "we first state the problems that should be discussed first."

Unless we are to concede that Aristotle, in an uncharacteristically self-assertive and authoritarian manner, simply *posits* the necessity of stating first the problems which should be discussed first and then, audaciously, continues Beta One by stating and discussing what we must, on the ground of their site of enunciation (i.e., Aristotle's authority), deem necessary problems, it seems best to situate the force of the normative injunction ("we *must* first state the problems which *should* be discussed first") as arising from, or at least professing to arrive from, a cultivated responsiveness to the science of wisdom and/or that which is disclosed therein. If we accept this interpretive hypothesis, in asking that we "first state the problems which should be discussed first," Aristotle does not expect us, who are at best incipiently emerging from the habitual hold of our regional concerns, to have even a vague inkling of the contours and order of such *aporias* or any great aptitude to discuss them well. Rather, it seems a great deal more plausible that we who are only initiating

---

[2] If we are to believe that only upon return from the completion of inquiry into the science of wisdom can one demand that problems are stated first that should be discussed first, and so if we are to conclude from this injunction that Aristotle is, or at least believes himself to be, returning from the culminating apex of insight into the science of wisdom, we would have to wonder what it is about the achievement of insight to the highest degree into the science of wisdom that sends him back? Why does Aristotle not rest content, reposing in a paroxysm of contemplative fulfillment?

[3] Whereas *pros theon* may be rendered as "in the name of the divinities," *pros tan . . . epistemen* may be rendered as "in the name of the science."

this inquiry are expected to "state the problems which should be discussed first" precisely by "stating" them along with Aristotle, by assenting to Aristotle's determination of these problems, at least for the time being, and by accepting Aristotle as a guide who will direct our ventures into the science of wisdom.[4] A troubling condition for thoroughgoing (self-)inquiry, Aristotle seems to suggest, is acceding to the perhaps irredeemable authority of inheritance, to the risk of receptivity.

To be sure, although Aristotle implores us to "state the problems which should be discussed first" as if what is stated and discussed first is a necessary prerequisite for the attainment of a predetermined end, this end to which we (are lead to) aspire is not necessarily the exhaustive finality of inquiry. Nor is it necessary that we think the end to come, the end in view of which it is necessary that we state and discuss certain aporias first, as a systematically organized set of contents that constitute "the science of wisdom"–at the very least, that would risk the grossest anachronism. It is not incidental that what is necessary is that we state and discuss *aporias* first. Regardless of how well these aporias are determined and discussed, perhaps they remain aporias none the less.[5] Perhaps what is at stake is less a methodologically regulated path to a predetermined end than an "ethical" reorientation, a concomitant change in the character of the inquirer and the inquiry. Furthermore, whether the discussion of aporias is confined to treatise Beta or in a way constitutes the entirety of *The Metaphysics* is extremely difficult to say, especially since it is yet quite unclear what constitutes a "discussion" of aporias[6] and thus quite unclear what would constitute the end of such a discussion.

Attending to the polysemic range of the dictate to "first state the problems which should be discussed first," it is quite indeterminate exactly what it would mean to *discuss first* the aporias laid down by Aristotle–especially since this call to order does not develop into a remarkably ordered discussion. The injunction may dictate something like ongoing, recursive inquiry: the discussion of aporias would be the first discussion of a great many, perhaps indefinitely many discussions required for a proper investigation of the science of wisdom, in which case such stating and discussing would be *merely*, however foundationally, first. In this case, the end of our inquiry, the trajectory from what is most known to us to what is most known according to itself, may be quite far from the stasis of investigative exhaustion. Insofar as the discussion remains concerned with aporias, it may remain, in principle, interminable.[7] On the other hand, the injunction to "first state the problems which

---

[4] Regardless of whether we are inceptively emerging from the hold of our regional concerns or we are experienced thinkers attuned in various ways to the question of being qua being, whether we are still for the most part held fast by our regularized interests and inquiries or initiated into the science of wisdom in our own ways, we would still do well to accede to Aristotle's determination and discussion of these aporias in order to inquire into the necessity to which they are said to respond.

[5] What it is to remain an aporia will be discussed below.

[6] Would this entail a dissolution of the aporias, a discerning of those questions that do not admit of thorough dissolution and those which do, a reflection that gives rise to another way of proceeding–a way that detours around the aporias, a listing and/or brief overview of certain aporias, a sustained engagement with the unsurpassability of the aporetic, a traversal of the aporia as such, some combination of the aforementioned possibilities, or something else altogether?

[7] Of course, the variegated destinies of the various aporias require a great deal of further attention. This paper only seeks to pave the way for such investigations. While some of the aporias formulated in Beta One

should be discussed first" may be understood as requiring us to engage in a discussion of a finite set of aporias in order to move on along a prescribed path to the peaks of insight. This is as yet undecided.

Crucially, the question of whether Aristotle's formulations and discussions of these aporias are *necessitated* by the science of wisdom would only be decidable, if at all, after we have tarried along the path he paves for us, only, if at all, after we too are able to respond to the science of wisdom and the *cosmos* it discloses as they are opened by the initial problems posed and the subsequent discussions and developments of those problems. The venture of Aristotle's discourse would be that only by proceeding in the manner that he lays forth could we either experience or fail to experience the retrospective necessity of the problems posed and the ensuing discussions. Only after we have followed Aristotle along the paths paved by the questions posed, only after we have become open to the phenomena investigated as well as the mode of their investigation, only then, if at all, may we undergo the failures or successes attendant thereto and on that basis decide upon the propriety of the initial claim too necessity. But it may (also) be that only having inquired along with Aristotle may we attain a more cultivated sense for the problematics incumbent to the science of wisdom and only then find ourselves in a position to re-begin with other problematics that we feel compelled to state and discuss first. If indeed we are as neophyte as the text suggests, then the condition for exceeding Aristotle's authority, the condition for beginning and/or proceeding otherwise, is to initially accede to Aristotle's trajectory such that it leads us to our own grounds for saying otherwise, to our own experience of the necessity of posing problems otherwise and/or engaging in discussions in a manner divergent from Aristotle's. For the meantime, in stating and discussing these problems as the ones which should be stated first, in accepting Aristotle as our guide, we ratify a normative orientation for our inquiry—already redoubling and thereby subverting its authority. Embracing the necessity of an initial ground-laying, we are saved from the vertiginous experience of inquiry without determinacy of direction. We thus acknowledge our utter dependence upon guides and grounds, upon previous thought and thinkers as a condition for inquiry, for thinking at all.

> They are concerned with matters about which some thinkers expressed different beliefs, and besides them, with some other matters which may happen to have been overlooked. (995a25-26)

As noted, the determinations of the aporias are not quite our own; we are to accept those laid down by Aristotle as provisionally, however necessarily, appropriate. But after following the paths of inquiry paved by Aristotle, we too may become "concerned with matters about which some thinkers [namely, Aristotle] expressed different beliefs, and besides them, with some other matters which may happen to have been overlooked." We may confirm the necessity to "first state the problems which should be discussed first"

---

are maintained in their original form as they are thought through later, others are significantly reformulated. It is thus incumbent upon us, if we are to explore the paths opened herein, to inquire into how and why these reformulations occur within the respective contexts of their elaborations. Further, if we are to pursue the trajectory broached herein, we will have to inquire into why some of the aporias laid out in Beta One later receive what may be called decisive treatment—even answers—while others are handled in a manner that more or less explicitly maintains their aporetic status.

precisely by reserving the prerogative to disagree with the propriety of Aristotle's specific determination and discussion of these problems. Aristotle's seeming didacticism paradoxically opens the way to a critical contestation of his teachings. If the *telos* of *physis* as such– if there is one–does not guarantee for *anthropoi* a linear progress toward wisdom, if some matters perhaps crucial for the inquiry into the science of wisdom may have been contingently overlooked ("may happen to have been overlooked") by our predecessors, it may be that Aristotle too contingently overlooks certain matters imperative for the inquiry into the science of wisdom. This is what his discourse gives to be seen, however dimly. Aristotle's (assimilated) authority is dislocated from the other side as it relays to (is re-assimilated by) his addressees. More precisely, Aristotle's authority manifests an uncanny structure: self-undermining yet persistent, it is a condition of its own transgression and so abides in what claims to exceed it.

Since it is undecidable from here whether or not various matters will have been overlooked, that is, precisely because the aporias which will be discussed first *may* have been taken up by previous thinkers in ways that are inaccessible to or misconstrued by our particular modes of inquiry as much as they "*may* happen to have been overlooked,"[8] and since regardless of whether or not such matters have been considered previously, contingent overlooking seems to remain an inevitable danger, we are bound to return, perhaps interminably, to the formulation and discussion of the initial aporias that structure our inquiry into the science of wisdom. The science of wisdom is perhaps a radically inceptive project–projecting us into a future of inquiry illimitable in principle. And even were we to later confirm the necessity of Aristotle's formulation and discussion of the guiding aporias, this necessity would only be confirmed or denied from the perspective of an inquiry emerging from Aristotle's initial statement and discussion of the aporias, the statement and/or discussion of which may inevitably, Aristotle intimates, simply overlook some crucial matters and may, in bringing certain problems into fine relief, concomitantly conceal others, which means that even then the inquiry may not rightly come to a rest.

Investigations that begin with aporias may remain irremediably partial and provisional, *but this is not to say without ends at all.*[9] Rather, it is to say that perhaps our ends are always responsive to our beginnings–beginnings formulated without the (perhaps ends-constitutive) knowledge acquired as we move toward our investigative ends, even if formulated in view of them, and thus perhaps perpetually in need of reformulation. We must then heed the formulation of initial aporias with the utmost attention, which may mean returning to them time and again in order to acknowledge the incessant task of the inquiry into the science of wisdom, the inquiry that *by necessity* begins with the stating and discussing of *aporias*. How far the determination of necessity seems to have drifted . . .

However, proceeding, let alone returning, will not be easy. This inquiry will likely provoke resistance insofar as we will be dealing with matters that "may happen to have been overlooked," that is, with matters that may be more or less, perhaps even thoroughly, unfamiliar. Seeking wisdom, of necessity we run headlong into the depths of obscurity. If the matters into which we investigate are rather distant from the themes that

---

[8] Notice the effort to attune us to opacity and obscurity as perhaps irreducible dimensions of insight, as shadows forever clouding the transparency of knowledge yet perhaps themselves knowable to some degree.

[9] Although "no one would try to do anything if [s/]he did not intend to come to a limit," the limit is not necessarily identical with an exhaustive stasis (994b14-15).

tend to dominate our concern, matters with respect to which we may have little or no footing, the vertiginous sense of beginning an inquiry without any known way of proceeding may generate quite some resistance, leading to the denial, trivialization, or facile mischaracterization of the problems rather than more serious confrontations with them.[10] Or so Aristotle intimates and the history of commentary on Beta One symptomatically corroborates. Thus without Aristotle's determination and discussion of the initial aporias, the starting point of inquiry may be experienced as abyssal, paralyzing rather than aporetic. Moreover, in that we will be "concerned with matters about which some thinkers expressed different beliefs," we will be taking a stand against the sedimented authority of doxa; and so, out of reverence for certain thinkers or commitments to particular thoughts, we may again find ourselves resisting.[11] "Concerned with matters about which some thinkers expressed different beliefs," thus with matters that are familiar but taken up in unfamiliar ways, we will be engaged in an inquiry that we are told in advance will be contestatory vis-à-vis received opinion, and as such, likely to evoke some measure of resistance. Were it not for Aristotle's claim to proceed via necessity, were it not for the channeling of our desire to know and our pleasure in having seen into the search for wisdom to the highest degree, that is to say, without the seductive allure of Aristotle's initial posture, what we called his seeming didacticism, we may not have the courage to proceed at all.

Gathered around the formulation and discussion of aporias, we are gathered into a community, a community of (self-)inquiry bound inexorably to no particulars of time or place. Though perhaps illimitable, such a community is not without criteria for participation. We are convoked to this community in virtue of a willingness to think with and against received opinion (and by implication, a willingness to work through the resistances this may provoke at various stages of inquiry). We are not gathered as a community of the purely contestatory, as if this were possible; this is no matter of negative self-identification or mere contentiousness. Our community is less an-archic than para-doxical. We begin with differences, with the possibility of resistances, with the abiding yet unsettled authority of received problematics and opinions, but we begin, even so, with guides and grounds because we begin in dialogue with our predecessors. And because we begin under the tutelage of Aristotle: in order to proceed, we will have embraced Aristotle's initial determination of "the problems which should be discussed first," etc.

---

[10] Precisely what such a "serious" confrontation may be remains a question to be explored throughout this paper.

[11] Compounding our difficulties, our concern "with matters about which some thinkers expressed different beliefs" may generate resistance from the opposite angle. Concerning ourselves with the diversity of opinions about matters of common concern, we will come to see that the seemingly established authority of doxa is never free from critical contestation, never beyond reproach. Exposed to the intervallic periodicity of established opinion and the ongoing dislocations of settled authority that subtend it, exposed to what may be the irreducibility of interpretive plurality about certain matters of ongoing interest, we may find ourselves strangely unsettled, resisting what seems to be the hounding out of authority from its historically established haunts or what we anticipatorily construe as the paralyzing effects of skepticism induced by a resolutely historical perspective. That is, resistances may arise out of piety as much as out of fear of the dissipation of the sort of authority that can command piety.

We are gathered as a community of (self-)inquiry in virtue having undergone an antecedent solicitation, in virtue of having been exposed to an unsettling force—one name or variant of which might be wonder, but in all cases it is a question of *eros*—to which we feel compelled— yet ill-equipped—to respond. The community in question is marked by a common compulsion to thoughtfully, inquisitively respond to something moving, affectively significant, inspiring, something demanding that the exhalation subsequent to this in-spiration is overfull with *logoi* that seek a responsiveness to the science of wisdom as much as possible.[12] Such a community, then, however illimitable, is hardly amorphous. Now, whether this in-spiration issues from Aristotle's didactic authority, from his proximity to what Lacanians would call the *sujet supposé savoir*, from a proleptic experience of the science of wisdom, or from the authority Aristotle assimilates and channels from the genuine successes of his investigations, remains to be determined. For now all we can say is that, thus gathered, we can confirm the necessity— in this case the affective necessity, the necessity of passionate compulsion—to state the aporias that should be discussed first (whatever they may be). As those tantalized by the prospects of wisdom to the highest degree (or its harbinger), as those desiring the pleasure of having seen to the greatest extent (or captivated by the bearer of the promise thereof), as those willing to stand out from the accepted positions of the communities in which we find ourselves,[13] we gather as the community of the aporia. It is perhaps only a community of the aporia that can be opened to an inquiry into the science of wisdom in its fullest, non-exhaustive dimension. Perhaps a reorientation of character—the ethical dimension—is a condition of insight here as elsewhere.

> Now those who wish to succeed well in arriving at answers will find it profitable to go over the *difficulties* well; for answers successfully arrived at are the solutions to *difficulties* previously discussed, and one cannot untie a knot if [s/]he is ignorant of it. (995a27-30)

Calling attention to "those who wish to succeed well in arriving at answers," Aristotle concerns himself with appetitive structure as it bears on the ethos of inquiry. Aristotle is here concerned with those who wish to "succeed well," that is, with ethos, character, and what gratifies. Of course, those to whom Aristotle refers may be inquirers who wish to bring their inquiring to a close, those who wish to repose in necessarily complete insight. But they also may be those who pursue the science of wisdom not simply out of a desire for answers as static finalities. Perhaps "those who wish to succeed well in arriving at answers" are not those who wholeheartedly desire the utter dissolution of aporias, the stillness of what once provoked and challenged, the exhaustion of striving, but rather those who desire another type of answer altogether: answers well arrived at. Over against those who only "wish to succeed . . . [by] arriving at answers," say, in order to bring the difficulties of inquiry to an end, over against those for whom the desire to bask in the accomplishment of full and final comprehension dominates so strongly that it promotes a self-subverting readiness to rest content with less than might be possible to achieve, there are perhaps "those who wish to succeed well *in arriving* at answers." These would be inquirers for whom what is at stake is their character upon arriving and the

---

[12] Cf. *Physics* 253a12-14: "the cause of . . . motion is not the animal itself [at least not in an unqualified sense] but perhaps its environment."

[13] Treatise Alpha has already established that this will be the case—at least for the most part.

character of their arrival, those for whom it is crucial that the provocation to inquiry is preserved, the initiating state of exposure is sustained *in the experience of arriving*. These would be inquirers who, no less enamored with the science of wisdom than those seeking contemplative completion—perhaps even more so—are, precisely in virtue of this desire, interested in the experience of arriving as in certain respects indistinguishable from sending. These would be lovers of the practice of inquiry, those who "love to have seen" [*eidenai*] both for its own sake and insofar as having seen, having made discriminations and determinations, generates refinements that allow for further differences to come into view, for further opportunities "to have seen," perchance for development. These inquirers would no doubt be eminently interested in the yield of their various regional inquiries, but their desires would not be rigidly attracted thereto, nor would they be monofocally set on the systematic integration of insights attained from regional investigations as if system and knowledge to the highest degree were simply *one*. Rather, these investigators may be lovers of the prospect of knowledge to the highest degree to such an exorbitant extent that they would be willing to consider knowledge attained as partial and provisional, as ever in need of refinement, if only to keep on their horizon the possibility of knowledge to an even greater degree.[14] A curious madness indeed.

To be sure, these two appetitive structures are not entirely incompatible. Perhaps the desire for and pleasure in the practice of inquiry as such, the desire for continual differentiation, specification, and openness to that which—putatively—remains forever on the horizon, can be the periodic *effect* of pursuing an inquiry predominantly organized by a desire for answers in the sense of a culminating terminus. Perhaps the transformation of desire, the generation of an ethos of incessant openness from out of a desire for totality, and this in the service of the science of wisdom, is, in part, the venture of *The Metaphysics*.[15] If so, the project would be, in principle, resistant to completion. And if so, if one of the essential movements of *The Metaphysics* is a to-and-fro between a urge to totalization and an interest in what stands apart, what remains abrasively particular and/or persistently opaque, perhaps the nature of dialectics needs to be reconsidered in its wake.

Perhaps, like those undertaking an effort geared to epistemic mastery, the latter sort of inquirers also "*wish* to . . .arriv[e] at answers," but are more circumspect about this desire. Perhaps, like those fixated upon the attainment of terminal conclusions, these inquirers "wish to . . . arriv[e] at answers," but do not allow this wish to overwhelm their "wish to succeed well" in arriving, do not allow this interest to deaden their receptivity to it potentially detrimental impact on its own fulfillment as well as to other goods. Perhaps these latter have come to believe—perhaps they have been lead to believe—that the only way to successfully arrive, to arrive well, is to remain open to, and sometimes this means vigilantly, willfully *keeping open*, questions of whether or not one has actually arrived and how one can arrive more successfully. Arriving well, for such inquirers, may involve re-traversing ground well covered, and not only in this respect would it be hardly the

---

[14] Here we see again how the regard directed beyond, the interest in transcendence, is itself manifest in the investigative return to what is familiar, how the pursuit of transcendence and the adventures of immanence are one.

[15] More on this thought below.

contrary of the experience of aporia.[16] "Those who wish to succeed well in arriving at answers," then, "will find it profitable to go over the *difficulties* [aporias] well." And if "to go over the aporias well" is an in principle interminable pursuit, if such an endeavor requires sustaining exposure to the interruptive and at times subversive efficacy of aporias, to the ongoing perplexities they induce, as much as to the ways they can be gotten around or worked through (e.g., specified, reformulated, partially resolved, mined for various resources) and the knowledge yielded thereby, if this "going over," in order to be done well, may be a simple glancing over as much as it may be an incessant retraversing (returning again and again to the initial formulation of the aporias so as to generate new and, hopefully, ever more refined lines of inquiry), what it is to arrive well seems, though not altogether unclear, radically underdetermined.

If the "solution to *difficulties* [aporias] previously discussed" is not the final resolution of the aporias, the dissolution of all disquietude, if we are still unclear what constitutes an adequate discussion of aporias (might this vary substantially from case to case?) and therefore remain uncertain whether or not we have attained to successful solutions insofar as "answers successfully arrived at are the solutions to the difficulties previously discussed," then it seems that, again, we must keep open (to) the question of whether or not we have actually arrived and how we can arrive more successfully. Although "one cannot untie a knot if [s/]he is ignorant of it," and so one must push toward the utmost specification of the problems at hand, it is as yet unclear, and perhaps will remain so, whether this analogy implies that the unbinding of the knot entails its successful (dis-)solution or rather requires the re-solve to confront the further problem of the threads constitutive of the knot as bound in their own way. With Aristotle as our guide, we encounter aporias again and again, as if there were nothing else.

Yet, as was noted earlier, Aristotle insists that we would not engage in any activity whatsoever if we did not intend to arrive at a limit. But perhaps a viable end is a provisional end, an end pervaded by the possibility of continuing otherwise: a self-surpassing end, but an end none the less. If the *telos* of all but the utterly simple is never exhaustive insofar as it is the actualization (*energia* naming a certain being-at-work, a continuity of directed motion) of a being that remains pervaded by potentiality, if teleological orientation (*entelekia*) names the prospective directedness of a process, the anticipated end in view of which the process takes upon a determinate shape and thus becomes knowable, then we must reconsider the way "*telos*" tends to resound with a sense of exhaustion and insurpassability. If, phenomenologically, an end is situated within a whole that exceeds it such that its status as an end does not exhaust its discernable operations within the whole, then an end is not in all registers identical with a final determination. If actuality precedes possibility for Aristotle such that the claim that we would not do things if we did not intend to arrive at a limit corresponds to a phenomenological perception of actions always arriving at ends within *physis*, this is quite different from claiming that actions necessarily arrive at exhaustive ends. Consequently, perhaps "to succeed well in arriving at answers" is not necessarily to succeed at the stopping point of inquiry beyond which nothing else can be

---

[16] Also, if arriving well implies re-traversing ground well covered, then the indistinguishability of arriving well from a stale, repetitive, obstinate going over of the same raises the specter of a madness from which the pursuit of insight would never be free.

known, beyond which no further determinations, differentiations, or qualifications are possible. Rather, answers may be contextually provisional—responsive to their beginnings and the interests borne thereby—and nonetheless ends. If there can be no full and final solution to a *difficulty* but only further inroads to exploring the depths of the problem [aporia] and those it branches off into, then a successful arrival at a solution is a non-arrival at investigative exhaustion. In a curious sense, the inquiry into the science of wisdom seems self-moving . . .

But what of the hierarchies established and ends posited by Aristotle throughout this inquiry? Are these to be understood as provisional and contextually relevant, that is, as hierarchies and determinations located in an in principle perfectible if interminable inquiry? Or are they responsive to a necessity that dictates a singular path toward knowledge in the highest degree from which deviation would amount to failure? Are the hierarchies (of the sciences, etc.) and conclusions of the various lines of investigation unsurpassable and irreplaceable within the inquiry into the science of wisdom or are they, precisely as elements of an *inquiry* into the science of wisdom that must begin with the statement and discussion of *aporias*, provisional and strategic resting points? Might these hierarchies and conclusions be conditioned by the (im)propriety of the specific inquiry that proceeds to their determinations? If so, what would guarantee their necessity?

Could it be that the various ends and hierarchies are elements of a strategy designed to mitigate the force of the various resistances that this particular inquiry risks eliciting? Again, might Aristotle be interested in putting a given desire for determinate ends, for hierarchies, generally, for the satisfactions of investigative conclusion, in the service of a project that may be, in principle, illimitable? If so, what would this tell us about the nature of the end of his pursuit? If these ends and hierarchies are in the service of advancing an inquiry that, if successful, would allow the inquirers following Aristotle's trajectory to return to the beginning of the inquiry in order to state the aporias which must be discussed first in a manner divergent from Aristotle's, if Aristotle understands the success of the inquiry in terms of cultivating the capacity to inquire in a manner other than, though hopefully building on, his own (that is, in terms of cultivating an openness to the emergence of phenomenon on the basis of an emphatic plurality of perspectives that would open the chance for the shortcomings of his investigations to be surpassed by its inheritors), then his push for the determinacy of conclusions to the highest degree, the thrust toward the hierarchization of the sciences, the systematic ruling out of infinite regresses, the decision that the best explanation is the one with the least number of premises, the expulsion of any unnecessary complexity, and so forth may be strategies to generate a taste for specification to the highest degree amongst those who follow him and therewith to induce the desire to attain an even greater degree of specification than his inquiry offers. To seek the utmost specificity while keeping an eye on the conditions from which this determinacy emerges (our premises, previous arguments, structural limitations, etc.) generates an historicization of our account (*logos*), reminds our *logos* of its origins, and thereby works against a fully originary or finalizing (thus perhaps unnecessarily abridged) discourse while at once working toward determinacy to the highest degree. If the success of an answer depends on the interpretation of what it is to arrive at a solution to *difficulties* posed and discussed, so long as we remain without secure ground for such an interpretation, our criterion for success remains indefinitely in question.

Perhaps, then, crucial to the successful performance of Aristotle's inquiries is the cultivation in his addressees of a desire for knowledge in the highest degree, a desire which may be actualized as an ethos of incessant, recursive inquiry. Perhaps Aristotle attempts to hierarchize, to specify, to rule out infinite regresses and superfluous concerns, and so forth out of an insistently ethical concern, out of a desire to cultivate a habit for or ethos of specification—and so to open us toward the potential need to undermine the hierarchies and determinacies he establishes along the path of inquiry he lays forth. Although Aristotle may not untie all of the knots emergent in the course of our inquiry, it still remains the case that "one cannot untie a knot if [s/]he is ignorant of it," and this guided inquiry at least allows for some familiarity with a great many of these knots and may even motivate us and provide some of the resources to detect knots indiscernible within Aristotle's account. For, to some extent, it is the desire for specificity that can eventually lead those who provisionally accept Aristotle's trajectory of inquiry to inquire otherwise. Thus it may be that *The Metaphysics* is formally self-undermining, potentially destructive of all its determinations, and as such, thoroughly committed to an investigation of the science of wisdom that seeks knowledge to the highest degree. Indeed, it may even be that the striving for knowledge to the highest degree *demands* the self-undermining of each and every singular discourse; perhaps there is an essential connection between wisdom and plurality. Aristotle's investigations into the science of wisdom, in determining that to which we may respond, in cultivating our response-abilities, in generating a habit and ethos of openness along with a concern for specification to the highest degree, may be thought, then, as an ethical project *par excellence*.

"Find[ing] it profitable to go over the *difficulties* well," we, as inquirers, undergo transformations in our appetitive structuration. Habituated to desiring ends as final resting points, we are opened to the labile desire for ends in their potential inexhaustibility and the satisfactions incumbent thereto.[17] Tarrying with Aristotle, we find that it may be to our profit to lay down our regular calculations wherein we can only accept as profitable that which is unequivocally and immediately so, that which fulfills a need defined in advance, and instead open to the possibility of an indefinitely deferred profit whose pursuit may be, para-doxically, profit to the highest degree. In going over the difficulties well, we inscribe hesitation as a condition for the success of our inquiries, inquiries so often characterized by over-great haste. Our desire for knowledge, perhaps due to our pleasure in "having seen," leads all too often to a rush for conclusions rather than a careful, hesitant approach to answers in many ways. Rather than returning to the inception of our inquiries and considering other, perhaps more fecund trajectories, we become enamored with the fruits of our inquiries and hold fast to them. Perhaps, returning to the issue of what it is to "succeed well in arriving at answers," success well arrived at is not a condition wherein all the relevant, pre-defined questions have been correlated with their "answers," but rather a condition wherein the texture of answering becomes a responsiveness to the questions posed, a responsiveness in which the answer's determinacy is in proportion to the determinacy of the question. This is perhaps the way in which aporias belong to their ends. When specific sets of questions posed are correlated with answers—such as "it is not impossible that ..." or "it may be the case and is not inconsistent that ..." or "such and such a thought does not run into the problems that our predecessors run into," or "from our inquiries we cannot conclude otherwise"—that are responsive to the quality of the questions, perhaps another mode of answering is at stake than that to which we are accustomed, and perhaps this mode of answering is inextricable from the attainment of knowledge to the highest degree. The cultivation of habits of answering, then, may be understood as a cultivation of proportional responsiveness, that is, as an ethical matter, an issue of justice.

---

[17] Cf. *Physics* 208a21: "time and motion . . . are infinite, and so is thinking."

> The *difficulties* raised by *thought* about its object reveal this fact: insofar as *thought* is in *difficulties*, it is like those who are bound; and in both cases one cannot go forward. (995a 30-34)

"Insofar as *thought* is in *difficulties* [*aporias*]," although one may not go forward, although one may be bound to aporias and the (in)determinacies of inquiry implied thereby, movement is not altogether paralyzed. Rather, in certain cases, the binding of thought, like the binding of limbs, hinders movement in some ways while focusing it in others.[18] Perhaps the aporetic bonds of thought, far from implying a simple paralysis, enable the concentration of thought in ways that would remain neglected given a more full range of motion. In the midst of our hasty rushing toward conclusions, perhaps it is the binding of thought to aporias that allows for the development of an even approximately sufficient clarification of the problems requisite for an investigation into the science of wisdom. Although thought remains ensnared by "the *difficulties*," perhaps beholden to the irreducible status of its aporetic beginnings, although thought may be prevented from an unabashedly forward motion, to be sure, forward is not the only relevant motion—especially with regard to inquiry.

"The *difficulties*" [aporias], we should note, are "raised by *thought* about its object," which is to say, these *difficulties* are products of thought internal to the attempt to articulate its object to the greatest extent. What stands revealed when "thought is in *difficulties*" is not only that "like those who are bound . . . one cannot go forward," but also that the difficulties impeding uninhibited progression are "raised by thought."[19] Paradoxically, the striving for utmost clarity gives rise to *difficulties* that require the project of clarification to focus on delimiting as precisely as possible the obstinate opacity of these *difficulties*. The aspiration for clarity, to remain true to its course, must swerve into its obverse: the precise clarification of concealment as concealment and opaqueness as opaqueness to the highest degree. The attempt to articulate the object of thought to the highest degree, paradoxically, suffuses thought with aporias and binds it to the study of those aporias. Compounding the paradox to the point of irony, the aporias internal to the attempt to specify the object of thought to the greatest extent may be understood as at once liberatory and binding (in aporetic appropriateness, as liberatory shackles); for, thought's self-binding to the specification of aporias consequent upon its commitment to clarification of its object to the highest degree appears as a mode of constraint that produces possibilities for thought that would likely remain suppressed by our habitual freedoms. Were thought able to simply gloss over the aporias to which it gives rise, were we to hastily march though problems on the way to exhaustive conclusions, thought, bereft of crucial opportunities for thinking the aporetic status of its objects, would remain precluded from determining its objects to the highest degree if doing so entails thinking the object *as* aporetic. *Difficulties*, although they may hinder a simply forward trajectory, open up lines of inquiry that structure our investigative topography and perhaps thereby facilitate investigative successes in their own way.

---

[18] Cf. Stephen Shainberg's (2002) *Secretary*.

[19] Such thought, to be sure, is itself beholden to phenomena and thus the *difficulties* are decidedly emergent from phenomena.

Insofar as "thought is like those who are bound," insofar as thought is attuned and responsive to aporias, a hasty rush forward is thereby hindered, and thought, emancipated by shackling, is allowed to be thoughtful all the more. Constraint becomes evident as a condition for self-actualization (once again). Binding may thus operate as a transfixed rapture, as an erotically charged attuning to the complexities of an object of inquiry, as a force liberating the energies of thought that become free to pervade their objects again and again. Directed inquiry here shades into reverie without regression, or at least this is the hope. Freed from the need to think only toward an exhaustive conclusion, liberated from the project of self-annihilation whereby thought dissolves in resolving its problems, thought, attentive to the aporias to which it is bound (perhaps attentive to such a degree that it is able to distinguish between problems that admit of a more thorough resolution and those that may not) is allowed to seek the greatest degree of specification of its objects. This would be the case even more so if the highest determination of the object of inquiry consists in its being spoken in many ways, that is, if the polysemic determinations of an object are intrinsic to its being articulated to the highest degree.

However, aporias also impose limitations. Too extreme a focus on a particular aporia or on the aporetic status of a particular object or range of objects, and all the more so, too extreme a focus on the aporetic dimensions of objects as such or the aporetic nature of inquiry may hinder progress in other directions. We are thus left to wonder: when is attunement to the aporias "raised by thought about its object" superfluous, or even worse, a mode of resistance to further developments and clarification there where they are possible, a hasty preclusion of the capacity "to go forward" when such a forward momentum is precisely what the inquiry requires? When is careful attention to the aporetic dimension of a particular investigation or to that of the general horizon of inquiry a mode of superficial stasis that forecloses careful consideration of issues looming on the horizon? Might over-enamored attention to aporias collude with various resistances to investigative progress? Might lavishing attention on the aporetic conspire with defenses against the contingent difficulties of working through and moving on? At this level of generality, all that can be said is that the productive and/or destructive status of attention to aporias remains, appropriately enough, undecided in advance, in its own way aporetic. We can not say for sure, once and for all, if aporias are on-balance helpful or harmful for thought. Attuned to aporias, thought seems both constrained and liberated. "One cannot go forward," but thought is nonetheless very much concerned with its object. On the other hand, perhaps contextualization would allow for more refined judgment.

> Accordingly one should study all the difficulties both for the purposes stated and because those who inquire without first going over the *difficulties* are like those who are ignorant of where they must go. (995a34-36)

"One should study all the difficulties" "for the proposes stated," that is, because (1) "answers successfully arrived at are solutions to *difficulties* previously discussed," (2) it is *necessary* that "we must first state the problems which should be discussed first," and (3) insofar as thought remains *simply* in difficulties, which is to say, wrapped up in aporias without generating any further determinacies or productive questions, "one cannot go forward" with the inquiry. "One should study *all* the difficulties": does this imperative not resist fulfillment? For how can one study all the difficulties if one is only beginning to inquire and is thus profoundly unaware of what the relevant difficulties are, let alone the proper order of their statement and discussion. If this account of the developments of Beta One is not wholly off target, appealing to Aristotle as an authoritative guide is not sure to resolve the difficulty. Since "those who inquire without first going over the *difficulties*," that is, *all* the difficulties, "are like those who are ignorant of where they must go,"[20] it seems that, if Aristotle's pedagogical practice is anything like what was sketched above, we will remain forever uncertain of the proper topography and trajectory of our investigation, consigned to dwell between ignorance and wisdom. It seems that we will remain liminal beings wondering whether we are being lead toward a specification of the science of wisdom to the highest degree or not. Recall that, as a matter of contingency or structural necessity, we may "overlook" the determination and study of one or more *difficulty* and thus deviate from the proper course, if there is one, from the beginning.

Consequently, the stakes of the question of to what extent we are to allow thought to tarry with any particular aporia are significantly raised. If "one should study all the difficulties" it is unclear whether that requires thought to "first go over the *difficulties*" in a careful although somewhat casual manner or rather "*study* all the difficulties" in a much more sustained engagement. Aristotle's habit in *The Metaphysics* of variously leaving and coming back to the same problem time and again is highly suggestive in this context. It remains quite indeterminate whether thought should be pushed from aproia to aporia in order to attain a synoptic view of *all* the relevant aporias of an inquiry (assuming that one's sense of relevance is absolutely astute from the beginning) or whether refusing to push thought beyond the aporia to which it is currently attuned until one is thoroughly satisfied—given that what seems to be a single aporia may resolve into many—is the only hope for the discernment of all the aporias relevant for the inquiry.[21] And even then, what sense of satisfaction would guarantee that the aporia is fully worked through, if there is such a thing as a thoroughgoing working through of an aporia? The tension is between the need for a survey that lays the ground for study and the need for study which determines the field to be surveyed.

Perhaps, given the seemingly irreducible ambivalences—the aporias—of the mandate to "study all the difficulties," it may be that to "study *all* the difficulties" requires more than one effort, and not just a two-track inquiry by a single inquirer. Perhaps what is required is a differential return to and development of the aporias structuring the inquiry, and perhaps this is connected with the illimitability of the community of the aporia.

> . . . besides, such persons do not even know whether they have found or not what they are seeking, for the end is not clear to them, but it is clear to those who have first gone over the *difficulties*. (995b1-3)

Sure enough, if one has not studied or at least "first gone over" all the aporias, "the end is not clear." But who has "first gone over [all] the *difficulties*" such that the end is clear? Is this to suggest that Aristotle, impelled by a force of necessity emergent from his unqualifiedly successful inquiry into the science of wisdom, has "gone over the *difficulties*" in their entirety, or at least to a sufficient degree? What in the character of his investigative performance would suggest this? If we are not to attribute an uncharacteristically hubristic tenor to Aristotle's intimation of investigative success, it may be best to understand that claim to "have first gone

---

[20] Concerning our status between ignorance and wisdom, compare *Symposium* 201dff.

[21] Aristotle's investigative performance throughout Beta is, to his credit, undecided between these options.

over the *difficulties* such that "the end is . . . clear" as involving not the secure knowledge of the issues which, once known fully, amount to wisdom to the highest degree, but rather involving clarity concerning the incessant task, the interminable, recursive end of the investigation into the science of wisdom. Is the clarity we seek clarity enough to locate that which would constitute the end of our inquiry or is it perhaps the clarity of the self-reflective realization that we cannot "even know whether . . . [we] have found or not what . . . [we] are seeking," that is, clarity concerning the difficulties of our condition? Taking the latter option seriously, it may be that, perhaps surprisingly, a form of self-knowledge is, in part, the end of the inquiry into the science of wisdom. Perhaps for those who have "gone over the difficulties" so as to become as clear as possible about their objects of inquiry, for those who attempt as much as possible to study all of the *difficulties* in the right order, success in arriving at the end names an affirmative appetitive comportment toward the interminability of the investigation. Over against the founding prejudice of those who "do not even know whether they have found or not what they are seeking" precisely as a result of their conviction that they are seeking an exhaustive determination of the aporias structuring the inquiry into the science of wisdom, perhaps "the end" is only clear, to the extent that it can become clear, in its indefinite deferral, which is to say, in its partial, ongoing obscurity. Even if so, is this the only end of the inquiry into the science of wisdom? Isn't the end, or at least an end, the determination of the primary mover to the highest degree? The end, whatever it may be, is, although necessary (or so Aristotle avers), apparently unverifiable: at the limit, a question. Such an end thus appears to be more of a methodological postulation in the service of an ethical and investigative project than the finality of totalized knowledge.

> Further, one who has heard all the arguments, like the one who has heard both parties in a lawsuit or both sides of a dispute, is necessarily in a better position to judge truly. (995b3-4)

"One who has heard *all* the arguments," presumably analogous to the one who has studied and/or "first gone over" all the difficulties, in fact, has not heard the totality of arguments. "One who has heard all the arguments" is rather "like the one who has head both parties in a lawsuit," that is, like one who has heard the sides admissible by the standards of the particular juridical apparatus. "Both parties in a lawsuit" may not be the totality of those involved in the issue at hand; for, to give an example from Aristotle's day, slaves, women, children, and foreigners (except under highly restricted conditions) were not admitted as parties in lawsuits. "One who has heard both parties in a lawsuit" is not "one who has heard all the arguments," but rather all of the arguments admissible. Similarly, "the one who has head both . . . sides of a dispute" may not have "heard all the arguments," for there may be more sides to the issue than are admitted by conventions of conversation (think here of Aristotle's failure to enter into dialogue with women when developing his treatises on sexual difference), and especially disputation. Or there may be some parts of an argument left unspoken for various strategic, ethical, or other reasons. "One who has heard all the arguments" and presumably by analogical extension, one who has studied "all the difficulties," is not one with unimpeachable access to a systematically complete totality but rather one who is acquainted with a contextually relevant whole. Those acquainted with *all* arguments (or aporias) in this sense end up (that is, arrive at a limit) not with methodically guaranteed certainty, not with definitive and final answers, but "in a better position to *judge*," perhaps in a "better position to judge truly."

As should be clear:

> Concerning all these problems, not only is it difficult to arrive at the truth, but it is not even easy to discuss the problems well. (995b4-5)

A COMMENTARY ON THERESA HAK KYUNG CHA'S *DICTÉE*
Michael Stone-Richards

Elle [la certitude] appelle, elle insiste, elle éclate dans chaque phrase qu'on lit. Mais elle reste sans objet. Si, après tout, cette certitude [d'être appellé] n'était rien? Si le plus vif de la mémoire était oubli sans fond? Alors la remémoration ne serait plus tentative d'arracher au temps perdu quelques souvenirs pour les revivre. Elle serait effort pour s'avancer toujours plus loin dans l'oubli.
—Michèle Montrelay, *L'ombre et le nom*, 1977

Comment savoir que ce qui fait retour est bien ce qui avait disparu?
–Jean-Francois Lyotard, *Lectures d'enfance*, 1991

[The feeling of certitude] calls out, it insists, it bursts out in every sentence which one reads. But it remains without object. / If, after all, this certitude [of being called] was nothing? If the keenest part of memory was endless oblivion? Then remembering would no longer be the attempt to pull some recollections from lost time in order to re-live them. It would be the effort to move oneself always further within oblivion.

How may it be known that what makes for a return is indeed that which had disappeared?

PART I[1]

The opening scene, event and sounds: pour quoi aller à la ligne . . .

1

Where does a work begin? The question may appear a simple one. Maybe, even, not the desired formulation, though a certain simplicity may have its value. It has never been a simple question, and even though a certain rhetoric of anti-origins has achieved the status of critical orthodoxy, it is clear, as romantic historiography would show, that the question of origins as formulated, or may be, as approached, by the early romantics, was but the outline of a problem engaging reader, response, writer, culture and historicity where the question of agency would indicate that agency did not reside exclusively in the writer-as-subject.[2] One might even go so far as to say that an understanding of formalism in aesthetic modernity—from Russian formalism and Surrealist automatism to the geology of language prevalent in J.H. Prynne's use of etymology[3]—is one that comprehends the modern artist as one who simultaneously investigates medium, as well as the conditions of articulation within a linguistically mediated historicity, from which would logically flow the problem of origination(s) as the means by which is encountered the related problem, namely, the (im)-possibility of there being a position from which to view the problem of origins.[4] No writing—or art—within an avant-garde or post-avant-garde, modernist or post-modernist mode has escaped this problematic, and it is something that has defined critical responsiveness. An aspect of this problem is the question of the relationship between reception of a work and the reading of a work, and it is this problem which I shall be confronting in a study of the poet, film-maker and artist Theresa Hak Kyung Cha (b. Pusan, Korea, 1951 - d. New York, 1982) whose book *Dictée*

---

[1] The work for this "Commentary" was begun whilst holding a position as visiting professor in English and Comparative Literature in the Department of English at Stonehill College, 2003-2005. I here express my gratitude to the College as also to Professor Barbara Estrin, Chair of the Department of English, for the support given me and my work. This is the first of a set of "Commentaries on Theresa Hak Kyung Cha's *Dictée*," partially to appear in Michael Stone-Richards, *Logics of Separation: Exile and Transcendence in Aesthetic Modernity* (forthcoming, Peter Lang). I am also grateful to the College for Creative Studies in making possible my visit in 2007 to the Cha archives at BAMPFA, University of California, Berkeley.

[2] Cf. Timothy J. Clark, *The Theory of Inspiration: Composition as a Crisis of Subjectivity in Romantic and Post-Romantic Writing* (Manchester: Manchester University Press, 1997); Philippe Lacoue-Labarthe and Jean-Luc Nancy, *L'Absolu littéraire* (Paris: Seuil, 1978).

[3] On the silent use of etymology in Prynne's poetry, "the unemphasized but radical demands it makes upon English etymologies," cf. the early response of Donald Davie in "The Hawk's Eye," *Thomas Hardy and British Poetry* (London: RKP, 1973), 115.

[4] Cf. Lacoue-Labarthe and Nancy, "Le système-sujet," *L'Absolu littéraire*, 39-52, and J.H. Prynne, following Jakobsen and Benveniste in the refusal of the arbitrariness of the sign in favor of a historically conditioned account of signification and reference, *Stars, Tigers and the Shape of Words* (London: Birkbeck College, 1993), and Émile Benveniste, "Nature du signe linguistique (1939)," *Problèmes de linguistique générale* (Paris: Gallimard, 1966), 49-55.

(1982) has continued to receive growing critical attention and a not insignificant aspect of which is centered around the question of the relationship between reception and reading.[5]

Consider, for example, Elaine Kim's opening declaration to the anthology co-edited by her, *Writing Self: Writing Nation*, tellingly titled, "Poised on the In-between: A Korean-American's Reflection on Theresa Hak Kyng's Cha *Dictée*":

> The first time I glanced at *Dictée*, I was put off by the book. I thought that Theresa Cha was talking not to me but rather to someone so remote from myself that I could not recognize "him." The most I could hope for, I thought, was to be permitted to stand beside her while she addressed "him." I was struggling at the time to define and claim a Korean American Identity that could protect me from erasure or further marginalization in my American life. What *Dictée* suggested, with its seemingly incongruous juxtapositions, its references to Greek etymology, and its French grammar exercises, seemed far afield from the identity I was after.[6]

In a later contribution to the same anthology, Shelly Sunn Wong provides a cogent reason as to why *Dictée* may not have been *receivable* in the context of Asian-American writing of the 1980s dominated as such writing was formally by realist autobiographical modes and in terms of gender politics by notions of Asian manhood:

> In this milieu, *Dictée*'s trenchant critique of identity and foundational discourses could hardly have made it a representative work within the
> context of existing Asian American political realities. However, perhaps
> because of its formal density and complexity, a complexity which resisted reductive generalizations of meaning, *Dictée*'s critics never vilified the work but simply set it aside.[7]

But what is this formal density and complexity, and what difference might it make to the understanding of reception to take into account a reading of the formal density and complexity of *Dictée*? Elaine H. Kim's more recent comment on Cha's work does little or nothing to address what it may be in the fabric or difficulty of the work itself that helps to generate or indeed to resist an audience or certain styles of reading, why indeed the framework of her own pioneering work of 1982, *Asian American Literature*, could not possibly have engaged *Dictée* and its distinctive forms of articulation, and consequently the modes of experience which it uncovers as shaping of a self in perpetual motion and exile encountered precisely because of the experience of avant-garde

---

[5] Cf. Elaine H. Kim and Norma Alarcon, eds., *Writing Self, Writing Nation: Essays on Theresa Hak Kyung Cha's Dictée* (Berekeley: Third Woman Press, 1994). Since this commentary was begun there has a appeared a study that looks at the visual dimension in *Dictée* as a critical politics of visibility. Cf. Thy Phu, "Decapitated Forms: Theresa Hak Kyung Cha's Visual Text and the Politics of Visibility," *Mosaic*, vol. 38, no. 1, March 2005. We shall discuss the status and role of the visual in *Dictée* below.

[6] Elaine Kim, "Poised on the In-between: A Korean-American's Reflection on Theresa Hak Kyng's Cha *Dictée*," *Writing Self, Writing Nation*, 3.

[7] Shelly Sunn Wong, "Unnaming the Same: Theresa Hak Kyung Cha's *Dictée*," in *Writing Self, Writing Nation*, 130. It could also be said, of course, that Cha, like say, Nam June Paik, did not figure in any of the networks of Asian-American realist writers or artists.

forms.[8] We are informed by Kim that Cha's "work . . . has been fought over by various parties that wish to claim it for themselves," aligning herself with "the contenders [who] include both Asian Americanists who believe that Cha's identity as a gendered and racialized Korean American[9] is crucial to the understanding of her work," as against "historians of avant-garde art who . . . fear that brainless advocates of 'identity politics' will flatten and reduce her work with their 'disheveled,' 'mawkish,' 'bumper-sticker'-level readings."[10] Who, though, could deny the *question*—which cannot be the fact—of gender in Cha's poetics, or that her own experience of the encounter with Korea—both idea and place—was characterized by hurt, regret, rejection and at times fearsome anger? It remains, though, to be seen whether Cha's poetics of exile, in terms of which difference and "Korea" needs be thought, would have been possible, made available without a certain avant-garde tradition as expressed, for example, by Susan Sontag in the limpid statement: "Most serious thought in our time struggles with the feeling of homelessness,"[11] or by Heidegger in his movement away from philosophy via poetry to thought, for, said Heidegger in the "Letter on Humanism," "Homelessness is coming to be the destiny of the world," and so one must learn to think the "The essence of the homeland [in terms of] the intention of thinking the homelessness of contemporary man."[12] Making *Dictée* legible by ascribing racialized Korean American gender simply begs the question or solves it by fiat. It is becoming increasingly clear that debates around *Dictée* are dominated by the question of reception and how, for some, reception may be conditioned, if not determined, by the rhetorical fabric and phenomenologies of com-position of *Dictée* itself and its work beyond genre, a work beyond—and against—genre issued from the formality inaugurated by early Romanticism and codified by modernism of which figures such as Blanchot, Duras, late Beckett, no less than Barbara Guest or Paul Auster (of "White Spaces") or, currently, Anne Carson and Mei-mei Berssenbrugge may be taken as emblematic.

Whilst it is assuredly—and demonstrably—not correct to say that the first responses to *Dictée* were de-contextualized appropriations, it borders on the anachronistic to say that the so-called neglect of Cha "in

---

[8] Cf. Elaine H. Kim, *Asian American Literature: An Introduction to the Writings and their Social Context* (Philadelphia: Temple University, 1982).

[9] And what would be "unracialized Korean"? And where does the stress fall: on the *unracialized* Korean American or on the unracialized *Korean American*?

[10] Elaine H. Kim, "Interstitial Subjects: Asian American Visual Art as a Site for New Cultural Conversation," in Elaine H. Kim, Margo Machida, and Sharon Mizota, *Fresh Talk, Daring Gazes: Conversations on Asian American Art* (Berkeley: University of California Press, 2003), 47.

[11] Susan Sontag, "The Anthropologist as Hero," *Against Interpretation* (New York: Farrar Straus Giroux, 1966), 69. Consider, too, the title of a major study of the poet of Négritude, Aimé Césaire, by M. a M. Ngal, *Aimé Césaire: un homme à la recherche d'une patrie* (Dakar-Abidjan: Nouvelles Editions Africaines, 1975). The Aimé Césaire who, in an interview with the *Magazine Littéraire*, could say, "Je n'ai pas du tout quitté la Martinique avec regret, j'étais très content de partir. Incontestablement, c'était une joie de secouer la poussière de mes sandales sur cette île où j'avais l'impression d'étouffer. Je ne me plaisais pas dans cette société étroite, mesquine; et, aller en France, c'était pour moi un acte de libération." "Un Poète politique: Aimé Césaire," Propos recueillis par François Beloux, *Magazine littéraire* n° 34 November 1969. This same person who did not quit Martinique with regret would be the poet who returned (*Cahier d'un retour*) in a lifelong quest for the *pays natal*.

[12] Martin Heidegger, "Letter on Humanism" (1947) in *Basic Writings* (Harper: San Francisco, 1993), 243 and 241.

debates concerning innovation in twentieth-century art and cultural politics of race can be explained in part by her opacity, incoherence, and seeming inaccessibility."[13] As the early response to *Dictée* and Cha's experimental film and performance work shows clearly, she was approached as a young emerging practitioner with a place in a community of avant-garde artists from San Francisco. With her move to New York (1980) and appointment as Instructor in video art at Elizabeth Seaton College and part-time work in the Design Department of the Metropolitan Museum (1981), followed in 1982 by a residency at Nova Scotia College of Art and Design, Cha was following a predictable institutional path for the talented, young emerging artist entirely typical of the period. Her association with the Tanam Press founded by Reese Williams gives her membership of a group and community where her work will have an audience, however small—that she, in line with avant-garde inculcation, did not expect otherwise is shown clearly by her letter to her mother written when she was a student in Paris[14]—but even more important where she will be assured a venue for the publication of her work, whence the substantial critical anthology *Apparatus: Cinematographic Apparatus: Selected Writings* (1981) edited by Cha at a time when the use of psychoanalysis by the new film theory had yet to be institutionalized and codified, followed by *Dictée* (1982), and no doubt there would have been others.[15] As it is,

---

[13] Thy Phu, "Decapitated Forms," 19. Cf. Helena Grice, who writes: "After graduating, Cha embarked upon a varied and experimental career as a film-maker and artist, and her work won several prestigious awards, including a Beard's Fund award in 1982. Her auto/biographical text *Dictée* was first published by Tanam Press in 1982, just before she was tragically killed in New York City, on 5 November of that year. Critical recognition of *Dictée* has thus largely occurred posthumously, with a range of articles discussing the text appearing with increasing frequency from 1983 onwards. This critical attention has recently *culminated* in the publication in 1994 of a collection of essays on *Dictée*, entitled *Writing Self, Writing Nation*." Helena Grice, "Korean American National Identity in Theresa Hak Kyung Cha's *Dictée*," in Alison Donnell and Pauline Polkey, eds., *Representing Lives: Women and Auto/biography* (Basingstokes and London: Macmillan Press, 2000), 43 (my emphasis).

[14] Cha writes to her mother from Paris in 1978: "I think I am getting some answers from deep inside. It will be blown out some day. I believe it. It is not only for myself. I like to let other people know that there is the pure, lily-like simplicity and beauty somewhere in the world. Of course, I will get a lot of sufferings and heartache because of the crazy and strange world but I will be satisfied with illuminating my ideas like a clear mirror *to one or two persons*. . . . Anyway if I am good someone will listen to my voice." *In Honor of Theresa Hak Kyung Cha* (1983, my emphasis. Privately published book in the Theresa Hak Kyung Cha Archives, Berkeley).

[15] Consider, for example, Reese Williams' reflections on the commencement and ending of Tanam Press in his "Preface" to *Fire Over Water* (dedicated "In Memory of Theresa Hak Kyung Cha"), the final volume produced by Tanam Press: "I remembered my first impulse to publish which took form as *Hotel* (Tanam Press, 1980). This book, a collection with seven contributors, was not "edited" in the usual sense of the word. Instead of selecting work that I felt merited greater attention, I invited seven people to create new work for *Hotel. It was understood that we would go with whatever they came up with, and that their "being together" would be the book*." Reese Williams, ed., *Fire Over Water* (New York: Tanam Press, 1986), 1 (my emphasis). To date there has been no consideration of the possibility that aspects of Cha's practice of photography in *Dictée* may well have been part of a shared practice with Reese Williams and others published by Tanam Press. To look at the books published by Tanam Press—beginning with Reese Williams' own works—*Figure-Eight: A Fable* (1981) and *A Pair of Eyes* (1983) and including Werner Herzog, *Of Walking on Ice* (1980) and *Screenplays* (1980)—is to see an ethos

we find in Cha's developing oeuvre a certain use of psychoanalysis, with a certain use of semiotics–inflected by Constructivist principles[16]–alongside a pervasive Jungianism entirely characteristic, indeed, definitive of the ethos of Tanam Press, though such a conjunction was also present in the work of Olson and certain of his collaborators such as Robert Duncan.[17] The death of Cha leaves in abeyance how this admixture of Jungianism, Constructivism, Semiotics and Psycho-Analysis could have been sustained given subsequent conceptual developments and alliances in what came to be known as "Theory."[18] It is as well, though, to recall P. Adams Sitney's statement of thesis for his study of Visionary Film:

> I will show in this book how the trance film gradually developed into the architectonic, mythopoeic film, with a corresponding shift from Freudian preoccupations to those of Jung; and then how the decline of the mythological film was attended by the simultaneous rise of both the diary and the structural film.[19]

---

centered upon the innovative use of photographic image and text in relation to film. Where, for example, Cha chooses not to identify any of the photographic sources for *Dictée*, Williams gives a whole page of credits for *A Pair of Eyes* (including a still from Godard's *Pierrot le Fou*), in contrast, no credits or sources are given for *Figure-Eight*.

[16] The same Constructivist principles whose trajectories may be situated relative to Gertrude Stein, International Constructivism, Dziga Vertov–compare, for example, James Cha's photograph of Cha's hands over a typewriter (1979) with stills of the typewriter from *Man with a Movie Camera* (1929)–along with Mallarmé's *Un Coup de dés* and which is practiced in the work of Lynn Hejinian, Marjorie Welish–above all her work as a painter–and the French (at times English?) writer, distinguished curator and Matisse scholar Dominique Fourcade.

[17] Here on might consider the significance of the use of hand of sheet mica from the Hopewell Culture as the cover of *Fire Over Water*, the discussion and (cover) illustration of this hand in Joseph Campbell's *The Way of the Animal Powers* (vol. I, 1983), and the profound significance of the work and iconography of the hand in the *oeuvre* of Cha.

[18] It should not, however, be thought, given the role of Lacan's thought in the development of "Theory" and Film Theory in particular, that there is necessarily incompatibility of Lacanian and Jungian thought on all points. It remains that Jung's questions to Freud on the nature of schizophrenia spurred Freud to think about the language of psychosis in such a way that it is arguable that the distinctive Lacanian conception of the psychoses in terms of paranoia would scarce make sense, and this all the more when it is realized just how much certain of the conceptual categories of Lacan's medical doctoral thesis is indebted to, and emergent from, the reigning Bleulerian nosographies of the later 1920s. Cf. John Forrester, *Language and the Origins of Psychoanalysis* (Basingstoke: Macmillan, 1980), 110-111ff, and cf. the interview with Wladimir Granoff, "Des années de très grand bonheur," *Le Désir d'analyse* (Paris: Aubier, 2004), 138. Jungianism, Freudianism and Lacanianism are on the similar territory precisely where it is a question of the archaic and the psychoses, which is also the terrain of *Dictée* from Demeter, to the illness of the Mother to the incipient madness revealed in the letter to Laura Claxton.

[19] P. Adams Sitney, *Visionary Film: The American Avant-Guarde*, 1943-1978 (Oxford and New York: Oxford University Press, 1979), 31.

In other words, the developments of avant-garde film, both before and after the rise of structural film, was one in which Jungian thought played a key role, one furthermore, as can be seen in the person of Stan Brakhage–and, in poetry, Charles Olson–that was in some respects shared with the development of American advanced painting of which Abstract Expressionism was only the most prominent component.[20] It remains that Cha died at the very moment where it could be reasonably assumed that, with an acknowledged body of work, she could have found an institutional base–if such indeed should have been her wish–with a body of work that could, in the customary way, have elicited response first in the restricted community of small presses and exhibitions before finding–or resisting–larger accreditation. Wendy Hui Kyong Chun is deeply unfair to an early response such as that of Michael Stephens–whose essay "Korea: Theresa Hak Kyung Cha" begins with a chapter entitled "Notes from an abandoned work"–for the terms of Stephens' response (Beckett, Olson, with the necessity of following Cha's movement toward the place of Korea) have in no way been superceded, and only very rarely deepened.[21] Chun is, however, pointing to an important issue about the reciprocal tensions between reception and the rhetoricity of the work–for which the inaugural model for later modernism is assuredly Mallarmé–when she says that though the "readings [of *Writing Self, Writing Nation*] are crucial, I also contend that DICTEE exceeds any project to tether it to Korean and Korean American experiences."[22] Likewise is Anne Cheng, in a probing essay, pointing to something important in her grounding of the récit *Dictée*–she is rare in referring to the work as Cha herself referred to it, namely, as a récit or narrative–when she begins by re-iterating what is already present in Stephens' (1986) essay, namely, that "Cha's 'novel' [the scare quotes are Cheng's] has more in common with poetic experimental writing dating back to the 1970s (Charles Olson, Robert Duncan) than with the majority of ethnic autobiographies flourishing in the 1980's," before commenting that "although, and perhaps precisely because, *Dictée* is not interested in identities, it is profoundly interested in the processes of *identification*."[23]

2

---

[20] On the use of Jungian terms of reference in American art of this period, cf. Michael Leja, *Reframing Abstract Expressionism: Subjectivity and Painting in the 1940s* (New Haven and London: Yale University Press, 1993), and also Daniel Belgrad, *The Culture of Spontaneity: Improvisation and the Arts in Postwar America* (Chicago: University of Chicago of Press, 1998).

[21] Cf. Michael Stephens, "Korea: Theresa Hak Kyung Cha: Notes from an abandoned work," *The Dramaturgy of Style: Voice in Short Fiction* (Carbondale and Edwardsville: Southern Illinois University Press, 1986).

[22] Wendy Hui Kyong Chun, "The Limits of Thinking Theory: Responding to the Theory/Practice Debate in Asian American Studies" (paper presented at the University of North Carolina, 1999), 14, <http://www.brown.edu/Departments/MCM/people/chun/papers/limits.PDF>.

[23] Anne Cheng, "History in/against the fragment: Theresa Hak Kyung Cha," *The Melancholy of Race* (Oxford: Oxford University Press, 2000), 140 and 141. Here might be the place to make a simple observation on the forms "DICTEE" and "Dictée": in French orthography, as Cha knew, the "é" requires no (acute) accent when capitalized and so I shall follow the practice of Cheng in writing "Dictée." That the capitalization DICTEE might be significant for its use of sans serif as a mark of a certain modernism would require further development, but it may also point out the use of capitals to suggest the title and movement of a film.

"Experience / whose line doth sound the depth of things"

There could be no better way, I would suggest, of beginning to respond to the question of density and complexity and the effects which flow therefrom than to confront the opening event of language in this work as it gives onto an opening scene, itself given over to another event where language and action resist each other in what I shall argue is part-and-parcel of a sustained thinking of logics of separation and the experience of resistance. As one turns the cover of the book of *Dictée*, the first leaf–call it the frontispiece–shows, not a photograph, but a *photocopy* (Fig. 1), that is, an image of diminished light which is a photomechanical copy in relation to a prior image.[24] Given the prevalence of this practice of image-making in the work of Cha (for example, *Chronology*, 1977) and her contemporaries, it can be inferred from the image-quality

Fig. 1: Theresa Hak Kyung Cha, Frontispiece, *Dictée*, 1982

and *texture* that it is the result of several copies of copies.[25] There is no doubt that any one literate in Korean (or even only familiar with the Korean alphabet Hangul) would readily recognize the writing presented in this

---

[24] Theresa Hak Kyung Cha, *Dictée* (New York: Tanam Press, 1982). All subsequent references to *Dictée* will appear in text as D followed by page number.

[25] This aspect of the image of the frontispiece as photocopy has not always been appreciated even as it has been felt. For example, "Theresa Hak Kyung Cha's *Dictée* begins with a blurred photograph," says Elisabeth A.

image as Korean, and not unlikely that any one literate in contemporary Korean history, which is to say, Korean history from the period of the Japanese colonial occupation of Korea, would recognize this image without necessarily being able to read the text, which is also to say that the image functions symbolically, not unlike the manner in which a Latin tag functions. Not unlike, but not exactly the same. The question, then, would not be first to do with decipherment, but rather that concerning the function of the image, or, in other words,

---

Frost, "'In Another Tongue': Body, Image, Text in Theresa Hak Kyung Cha's *Dictée*," in Laura Hinton and Cynthia Hougue, eds., *We Who Love to Be Astonished: Experimental Women's Writing and Performance Poets* ((Tuscaloosa and London: The University of Alabama Press, 2002), 181, whilst another, earlier commentator, Eun Kyung Min, will observe that "The frontispiece to *Dictée* consists of a grainy reproduction of writing in Korean script" (Eun Kyung Min, "Reading the Figure of Dictation on Theresa Hak Kyung Cha's *Dictée*," 313) and Juliana Spahr will note this "single, originary photograph (which looks badly photocopied and several generations from the original)," commenting upon "its blotchiness and obvious distance from the original [which] suggests an impure product, an image that is several removes even from Cha" ("Teretium Quid Neither One Thing Nor the Other," 150).

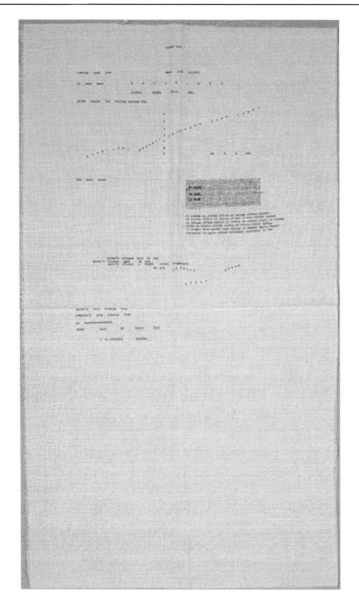

Fig. 2 Theresa Hak Kyung Cha, *Tongue Tied*, 1976. Typewritten text on white cloth, 26 X 15. Collection Berkeley Art Museum

its depiction, and in this respect the quality of the depicted image most pertinent to the argument to be developed in this essay is its texture or the working and wearing away of surface: it is faded, appears rubbed down, worn in such a way as to minimize the perceptible and articulable difference between "writing" and support, between lighter and darker, in such a way, in short, as to make the document presented appear, on the one hand, faded, but also, on the other hand, fragile, indeed, papyrus-like, as though an archeological document, suggestive of the very texture of memory fading to the archaic. But the archaic of what? After title page and copyright declaration, comes a dedication (a declaration of filial piety) "To my mother and father," then a blank, white page followed, on an unnumbered page, by the invocation as epigraph, attributed to Sappho:

> May I write words more naked than flesh,
> stronger than bone, more resilient than
> sinew, sensitive than nerve

Another blank page (all white), followed on the right by two columns *in parallel*: on the left column, the names of the muses (with a variant muse "Elitere"—in French, "Eutere" is a variant of "Euterpe") and their corresponding domains, terrains of privilege: Clio/History, Calliope/Epic Poetry, Elitere/Lyric Poetry, etc., Blank, and then, page 1—there is no use of roman numerals for numbered pages—the opening event:

> Aller à la ligne   C'était le premier jour   point
> Elle venait de loin   point   ce soir au dîner   virgule
> les familles demanderaient   virgule   ouvre les guil-
> lemets   Ca c'est bien passé le premier jour   point
> d'interrogation   ferme les guillemets   au moins
> virgule   dire le moins possible   virgule   la reponse
> serait   virgule   ouvre les guillemets   Il n'y a q'une
> chose   point ferme les guillemets   ouvre les guille-
> met   Il y a quelqu'une   point   loin   point   ferme
> les guillemets

> Open paragraph   It was the first day   period
> She had come from a far   period   tonight at dinner
> comma   the families would ask   comma   open
> quotation marks   How was the first day   interroga-
> tion mark   close quotation marks   at least to say
> the least of its possible   comma   the answer would be
> open quotation marks   there is but one thing   period
> There is someone   period   From   a far   period
> close quotation marks

Between the tercet opening "May I write words more naked than flesh" and "Aller à la ligne" with its accompanying English parallel—the issue of precedent order or no will remain open—is a world of difference, a difference in no small part embodied in and articulated through rhythm and breath: the vocalic ease of the epigraphic verse

> May I write words more naked than flesh,

> stronger than bone, more resilient than
> sinew, sensitive than nerve

paves the way for the encounter with a multiply-domained phenomenology of resistance: the absence of rhythmic ease, the presence of saccadic breath, along with syntactic and visual dissonances brought about, we shall begin to apprehend, by the layout of linguistic use and mention as though the one might be continuous with another, without that is, any marker of hierarchy, and all in such a way as to emphasize, foreground and to dramatize the materiality and physicality of language. In his discourse on "Différance" pronounced in the halls of the Société française de philosophie in 1968, Jacques Derrida had tried to habituate his audience to the silent and necessarily unpronounceable *a* of *différance* by citing the examples of diacritical or phonetic marks which, though necessary for the functioning of language, cannot themselves be pronounced, which are necessarily inaudible, silent. Indeed, Derrida pointed out, the kind of non-phonetic markings which he has in mind such as punctuation or spacing can scarcely be considered signs properly so-called.[26] *Dictée*'s opening onto *Aller à la ligne / Open paragraph*, makes the material infrastructure of diacritical markings (*point, virgule / period, comma*) audible but in such a way that the diacritical markings are themselves without such markings as would enable the hearer readily to discern phonological hierarchy the effect of which, the first principle of Cha's poetics, is to make *mention* continuous with *use* in a scene of utmost complexity and richness. The scene, the opening event of language, which may be construed as a figuration of a primal scene of language acquisition, is not singular but multiple and constitutes at the same time, possibly, the second instantiation of what the title "Dictée" might encompass—blurring the line between use and mention—firstly, the invocation to the muse, in this case, by indirection to Sappho, the tenth Muse, where what the poet writes is dictated by the Muse; then, too, "Dictée" may refer to the act of learning by dictation. The framework of utterance, of enunciation, then, is at the level of an imaginary, and the site of transmission of knowledge.[27]

What is presented in this opening scene, this opening tableau? The emergent scene is that of a person (which may be, but by no means exclusively, figured as a foreign exchange student) in a foreign land, in the evening at dinner with a host family anchored in a French-language landscape who begin to put questions to the visitor (she who *venait de loin / had come from afar*) about her/*the first day*, since the absence of phonological hierarchy results in the effect of *she* being enclosed, wrapped in the day. There is no suggestion within the depicted scene of fluency on the part of the visitor who responds to the *questioning*, and the difficulties and resistances of utterance are doubled, shadowed in the foregrounding of orthography in that way in which when one is learning a language one can become acutely aware of its physicality and individuality as one makes each utterance an intended, explicit, and projected effort before speech, in other words, as though one thinks about and translates from one's native language into the foreign tongue before utterance, the effect of which is always to slow down utterance, to make sentences thereby devoid of rhythm, in short clumsy, and as a result to feel the physicality of language as obstacle through clumsiness of speech, hence to the question posed "au moins / virgule dire le moins possible," the hesitancies and doubts of which are shadowed in the *effort* of "at least to say" and "the least of it possible." Just as use and mention are subject to cultural as well as

---

[26] Cf. Jacques Derrida, "Différance," *Marges de la philosophie* (Paris: Seuil, 1972), 5.

[27] In every class in which I have taught *Dictée*, students, in order to come to terms with, to make more tractable, this opening text, have re-written the passage without the mention of orthographical terms as injunctions, thereby shifting the visual arrhythmia of utterance and image to a presentation scene.

linguistic conventions—for instance, intonation alone may suffice in certain contexts to mark mention rather than use—reading on the page is no less conventionalized: English and French, by convention, require reading from left to write, top to bottom. The presentation of "Aller à la ligne" *followed* by "Open paragraph," encourages the idea—that is, encourages by convention—that *Open paragraph* is a translation of what precedes it, namely, the passage beginning *Aller à la ligne*. Had the page begun with *Open paragraph*, then a conventionalized reading would instead have encouraged one to believe rather that *Aller à la ligne* is a translation of what preceded, namely, *Open paragraph*. Note, though, that from the first there is richness, complexity and much that makes it difficult to sustain the English as an evident translation of the French, for "Aller" is an infinitive which homonymically is the imperative "Allez": "to go to the line" is not "Go to the line!" "Open paragraph" may sound contextually legitimate, but it is this contextualism that gives the idea of a separate subsequent translation by eschewing, putting aside the literalism of the terms present, a literalism that is essential to Cha's poetics. In view of the fact, too, that there are many passages elsewhere in *Dictée* where the English is composed within the shadow of French syntax—and vice versa—it is by no means obvious that *Open paragraph* is simply a translation of a prior French passage, i.e., that it comes second, and not, in other words, to be taken holistically, harmonically, one might say, together with *Aller à la ligne* as though once read the reader should then grasp the two passages, in English and French, as two simultaneous scenes unfolding in parallel if not side by side (left to right) then as though on a screen split horizontally (top and bottom) as though watching a foreign film with sub-titles or in which the French and English would precisely be *not* subtitles but *as* they are; rather, the passages are in parallel because in parallel temporalities yet linked at a point of common perception, as though the page could be folded to show the two passages as near mirror images one of the other without knowing which image is the reflection of which substance. The mark of this possibility, to which we shall return below, is the use of literalism as a technique in Cha's poetics: it is intended to be "Aller à la ligne": both "to go to the line" and "Go to the line!" which literally is not "open paragraph."

    The opening event and scene is a primitive scene in that the reception of a stranger (from a far) is a mytheme, above all when the stranger is met at evening's fall— "at the end of a day's reaches"[28]—and thus at the phenomenological threshold of day and night.[29] This opening is also primitive in that it dramatizes language in a place of emergence where time is not wholly present, and hence when translation not yet fully

---

[28] This verse is from Robert Duncan's "Tribal Memories   Passages 1," which opens:

    And to Her-Without-Bounds I send,
      wherever She wanders,   by what
          campfire at evening,

    among tribes setting each the City where
        we Her people are
    at the end of a day's reaches

(Robert Duncan, *Selected Poems* [New York: New Directions, 1993], 78).

[29] Given the prevalence of filmic techniques and issues in film theory in *Dictée*, we might here speak not only of the phenomenological threshold of day and night but equally, that is to say, at the same time, of light and darkness, that is, the conditions of entering or leaving a movie theatre.

operative: "Il y a quelqu'une   point   loin / There is someone   period   From   a far   period"; it is, finally, but by no means least, a primitive scene because in poetically blurring the distinction between use and mention—re-writing this passage to make graphic the orthography is but an escape, as it were—not only is the materiality and physicality of language made a substance and subject of language, but, crucially, language use is made subject to a *threshold experience* the exploration of which will result in a distinct spatiality and anachrony of time—the emergence of a *passé anachronique*—as can be seen in the pages following "Aller à la ligne," after, that is, a blank on page four, titled "Diseuse," for the blank white page following "Aller à la ligne" marks a transition of register, a distance crossed, but it also carries expressive value, that of a pause, a calm between two different forms of complex deployments of breath and syncopated breathing as the line (*ligne*), marker and holder for threshold and transitional placement, moves experience, the experience of the reader-viewer-audience, to allude to Jonson's *Under-Woods*, "whose line doth sound the depth of things." For the movement of line is at once punctually horizontal—upon and across the white surface of the page—and vertical, as the image upon a screen where the apparatus, the materiality supporting the cinematic situation, is laid bare in precisely the manner in which the materiality of language has been laid bare through the phonologically non-hierarchical deployment of use and mention. The event of language is carried through and by the material equivalence of the page to the screen in the approach to the line—*Aller à la ligne*—and the scene of the paragraph opened, that is, an event in the beyond (*para*) of writing (*graph*) is announced, whence, beginning from the event of language, the encounter with resistance and difficulty as embodied in the fractured and fracturing forms of the "Diseuse," a figure, as we shall come to see, which embodies the forms of fortune teller (Diseuse de bonne aventure), shaman (Mudang), and récitante (Sprechstimme).

3

One way in which *Dictée*'s exploitation of a materiality of equivalence between screen and page can be appreciated is by considering aspects of the sixth division of *Dictée* titled "Erato   Love Poetry" which will enable us to return to an understanding of the function of the photocopied image used as frontispiece for the work. The parallelisms of which we have been speaking—night and day, light and darkness, spatial parallels, etc.—are immediately presented on pages 94 and 95 which must be apprehended simultaneously and not in sequence: the left page containing 24 lines beginning "She is entering now" juxtaposed with the right page of five lines interspersed with paragraphs of white beginning "Columns. White. Stone." The simultaneity of presentation and apperception is then underscored by imagery within the page, that is, the columns which are both vertical (hence top to bottom of the page) and horizontal (there is more than one, and hence an implied rhythm). The reading is not left to right, that is, from page 94 to page 95: either it is simultaneous—it could also be at the same time the script of a scenario—or, the materiality of the hand and the page is thematized as the sequence of reading moves to alternate paging thereby making one aware of the hand turning the page simultaneously with the eye searching for a point of continuation. So, for example, page 97 which is blank until three lines which *fall* at the bottom of the page, ends "With the hand placed across on the other's lips, moving, form- " which then continues at the top of page 99: "ing the words." The top half of page 99 is a paragraph of lines, followed by a paragraph of blank, whilst page 98, to which the technique of reading that the text imposes returns us, opens on a paragraph of blank followed by two paragraphs of lines in the latter half of the page, in other words, an inverse mirror image. This particular mode of patterning continues for much of "Erato

Love Poetry" with variations on the patterning, and variations of implied acts of mimetic accompanying. The connotations which mark out the possibilities of mimetic doubling are many: the use of white in the punctuation of the page as marking the implied imagery of white columns, for example, or large vertical white pages with few lines of text at the bottom as marking the *fall* of the verticality of white columns; throughout *Dictée* is strewn imagery of surfaces, kinds of surfaces, "Stone. Abrasive and worn" (D 95), "Fine grain sanded velvet wood and between the frames the pale sheet of paper" (D 131), and words too can be a surface hence like columns can be weathered, whence, "Words cast each by each to weather" (D 177), and the white page can stand in for and accompany, even enact the apperception of such surfaces, resistant, as with stone, or instead as a medium of suspension, where someone may be "suspended, in a white mist, in white layers of memory. In layers of forgetting, increasing the density of mist, the opaque light fading to absence, the object of memory" (D 108); or it is a white cloth, "Whitest of beige" (D 113). It is, too, a membrane, whence "Contents housed in membranes" (64). Above all, however, is the white page a screen—"Whiteness of the screen" (D 95)—in relation to which the play of black and white is materially equivalent to the play of black ink on white page, the support on to which a medium (ink, light, blood) may spill: From the opening of "Urania Astronomy," for example, "Contents housed in membranes. Stain from within dispel in drops in spills. . . . *Stain begins to absorb the material spilled*" (D 64 and D 65).

For much of "Erato Love Poetry" there is a very careful play upon devices of framing as means of staging the question of transition and threshold and liminal experience (or suspension). Nominally, the transition is between what is outside and what is inside a film, who—or what—is viewing and who—or what—is being viewed, then, between entering a movie theatre and entering a filmic space. The parallelism of these *situations* is carried through syntactical parallelism. The division opens:

> She is entering now. Between the two
> white columns. White and stone.
> Abrasive. Worn.
>
> The doors close behind her.   She
> purchases the ticket, a blue one. She
> stands on line, and waits. Etc

> Columns. White. Stone. Abrasive and
> worn. touch [etc.].

Once entered, there is a startling moment which figures the moment of transition, spatially, temporally, phenomenologically and, crucially, topographically:

> [she] climbs three steps into the room. The whiteness of the screen takes her back wards almost half a step.

The slight spacing between "back" and "ward" should not go unnoticed, is not a fault of typography—in the right column we have "Takes her backwards"—since this marks a journey, a moment of haltingness, a psychic movement hinted at in the near implicit slant rime of *half a step* with *half asleep*, as the mark of a zone of transition that is phenomenological and now topographical in the Freudian sense of this term, for the hinted near rime of "back [pause] ward almost half a step [to half asleep]" articulated the transition with which Cha's generation of film theorists influenced by Roland Barthes were deeply preoccupied, namely: is the entering into the space of the cinematic experience—or, the space projected through the cinematic apparatus—a regressive experience, a regression from the Symbolic to the Imaginary? Or is it indeed the source of, the transition to, a distinctive pleasure of the Imaginary? That this is the domain of questioning and experience pertinent to this division of *Dictée* is re-inforced in the continuation of the narrative through the crossing of threshold without markers of distinction:

She enters the screen from the left, before the titles fading in and fading out.

Whiteness of the screen. Takes her backwards.

Later we will learn, tracking the movement of a character on-screen, "Then you, as viewer and guest, enter the house," (D 98) thereby foregrounding the issue of cinematic identification made possible through the entering, fading in and fading out. The *fading in and fading out* is the mark of a phenomenological experience, potentially a topographical stage (of reversion, regression to the Imaginary), but also the marker of a discourse: of the status of black-and-white-film, and of the status of cinematic experience. Hence of the title of his essay contribution to *Apparatus*, "Blinking, Flickering and Flashing in the Black-and-White Film," Marc Vernet comments;

> "Black-and-white" is hyphenated because it is not so much a question of their opposition as it is of their conjunction – their fusion, one in the other at the same time.
>
> "Blinking, Flickering, and Flashing," thinking first of Gaston Bachelard, of his work entitled *La flamme d'une chandelle*.[30]

If the allusion to Bachelard may be construed as a marker for the register of the imaginary—not necessarily to be taken in the same sense as Lacan's *Imaginaire*—then the fusion of the black-and-white in film, and behind it, the implicit reference to the scenes of blinking eyes intercut with shutter blinds from Vertov's *Man with a Movie Camera* (1929),[31] serve to situate the problematic of the imaginary with the symbolic which for *Dictée* is worked through a consistent parallelism of screen and page, whence the attention to the formality, the grain of light and dark, black and white where word and filmic image meet, after *she* has

> [entered] the screen from the left, before the titles fading in and fading out. The white subtitles on the background continue across the bottom of the screen. The titles and names in black appear from the upper right hand corner, each letter moving downwards on to the whiteness of the screen. She is drawn to the white, then to the black. In whiteness the shadows move across, dark shapes and dark light. (D 94)

---

[30] Marc Vernet, *Apparatus*, 357.

[31] The passage from Henry James contains the following variations on the metaphorics of shades, reflections, pulse and half lights: "At the end of two flights he had dropped to another zone, and from the middle of the third, with only one more left, he recognised the influence of the lower windows, of half-drawn blinds, of the occasional gleam of street-lamps, of the glazed spaces of the vestibule" (James, cited in Cha, *Apparatus*, 411).

What is here presaged, in an almost glorified myopia of insight, is the near dissolution of word into texture, light and shade: dark shapes and dark light, itself articulating the (irresistible?) temptation: *She is drawn to the white, then the black*, leading to a situation where "In the whiteness the shadows move across, dark shapes and dark light," that is, a situation of primal, maybe even foundational indistinction and indifferentiation. *She is drawn to the white, then the black*. In Barthes' essay "Upon Leaving the Movie Theater," which forms the programmatic introduction to Cha's *Apparatus*, the question is posed:

> A filmic image (sound included), what is it? A lure [*leurre*]. This word must be taken in its psychoanalytic sense. I am locked in on the image as though I were caught in the famous dual relationship which establishes the imaginary. The image is there before me, for my benefit: coalescent (signifier and signified perfectly blended), analogical, global, pregnant. It is a perfect lure [*leurre* is also *bait*]. I pounce upon it as an animal snatches up a "lifelike" rag.[32]

That there is an older, definitive form of this question was something clear to the film theorists of Cha's generation. There are, in effect, not one but two contributions that Cha makes to her edited anthology *Apparatus*: first, the conceptual constructivist work "Commentaire" which has received acknowledgement,[33] but also another work—which I do not believe has been recognized as such—dispersed in sections throughout the anthology consisting of quotations. Instead of writing introductions to each work or section of the anthology, Cha, as editor, interposes, like found objects, black pages on which are written in white, quotations. Using only the information provided in Cha's texts, in order, they are quotations from Plato, *The Republic*, vii, 514, trans. by Francis M. Cornford (*Apparatus* 23), Diderot (*Apparatus* 39), Balzac (*Apparatus* 65), Apollinaire, "Le Roi Lune" (1902-1908) (*Apparatus* 371), and Henry James, (*Apparatus* 411).[34] In other words, it is not incidental that alone of all the passages Plato's *Republic* with the passage from Apollinaire's "The Moon King" are named, even as the quoted passage from *The Republic* would have been readily recognized as the ur-text on the "Allegory of the Cave":

> Next, said I, here is a parable to illustrate the degrees in which our nature may be enlightened or unenlightened. Imagine the condition of men living in a sort of cavernous chamber underground, with an entrance open to the light and a long passage all down the cave. Here they have been from childhood . . .[35]

From Plato's "Allegory of the Cave," all the subsequent quotations—from Diderot, Balzac, Apollinaire, and James—are concerned with illusionism, specters, ghosts, shadows and, if not imprisonment, then with constraint, in other words, with the whole panoply of ontological fictions which extend, or stretch, existential commitment beyond substance, and further with how, and in what support, something is projected the source of which may not be known but which may yet be recorded. In the case of the passage form Balzac this leads

---

[32] Roland Barthes, "On Leaving the Movie Theater" (1975), in *Apparatus*, 3.

[33] Cf. John Cho, "Tracing the Vampire," *Hitting Critical Mass: A Journal of Asian American Cultural Criticism* 3 (1996), 87-113.

[34] The Cha archives, though, provides a file with the sources of the quotations.

[35] Plato, *The Republic*, as cited in Cha, *Apparatus*, 23.

to the view that the future is no more difficult to know than the past, which, in the terms being developed here, is to say that the conditions of film lead to or presuppose an anachrony of the syntax of time, a capacity identified with the seer by Balzac, with the Diseuse by Cha:

> That certain beings should have the power of foreseeing events in the germ of causes, just as the great inventor perceives an art of science in some natural phenomenon unobserved by the ordinary mind [let us note that for Vertov this particular capacity of perception will be a mark of the superiority of the cinematic eye, MSR], this is not one of those violent exceptions to the order of things which excite unthinking clamor; it is simply the working of a recognized faculty, and of one which is in some measure the *somnambulism of the spirit*. . . . Observe also that to predict the great events of the future is not, for the seer, any greater exhibition of power than that of revealing the secrets of the past.[36]

Above all, these passages are concerned with the uncanny as a condition not merely of film, but with filmic temporality as a mark of threshold experience, itself an experience for which there is no clear marker—no clear and distinct idea—to disambiguate illusion from reality, whence the passage from James, describing the terms of an encounter, the terms of which, as with the "Allegory of the Cave," recall "the marble squares of [one's] childhood"—which are surely also the squares and piazzas of de Chirico—in which the protagonist finds himself confronted with someone, or something, "Rigid and conscious, spectral yet human, a man of his own substance and stature."[37] Everywhere in these quotations the presence of the uncanny, which is to say, filmic effect, is linked to the imaginary and the possibility of illusionism—hence the significance of Apollinaire's title "Le Roi Lune : the Moon King," which now returns us to what Barthes characterized as the pre-hypnotic condition of the cinematic condition:

> There exists a "cinematic condition": and this condition is prehypnotic. Like a metonymy become real, the darkness of the theater is foreshadowed by a "crepuscular reverie," (preliminary to hypnosis, according to Freud and Breuer) which precedes this darkness and draws the subject, from street to street, from poster to poster, to abandon himself into an anonymous, indifferent cube of darkness where the festival of affects [fêtes d'affects] which is called a film will take place.[38]

The implicit identification made by Barthes, and through him subsequent film theorists such as Jean-Louis Baudry, between the analytic situation and the cinematic apparatus or situation is such as to say that the movement of affect that is known as the transference is wholly a function of the cinematic situation itself. Thus just as the love produced in transference is a false love produced by the very framework of the analytic situation itself, likewise the transference produced in film experience is wholly a by-product of the cinematic situation, and hence the interpretation of the transference required in analysis must find its equivalent in the

---

[36] Balzac as cited in Cha, *Apparatus*, 65. My emphasis.
[37] Henry James, as cited in Cha, *Apparatus*, 412.
[38] Barthes, in *Apparatus*, 1.

cultural work of the critical interpretation of the condition of film, of the cinematic apparatus.[39] The whole project of film theory since the 1970s is encapsulated in these few lines from Barthes:

> How does one pry oneself from a mirror? Let me risk a response that will be a play on words: it is by "taking off" (in the aeronautic and the hallucinogenic sense of the term). It is true that it is possible to conceive of an art that would break the circle of duality (dual circularity), filmic fascination, and would loosen the glue's grip, the hypnosis of verisimilitude (of analogy) by resorting to some (aural or visual) critical faculty of the spectator–isn't that what is involved in the Brechtian effect of distancing? There are many things that could facilitate the awakening from hypnosis (imaginary/ideological); the very technique of epic art, the spectator's culture, or his ideological vigilance; unlike classical hysteria, the imaginary disappears the moment it is observed.[40]

That *Dictée* is engaging in these conceptual and aesthetic issues is not in doubt, rather it is how it engages them, how, in other words, it works, brings it off, to allude to Barthes, once more. First, let it be noticed that *Dictée*, following Barthes's "Upon leaving the Movie Theater," implicitly distinguishes between *object* and *situation* in the organization of the filmic space. Comparing televisual and cinematic space, the first difference, says, Barthes, is the absence of darkness when watching television. "Consider, on the other hand, the opposite experience, the experience of TV . . . : nothing, no fascination; the darkness is dissolved, the anonymity repressed, the space is familiar, organized (by furniture and familiar objects), tamed."[41] We have previously observed the manner in which certain pages in "Erato   Love Poetry" not only imply but necessitate a parallel apprehension, as also the manner in which the text moves in sequence from, say, 98 to 100, from 97 to 99. We are now better placed to understand the significance of this formal structuring, to understand, in other words, what is being articulated through this structuring movement, above all as this relates to our argument that in *Dictée*, from its inception, its opening scene, there is implicitly deployed a conception of the material equivalence of screen and page. What we are now in a position to appreciate is that the alternation of page sequence is the way in which *Dictée* conveys autonomy of voice, that is, sound, from image, that is, what is projected onto the screen, without it always being utterly clear which is which, which is also to say that the exploitation of a relative autonomy of voice from image goes hand-in-hand with the interruption of the diegesis.[42] (Here it can be said that Cha's poetics deploy the avant-garde experiments with sound as an independent phenomenon to be found variously in the films of Guy Debord (Fig.3), Lettrisme, Marguerite Duras, Alain Resnais all the way back to Russian experiments in asynchronism as a principle of sound film). So we see an argument developed, say, from 98 to 100 which functions as a commentary:

---

[39] Cf. Sigmund Freud, "Further Recommendations in the Technique of Psycho-Analysis. Observations on Transference-Love (1915)," *Collected Papers*, vol. II, ed. Joan Riviere (London: Leonard and Virginia Woolf at the Hogarth Press and the Institute of Psycho-Analysis, 1924), 387.

[40] Barthes, in *Apparatus*, 4.

[41] Barthes, in *Apparatus*, 2.

[42] So, much of "Erato   Love Poetry" consists of large passages taken from Sainte Thérèse of Liseux's *The Story of a Soul*, with cinematic directions, with passages of description drawn from Dreyer's *Gertrude*.

> One expects her to be beautiful. The title which carries her name is not one that would make her anonymous or plain.

This commentary (whether as voice-over soundtrack, or as internal voice) continues:

> Then you, as a viewer and guest, enter the house. It is you who are entering to see her,

at which point we recover Barthes' distinction between object and situation—and here attention should shift to the stripping away of objects:

> Her portrait is seen through her things, that are hers. The arrangement of her house is spare, delicate, subtly accentuating, [turn leaf to page 100] rather, the space, not the objects that fill the space.

Simultaneously, pages 95, 97, 101 *see* the unfolding of a projected story the terms of which will return the reader of *Dictée* to its beginnings: rhetorically in the non-hierarchical deployment of use and mention in *Aller à la ligne / Open paragraph*; phenomenologically in the experiences portrayed under the inaugurating figure of the Diseuse, namely, the *pain* to speak, but above all in the frontispiece. For if pages 94, 96, 98, 100 of "Erato Love Poetry" convey a commentary, then pages 95, 97, 101 convey *in the same time* the projected story of:

> Mouth moving. Incessant. Precise. Forms the words heard. Moves from the mouth to the ear. With the hand placed across on the other's lips moving, form- [turn leaf from page 97 to page 99] ing the words. She forms the words with her mouth as the other utter across from her.

Which, as we shall see below, recapitulates and extends the inaugural experience of the "Diseuse" (D 3-5) in which is portrayed "She [who] mimicks the speaking . . . [whose] lower lip would lift upwards then sink back to its original place" (D 3). This synchrony of page and screen—what *Dictée* names as "the other overlapping time" (D 99)—would thus be to make of "Erato   Love Poetry"– and much else in *Dictée*–a double channel work of sound and image, which then allows one *to hear* that commentary spoken as, indeed, a form of *dictation*–and *commentaire* (see fig. 3. Guy Debord, scenario from *Critique de la séparation*, 1961).[43]

---

[43] This relating of "Diseuse" and "Erato   Love Poetry" is a structural feature of the poetics of *Dictée*, the *the other overlapping time* being an example of atonal (eternal) structure in which comparable events and actions are repeated as variations of a given form or structure, or repeated–resurrected–as a means of difference-in-sameness. Another example of this atonal variation is the treatment of movement, blood and sound in "Melpomene   Tragedy" (82) and "Terpsichore   Choral Dance" (162).

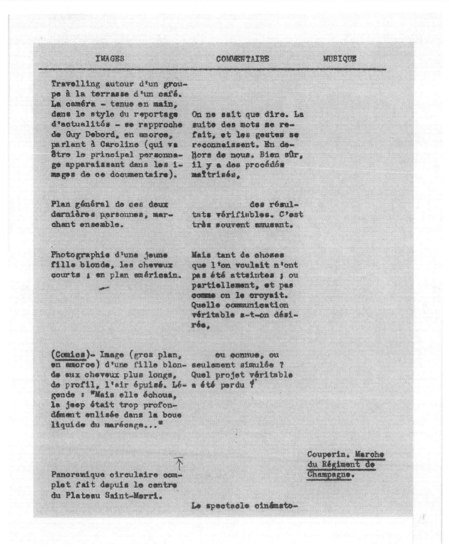

Fig. 3: Guy Debord, scenario from *Critique de la séparation*, 1961

The separation, however, between commentary and story, is not straightforward—is, indeed, partly fictional—for we see (or glimpse) and hear (or catch) on both sides of the screen/page, within both channels, as it were, "Drawn to the white, then the black . . . dark shapes and dark light" (D 95 and D 94), all the more so when such "dark shapes and dark light" are apprehended as also acoustic shapes and light, which is to say in terms of timbre (of the voice or sound emanating from some other source).[44] Consistent with the separation of sound and image in the tradition of advanced film important to Cha—pre-eminently Duras and Resnais' *Hiroshima mon*

---

[44] One of the early intertitles of Dreyer's *Vampyr* reads: "In the moonstruck night light and shadow, voices and faces, seemed to take on meanings" (Carl Theodore Dreyer, *Vampyr* [1932]).

amour (1959)—there is also a separation in "Erato   Love Poetry" not only of sound and image but of diegesis: the two narratives—or scenarios—in parallel throughout this division are figured in a telling way: the opening photograph on page 93 is a photograph—as some have correctly seen—of St Thérèse of Lisieux, but what has not been understood is its function, namely, that it is a photograph of St Thérèse of Lisieux as Joan of Arc (1894) (with flag and sword) in the performance of a play she wrote for her sister.[45] "Erato   Love Poetry" closes with a still photograph of Maria Falconetti as Joan of Arc in Dryer's *La Passion de Jeanne d'Arc* (1928) which serves to underline the fictionality and artifice in construction of *Dictée*, but no less the rich projective possibilities of the interplay of complex temporality and performative masks which refers always to the mediumicity of the apparatus and the practice of what may be characterized as a phenomenology of saturated description.[46]

The technique, the form, the problematic of *Dictée* are, it may now be appreciated, announced, declared from the near opening of the work in its epigraph attributed to Sappho:

May I write words more naked than flesh,
stronger than bone, more resilient than
sinew, sensitive than nerve

What is here presented may be understood as the infrastructure of the body: flesh, bone, sinew, nerve; just as "Urania   Astronomy" provides the reader with a plate (D 74) showing the infrastructure of breathing: nasal

---

[45] On this photograph, cf. Megan Sexton's poem, "A Photo of St. Thérèse of Lisieux dressed as Joan of Arc, 1894," *The Southern Review*, Winter 1998; and for another photograph from the play showing St. Thérèse as Joan in chains against the same wall as that shown in *Dictée*, 93, cf. <http://www.sttherese.com/St%20Therese%20Calendar%202007.pdf>.

[46] The text, and strategies, of "Erato   Love Poetry" are much richer, more complex, even, than my presentation and analysis would suggest. Throughout this study, there is mention of Dreyer and Huillet and Straub. The work to be done on Cha's poetics would require much deeper research into her understanding of Dreyer, Huillett and Straub, each of whom has produced a new conception of realism in which textual realism (what I have termed a phenomenology of saturated description) is crucial, for which the style of dramaturgy would, in traditional terms, seem almost stilted, wooden—I should say post-symbolist—all the more so as the appreciation of *Gertud* fell to a younger generation of writers, artists and critics. At the final stage of preparing this manuscript there appeared an important study by James Schamus of *one* scene from Dreyer's *Gertud*—drawing upon and extending the phenomenology of saturated description internal to *Getrud*—which I think would be a key starting-point for a renewal and extension of Cha studies. Cf. James Schamus, *Carl Theodor Dryer's Gertud: The Moving Word* (Seattle: University of Washington Press, 2008). On styles of acting and dramaturgy in Symbolist acting—the influence of which is still available in the work of a Beckett—cf. František Deak, *Symbolist Theater: The Formation of an Avant-Garde* (Baltimore: The Johns Hopkins University Press, 1993); on the transformation of one style of impersonality in Symbolist dramaturgy to another style of impersonality in Constructivist dramaturgy, cf. Edward Braun, "1905: The Theatre Studio," and "1921-1923: Biomechanics and Constructivism," *Meyerhold: A Revolution in Theatre* (London: Methuen, 1995).

ISSN 1942-3381   Michael Stone-Richards

passage, oral passage, pharynx, larynx, trachea, etc. along with other plates showing the anatomical infrastructure that supports the actions of breathing, likewise in "Erato   Love Poetry" the language of cinema experience is not made separate from its technical language of process, its infrastructure:

> Extreme Close Up shot of her face. Medium Long shot . . . She enters from the left side, and camera begins to pan on movement . . . Camera holds for a tenth of a second. . . . The clock in Extreme Close Up. . . . Camera is stationary . . . The screen fades to white. (D 96)

Hence again, the opening scene, page one of *Dictée*

> Aller à la ligne   C'était le premier jour   point
> Elle venait de loin   point   ce soir au dîner   virgule
> les familles demanderaient   virgule   ouvre les guil-
> lemets   Ca c'est bien passé le premier jour   point
> d'interrogation   ferme les guillemets   au moins
> virgule   dire le moins possible   virgule   la reponse
> serait   virgule   ouvre les guillemets   Il n'y a qu'une
> chose   point ferme les guillemets   ouvre les guille-
> met   Il y a quelqu'une   point   loin   point   ferme
> les guillemets

> Open paragraph   It was the first day   period
> She had come from a far   period   tonight at dinner
> comma   the families would ask   comma   open
> quotation marks   How was the first day   interroga-
> tion mark   close quotation marks   at least to say
> the least of its possible   comma   the answer would be
> open quotation marks   there is but one thing   period
> There is someone   period   From   a far   period
> close quotation marks

which presents the diacritical infrastructure of language which cannot be sounded in use but without which sense cannot be heard. Each of these parallelisms encompassing body, language, page and screen foregrounds the *apparatus* of representation and articulation in such a way that method is made a subject and the subject an action in the text–the scenario of *Dictée*.

4

There is, in other words, a performative confounding of use and mention, a confounding of object language and metalanguage, through which is figured a chiasmic relation of orders: sound and image, commentary and story, going in-and-out of black-and-white, perception and apperception, attention and subliminality. This is, indeed, the subject of Cha's 1980 work *Commentaire* (as it were, her second contribution to *Apparatus*), a work of sixty-eight pages consisting of four black and white photographs by Reese Williams and Richard Barnes and two stills from Carl Theodor Dreyer's *Vampyr* (1932, black and white). The work opens on a full black page, and closes on a full white page, with page two of black ground showing a still of the Vampire from Dreyer's *Vampyr*.[47] The head of the Vampire (Fig. 4) is so positioned that it looks upside down, but this is so because in the film the Vampire (protagonist) is holding a candle looking into a coffin at the (presumed) body of the character Allan Gray (antagonist). The other still from *Vampyr* comes five pages from the end and shows the face of Allan Gray (Fig. 5) in the coffin. The viewer can now begin to understand the earlier (phenomenologically) inverted position of the Vampire-- which doubles as a figure of retinal inversion[48]-- for the coffin has a square window cut into it revealing Gray's face – the viewer (no less than the audience, in other words) is in the coffin of the apparatus. The particular moment from which the still (Fig. 5) is taken is crucial in Cha's deployment of liminality: the antagonist Allan Gray, in pursuit of the Vampire, becomes weakened, sits down on a bench as his body dissociates (separates) into an out-of-the body experience: his spectral figure continues the search for Gisèle, the younger daughter of the manor taken by the Vampire's assistant, whilst his own physical body is taken and placed into the coffin. The still of Allan Gray in the coffin is precisely the moment where his coffin is being carried in a night landscape of clouds and moonlight. Though presumed dead, his eyelids remain open and the camerawork seeks to capture not only the texture of the movement of the coffin being carried, but also to capture—as figured through the eyes of Allan Gray—the blurring of the landscape underneath the coffin riming with the vision of the cloudy, moonstruck night: this is what is depicted in *Commentaire*'s use of this passage as a film still: the clouds as though they formed landscape in movement under the coffin. This key moment of liminality figures the preoccupation with threshold, both phenomenological thresholds and linguistic thresholds, that is the dominant subject of *Commentaire* which is taken up again in *Dictée*–and not only in the more obviously cinematic passages, for here it can be comprehended that Cha's poetics, in exploring the modes of liminality and threshold experience, is moving toward the de-marcation of a zone of transcription—what I have suggested may be conceived as a *pays de l'autre*– populated by figures of the third and thirdliness: the Mother depicted in *Dictée* in a state of *sinbyong*,[49] the Diseuse of *Dictée*, Allan *Gray* [sic] of *Vampyr* (as deployed in *Commentaire*), precisely where Gray is neither living nor dead, precisely where the Diseuse is neither wholly in this world nor the next, but a vehicle for the embodiment of acoustic forces, and precisely where the Mother is the third moment between the mystical morphology of simultaneous movement and stillness (cf. D 50-51).[50]

---

[47] Uniquely in *Apparatus*, the only unpaginated pages are those of *Commentaire*, running from 260-328, and the black pages on which the quotations from Plato, Diderot, Balzac, Apollinaire and James are written, pages of quotations which I have referred to as akin to found objects, and which I have suggested are to be taken collectively as a work (intervention) by Cha.

[48] That is, whether for camera obscura, camera, or film production, which thus opens the possibility of a related alterity between Allan Gray and the Vampyr.

[49] *Sinbyong* is the Korean term for the illness experienced by a woman (an more rarely a man) which marks her as as Mudang or Shaman.

[50] Within modernist poetry, this notion of the third plays a key role in certain inaugural works such as T.S. Eliot's *The Waste Land*, especially in the division of "What the Thunder Said":

Fig. 4 (left): Opening still (Vampire) from *Commentaire*, 1980
Fig. 5 (right): Closing still (Allan Gray), from *Commentaire*, 1980

> Who is the third who walks always beside you?
> When I count there are only you and I together
> But when I look ahead up the white road
> There is always another one walking beside you
> Gliding wrapt in a brown mantle, hooded
> I do not know whether a man or a woman
> —But who is that on the other side of you?

(*The Waste Land* [1922], ll.360-66, in *Collected Poems: 1909 - 1962* [New York: Harcourt Brace and Company, 1991]). Within the philosophical discursive form of this modernist sensibility, one finds the notion of the third (and thirdliness) variously articulated in Blanchot (and through him Derrida), psychoanalytically (in Wladimir Granoff's magisterial *La Pensée et le féminin* [Paris: Minuit, 1976]), and in Gillian Rose where the third is part of her conception of configurated middle. See Gillian Rose, *The Broken Middle* (Oxford: Basil Blackwell, 1992).

In its most banal sense (as depicted in Fig. 3 and our discussion above), *commentaire* means the voice-over accompanying a passage of film; but once Cha's work is situated within the experimental cinematic tradition which separates the voice from the image and which renders autonomy to voice over image, it becomes possible to appreciate *Commentaire* as a work of voice, a work in voice, and a work in the decomposition (separation) of voice into voices through the combinatorial possibilities of phonemes on a ground that may be configured as page (black or white), or film screen or dream screen. (There is a key moment in Dreyer's *Vampyr* when faint voices are heard by the characters—of Allan Gray with the Vampire's assistant—and the question is asked, "Did you hear?—The child.") Thus from the opening of *Commentaire* in terms of the parallelism between screen and page, on page four we come on the word (black on white) **COMMENTAIRE,** which will be decomposed, re-combined and put through assorted permutations: sometimes broken down to: "comment, taire," followed phonetically by, "comment taire," which immediately makes the commentary silent (as the screen of *Vampyr* is silent): but also "comment," the French how, why, what,[51] followed by "taire," to say nothing of, not to say *or* tell *or* mention, to pass over in silence, but also to conceal, to suppress—to suppress what? Well, the comment (as the English to comment), but also that on which the voice of cinematic experience is built, namely, the childhood of experience. At other times, the generative principle of combinatorial movement—extending the principle of double channel work—might be by associative homology (or homophony) between French and English: from TAIRE, to TEAR;[52] or, white on black, a particle, such as "comment" (in French), is tacitly taken over into English: AS, LIKE / HOW to suggest modality: conjunctively, then adverbially. These associative possibilities which are based upon the principle of double channel work make it all but impossible to know how the words of *Commentaire* could be pronounced by one person, as distinct from plural soundings and voices, though the implied temporality of multiple voices would not, in principle, present a problem for cinematic rendition—which is to say, that *Commentaire* rejoins the poetics of (im)-possible articulation essayed by Mallarmé but which is taken up as an explicit model for film construction and experience by two other collaborators to Cha's *Apparatus*, namely, Danièle Huillet and Jean-Marie Straub, whose "Every Revolution Is a Throw of the Dice"[53] immediately follows Cha's *Commentaire*. The

---

[51] The range of *comment* in French is far wider, especially when used for emphasis.

[52] Here may be the occasion to suggest how one might construe "Elitere" the name given by Cha instead of Euterpe for the Muse of Lyric Poetry. Since *Elitere* is made up— though I am open to correction—one approach would be to read it homonymically beginning with the fact that French as well as English possess a variant for Eurtepe, namely, *Eutere*. Reading *Elitere* homonymically we construe: *elle y taire / tears*: there she weeps, there she says nothing, passes over in silence. Elitere, the Muse of lyric poetry—a late Classical attribution for the earlier Muse of Music—thus comes to present lyric poetry as not only the giving of pleasure or delight, but as a poetry of circumscribed and affective silence upon a site of Anamnesis.

[53] Cf. Danièle Huillet and Jean-Marie Straub, "Every Revolution Is a Throw of the Dice," *Apparatus*, 329-354. This text—a scenario—opens with a consideration of 'The Typography of the *Coup De Dés*': "An original page from Stéphane Mallarmé's *Coup de dés* (whose ninth folio is reproduced below) can serve as a starting-point for a demonstration of the *parallel construction* of Jean-Marie Straub's latest film (color, 35 mm, 11 min)" (my emphasis). One might also bear in mind Pierre Boulez' setting of Mallarmé's sonnet "Une dentelle s'abolit" as a parallel exploration through music of the (im)-possibility of plural, simultaneous voicings. Cf. Pierre Boulez, "Improvisation sur Mallarmé II: Une dentelle s'abolit," with soprano Phyllis Bryn-Julson and the BBC Symphony Orchestra, on *Pli Selon pli*, Erato (CD), 1983.

approach to near impossibility of vocal articulation thus enables *Commentaire* to make the syllable and phoneme visual and moving and thereby to make the visual speak, and thus moves poetry toward cinematic experience through a play of word and world of which gesture is a middle term. One of the many ways in which this play of world and word is conveyed is in the *écriture* (that is, rhythm) of the implied gesture of the implied (brushlike) handwritten moments in *Commentaire* among which are *noir, noirceur, blanc* but also *blanchir, blanchiment, blanchissement* and *blancheur*, for these gestures in Cha's *Commentaire* allude to a beautiful observation by François Truffaut in his essay on "La Blancheur de Carl Dreyer (The Whiteness of Carl Dreyer)" that "When I think of Carl Dreyer, what comes to mind first are those pale white images, the splendid voiceless close-ups in *La Passion de Jeanne d'Arc* that play back exactly the acerbic dialogue at Rouen between Jeanne and her judges."[54] Truffaut continues by extending his associations of Dreyer and whiteness, *blancheur*, to comment upon whiteness (instead of black) as indicative of a form of burial–and one is reminded of the use of white as a color of mourning or death in many ancient traditions as well as in certain moments of modern painting such as Newman - before finally suggesting how the movement of the camera in *Vampyr* achieves an autonomy from simple reference by a play of forms and gestures in the allusion to handwriting ("a young man's pen"): "Then I think of the whiteness of *Vampyr*, though this time it is accompanied by sounds, the cries and horrible groans of the Doctor (Jean Hieromniko), whose gnarled shadow disappears into the flour bin in the impregnable mill that no one will approach to save him. In the same way that Dreyer's camera is clever in *Jeanne d'Arc*, in *Vampyr* it *frees itself and becomes a young man's pen as it follows, darts ahead of, prophesies the vampire's movements along the gray walls.*"[55]

Within *Commentaire* there are several modes of play in question: (1) The combinatorial play of word and syllable (and phoneme); (2) the play through the implicit parallelism of page and screen of the transposition of black and white, noire et blanc at the level of the page; (3) the play of black and white, noir et blanc at the level of the word or phoneme; (4) the implied play of reference and extension–a play of forms–and it is in this context that the photographs by Williams and Barnes are important: one set of two photographs (Reese Williams?) depicts first a blank white screen in an urban setting framed by palm tress, then the interior of a half-empty theatre with, again, a blank white screen, whilst the other photographs (Richard Barnes?) depict first a whitewashed wall with peeling paint, and a second photograph which consists of a blown-up detail (in grayer tonality) of a portion of the right side of the same wall;[56] (5) finally, as a variation upon the concern with combinatorial method linked to gesture, there is a pervasive play of framing. This elaborated play of combinatoriality is of interest here in terms of the developing argument about threshold, for

---

[54] François Truffaut, "The Whiteness of Carl Dreyer" (1969), *The Films in My Life* (translated by Leonard Mayhew) (New York: Simon and Schuster, 1978 and Da Capo Press, 1994), 48. On cinematic whiteness, also cf. Christa Blumlinger, "Blancheur d'images," in *Jean-Luc Godard: Documents* (Paris: Centre Georges Pompidou, 2006), 337-339.

[55] François Truffaut, "The Whiteness of Carl Dreyer," 48. My emphasis.

[56] The name of the village in which the action of the *Vampyr* takes place is *Courtempierre* which, on one literal reading, could be short-weather-stone. It is also (more) relevant to consider that the photographs in Cha's work of clouds are acknowledged to have been taken by her husband Richard Barnes, and it is my suggestion here that the photographs of the wall function both as figures of resistance (a block to a certain kind of play of extension) as well as an invitation to extension through imaginative projection (like the wall–and clouds–of Leonardo).

ISSN 1942-3381   Michael Stone-Richards

what *Commentaire* achieves as its subject, following Dreyer, is a spectralization (the graying, as it were) of voice and image—Barthes' "Like a metonymy become real"—as a means of exploring the attempted materialization of non-material substance, the moving stuff that is voice (sound) yet not wholly within voice (the child), as though voice might itself be the source of spectrality.[57] The most exemplary figure of this movement of non-material substance is (Fig. 5) the still frame used by *Commentaire* of Allan Gray being carried in his coffin, for this is the image and moment, *Commentaire* seems to suggest, that most concentrates the formal modes of Dreyer's compositional approach: in phenomenological terms, liminality; in formal terms framing: there are few films where the play of self-conscious framing through camerawork (rather than editing) is so astounding and poetic: from the opening scenes of the lake so framed as to be an oblong plane, then the succession of windows, doorways, skylights, shutters, squares within walls, openings within walls, windows sectioned into four, followed by one square window above two smaller square windows, trapdoors, the window cut-out from the coffin, the various square(s) now echoing the square of the shadowy edges of both windows and projected light on screen.[58] With a basic set of combinatorial terms—black, white; word, syllable; page, screen—*Commentaire* takes up the play of framing from Dreyer's *Vampyr* through the edge of page (and screen): the word moved to the edge of the page, turned to the next (HOW TO), through the variation of width to black borders; through tonal texture as transition between black and white (the descending gray lettering for

WENT PAST

MINUTE

OR

MOMENT),

---

[57] Which, in psychoanalytic terms, would be to comprehend voice as a superego (and archaic) formation (André Green) or as the residue following the murder of the child necessary to reach symbolicity (the Serge Leclaire of *On tue un enfant*).

[58] And does the following succession of screens, veils and doors from "Aller/Retour" (meaning *roundtrip*) not recall the movement of Dreyer's framing?:

> Inside. Outside.
> Glass. Drape. Lace. Curtain. Blinds. Gauze.
> Veil. Voile. Voile de mariée. Voile de religieuse
> Shade shelter shield shadow mist covert
> screen screen door screen gate smoke screen
> concealment eye shade eye shield opaque silk
> gauze filter frost to void to drain to exhaust

(Theresa Hak Kyung Cha, ""Elitere   Lyric Poetry," *Dictée*, 127).

with

SILENCE

at the utmost edge of the page (screen) now working lexically, thematically and phenomenologically in terms of absence such that the use of SILENCE is not readily distinguishable from the mention of "SILENCE," no more than the screen from the page, absence of sound from the silencing of sound or the impossibility of sounding: the last four words of *Commentaire*–each occupying a single page–are TIME TAKES TO HUSH, followed by a double page of white bordered with black–like those *cartes de visite* which once upon a time announced not the visitor but the death of the person whose name is borne upon the card–immediately followed by the frozen image–*temps figé*–of Allan Gray's framed head seen through the window of his coffin. The direction of these words pointing both beyond themselves (reference) to a possible event, or to the medium (in the apparatus of cinema or reading and thus as signification), in an economy of spectrality conditioned by the indistinguishability of use and mention, for by the end of *Commentaire* no means are available, no indication discernable for it to be known if it is meant be spoken or is itself a silent work of movement–the hand turning the page as a primitive stand-in mechanism for the rolling projector–no less than a metacommentary on the status of being a "Commentaire" (as Fig. 3 above, for example).

5

Here, I should like to pay closer attention to the terms *use* and *mention* in this economy of articulation and spectrality (the cave, de-materialization, light and dark). The concept of use and mention as logical categories as developed in Bertrand Russell's theory of descriptions (or logical types) was a means of avoiding logical paradoxes of the sort "The set of all sets which is not a member of itself." It was shown by Russell that by recognizing hierarchies or (types) of statements it could be appreciated that the statement "X is a member of Y" is not the same kind of statement, did not carry the same status as, "The set of all sets that is not a member of itself." In transposing from the logical to the semantic this clarification of types of statements, logicians and semanticists came to be able to clarify what it means to say that the use of a statement is distinct from the mention of–discussion about–a statement, in other words to create a metalanguage (mention) the conditions of use of which are distinct from statements in the object language (the language of use). There are, though, circumstances in which no clear distinction can be drawn between use and mention, between language and metalanguage, between act and reflection upon the act, between medium and support: Lacan's formula for this was that in matters of unconscious activity *Il n'y a pas de métalangage*; for Derrida and his followers, this became the recognition that there is no means available for distinguishing in principle the primary from the secondary (text), or in terms of genre, the poetic from the philosophical; a Cavell re-situates these matters at a phenomenological level made continuous with a drama of epistemology, namely, that skeptical claims against knowledge cannot in principle be defeated in order to vindicate the possibility of a secure mode of knowing, for the medium in which epistemic claims are made is continuous with and made possible by the same medium in which knowledge is undergone. All of these forms are implicitly articulations of the awareness of the necessity of separation from a medium as condition of there being knowledge at all which nevertheless recognizes that the medium from which separation is sought is the stuff of knowledge itself. In modern philosophy, Hegel has set the terms of this drama, a drama of immediate experience, but it can be said that avant-garde experience in its push for forms of simultaneity of experience—collage, montage, *cadavre exquis*, spatialization of time, the anachrony of the unconscious, and myth—as encapsulated emblematically in Breton's search for "un nouveau temps du verbe être (new tense [time] of the verb to be)"[59] has found in film the form for the pursuit of a dramatological epistemology of separation and limitation, separation and binding, separation and release, the acknowledgement that the presupposition of knowledge is at one and the same time the repressed of knowledge. On a certain interpretation, Plato's "Allegory of the Cave" is not merely—or only—a pre-figuration of a thinking of the unconscious or of the ontology of filmic *aisthesis*, but an implicit recognition, admittedly against the grain, of the unconscious conditions of knowledge.[60] Whence Jean-Louis Baudy, in his essay "The Apparatus," an extended reflection on the metapsychology of the conditions of the cave/unconscious and sleep:

> One constantly returns to the scene of the cave: real-effect or impression of reality. Copy, simulacrum, and even simulacrum of simulation. Impression of the real, or more-than-the-real? From Plato to Freud, the perspective is reversed; the procedure is inverted—so it seems.[61]

So it seems, indeed. What Baudry is working toward is an insight that has long been part of Surrealist experience and slowly articulated into philosophical discursivity through Lacan, Girard, Derrida and indeed others, and it is an insight that is profoundly Hegelian, namely, the doctrine of negative infinity: opposites born of human temporalisation are opposites only in appearance, that no negation by the simple act of negation can escape that which would be negated for all are constrained by a common medium, whence the inavoidance of the question of violence in representation: Is violence inherent in the very coming into being of representation (as it is, say, for a Melanie Klein no less than a Lacan), or is violence a function of a given social (patriarchal) arrangement, as a certain Feminism or Marxism – not to be confused with "Communism" – might imply? Let us quote Baudry at length from his opening page on "The Apparatus" as he works his way through the vocabulary of staging, places—to be more precise, the metapsychological *question* of *lieux*—[62] and the gradual dissolution of left and right positionalities:

---

[59] André Breton, "RÉVE," *Littérature*, nouvelle série, no. 7, December 1922.

[60] Though it should be pointed out that an older tradition of interpretation of Plato—as found in the anthropologically inflected Jane Ellen Harrison no less than a Simone Weil—would not find such a view at all against the grain, for in this tradition Plato's work made little sense when separated from the Orphic tradition or the traditions of initiation associated with the Pythagoreans. Cf. Jane Ellen Harrison, *Epilegomena to the Study of Greek Religion* (1921), and *Themis: A Study of the Origins of Greek Religion* (1912, 1927) (New York: University Books, 1962).

[61] Jean-Louis Baudry, "The Apparatus," in Cha, *Apparatus*, 41.

[62] Cf. Pierre Fédida, "Théorie des lieux," *Le Site de l'etranger*: La situation psychanalytique (Paris: PUF, 1995), 267-298, and on the metapsychology of sleep, Pierre Fédida, "Le Conte et la zone de l'endormissement," *Corps du vide, espace de séance* (Paris: Jea-Pierre Delarge, 1977), 155-191.

From Plato to Freud, the perspective is reversed; the procedure is inverted—so it seems. The former comes out of the cave, examines what is intelligible, contemplates its source, and when he goes back, it is to denounce to the prisoners the apparatus which oppresses them, and to persuade them to leave, to get out of that dim space. The latter, (on the contrary, - no, for it is not a matter of simple opposition, or of a simplifying symmetry), is more interested in making them go back there precisely where they are; where they didn't know how to find themselves, for they thought themselves outside, and it is true that they had been contemplating the good, the true and the beautiful for a long time. But at what price and as a result of what ignorance; failure to recognize or repress, compromise, defense, sublimation? Like Plato, he urges them to consider the apparatus to overcome their resistances, to look a little more closely at what is coming into focus on the screen, the other scene. The other scene? What brings the two together and separates them? For both, as in the theater, a left side, a right side, the master's lodge, the valet's orchestra. But the first scene would seem to be the second's other's scene. It is a question of truth in the final analysis, or else: "the failure to recognize has moved to the other side." Both distinguish between two scenes, or two places, opposing or confronting one another, one dominating the other [even as these] aren't the same places.[63]

"One constantly returns to the scene of the cave," says Baudry, and this is indeed, the *place where Dictée* opens, its primal scene, and with it the presence of childhood. We note, again, the prevalence in the found quotations of *Apparatus* of the strategic presence of childhood proximate to the form of the cave—for is this not part of the irony that the cave in the "Allegory of the Cave" may well itself be a Form/Idea?—thus: Plato: "Here they have been from *childhood*"; Diderot: "I had the impression of being inside a place that is called this philosopher's cave (Plato's). It was a long and dark cave. I was seated among many men, women and *children*" (39); and finally from James: "the marble squares of [one's] *childhood*." Though there has been some discussion about when the inscribed message of the Frontispiece of *Dictée* (Fig. 1) could have been written, it is accepted that the statement which can be translated as "Mother / I miss you / I am hungry / I want to go home" is figured as a cut into the wall of a coal mine in Japan where, it is to be understood, the Japanese had abducted Koreans for slave labor. This is how Cha would have understood it—but this is not, for *Dictée*, its first significance, its function. The surface of the image—as we have said above, a *photocopy* and not a photograph—brings attention to itself, its disintegration of boundaries, its appearance of decay, its darkness with glimpses of light-words: the image in a state mid-way between recuperation and loss, between light and dark is the cave—the coal mine—wherein or whereupon a cinematic situation, that is, a wall-support, obtains for the projection through a light-source of images of which we—the audience—have only this surviving film still, *of a source of which we are necessarily ignorant.* This could not have been known *ab initio,* from the beginning of the first reading of *Dictée,* for we had to allow the work to instruct us in the appropriate mode of attention, we had to come to understand the work as performing a material equivalence between screen and page, commentary and voice, sound and image such that we could then understand the Korean inscription—to be read from right to left and top to bottom—as being echoed in the diegetic commentary of "Erato   Love Poetry":

---

[63] Jean-Louis Baudry, "The Apparatus," in Cha, *Apparatus*, 41.

The titles and names in black appear from the upper right hand corner, each letter moving downwards onto the whiteness of the screen (D 94)

The same form of movement that is exploited in a work such as (Fig. 2) *Tongue Tied*, the obscurity of which dissolves before the eyes as one suddenly realizes that it is to be read from right to left twisting (diagonally) from top to bottom, for example:

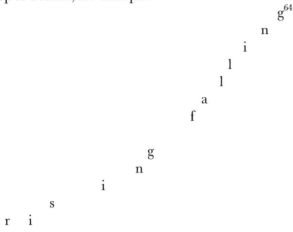

---

[64] Compare, in this respect, e.e. cummings (as quoted in *Paterson*, itself quoted from an interview between Mike Wallace and William Carlos Williams):

(im)c-a-t(mo)
b,i,;l:e
FallleA
ps!fl
OattumblI
sh?dr
IftwhirlF
(UL) (IY)
&&&

which may be provisionally transcribed to ease out the perceptual tease: "cat immobile Fall leaps Float tumble sh? [? = balloon string, or ball of string, say] drift whirl Fully and etc etc." To re-introduce the formatting and silent signs (brackets, dashes, question mark, ampersand) is to begin to recognize in what the poetry consists, namely, the sudden perception of silence in slow motion—thus "sh" becomes the beginning of the sound (exclamation) to enjoin silence!—the ever so slightly delayed recognition almost concurrent with the event of (just past) immediate experience. The ampersand not only repeats the gesture but indicates the shape of the cursive movement apperceived: fall, leap, float. Cf. William Carlos Williams, *Paterson* (1958), Book Five (Harmondsworth: Penguin Books, 1983), 224.

The commentary–not unlike *Commentaire* and Dreyer's *Vampyr*–is juxtaposed with the projected story wherein:

> The shadows moving across the whiteness, dark shapes and dark light (D 95).[65]

The coal mine of the figured frontispiece is but the configured cave for the *scene of childhood*, its place, its losses, fragilities and possibilities, the figure of *a source of which we are necessarily ignorant*, no less than its alterity and otherness from "us," from "where" we are "now";[66] it is to make of the cinematic situation what Pierre Fédida said of the analytic situation, it is *le site de l'étranger*. To return to Baudry's entering himself into the re-cognition that there is no scene–no truth–separate from alterity:

> The other scene? What brings the two together and separates them? For both, as in the theater, a left side, a right side, the master's lodge, the valet's orchestra. But the first scene would seem to be the second's other scene. It is a question of truth in the final analysis, or else: "the failure to recognize has moved to the other side." Both distinguish between two scenes, or two places, opposing or confronting one another, one dominating the other [even as these] aren't the same places.[67]

We might now look at (Fig. 6) the photograph on the cover of *Dictée* and recognize[68]–even before the specific location can be *named*–that what is depicted are (archaic) tombs, which is thereby to make of *Dictée* not only a commemoration, but more specifically a *tombeau*, the inside–or otherside–of which is the speckled play of light and dark in the image of the frontispiece (Fig. 1), marking a moment and space of transition, which would be also to imply not merely a movement through otherness but a *form of descent* through what the work itself names as a "Tombe des nues de naturalized" (D 20) to the first encounter with the day, that is, the very light of day–

---

[65] Within this play of dark and light there are multiple allusions to key moments, scenes and debates in film history where the status of the spatiality of the image-projection–the *lieu* of the cinematic image–is the question which, unavoidably, cannot be held separate from questions of receptivity. Consider, for example, the opening extract of Reese Williams' *A Pair of Eyes*: "Screen, the receptive, comes up from Silence, as pinning rebus of the perfected cries of monkeys and dogs, an unknowable space, vast enough for the words, *mother, father, soul, home* and *world* to continue branching forever without meeting a blockage." This passage is printed facing a blown up black and white film still from Godard's *Pierrot le fou* (as identified by Reese in a note). Reese Williams, the second cycle from *A Pair of Eyes* (n.p., in *Wedge*: nos. 3,4,5, 1983, Partial Texts: Essays and Fictions). This same issue of *Wedge* contains Cha's *Clio History* (with calligraphy in seal script) as Wedge Pamphlet no.8

[66] Though there is not space to do so, it would be of great value to consider Renée Green's juxtaposition of Robert Smithson (of great import, I would suggest, to both Cha and Reese Williams) and Cha in her video installations "Partially Buried in Three Parts" (1996-99) which raises important questions concerning *natal patria* and the (im)-possibility of return to the place of birth.

[67] Jean-Louis Baudry, "The Apparatus," in Cha, *Apparatus*, 41.

[68] And might we not know be able to see the image as so constructed, so cropped as to suggest the angle – and view – of wide screen cinemascope, the tombs receding in perspective, moving away *à perte de vue*?

C'était le premier jour[69]–as though the first, which is to say originary day of a new existence, that is, a dying to new birth, before the second encounter, namely, the encounter with *families* (*les familles* : *the families*)–surely the plural is here significant–whose questions to the one who had come "From A Far" (D 20) would indeed be questions of relation: nationality, kindred and blood relation, questions, then, of ancestry through and "From a far period" (D 1), an anthropologically primitive form of enunciation and relating which shadows from beginning to end the attempts of utterance in *Dictée*, as prayer, as invocation, but also submission as act of humility. Consider, for example, the following commonplace from the great ethnographer Germaine Dieterlen, commenting upon a scene which she witnessed through listening, that "for those interested, a prayer, an invocation, are effective for those who hear them. One evening [Un soir], very late in the night, I heard singing. It was a man come from afar [venu de loin] to honor his late mother. Near the house where she was born, he sang the title [devise][70] of her family and repeated his song tirelessly."[71] This encounter is the form of the encounter in which *she who had come from afar / Elle [qui] venait de loin* participates in *Dictée* as part of the experience of transition and *katabasis*. The speckled play of light and dark of the frontispiece, thus, encompasses, through the form of a cave, the suggestion of a place of birth and transformation, at the same time that it suggests the origin of filmic experience in light and dark as a form or kind of *ur-writing*–for this is what much of the film theory of Cha's generation is hinting at, working around, through the exploration of the cinematic condition and situation as a recapitulation of the unconscious, namely, that archi-writing and film originate in the same *place*, share the same childhood, the same displacements–

---

[69] Consider, here, Wallace Steven' verse that "The oldest-newest day is the newest alone," "An Ordinary Evening in New Haven," *The Auroras of Autumn, The Collected Poems* (New York: Knopf, 1982), 476. Consider, too, Aimé Césaire's variation on the structurally same topos of first day, from his "Poésie et Connaissance (Poetry and Knowledge)": "Et voilà qui nous ramène aux premiers temps de l'humanité. . . . Même, je crois que l'homme n'a jamais été plus près de certaines vérités qu'aux jours premiers de l'espèce. Aux temps où l'homme découvrait avec emotion le premier soleil, la premiere pluie, le premier soufflé, la première lune. Aux temps où l'homme découvrait dans la peur et le ravissement, la nouveauté palpitante du monde." Aimé Césaire, "Poésie et connaissance," *Tropiques*, no.12 January 1945, 158. Another, especially beautiful variation upon the topos of the first day, is Maurice Blanchot's closing chapter XII of *Thomas l'Obscur* which renders the first day as simultaneously a katabasis and a regression in time, to a condition where all things interpenetrate–on the model of sound–in the realization of a song of creation. Cf. Maurice Blanchot, *Thomas l'Obscur* (Nouvelle version) (Paris: Gallimard, 1950).

[70] Dieterlen's French is *devise* which is also *devise* in English meaning the law to transmit or give property by will, hence my use of "title" as to give, transmit, confirm, establish title.

[71] Germaine Dieterlen, "Entretien avec Germaine Dieterlen à propos de Marcel Griaule et du cinéma ethnographique," in C.W. Thompson, ed., *L'Autre et le sacré: Surréalisme, cinéma, ethnologie* (Paris: L'Harmattan, 1995), 441.

Michael Stone-Richards

Fig. 6. Theresa Hak Kyung Cha, detail, Cover, *Dictée*, 1982

whence the quest and search to capture in acoustic and visual traces (Fig. 8) the forming of words, the birth to language as Memory, as a species of Anamnesis:

> Mouth moving. Incessant. Precise. Forms the words heard. Moves from the mouth to the ear. With the hand placed across on the other's lips moving, form- [turn leaf from page 97 to page 99] ing the words. She forms the words with her mouth as the other utter across from her. She shapes her lips accordingly, gently she blows whos and whys and whats. On verra. O-n. Ver-rah. Verre. Ah. On verra-h. Si. S-i. She hears, we will see.

There is so much being deployed in and through this passage - use of double channel, confounding of use and mention, synaesthesia—but attention should be drawn to the hint at, the approaching of and play with a dissolution of word not merely to syllable (phonology) but the re-turn to or emergence of breath (gesture): in shape: "Ver-rah," in sound: "Ah." Breath, then, as threshold - but as we shall see in the following section devoted to a close reading of the continuation of the opening of *Dictée*, the section entitled "Diseuse," amongst the key moments explored is that of pain as a threshold phenomenon: pain as physiological, pain as psychological, through which a work of cultural pain is articulated.

Michael Stone-Richards

Fig. 7 Detail, "Polymnia   Sacred Poetry," *Dictée*

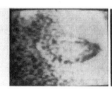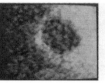

Fig. 8. Theresa Hak Kyung Cha, *Mouth to Mouth*, 1975. Single-channel videotape with sound (of Korean vowels). Collection Berekely Art Museum.

6

From this account of the opening scene and the event of language we shall proceed to an examination and reading of *Dictée* as a work of, a reflective movement around the conditions of communication (use, mention) in relation to conditions of crisis (forms of pain), in other words, as a work of liminoid moments in Victor Turner's sense of this term, that is, moments of individual and cultural qualitative change, crisis, collapse and re-definition. This is what is encompassed in speaking of *logics of separation*. In this light, though we shall consider questions of the genre of *Dictée*—what it means to say that Dictée is a *récit*—as preparatory to an approach to the dominant and three interrelated moments of liminoid forms of communication as especially emblematic of the accomplishment of *Dictée*: (1) The birth and accession to a heightened condition of communication in the Diseuse where pain may be ambivalently embodied through a depiction of physical hurt and sickness; (2) the scenes depicting the sickness and illness of the Mother, but with this difference that the experience of sickness is now a sign of election, of sickness as a state of what in Korean is termed *Sinbyong*; and something, as far as this study is aware, which has hitherto gone unnoticed, namely, (3) the hints, glimpses and proximities of madness in *Dictée*, above all as these come to be concentrated in the person revealed through a letter to Laura Claxton. Underlying these concerns from beginning to end, we shall argue, is a critical theory through a poetics and staging of breath and translation (Laplanche) in the temporality of *passé anachronique* (Fédida). In the process we shall come to re-think the project of Theresa Hak Kyung Cha as this leads to her conception of exile, historicity and the implications of alterity that emerge from her *oeuvre*. By way of introducing this account of the role of liminoid states cutting transversally across pain and communication, Sinbyong and madness, we shall close by concentrating on a scene depicting the accession to alterity and symbolicity through the acoustic mask of the Diseuse, *she who mimicks the speaking*.

Fig. 9. The framing of *Dictée*: the wide-angle (cinemascope) effect of perspective.

ISSN 1942-3381

Michael Stone-Richards

PART II

She mimicks the speaking: Diseuse

7

Above, in my commentary upon "Aller à la ligne," I had said that there is no suggestion within the depicted scene of fluency on the part of the visitor in the opening scene, and there is little doubt that an initial and legitimate response to this would be to think that this is so because the subject is that of language-acquisition—French, say, though by no means necessarily so—and thus any lack of fluency would be but a mark of wanting mastery. A close reading, however, gives no clear warranty for such a view: amongst the many reasons that there may be for want of linguistic fluency, there may be physiological as well as cultural factors, or, put in other words, the *one from afar* may be in some kind of altered state as well as an environment, a place, in some way new; there may, indeed, have been some kind of trauma which might necessitate the acquisition of a language in non-pathological contexts: one thinks, here, of the aphasias, the many neurological syndromes that mark an impairment of language use—of which Bergson and Cassirer were amongst the first to realize the philosophical significance—as well as physiological shortcomings. It is clear that such concerns belong to *Dictée* as well as to Cha's larger preoccupations—possibly, even, derived from Roman Jakobson—as can be understood by the chapter of "Urania   Astronomy," prefaced by a Chinese acupuncture chart, and which opens on the following scene:

> She takes my left arm, tells me to make a fist, then open. Make a fist then open again, make the vein appear through the skin blue-green-purple tint to the translucent surface. (D 64)

The actions which make up this scene are readily recognizable, and available: a subject, in this instance, a medical subject, follows the instruction—"She takes my left arm, tells me to make a fist, then open. Make a fist then open again"—consistent with testing for blood pressure in order to show the color of the veins which will then be prepared for the extraction of blood: "She taps on the flesh presses against it her thumb. . . . She takes the cotton and rubs alcohol lengthwise on the arm several times. . . . She takes the needle with its empty body to the skin." If, though, this is the scene, the scene carries something else—for there is "No sign of flow"—namely, the way in which parts of the body (in one sense, given the right circumstances, any part of the body) in a form of corporeal *plasticity* may become lighter as a condition of something else happening, coming about through it, what, later on in the same section, would be characterized as "One empty body waiting to contain" (simply, no more than potentially *to contain*: simply the infinitive as the condition), all the more so where that which extracts—which is not to be identified with the needle for *the needle* is but a metonym for the fact of agency—is not unrelated to what remains empty, expectant, whence, at the end of the first division of "Urania Astronomy" we find:

> Something of the ink that resembles the stain from the interior emptied onto emptied into upon this boundary this surface

quickly followed by "More. Others," the periods serving rhetorically to enclose in such a way as to make for shortness of breath,[72] that is, an unconnectedness with an outside, whence the imprecation, the *forceful* wish, as though, in certain instances, akin to an exorcism or execration:

>   Expel. Ne te cache pas. Révèle toi. Sang. Encre.
>   [Expel. Do not hide yourself. Reveal yourself. Blood. Ink.]

so that, as is shown in the closing utterance of the division, there can be revealed that which is "Of its body's extension of its containment."

The issue in *Dictée* will be the way in which Cha's poetics consistently allow the physiological and the spiritual, the physical and the psychological to become blurred, to become, as it were, part of a calculated vacancy the various modes and types of which fly under the conceptuality and metaphor of materiality—of language or apparatus or body.

If this physicality may point to language use in terms of embodiment, or, more precisely, failure of the physical body as necessary preparatory to elevated modes of embodiment - the container must be emptied in order to receive as well as to extend itself, for example - we might come to understand *Dictée*'s formal density as cultural, linguistic and experiential, and the "Diseuse"—whose significations are multiple throughout—becomes the figure of this threshold, this movement of liminal and liminoid experiences for which the body (a cultural, physiological and linguistic body, the body marked by punctuation and voids) becomes the means of passage and transition. Let us take the "Diseuse" section of *Dictée* (D 3-5), which follows the blank page (D 2) after *Aller à la ligne*. Immediately we are told:

> She mimicks the speaking. That might resemble speech. (Anything at all.) Bared noise, groan, bits torn from words. Since she hesitates to measure the accuracy, she resorts to mimicking gestures with the mouth. The entire lower lip would lift upwards then sink back to its original place.

At this point in the physical act of reading, it is by no means clear that it would not be the question of someone, a person, learning a language, and going through the range of mimicry, physical and linguistic, required to embody language as speech. That this moment, this passage of *Dictée*–of the Diseuse–is of central importance in the development and comprehension of Cha's enterprise is shown by the frequency with which commentators have turned to it. In her forceful essay, Ann Cheng interprets it thus:

> The opening pages of *Dictée* demonstrate the emergence of the speaking subject as echo: "She mimicks [sic] the speaking. That might resemble speech. (Anything at all.) Bared noise, groan, bits torn from words. Since she hesitates to measure the accuracy, she resorts to mimicking gestures with the mouth. The entire lower lip would lift upwards then sink back to its original place. She would then gather both lips and protrude them in a pout taking in the breath that might utter something. (One thing. Just one.) But the breath falls away. With a slight tilting of

---

[72] We shall return below to a consideration of the physiological significance of shortness of breath.

her head backwards, she would gather the strength in her shoulders and remain in this position." The Beckettian, infantlike creature coming to speech dramatizes the beginning of speech as imitation. Since listening remains one of the only physical activities of the human body that occurs simultaneously inside and outside the body, we might understand listening here to be initiating a boundary contestation. The sound that penetrates the infant is also the sound after which the infant fashions him/herself; the moment of shattering retroactively constitutes the possibility of boundary not experienced before. The infant mimes the sound he/she hears and, in the act of mimicry, experiences him/herself as at once possible and other—what Lacan calls the loss of self to self. . . . there is no speaking subject as such that is not already an echo.[73]

Now, Cheng is undoubtedly right that there is a marked preoccupation in Cha's poetics with movements of echo, and more broadly with modes of sounding; likewise is Cheng correct to say that there are concerns, here and elsewhere in Cha, with mimetic capacities, a pervasive concern with the childlike, and a deep and defining concern as well as with modalities of passage and transition between interior and exterior. For this preoccupation with transition and passage listening will become a privileged figure, a figure, too, for the emergence of *subjection*. It is, though, also noticeable, that any source of "the speaking" that might be mimicked in this passage—and Cheng's *sic* serves to mark the antique orthography of *mimick* which should alert us to something happening—is either withheld or is not available there precisely where one might infer a (native) speaker or child in the pocess of learning or acquiring a language. This leads the auditor or reader, as a result, to realize that precisely where speaking is presented but not configured with an identified or identifiable subject we find that resemblance and measure, which is to say, the affective proportionalities that make for mimetic identification, begin to move away from the sense of apperception—one notices that Cha's text parenthesizes what resemblance strives after as "Anything at all." Indeed, the terms of affective proportionalities, that is, mimesis, sought after begin to move from the initial sense of the concrete as the increasingly foregrounded and *dramatized* failure of enunciation would seem not so much imminent (an event coming about), as immanent (but contrasively something unfolding). The mark of this immanence is the semantic ambiguity, and hence richness, due to the rhetorical use of punctuation. For example:

> She mimicks the speaking. That might resemble speech.

Is "that" a relative pronoun? And if so, for what does it stand in? Does it stand for *the speaking* or *the act of mimicking, the speaking which might resemble speech*? As it is, there is no grammatical marker to facilitate the distinction (say, between relative and demonstrative) and this is a consistent aspect of Cha's technique, a singular way in which she makes her verbal acts rich and dense, at once an event in which and through which the linguistic and the phenomenological overlap.

---

[73] Anne Cheng, "History in/against the fragment: Theresa Hak Kyung Cha," *The Melancholy of Race* (Oxford: Oxford University Press, 2000), 161-62.

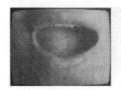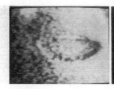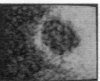

Fig. 8. Theresa Hak Kyung Cha, *Mouth to Mouth*, 1975. Single-channel videotape with sound (of Korean vowels). Collection Berkeley Art Museum.

The division titled *Diseuse*, though, however richly, however densely and, indeed, however chromatically, presents a form of experience at the same time that this experience, and the poetic experience which it doubles, seeks a form of language; hence, significantly, the work begins in the prepredicative dimension of experience *par excellence*, namely that of sound, with the co-presence of the social dimension of experience ironically intimated through *distortion*—whence the import of resemblance as the mark of mimetic capacities. "She mimicks the speaking," for speaking is not hers, and her action is one of a resemblance which is not yet an exact resemblance. Instead there are: "Bared noise, groan, bits torn from words" (D 3). This is the prepredicative dimension of the cry, noise and sound before sound becomes intelligible whether as music, song or, indeed, speech. It is, too, crucially, the *dimension of pain* laid bare as "noise, groan, bits *torn* from words" (my emphasis). The activity of resemblance is an effort, a work of the body—underwrit by pain—for she would mimick not only speech, for "she resorts to mimicking gestures *with the mouth*" (my emphasis). This centering of the means of measure along with the processes of resemblance on the mouth (Fig. 8) indicate something of the positionality of the body and the intention incarnate in its being as there is slowly introduced the suggestion of a prospect in which she is both acting and observing her action whoever or whatever else might be present to witness the sociality of the situation, an observation, a self-observation that begins to move outside of chronological time into an anachrony of time (Fig. 8), as much part of the page as part of the screen (see for example, D 97-99): "The entire lower lip would lift upwards then sink back to its original place" (D 3). And always, the effort is one of resemblance as "She would then gather both lips and protrude them in a pout taking in the breath that might utter some thing." And as though to emphasize that it is *some thing*, and not "something," the parenthesis tells us: "(One thing. Just one.)" The lip that falls "back to its original place" becomes shaped as that which is physical opens, gives way to air, that is, breath: "She would then gather both lips and protrude them in a pout taking in the breath that might utter some thing. (One thing. Just one.) But the breath falls away." With the lip back in place without utterance of any kind, and breath—now the marker of transition, of passage—become in a sense thingified, some thing that may fall away, attention shifts to the Diseuse in changed physical configuration: *With a slight tilting of her head backwards, she would gather the strength in her shoulders and remain in this position* (my italics). But these are neither the actions nor the operant intentionalities of a child learning to speak. It is with this poised, positioned passivity of the Diseuse that we, as readers—or implied auditors in a powerful dramaturgy—begin to apperceive the kind of archaic sounding (or archaic utterance) that might be mimicked, for to this poised passivity is conjoined the indefinite and the anonymous:

> *It murmurs inside. It murmurs. Inside is the pain of speech . . . It festers inside. The wound, liquid, dust. Must break. Must void.*

As the internal pain grows commensurate with the desire to speak, the body undergoing, subject to these (physiological and psychic) experiences prepares itself for an event, an event wished for, anticipated, even if feared:

> From the back of her neck she releases her shoulders free. She swallows once more. (Once more. One more time would do.) In preparation. It augments.

And one observes the return of sounds, but no longer the sounds of groans or bared noise, but instead pitch and drone, that is, the self now entering a new structuring field of musicality, not yet this or that particular music, but of the elements which transform the inarticulacy of sound from background field of indetermination to field of attention. Whence: "It augments. To such a pitch. Endless drone, refueling itself. Autonomous. Self-generating," for now the entry into the autonomous field of musicality–autonomous, self-generating–is to have entered an experience that figures the sustaining field of social attention that is the habitus for musicality, for it is only when sound, begun as bared noise, as groan, as bits torn from words, becomes the right pitch, the right drone that effort (will) can be let go and others enter (passivity). So:

> Swallows with last efforts last wills against the pain that wishes it to speak.
>
> She allows others. In place of her. Admits others to make full. Make swarm. All barren cavities to make swollen. The others each occupying her. Tumorous layers, expel all excesses until in all cavities she is flesh.

The right degree of pitch reached and sustained – the very definition of *drone* – not only can others enter in, and all the autonomous, self-generating forms attendant with them, but *she* can now (*inside the pause*) transcend her simple passivity and enter in to others (*inside her*), *re-find* the utterance of which she had been dispossessed (*the voice wraps another layer. Thicker now even. From the waiting*), indeed, become echos of herself as well as echos for others, for this is where *Dictée* begins to show what is actualized in echo as medium for the play of acoustic mirroring, for call (*she might make the attempt then*) and response (*the echo part. At the pause*):

> She allows herself caught in their threading, anonymously in their thick motion in the weight of their utterance. When the amplification [of the drone, of pitch] stops there might be an echo. She might make an attempt then. The echo part. At the pause. When the pause has already soon begun and has rested there still. She waits inside the pause. Inside her. Now. This very moment. Now. She takes rapidly the air, in gulfs [also implicitly, in gulps], in preparation for the distances to come. The pause ends. The voice wraps another layer. Thicker now even. From the waiting. The wait from pain to say. To not to. Say.

"She takes rapidly the air in gulfs, in preparation for the distances to come": this is where though the ambiguities–of pain, of sound, of utterance–are not resolved, are indeed not meant to be resolved, it becomes clear what *kind of experience* is being articulated through the Diseuse, namely, a shamanistic displacement. Compare, for example, the following passage form J. H. Prynne's early period poem on shamanistic displacement, "Aristeas, in Seven Years" (1969), and we comprehend a comparable set of typologies at work:

> Gathering the heat to himself, in one thermic
> hazard, he took himself out: to catch up with
> the tree, the river, the forms of alien vantage
> *and hence the first way*
>   by theft into the upper world . . .
>
> And his songs were invocations in no frenzy
> of spirit, but clear and spirituous tones from the
> pure base of his mind; he heard the small
> currents in the air & they were truly his aid.
> In breath he could speak out into the northern
> air and the phrasing curved from his mouth
> and nose, into the cold mountain levels.[74]

Let us note, too, that just as for *Dictée* the physiological and the psychic are intertwined, likewise in "Aristeas, in Seven Years" there is the same intertwining of the physiological and the psychic signaled through the use of *base* to convey not only root, source, support but ganglial root, nervous system which translates nervous (neurological) pain into songs and invocations, the nervous pain that makes the mind and body sufficiently sensitive to hear "the small / currents in the air": this is the taking of the distances to come.[75] That Cha should be exploring this terrain along with a poet such as Prynne should be no surprise, for they share many of the same models in American poetry in a period when American poetry (of the 1960s-70s) made deep inroads into the physiology, psychology and culture of shamanism, something Donald Davie observed, commenting on "Aristeas, in Seven Years," placing it "Among the many shamanistic poems which have been such a feature of recent years in Anglo-American poetry."[76] The Ethnopoetics movement and journal organized by Jerome Rothenberg and canonized in his anthology *Technicians of the Sacred* (1968) is but the most public face of this set of preoccupations which extended to film, installation and performance–the very domains of Cha's interdisciplinary practices.[77] (The sign for the avoidance of exoticism is precisely the insistence on the material foundation of ec-static experience–a universal phenomenon–namely, its physiology, the neurology of synaptic firing, the developed techniques of breathing as access to autonomy (the nervous system) and as a figure of

---

[74] J. H. Prynne, "Aristeas, in Seven Years," *The White Stones* (1969), *Poems* (Newcastle upon Tyne: Bloodaxe Books, 1999), 90 and 91.

[75] In this configuration, one might also consider Aimé Césaire's assessment of the role of the body in black American poetry in the incarnation of ec-static experience, precisely where materiality and spirituality meet each other, namely, in the *nervous system*, "this point of the lowest humanity." Aimé Césaire, "Introduction à la poésie nègre americaine," *Tropiques*, no. 2, July 1941, 41.

[76] Donald Davie, *Thomas Hardy and British Poetry*, 128. One might also consider the many works of avant-garde music which, in one way or another, take their orientation from shamanistic forms of which Joan La Barbara's *Shamansong* of 1991 would be one obvious example amongst many.

[77] See, for example, the exhibition catalogue, *Masks, Tents, Vessels, Talismans* (Philadelphia: ICA, 1979–1980) with essay by Janet Kardon, "The Ethnographic Model."

feed-back within the self as a set of subsystems and between selves and cosmos, the control of blood-flow and circulation before the construction of culturally specific significations of vacancy, trance and possession.)

The characteristic intermingling of physiology and culture in *Dictée*, of which "Diseuse" is a determinant moment in the generation of the work, begins to reach a point of pressure in the experience of embodiment: the weight "stretches evenly, the entire skull expanding tightly all sides toward the front of her," and soon "*Inside her voids,*" (D 5) the body takes on, assumes—*She relays the others*—weight and pressure, but it does so in a way that shows the pressures to be moving simultaneously in contrary directions: but soon it is a pressure that turns "her inside out in the same motion, shifting complete the whole weight to elevate upward" (D 5). The body is everywhere wrought and figured in contradictory directions simultaneously, and it is this giving over of the body to contradictory motions, voids and voicings that marks the effort of *Dictée*, of the Diseuse: the scene depicted, re-enacted is an initiation scene as a body is emptied in preparation for the entry of a greater force: this is an out-of-the-body experience, which, in time, may be more specifically culturally located as a Korean *naerim-kut* during which there is an initiation for a Shaman (in Korean, a Mudang) in preparation for the displacement and vacancy of the body preparatory to possession. The kinds of contradictory energies of displacement and possession depicted in "Diseuse" are to be found also depicted in the great final chapter, "The White Darkness," of Maya Deren's *Divine Horsemen: The Living Gods of Haiti*. The sense of relay and habitus in the self-awareness in trance and possession:

> As sometimes in a dream, so here I can observe myself . . .
>
> It is when I turn, as if to a neighbor, to say, "Look! See how lovely that is!" and see that the others are removed to a distance, withdrawn to a circle which is already watching, that I realize, like a shaft of terror struck through me, that it is no longer myself whom I watch.[78]

The crossing of the *line—pourquoi aller à la ligne?*— into lived separation and doubling:

> No sooner do I settle into the succor of this support than my sense of self doubles again, as in a mirror, separates to both sides of the invisible threshold.

The experience of voids—"How," asks Deren, "could I know a void as void?"[79]—and dead space with *dead time*:

> I feel that the gaps will spread and widen and that I will, myself, be altogether lost in that dead space and that dead time.

The experience of voices and sounds:

> these . . . voices—great, insistent, singing voices—whose sound would smother me. . . . The singing is at my very ear, inside my head. This sound will drown me![80]

---

[78] Maya Deren, "The White Darkness," *The Divine Horsemen: The Living Gods of Haiti* (1953) (New York: McPherson and Company, 1970), 258-59.

[79] Maya Deren "The White Darkness," 260.

The tension of surfaces:

> My skull is a drum . . . The white darkness . . . is a great force which I cannot sustain or contain, which surely will burst my skin.[81]

And finally, the experience of the anachronization of time as chronology and sequence give way, sometimes to inversion, sometimes to simultaneity, sometimes to totality: for "Diseuse": "All the time now. All the time there is. Always. And all times"; for "The White Darkness":

> the body growing lighter with each second . . . the sound grown still stronger . . . then suddenly: surface; suddenly, air; suddenly: sound is light,   dazzling white.[82]

That Cha's poetics of the Diseuse is a literary use of the anthropological experience of vacancy preparatory to trance and possession is further underscored by the not infrequent use of out-of-the-body experience *specifically as a form of inaugural experience*: this is present in many of the key inaugural texts of modernism: in H.D.'s (late Modernist) *Helen in Egypt* above all in the encounter between Helen (*both phantom and reality*) and Achilles in the Underworld, the Underworld which is precisely the domain and *state* which, being that of an anachronized time, permits a new agency to Helen who is still Helen of Sparta, Helen of Troy, "Helena, hated of Greece," but also Helen capable of "the difficult task of translating a symbol of time, into timeless-time."[83] It is to be found, too, in Eliot's *The Waste Land*, beginning with its epigraph from Petronious on the Cumean Sybil trapped in a state of aimless transition (in-betweeness) waiting for, but also in a permanently deferred death, which figure is replicated in the forms of Tiresias, Phlebas the Phoenician, and the girl of the Hyacinth Garden, "neither / Living nor dead," who yet "knew nothing, / Looking into the heart of light, the silence."[84] There is, though, another modernist work along with *The Waste Land* and *Helen in Egypt* which, in addition to Deren and the tradition identified with *The Waste Land*, I believe to be essential to the poetics of Cha, namely, the opening of Pound's Canto I, the Nekuia episode from Book 11 of the *Odyssey* only partially translated by Pound, beginning, famously, *in medias res* (as figures of separation and separatedness) and closing on a colon. We begin with the libations poured to the ancestors:

> Here did they rites, Perimedes and Eurylochus,
> And drawing sword from my hip
> I dug the ell-square pitkin;
> Poured we libations unto each the dead

---

[80] Maya Deren, "The White Darkness," 259-60.
[81] Maya Deren, "The White Darkness," 260.
[82] Maya Deren, "The White Darkness," 261.
[83] H. D., *Helen in Egypt* (New York: New Directions, 1961, 1974), 13.
[84] T.S. Eliot, *The Waste Land*, ll. 41-42 in *Collected Poems, 1909-1962* (New York: Harcourt Brace, 1991), 54.

followed by the *passage* into this world from the next, another world (*pays de l'autre*) always present in parallel, always present in latency:

> Dark blood flowed out in the fosse,
> Souls out of Erebus, cadaverous dead, of brides
> Of youths and of the old who had borne much;
> Souls stained with recent tears, girls tender,
> Men many, mauled with bronze lance heads,
> Battle spoil, bearing yet dreory arms,
> These many crowded about me; . . .
> I sat to keep off the impetuous impotent dead,
> Till I should hear Tiresias,[85]

in other words, until the true prophetic voice should arise. In *Dictée*, this true prophetic voice will devolve to the Diseuse, and the mimicking speech both her invocation (Muga, the song sung by a Korean Shaman) and her incarnation as Diseuse (Mudang). Here, "Polymina   Sacred Poetry," the closing division of *Dictée*, makes clear the role of shamanism, that the Diseuse is, in a manner of speaking, a form of Princess Pari (Pari Kongju), the deity at the source of Korean shamanism whose epic is sung in the *kut* for the dead to guide their souls to the Heavenly Kingdom.[86] In the classical tale of Princess Pari, she is abandoned by her parents (Pari may be translated as Abandoned One), the King and Queen, because she is not a boy. When, however, the King and Queen fall ill, only the Abandoned One, Pari, will undertake the risk, that is, the *journey*, to find the medicinal water that alone can save them. She journeys to the underworld and after many trials—over nine years in all[87]—she returns only to find her parents dead, but is able to revive them with the waters. Hereafter, Pari becomes the goddess and guide of the Underworld. It is this story, of Abandonment, made materially equivalent to the story of Demeter and Persephone, that is, an allegory of Separation, that structures the closing of *Dictée*, where a child, in search of medicine for her mother, encounters "A young woman [who] was dipping into the well all alone and filling two large jars that stood beside her" (D 167).[88] There is a moment of transition and passage,

---

[85] Ezra Pound, *Canto I (A Draft of XXX Cantos, 1930)*, *The Cantos* (London: Faber, 1975), 3-4.

[86] Cf. James Huntley Grayson, *Myths and Legends from Korea: An Annotated Compendium of Ancient and Modern Materials* (New York and London: Routledge, 2001), 352. For a version of the tale cf. "Princess Pari," trans. Lee Tae-Dong, *Korea Journal*, vol. 18, no. 6, 1978, 52-57.

[87] "Gow Gee Lin Wan   Ninth, Unending series of nines, or nine points linked together," it is written in *Dictée* (173): the novena (of Mary), the nine days of Devi, or the "Nine days queen Deo [Demeter] wandered over the earth / Constantly searching." "Hymn to Demeter," ll. 46-47 in *The Homeric Hymns*, Thelma Sargent, translator (New York: Norton, 1975).

[88] Here compare the "Hymn to Demeter," where Demeter, "Her heart overflowing with sorrow . . . sat by the path / Near the Well of the Maiden, where housewives came to draw water." "Hymn to Demeter," ll. 108-109. But also, compare the opening of Joan of Arc's dictated life: "Not far from Domremy there is a tree called the Ladies' Tree, and others call it the Fairies' Tree, and near it there is a fountain. And I have heard that those who are sick with fever drink at the fountain or fetch water from it, to be made well" (*Joan of Arc: In Her Own Words*, compiled and translated by Willard Trask [New York: Books and Co, 1996], 4).

of literariness and phenomenological transfiguration, as landscape becomes screen and thus support of projections, for the day is hot, "The sun became brighter at an earlier hour," and so

> The heat rises from the earth, diminishing the clear delineations of the road. The dust haze lingers between earth and sky and forms an opaque screen. The landscape exists *inside the screen* [my emphasis]. On the other side of it and beyond. (D 167)[89]

The child and the young woman *mirror* each other, for "She too was wearing a white kerchief around her thick black hair braided in a single knot down her back, which swung forward when she leaned against the well" (D 167). The supernatural presence of the young woman at the well is marked in simultaneously linguistic, phenomenological and filmic registers: "Her eyes were dark and they seemed to glow from inside the darkness" (D 169). The child relates her story to the young woman "who listened and when the child finished her story, she nodded and gently patted the child's head. She then brought over a basket and sat down beside her. The basket was filled with many pockets and she began to bring out one by one each pocket drawn with a black string. She said that these were special remedies for her mother and that she was to take them to her" (D 169). The young woman gives instructions to the child on the preparation of the special remedies and presents the child with a tenth pocket (*pojagi*), a gift, then said that the child should "go home quickly, [and] make no stops and remember all she had told her" (D 170).[90] As the child begins to leave, there is another moment of transition and passage, bearing with it the time of the encounter, as "Her steps seemed to move lighter than before. After a while she turned around to wave to the young woman at the well. She had already left the well. She turned and looked in all directions but she was not anywhere to be seen" (D 170).

The close of *Dictée* makes clearer the framing devices at play from beginning to end, for, consistent with the interpretation offered above of the frontispiece (Fig. 1) and the cover of *Dictée* (Fig. 6) as *tombeau* through which transition (which is to say, a *katabasis*) occurs to a new day—*C'était le premier jour*—to an encounter with ancestral specters, it may be said that *Dictée* offers its own variation upon the Nekuia episode in order to meet with, to embody "Souls stained with tears, girls tender, / Men many, mauled with bronze lance heads" as can been seen through the many forms of dismembered and sacrificed bodies strewn throughout *Dictée*, but above all as captured in the extraordinary phenomenon of Korean *Girl Martyrs for Liberty* in the context of the

---

[89] Which echoes Jean-Louis Baudry on the metapsychology of place discussed above.

[90] On the dismissive movement away from the encounter with the stranger, that is, with the suddenness of return from the sacred to the profane (see, as a type, the *Noli me tangere* episode of Jesus healing in Mark 5, 30-34, or Mark 7, 29-30) compare in this respect Cha with Prynne's,

> Go home said the
>   stranger to the
> Boy's mother he's too
>   weak & she
> cried bitterly & led
>   him to the door.

(J. H. Prynne, "Voll Vierdienst" [c. 1968], Poems, 36).

Japanese colonial response to the peaceful demonstrations which came to be known as the March 1, 1919 events which produced the Korean Jeanne d'Arc: Yu Guan Soon.[91] We might now comprehend another central aspect of the framing function of the photographic iconography of *Dictée* beginning with the archaic tombs on the cover (Fig.6), through the figuration of transition (*katabasis*) in the speckled light of the frontispiece (Fig 2) with a return, in the final photographic plate internal to the book (Fig. 7), to the kind of space of the archaic and the mythographic in "Polymnia   Sacred Poetry," which is to say, that the final scene effects a framing as the end recalls the opening: (Fig. 9) Space-Transition-Other-Space; then: a presentation of the invisible through a figuration of a threshold-line, without it being clear whither the direction: from the tomb or into the tomb; into this space or out of this space, within time or out of time, and its ruins . . .

8

The Genre of *Dictée* (I)

These works which help to situate the poetic practice of *Dictée* are indeed canonical works of High Modernism, but what Cha's work isolates, identifies and extends (since every significant work must re-define its relation to a medium that makes it possible) is the functioning of a device at once rhetorical: breath (its absence in "The White Darkness," its insufficiency in *Helen in Egypt*, its fading in the girl from the Hyacinth Garden, its cosmological property in *Canto I*); anthropological: the role of out-of-the-body experiences to mark an inaugural moment; and finally, prosodic: the caesura as figure of separation, sameness-in-difference, and as allowing presence to the distance and proximity between living and dead. It will be noted, though, that the personae in these works do not sing–"Deren" hears voices and song–whereas in *Dictée*, precisely what is thematised in the Diseuse is the line between speech and song, and it is here that another model–which is shadowed by Korean forms in the *P'ansori*–may be brought to bear upon the articulations of *Dictée*, namely the figure of the Récitant from Victor Segalen's *Les Immémoriaux* (1907) who performs in "gestes rigoureux, des incantations cadencées (rigorous gestures, cadenced incantations)":[92] the Récitant, Térii, belongs to an order of Maori society, the haèré-po (night-walkers), whose business it is to relate–*relay*, one should say following the diction of *Dictée*, relay in "Recitation. Evocation"[93]–the immemorial stories of the tribe's foundation: "And it is the business of the night-walkers, the haèré-po with long memory, from altar to altar and from sacrificer to disciple, to give themselves over to the first stories and the exploits [gestes: deeds] which must not die." In

---

[91] See Appendix I and for a fuller discussion of the extraordinary phenomenon of Girl Martyrs for Liberty, cf. Michael Stone-Richards, "Le temps de l'autre (II): French, Roman Catholicism and the Language of Religion," *Logics of Separation: Exile and Transcendence in Aesthetic Modernity* (forthcoming Peter Lang).

[92] Victor Segalen, *Les Immémoriaux* (1907) (Paris: Plon, 1956), 4. On *Les Immémoriaux*, cf. Giorgio Agamben, "L'Origine et l'oubli: Parole du mythe et Parole de la Littérature," *Image et mémoire: Ecrits sur l'image, la danse et le cinéma* (Paris: Desclée de Brouwer, 2004), 71-85; and cf. James Clifford, "A Poetics of Displacement: Victor Segalen," *The Predicament of Cultue: Twentieh-Century Ethnography, Literature, and Art* (Cambridge: Harvard University Press, 1988), 152-163.

[93] "She relays the others, Recitation. Evocation. Offering. Provocation. The begging. Before her. Before them." Theresa Hak Kyung Cha, "Diseuse," *Dictée*, 4.

recounting, in "rigorous gestures, cadenced incantations," the first stories of the tribe, the Récitant is also perpetuating the Origin of Word and Speech, and as though the existence of the tribe is linked to this Word and Speech, continuity and fluency of recitation is a condition of performance, whence the pain (épreuve: ordeal) as "suddenly the récitant began to stumble ... He stopped, and, refocusing his attention, restarts the narrative of ordeal. . . . A silence weighed, with a touch of anguish. Aie! what was presaged by the forgetting [l'oubli: oblivion] of the name?"[94]

The failure of articulation in recitation returns us to one of the central preoccupations of breath as a means of approach to another sense of the kind of work that is *Dictée* and the sources of its mode of articulation. There is in *Dictée* a clear staging of the status of breath: the physicality and materiality of breath is given an ostensive presentation, boldly and baldly, in a diagram in the division devoted to "Urania Astronomy" (D 74). Look, here is the physiology of the production of breath: the passages (nasal and oral), the larynx, the trachea which carries air to the lungs, etc. There is, too, as we have already mentioned, the pervasive rhetorical use of punctuation by which is staged the articulation of breath and the control of breathing, the poetic manifestation of which is rhythm: rhythms of dis-articulation, dis-continuity, inter-ruption and inter-ference, rhythm, in short, undoing measure (proportionality and resemblance) in the laying bear of the material conditions for the production of song from sounds, groans, pain, immediacy and haltingness, a song, that is to say, which is not lyric fluency, as song approaches speech and speech reaches song. This is *Dictée*'s (and Cha's) *Sprechstimme*—and at the same time a parallel with Korean *P'ansori*[95]—a term created by Arnold Schönberg for the new mode of articulation for the kind of performance voice inaugurated in his chamber work *Pierrot Lunaire*, op. 21 (1912), a setting of 21 poems by the Belgian Symbolist Albert Giraud in a German translation by Erich Hartleben. Sprechstimme is a form of handling of the voice through pitch in such a way that it does not become singing proper but no longer remains speaking, but is speech sound producing *Sprechgesang*, speechsong. A very important aspect of the development of Sprechstimme, as Pierre Boulez has noted, is its development from the mode of recitation performed by the diseuse of late nineteenth- early twentieth-century European cabaret culture,[96] for precisely the significance here of the diseuse—or diseur, since there were male performers, too—is that she was not a singer: Yvette Guilbert was a *diseuse fin de siècle*, Damia a

---

[94] Victor Segalen, *Les Immémoriaux*, 7.

[95] *P'ansori*: *Pan* means a place of gathering and *sori* means song. The *P'ansori* is a dramatic form of recitation in Korean folk culture performed by one *Sorrigun* (singer, male or female) accompanied by one *Gosu* (drummer) on a small barrel drum. The recent, and successful, Korean film *Chunhyang* (2000) directed by Im Kwon-Taek dramatized one of the five existing forms (Madang) of the *P'ansori*. For a "classical" treatment of the vocal recitation of the P'ansori form, one may consult the performance of Kim so-hee on *P'ansori: Korea's Epic Vocal Art and Instrumental Music*, Elektra/Wea, 1990 (compact disc), and the short story by Yi Ch'ŏngjun, "Sŏp'yŏnje. La Chanteuse de p'ansori," in Patrick Maurus, ed., *La Chanteuse de p'ansori: Prose coréenne contemporaine* (Arles: Actes Sud, 1997), 215-230. I should not, of course, have been at all surprised when Patrick Maurus, in an editorial note to "La Chanteuse de p'ansori," described P'ansori as a "narrative sung, or song narrated, perhaps as well considered as a sort of opera in solo, alternating songs, arias often close to *sprechgesang*." Patrick Maurus, *La Chanteuse de p'ansori*, 231, n.2.

[96] Cf. Pierre Boulez, "Dire, jouer, chanter (sur le *Pierrot lunaire* et *Le Marteau sans maître*)," *Regards sur autrui* (Paris: Christian Bourgois, 2005), 75-93. For a further development of this theme of Sprechstimme emerging from the cabaret diseuse, cf. Michael Stone-Richards, "Cette musique de l'inconscient," forthcoming.

singer. At its most minimal, the diseuse was a reciter of melodramas performed to musical accompaniment, and the accomplished diseuse was a skilled vocalist: whether of monologues in the genre of music-hall recitation or of melodies that are no more than elevated speech. In the elaborated figures of and on sound patternings that are strewn throughout *Dictée*, it should not be surprising that Sprechstimme is encountered, indeed, taken as a musical as well as both a linguistic and cultural model. Thus in the division "Terpsichore Choral Dance," which contains the most sustained presentation of soundings in *Dictée* and Cha's oeuvre–including the performances that remain in recorded forms–we encounter the search for "Other melodies"–and it is not possible that for Cha *melodies* does not here connote the genre of French art song–"Other melodies, whole, suspended *between song and speech*" (D 162, my emphasis). In the broadsheet announcing the publication of *Dictée*, there is also another allusion to Schönberg, this time as part of a concern with what is called the grammar of time–and which we have above characterized as the anachronization or degrammaticalization of time: "Dictee simultaneously experiments with time; Time which the characters experience . . . in Korean history, in 'mythological' Time. The grammar is applied in ways to establish a chronology which expands or condenses time, or makes it constant, atonal / eternal." This grammar of time proposes that temporality be felt not in terms of past, present and future, but, being anachronized, be felt instead in terms of modes, modes of atonality, condensation, constancy - and are these not also modes of gestation?[97]–producing thereby experiences which might then be best depicted in musical terms: its vocal articulation would be the steady monotony which is yet capable of sudden and radical shifts (whole octaves) that is Sprechstimme (or the non-diatonic performance of a Récitant such as Terrii in *Les Immémoriaux*, or the timbral performance of a cabaret diseuse), or the decentered movement of tonal (pitch) clusters each of which may be a new point of origination (*For the next phase. Next to last. Before the last.*) the mutual vibrations of which will condense "In deep metal voice" (D162), be constant in variation, whence the transferred patternings of "deep metal voice spiraling . . . shiver the air in pool's waves" (D 162), but also atonal, a principle of generation through repetition and reversibility–like tone rows. This grammar of time can produce "Other melodies," which is to say, other acoustic times, other temporalities, of *equal* importance, hence "Other melodies, whole," and if whole then in an-other sense they must resist ordinary time and so they are "Other melodies [that] in still the silence," not simply "instill" but "in still" actualize that which is still, unmoving, and which, now making breath material, do so with silence. The tension–and *Dictée* will speak of as well as announce "*the labor of figures*" (D 161)– is that between a voice of invocation, which is linked to "*The labor of voices*" (D 161), and a medium of stillness, which is figured here as the tension and passage between music and painting: *intones, in tones* (of sound) and *in tones* (of color)– the two caught in a spatiality of vibration at an abstract remove, which is the spiritual (meditative) distance. So:

> Water inhabits the stone, conducts absorption of implantation from the exterior. In tones, the inscriptions resonate the atmosphere of the column, repeating over the same sounds,[98] distinct

---

[97] For a very complex development of the figure of gestation–linked to sound with more than a hint of theurgical invocation in the manner of the Mallarmé of "Prose (pour des Esseintes)"–see "Terpsichore Choral Dance," *Dictée*, 156-162.

[98] Following through the analogy between paint and sound, layers of sound (repeating over the same sounds) would be sounds of *repentir*.

words.[99] Other melodies, whole, suspended between song and speech in still the silence. (D 162)

The explorations of atonality, ec-static movement and displacement in *Dictée* find themselves part-and-parcel of a continuous exploration of image and materiality: the *writing* of ink and blank page in parallel with the *light* of the black and white cinematic screen, framed by white, stone architectural columns. What is essential to the various modalities of exploring materiality—breath, ink, page, diacritical markings, sounds, close ups, nerve, sinew, etc.—is the underlying concern with what I have characterized variously as anachrony, anachronization of time, or, following Pierre Fédida, the eruption of the *passé anachronique* into the movement of the present which permits a view upon time as timeless (*zeitlos*), without governance, the image of which is the taking of distance in shamanistic displacement.[100] I should like to consider the significance of this term, *passé anachronique*, more carefully.

9

The Genre of *Dictée* (II)

The term *passé anachronique* is Pierre Fédida's translation of Freud's *zeitlos*. For Freud, the unconscious is by definition *zeitlos*, that is, without time, timeless, though its continuum with the preconscious means that it is not unrelated to temporality, indeed, through the preconscious the unconscious registers movements of pulse, fading and blinking—the very diction of 1970s film theory—but not the continuity of perceptual (temporal) succession for "die unbewußten Seelenvorgänge an sich 'zeitlos' sind (unconscious mental processes [by themselves] are 'timeless')."[101] In translating *zeitlos* as *passé anachronique*, that is, a past with-out time, Fédida means to address (through the negative *ana-*), first, the sense in which unconscious elements, being independent of time, can also be understood to be independent of structure, which then enables him to foreground the active way in which the force of the unconscious intervenes, pierces, into the movement of self-consciousness disrupting thereby its habituations at any point or time: little surprises, those slips of the tongue as well as the more expansive experiences that we designate uncanny, déjà-vu where suddenly perceptions slip one into another, where something dreamt becomes something lived and something lived something dreamt, the passage of the one into the other become marked by indistinction. Such experiences, from the slight to the expansive, come about, says Fédida, because the intrusion of the movements of the unconscious into the

---

[99] Here we might notice the implicit rhyme—the vibration—of *words* with *chords*, which would evoke an intersection of horizontal and vertical listening.

[100] Cf. Pierre Fédida's intervention in the debate with Jean Laplanche on *après-coup* in Jean Laplanche, "Temporalité et traduction," *Psychanalyse à l'université*, vol.14, no.3, January 1989, 42-45. Fédida's intervention has been translated, with introduction, by Michael Stone-Richards as "From *après-coup* to *passé anachronique*: An intervention by Pierre Fédida," in D.S. Marriot, ed., *Psychoanalysis and Poetics, Fragmente*, vol. 8, Summer 1998.

[101] Cf. Sigmund Freud, *Jenseits des Lustprinzips* (1920), Gesammelte Werke, Band XIII (London: Imago Publishing, 1940, 1947), 27-28, and *Beyond the Pleasure Principle*, Pelican Freud, vol. 11, *On Metapsychology* (Harmondsworth: Pelican, 1987), 299-300.

movement of self-consciousness results in a transference of the properties of the place of the unconscious (chora) into the spatiality of perception leading to a de-grammaticalization of the syntax or governance of social time.[102] This he terms the anachronization of time; and when the past - memory, recollection, even the archaic - is lived continuously with the present or as presentness such that presentness is not marked as such, in the way in which the confusion of use and mention is made possible by the absence of phonological hierarchy – consider, too, analytically, the re-living of the past in the experience of the transference, or the sudden re-living of a trauma - then we have a *passé anachronique*. Such a conception of the *passé anachronique* has implications not only for experience at an individual level but addresses that important question – important to Freud and Jung equally - touched on since the final chapter of *The Interpretation of Dreams*, namely, how is it possible that in the dreams of an individual there may be found symbols of ancientness of which the individual could not have had any personal knowledge, the problem, in other words, of the inheritance and transmission of phylogenetic traces. It is a small step from the recognition of the problem of the inheritance of phylogenetic traces to a preoccupation with the language of myth (or rites) as living anachronism.[103] In this latter respect, it must be appreciated, that Cha's thinking—as witnessed in her MFA thesis, "Paths," and many other working documents in the Cha archives at Berkeley—is clearly Jungian rather than Freudian, and very likely mediated by aspects of the work of Joseph Campbell.[104] But in the way in which she deploys the topoi of vacancy, illness as elective sign, and out-of-the-body experience there is not theoretical specificity, rather the form of shamanistic displacement affords *Dictée* a structural means of controlling and deploying the anachronization of time, for once time is anachronized, and the *passé anachronique* thereby opened up, another topos is deployed, namely, displacement as voyage of an exilic, ec-static self where the future (*Diseuse de bonne aventure*) is no less open than other pasts (as the passage from Balzac used in *Apparatus* argues quite forcefully): hence the exilic voyage revives in nine divisions, each of which is presided over by a (Greek) Muse, nine narratives (i.e., récits) giving stories, histories and experiences through the (acoustic) masks (or voices, as Cha puts it) of Korean women,[105] counter-pointed from the ancient past to the contemporaneous present (which is always the *time of writing*, the time of the récit): beginning with (1) the 17 year old Korean revolutionary Yu Guan Soon—the picture of her on page 24 is a detail from a photograph of thirteen women carefully cropped to present nine young women used on the back cover of the book—who may be counterpointed with Jeanne d'Arc (and implicitly also with St

---

[102] Cf. Pierre Fédida, "Théorie des lieux," *Le Site de l'étranger: La situation psychanalytique* (Paris: PUF, 1995).

[103] For a development of this view of anachrony and phylogenetic traces in relation to myth and bisexuality, cf. Pierre Fédida, "D'une essentielle dissymétrie dans la psychanalyse," *L'Absence* (Paris: Gallimard, 1978), 245.

[104] Cf. The Theresa Hak Kyung Cha Archive at the Berkeley Art Museum / Pacific Film Archive, University of California <http://www.bampfa.berkeley.edu/collections/bam/texts/cha.ead.html>.

[105] In the broadside announcing the publication of *Dictée*, we read: "*Dictée* is a series of narratives in nine parts with each of the Nine Muses identifying each of the sections . . . The narratives trace names, events & histories of existing persons, individual personages in history & other fictitious characters embodied in nine female voices." When Cha here speaks of fictitious characters embodied in female voices, we should bear in mind the importance of Beckett, Duras and Yourcenar, above all the Yourcenar of *Mémoires d'Hadrien* which Yourcenar characterized as the "Portrait d'une voix." See Marguerite Yourcenar, *Carnet de Notes, Memoires d'Hadrie* (Paris: Gallimard, 1963).

Thérèse of Liseiux);[106] (2) the Mother, who in the developing symbolism of three and nine may be taken as the simplest form of the timeless complex Mary-Demeter-Devi;[107] (3) a re-counting of Korea occupied by Japan and betrayed by an American government, a Korea since time immemorial caught between China and Japan; (4) the voyage moves from history to the skies in the form of an exploration of the proportionality of macrocosm and microcosm (i) through the image of the eternal starry sky as a membrane implicitly compared to the membrane of human skin (a medium of primal inscription) and (ii) language as a combinatory method (French into English, English into French, French and English in and as parallel, and so on) for movement between points of any structure of topological equivalence (for example, where microcosm = macrocosm) ("Urania   Astronomy"); (5) a return from the west to Korea eighteen years after the first departure; (6) a presentation of *sympathetic* states articulating women in states of psychological *collapse* (the letter to Laura Claxton (D 146-48),[108] or the Mother on the threshold of a possession by divine sickness or *sinbyong* (D 50-53, but also D 3-5); (7) journeys into mythical—i.e., timeless—time ("Polymnia   Sacred Poetry") resulting in the feeling of re-joining the whole (the ten cosmic circles) before the culmination through the *time of writing* in re-birth (the condition of natality) and the recovery of the myth and language of childhood ("Lift me up mom," D 179).

The above schematization represents the basic structure of movement permitted by the anachronization of time, an experience brought about through the Diseuse, she who is invoked in order to "break open the spell cast upon time" (D 123), to overcome *dead time*. We might put this schematization of exilic, ec-static voyage in thematic terms as follows. Once the mimicking subject of "Diseuse" finds itself sufficiently undone, exposed, voided, emptied, sufficiently absorbed into and by the anonymity of what is—the *il y a*—not to be confused with the social anonymity of the *they*, then the processes of subjection at work in the time of com-position and the time of writing, lead to an altered sense of the appropriation of subject, for we note the dominance in *Dictée* of the following: (1) scenes of inculcation: language and religion; (2) sacrifice (Yu Guan Soon, Jeanne d'Arc, the crucifixion of *Korean Christians* as represented in the photograph on page 39);[109] (3) liminoid states, that is, states of psychological and social crisis which result in a disintegration of current values and ideas of selfhood before the re-emergence of new values and ideas of selfhood (this is captured under the Korean term of *sinbyong*, the divine sickness that marks a person as being called to be a Mudang—the Mother, possibly, the Diseuse, certainly; or as in the case of the letter to Laura Claxton, the proximity of madness); (4) the play of forms, mythical and anthropological: Mary-Demeter, or the Novena of Roman liturgy compared to, or as an instance of, the Hindu devotion in the festival of Navaratri in which the goddess

---

[106] "Jeanne d'Arc" is also and at the same time a film by Carl Th. Dreyer, *The Passion of Joan of Arc* (1928), 35 mm Black and White. In *The Story of a Soul*, St. Thérèse of Lisieux had written: "When I read stories about the deeds of the great French heroines—especially the Venerable Joan of Arc, I longed to imitate them and felt stirred by the same inspiration which moved them" (St. Thérèse of Lisieux, *The Story of a Soul*, trans. John Beevers [New York: Image Books, 1957]), 49.

[107] Devi, the universal mother the worship of whom, says the Kena Upanishad, leads to knowledge of the self.

[108] Cf. Appendix II below.

[109] On which photography cf. Cf. Michael Stone-Richards, "Le temps de l'autre (II): French, Roman Catholicism and the Language of Religion," *Logics of Separation*: Exile and Transcendence in Aesthetic Modernity (forthcoming Peter Lang).

in the form of the Universal Mother (Durga) is worshipped for nine nights;[110] (5) the many scenes of childhood from inculcation to recovery—for example, the child speaking to the mother the mother's own story, rather than the child learning of its own past from the mother (D 45 ff.); and (6) history: French, Korean, Koreans of Hawai'i.

If the anachronization of time may be seen as not only a thematic aspect of *Dictée* but part of its structural production and generative strategy, then the way is open to see this anachronization as the means by which the récit or narrative form of *Dictée* becomes porous, not only to the power of memory, but also to a temporality of the now, the present, and as such capable of approaching at moments the conditions of autobiography, or diary or recollection, no less than the condition of history, or Bildungsroman, etc., for the movement of anachronization makes the time of the writing concurrent with the action of depiction—this is the conception of the récit (narrative) and thirdliness which Maurice Blanchot finds embodied variously in Rimbaud's *Une Saison en enfer*, Proust's *A la recherche du temps perdu*, and Breton's *Nadja* (underwrit, to be sure, by a certain interpretation of *The Odyssey*),[111] for "the récit . . . is the récit of an exceptional event which escapes the

---

[110] This observation on the role of play of forms in *Dictée* cannot be over-emphasized as it touches on the status of Cha's style and poetics. There is much confusion, I would suggest, about the status of Korea and things Korean in Cha's poetics. Clearly Korean history is of great importance and I shall have more to say about this, but "Korea" is not more important than the traditions of writing which inform *Dictée*, which, on the strong argument I have proposed, make the recovery of Korea possible. *Dictée* is a supremely literary work and the play of forms is one very telling example of this: Mary is Demeter is Devi in some very obvious sense. So, what of the Korean tale of Princess Pari that is found in "Polymnia   Sacred Poetry," the story of the meeting around the well? This is taken by many as a mark of the Koreanness of Cha/*Dictée*, and it is telling that those who make this argument always omit the many references to "screen" in this division of *Dictée*, its many internal references back to the scenes of *sinbyong* depicted in "Calliope   Epic Poetry," do not, in other words, read the work as an artifact self-conscious in its construction. For not the least of it is that the opening pages of the dictated life of Joan of Arc contain very similar scenes about the childhood of Joan of Arc in Domremy: "Not far from Domremy there is a tree called the Ladies' Tree, and others call it the Fairies' Tree, and near it there is a fountain. And I have heard that those who are sick with fever drink at the fountain or fetch water from it, to be made well" (*Joan of Arc: In Her Own Words*, compiled and translated by Willard Trask [New York: Books and Co, 1996], 4). Demeter is also to be found near a well. The anthropologically stable pattern is: drawing water is woman's work, but the anthropologically inflected poetics is: the well becomes the place of encounter, hence, it is where Jesus meets the woman as outcast in the gospel according to *John* 4: 6-30 where Jesus meets the woman of Samaria at Jacob's well. The play of forms is the manner of *Dictée*, and all the more so because it points to certain anthropological interests central to Cha's poetics and the poetics of her generation. This is in part what I intend by *Dictée's* use of variation in mythical forms as an eidetic phenomenology of myth.

[111] The contemporary writer more than any other whose work embodies this conception of the récit as a work of mixed genre in which the time of writing is the relation itself is W.G. Sebald, and in a manner that is manifestly continuous with the Surrealism of *Nadja*, if at a times more attenuated. One thinks of such works as *Vertigo* (1990), *The Emigrants* (1992), and *The Rings of Saturn* (1995). There are the found documents, photographs, objects, letters, the moments of the narrative that are essay-like, then the mark of a diary, or moments that bear the diction of autobiography, carrying the implication of an "I" in such a way that the

forms of every day time and the world of habitual truth, perhaps of all truth";[112] in escaping the time of habits, the time of the everyday world and habitual truth, in its mode of anachronization, therefore, the "récit is not the relation of an event, but this very event, the approach of this event, the place where this event is called to produce itself, an event still to come and by the alluring power of which the récit itself can hope to become realized."[113] The anachronization of time, as a result, entails the process of authorship into a consciousness of the weight and process of writing which in *Dictée* is deployed through a presentation which manages to encompass both a stringent materiality—of word, of medium, of apparatus—as well as states and forms of experience—*sinbyong*, vacancy, shamanistic possession and displacement, madness, no less than variations on the myth of childhood so central to modern poetry from Baudelaire through Saint-John Perse, Surrealism, Négritude and beyond to Yourcenar and Duras so important to Cha. Above all, the understanding of the anachronization of time, the *passé anachronique*, permits one to grasp the role of film and cinematic experience— structural film and its theory—in the deployment of collage and montage as both technique and form, in the approximation of page and screen, and the persistently worked parallelism of the material and the psychic as a

---

reader cannot tell from the work itself where the ontology of the "I" is to be situated, and all is written in a tone or key of the memorial. One major difference, of course, between Sebald and Cha is that though wit there is in Cha, there is never a trace of cruel humor—*l'humor noir*—and the irony of Sebald is not Cha's; also, where in Sebald it is clear that certain objects, documents or photographs are chanced upon or found objects, this is rarely if ever the case for Cha where every document (from a photograph of St. Thérèse of Liseux to a Chinese acupuncture diagram) is meant to be identifiable.

[112] Maurice Blanchot, "La loi secrète du récit," *Le Livre à venir* (Paris: Gallimard: 1959), 13. It is interesting to note just how very rare it is, in Cha's *oeuvre*, to encounter the banal everyday, the everyday in its plainness without any claim for its value. The rhythms and diction of the everyday as we find them, say, in an avant-garde poet such as the late Frances Chung has no counterpart in Cha's *oeuvre*:

> The echoes of the night trucks
> bouncing off the cobblestones
> on Canal Street play on the
> silences in my bones. Playing
> games with the red and green
> light on the corner of Mott and
> Canal, we find an excuse to run –
> we who know that those who are
> brave cross Mott Street on a
> diagonal.

(Frances Chung, "The echoes of the night trucks," *Crazy Melon and Chinese Apple: The Poems of Frances Chung* [Hanover and London: Wesleyan University Press, 2000], 4). The many scenes of childhood or interaction with the figure of the Mother in *Dictée* are always underwrit by transfigurative possibilities, as I argue elsewhere. See Michael Stone-Richards, "Sickness as election: Mother, *Sinbyong*," and "Sickness: the approach of madness: Laura Claxton," *Theresa Hak Kyung Cha: Commentaries* (forthcoming).

[113] Maurice Blanchot, *Le Livre à venir*, 14.

means for exploring that condition where, in the words of Saint-John Perse, "L'exil n'est point d'hier! l'exil n'est point d'hier!" (Saint-John Perse, *Exil*, II), and this is so for one carries within oneself the memory of that to which no return can be made—exile, then, is lived as an existential interval—for exile is not elsewhere (of yesterday, for example), but always here and now because of "yesterday" become irretrievable save through memory, whence the force of Lyotard's question: "How may it be known that what makes for a return is indeed that which had disappeared?" The persistent parallelism of materiality and psychic forms enables, finally, a strong sense of the term *dictée* to emerge, namely, as *trans*-scription, the possibly alternative inscription (proto-writing) made possible in/through trance-like states, through states that fail to be encoded in the socially available registers—whence the role of gender as intrinsic to the very form of the narrative of *Dictée*—no less than in states of collapse of signification (de-translations, as Jean Laplanche terms it) seeking new forms and articulations (re-translations). The opening scene and event of language of *Dictée*—the action of the text—gives onto, opens itself to, envisions these structural possibilities and imaginative variations within an interval, an opening, of acoustic distanciation and an eidetic phenomenology of myth. Such are the issues propadeutic to any further study of how rhetoricity—complexity and density, what *Dictée* characterizes as the modes of *thick weight*—becomes part of the way of understanding historicity and reading in *Dictée*.[114]

---

[114] Cf. Michael Stone-Richards, "Le temps de l'autre (I): Translation as model" and "Le temps de l'autre (II): French, Roman Catholicism and the Language of Religion," *Logics of Separation: Exile and Transcendence in Aesthetic Modernity* (forthcoming Peter Lang).

APPENDIX I

F.A. McKenzie, *Korea's Fight for Freedom* (New York and Chicago: Fleming H. Revell Company, 1920; rpd. Seoul: Yonsei Univesity Press, 1969 and 1975 in the Series of Reprints of Western Books on Korea) and The Project Gutenberg EBook of *Korea's Fight for Freedom*, by F.A. McKenzie (for the use of anyone anywhere at no cost and with almost no restrictions whatsoever. You may copy it, give it away or re-use it under the terms of the Project Gutenberg License included with this eBook or online at www.gutenberg.net).

Title: *Korea's Fight for Freedom*
Author: F.A. McKenzie
Release Date: September 3, 2004 [EBook #13368]

XVII

GIRL MARTYRS FOR LIBERTY

The most extraordinary feature of the uprising of the Korean people is the part taken in it by the girls and women. Less than twenty years ago, a man might live in Korea for years and never come in contact with a Korean woman of the better classes, never meet her on the street, never see her in the homes of his Korean friends. I have lived for a week or two at a time, in the old days, in the house of a Korean man of high class, and have never once seen his wife or daughters. In Japan in those days--and with many families the same holds true to-day--when one was invited as a guest, the wife would receive you, bow to the guest and her lord, and then would humbly retire, not sitting to table with the men.

Christian teaching and modern ways broke down the barrier in Korea. The young Korean women took keenly to the new mode of life. The girls in the schools, particularly in the Government schools, led the way in the demand for the restoration of their national life. There were many quaint and touching incidents. In the missionary schools, the chief fear of the girls was lest they should bring trouble on their American teachers. The head mistress of one of these schools noticed for some days that her girls were unusually excited. She heard them asking one another, "Have you enrolled?" and imagined that some new girlish league was being formed. This was before the great day. One morning the head mistress came down to discover the place empty. On her desk was a paper signed by all the girls, resigning their places in the school. They thought that by this device they would show that their beloved head mistress was not responsible.

Soon there came a call from the Chief of Police. The mistress was wanted at the police office at once. All the girls from her school were demonstrating and had stirred up the whole town. Would the mistress come and disperse them?

The mistress hurried off. Sure enough, here were the girls in the street, wearing national badges, waving national flags, calling on the police to come and take them. The men had gathered and were shouting "Mansei!" also.

The worried Chief of Police, who was a much more decent kind than many of his fellows, begged the mistress to do something. "I cannot arrest them all," he said. "I have only one little cell here. It would only hold a few of them." The mistress went out to talk to the girls. They would not listen, even to her. They cheered her, and when she begged them to go home, shouted "Mansei!" all the louder.

The mistress went back to the Chief. "The only thing for you to do is to arrest me," she said.

The Chief was horrified at the idea, "I will go out and tell the girls that you are going to arrest me if they do not go," she said. "We will see what that will do. But mind you, if they do not disperse, you must arrest me."

She went out again. "Girls," she called, "the Chief of Police is going to arrest me if you do not go to your homes. I am your teacher, and it must be the fault of my teaching that you will not obey."

"No, teacher, no," the girls shouted. "It is not your fault. You have nothing to do with it. We are doing this." And some of them rushed up, as though they would rescue her by force of arms.

In the end, she persuaded the girls to go home, in order to save her. "Well," said the leaders of the girls, "it's all right now. We have done all we wanted. We have stirred up the men. They were sheep and wanted women to make a start. Now they will go on."

The police and gendarmerie generally were not so merciful as this particular Chief. The rule in many police stations was to strip and beat the girls and young women who took any part in the demonstrations, and to expose them, absolutely naked, to as many Japanese men as possible. The Korean woman is as sensitive as a white woman about the display of her person, and the Japanese, knowing this, delighted to have this means of humiliating them. In some towns, the schoolgirls arranged to go out in sections, so many one day, so many on the other. The girls who had to go out on the later days knew how those who had preceded them had been stripped and beaten. Anticipating that they would be treated in the same way, they sat up the night before sewing special undergarments on themselves, which would not be so easily removed as their ordinary clothes, hoping that they might thus avoid being stripped entirely naked.

The girls were most active of all in the city of Seoul. I have mentioned in the previous chapter the arrest of many of them. They were treated very badly indeed. Take, for instance, the case of those seized by the police on the morning of Wednesday, March 5th. They were nearly all of them pupils from the local academies. Some of them were demonstrating on Chong-no, the main street, shouting "Mansei." Others were wearing straw shoes, a sign of mourning, for the dead Emperor. Still others were arrested because the police thought that they might be on the way to demonstrate. A few of these girls were released after a spell in prison. On their release, their statements concerning their treatment were independently recorded.

They were first taken to the Chong-no Police Station, where a body of about twenty Japanese policemen kicked them with their heavy boots, slapped their cheeks or punched their heads. "They flung me against a wall with all their might, so that I was knocked senseless, and remained so for a time," said one. "They struck me such blows across the ears that my cheeks swelled up," said another. "They trampled on my feet with their heavy nailed boots till I felt as though my toes were crushed beneath them.... There was a great crowd of students, both girls and boys. They slapped the girls over the ears, kicked them, and tumbled them in the corners. Some of them they took by the hair, jerking both sides of the face. Some of the boy students they fastened down with a rope till they had their heads fastened between their legs. Then they trampled them with their heavy boots, kicking them in their faces till their eyes were swelled and blood flowed."

Seventy-five persons, forty men and thirty-five girls, were confined in a small room. The door was closed, and the atmosphere soon became dreadful. In vain they pleaded to have the door open. The girls were left until midnight without food or water. The men were removed at about ten in the evening.

During the day, the prisoners were taken one by one before police officials to be examined. Here is the narrative of one of the schoolgirls. This girl was dazed and almost unconscious from ill-treatment and the poisoned air, when she was dragged before her inquisitor.

"I was cross-questioned three times. When I went out to the place of examination they charged me with having straw shoes, and so beat me over the head with a stick. I had no sense left with which to make a reply. They asked: "'Why did you wear straw shoes?'

"'The King had died, and whenever Koreans are in mourning they wear straw shoes,'

"'That is a lie,' said the cross-examiner. He then arose and took my mouth in his two hands and pulled it each way so that it bled. I maintained that I had told the truth and no falsehoods. 'You Christians are all liars,' he replied, taking my arm and giving it a pull.

". . . The examiner then tore open my jacket and said, sneeringly, 'I congratulate you,' He then slapped my face, struck me with a stick until I was dazed and asked again, 'Who instigated you to do this? Did foreigners?'

"My answer was, 'I do not know any foreigners, but only the principal of the school. She knows nothing of this plan of ours!'

"'Lies, only lies,' said the examiner.

"Not only I, but others too, suffered every kind of punishment. One kind of torture was to make us hold a board at arm's length and hold it out by the hour. They also had a practice of twisting our legs, while they spat on our faces. When ordered to undress, one person replied, 'I am not guilty of any offence. Why should I take off my clothes before you?'

"'If you really were guilty, you would not be required to undress, but seeing you are sinless, off with your clothes,'"

He was a humorous fellow, this cross-examiner of the Chong-no Police Station. He had evidently learned something of the story of Adam and Eve in the Garden of Eden. His way was first to charge the girls–

schoolgirls of good family, mind you--with being pregnant, making every sort of filthy suggestion to them. When the girls indignantly denied, he would order them to strip.

"Since you maintain you have not sinned in any way, I see the Bible says that if there is no sin in you take off all your clothes and go before all the people naked," he told one girl. "Sinless people live naked."

Let us tell the rest of the story in the girl's own words. "The officer then came up to where I was standing, and tried to take off my clothes. I cried, and protested, and struggled, saying, 'This is not the way to treat a woman.' He desisted. When he was making these vile statements about us, he did not use the Korean interpreter, but spoke in broken Korean. The Korean interpreter seemed sorrowful while these vile things were being said by the operator. The Korean interpreter was ordered to beat me. He said he would not beat a woman; he would bite his fingers first. So the officer beat me with his fist on my shoulders, face and legs."

These examinations were continued for days. Sometimes a girl would be examined several times a day. Sometimes a couple of examiners would rush at her, beating and kicking her; sometimes they would make her hold a chair or heavy board out at full length, beating her if she let it sink in the least. Then when she was worn out they would renew their examination. The questions were all directed towards one end, to discover who inspired them, and more particularly if any foreigners or missionaries had influenced them. During this time they were kept under the worst possible conditions.

"I cannot recount all the vile things that were said to us while in the police quarters in Chong-no," declared one of the girls. "They are too obscene to be spoken, but by the kindness of the Lord I thought of how Paul had suffered in prison, and was greatly comforted. I knew that God would give the needed help, and as I bore it for my country, I did not feel the shame and misery of it." One American woman, to whom some of the girls related their experiences, said to me, "I cannot tell you, a man, all that these girls told us. I will only say this. There have been stories of girls having their arms cut off. If these girls had been daughters of mine I would rather that they had their arms cut off than that they faced what those girls endured in Chong-no."

There came a day when the girls were bound at the wrists, all fastened together, and driven in a car to the prison outside the West Gate. Some of them were crying. They were not allowed to look up or speak. The driver, a Korean, took advantage of a moment when the attention of their guard was attracted to whisper a word of encouragement. "Don't be discouraged and make your bodies weak. You are not yet condemned. This is only to break your spirits."

The prison outside the West Gate is a model Japanese jail. There were women officials here. It seemed horrible to the girls that they should be made to strip in front of men and be examined by them. Probably the men were prison doctors. But it was evidently intended to shame them as much as possible. Thus one girl relates that, after her examination, "I was told to take my clothes and go into another room. One woman went with me, about a hundred yards or more away. I wanted to put my clothes on before leaving the room, but they hurried me and pushed me. I wrapped my skirt about my body before I went out, and carried the rest of my clothes in my arms. After leaving this room, and before reaching the other, five Korean men prisoners passed us."

For the first week the girls, many of them in densely crowded cells, were kept in close confinement. After this, they were allowed out for fifteen minutes, wearing the prisoners' hat, which comes down over the head, after breakfast. Their food was beans and millet. It was given to the accompaniment of jeers and insults. "You Koreans eat like dogs and cats," the wardresses told them.

The routine of life in the prison was very trying. They got up at seven. Most of the day they had to assume a haunched, kneeling position, and remain absolutely still, hour after hour. The wardresses in the corridors kept close watch, and woe to the girl who made the slightest move. "They ordered us not to move a hand or a foot but to remain perfectly still," wrote one girl. "Even the slightest movement brought down every kind of wrath. We did not dare to move even a toe-nail."

One unhappy girl, mistaking the call of an official in the corridor, "I-ri-ma sen" for a command to go to sleep, stretched out her leg to lie down. She was scolded and severely punished. Another closed her eyes in prayer. "You are sleeping," called the wardress. In vain the girl replied that she was praying. "You lie," retorted the polite Japanese lady. More punishment!

After fifteen days in the prison outside the West Gate, some of the girls were called in the office. "Go, but be very careful not to repeat your offence," they were told. "If you are caught again, you will be given a heavier punishment."

The worst happenings with the women were not in the big towns, where the presence of white people exercised some restraint, but in villages, where the new troops often behaved in almost incredible fashion, outraging freely. The police in many of these outlying parts rivalled the military in brutality. Of the many stories that reached me, the tale of Tong Chun stands out. The account was investigated by experienced white men, who shortly afterwards visited the place and saw for themselves.

The village of Tong Chun contains about 300 houses and is the site of a Christian church. The young men of the place wished to make a demonstration but the elders of the church dissuaded them for a time. However, on March 29th, market day, when there were many people in the place, some children started demonstrating, and their elders followed, a crowd of four or five hundred people marching through the streets and shouting "Mansei!" There was no violence of any kind. The police came out and arrested seventeen persons, including five women.

One of these women was a widow of thirty-one. She was taken into the police office and a policeman tore off her clothes, leaving her in her underwear. Then the police began to take off her underclothes. She protested, whereupon they struck her in the face with their hands till she was black and blue. She still clung to her clothes, so they put a wooden paddle down between her legs and tore her clothes away. Then they beat her. The beating took a long time. When it was finished the police stopped to drink tea and eat Japanese cakes, they and their companions--there were a number of men in the room--amusing themselves by making fun of her as she sat there naked among them. She was subsequently released. For a week afterwards she had to lie down most of the time and could not walk around.

Another victim was the wife of a Christian teacher, a very bright, intelligent woman, with one child four months old, and two or three months advanced in her second pregnancy. She had taken a small part in the demonstration and then had gone to the home of the mother of another woman who had been arrested, to comfort her. Police came here, and demanded if she had shouted "Mansei." She admitted that she had. They ordered her to leave the child that she was carrying on her back and took her to the police station. As she entered the station a man kicked her forcibly from behind and she fell forward in the room. As she lay there a policeman put his foot on her neck, then raised her up and struck her again and again. She was ordered to undress. She hesitated, whereupon the policeman kicked her, and took up a paddle and a heavy stick to beat her with. "You are a teacher," he cried. "You have set the minds of the children against Japan. I will beat you to death."

He tore her underclothes off. Still clinging to them, she tried to cover her nakedness. The clothes were torn out of her hands. She tried to sit down. They forced her up. She tried by turning to the wall to conceal herself from the many men in the room. They forced her to turn round again. When she tried to shelter herself with her hands, one man twisted her arms, held them behind her back, and kept them there while the beating and kicking continued. She was so badly hurt that she would have fallen to the floor, but they held her up to continue the beating. She was then sent into another room. Later she and other women were again brought in the office. "Do you know now how wrong it is to call 'Mansei'?" the police asked. "Will you ever dare to do such a thing again?"

Gradually news of how the women were being treated spread. A crowd of five hundred people gathered next morning. The hot bloods among them were for attacking the station, to take revenge for the ill-treatment of their women. The chief Christian kept them back, and finally a deputation of two went inside the police office to make a protest. They spoke up against the stripping of the women, declaring it unlawful. The Chief of Police replied that they were mistaken. It was permitted under Japanese law. They had to strip them to search for unlawful papers. Then the men asked why only the younger women were stripped, and not the older, why they were beaten after being stripped, and why only women and not men were stripped. The Chief did not reply.

By this time the crowd was getting very ugly. "Put us in prison too, or release the prisoners," the people called. In the end the Chief agreed to release all but four of the prisoners.

Soon afterwards the prisoners emerged from the station. One woman, a widow of thirty-two who had been arrested on the previous day and very badly kicked by the police, had to be supported on either side. The wife of the Christian teacher had to be carried on a man's back. Let me quote from a description written by those on the spot:

"As they saw the women being brought out, in this condition, a wave of pity swept over the whole crowd, and with one accord they burst into tears and sobbed. Some of them cried out, 'It is better to die than to live under such savages,' and many urged that they should attack the police office with their naked hands, capture the

Chief of Police, strip him and beat him to death. But the Christian elder and other wiser heads prevailed, kept the people from any acts of violence, and finally got them to disperse."

Appendix II

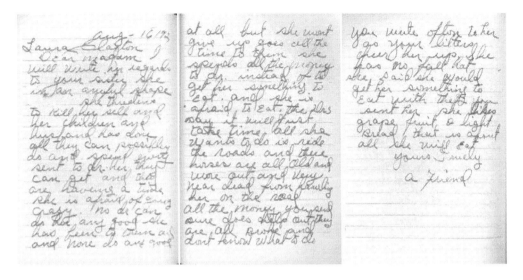

Theresa Hak Kyung Cha, Letter to "Laura Claxton," from
"Thalia   Comedy," *Dictée*, 146-48

Transcription

Aug. 16 192 [?]

Laura Claxton,
   Dear madam I will write in regards to your sister she in an awful shape   she threatens to kill her self and her children and husband has done all they can possibley do and spend every sent to dr. her they can get and they are having a time. She is afraid of going crazy. No dr. can do her any good she has been to them all and none do any good at all but she wont give up goes all the time to them she spends all the money to dr. instead of to get her something to eat. And she is afraid to eat. The drs say it will just take time. All she wants to do is ride the roads and there horses are all old and worn out and very near dead from hawling her on the road All the money send sure does help out They are all Broke and dont know what to do You write often to her as your litters cheer her up. She has not fall hat   . she said she would get her something to eat with the $2 you sent her
   she likes grape fruit & light bread . that is about all she will eat

        Yours Truly

            A Friend

APPENDIX III

Benjamin COTTAM. *Theresa Hak Kyung Cha–Dead Artist,* 2003, silver point on prepared paper, 4 X 3.25 inches (10.2 X 8.3 cm) (Private Collection, Michigan).

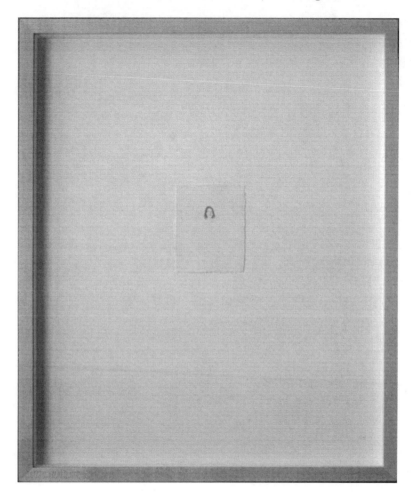

Michael Stone-Richards

Michael STONE-RICHARDS is Associate Professor in the Dept of Liberal Arts, College for Creative Studies, Detroit, where he teaches critical theory and comparative literature. Stone-Richards is a founding member of the Program Committee of the Museum of Contemporary Art, Detroit (MOCAD) and a member of the board of the Friends of Modern and Contemporary Art at the DIA (Detroit Institute of Arts). He has published widely in English and French in Critical Theory, Surrealism, and the European avant-garde. His most recent essays have been on Du Bois and Fanon (*Cambridge Companion to Du Bois*) and Giacometti (*Giacometti: Critical Essays*). Amongst forthcoming work will be his book *Logics of Separation: Exile and Transcendence in Aesthetic Modernity* (Peter Lang) and essays on Prynne, Debord and Simone Weil, along with translations of Jean Starobinski on "Freud, Breton, Myers" and Antoine Berman's "L'Âge de la traduction."

About

Glossator publishes original commentaries, editions and translations of commentaries, and essays and articles relating to the theory and history of commentary, glossing, and marginalia (catena, commentum, gemara, glossa, hypomnema, midrash, peser, pingdian, scholia, tafsir, talkhis, tika, vritti, zend, zhangju, et al). The journal aims to encourage the practice of commentary as a creative form of intellectual work and to provide a forum for dialogue and reflection on the past, present, and future of this ancient genre of writing. By aligning itself, not with any particular discipline, but with a particular mode of production, *Glossator* gives expression to the fact that praxis founds theory.

Glossator welcomes work from all disciplines, but especially from fields with strong affiliations with the commentary genre: philosophy, literary theory and criticism, textual and manuscript studies, hermeneutics, exegesis, et al.

What is commentary? While the distinction between commentary and other forms of writing is not an absolute one, the following may serve as guidelines for distinguishing between what is and is not a commentary:

- A commentary focuses on a single object (text, image, event, etc.) or portion thereof.
- A commentary does not displace but rather shapes itself to and preserves the integrity, structure, and presence of its object.
- The relationship of a commentary to its object may be described as both parallel and perpendicular. Commentary is parallel to its object in that it moves with or runs alongside it, following the flow of reading it. Commentary is perpendicular to its object in that it pauses or breaks from reading it in order to comment on it. The combination of these dimensions gives commentary a structure of continuing discontinuity and a durable utility.
- Commentary tends to maintain a certain quantitative proportion of itself vis-à-vis its object. This tendency corresponds to the practice of "filling up the margins" of a text.
- Commentary, as a form of discourse, tends to favor and allow for the multiplication of meanings, ideas, and references. Commentary need not, and often does not, have an explicit central thesis or argument. This tendency gives commentary a ludic or auto-teleological potential.

Glossator publishes a themed issue each Spring and periodic open issues in the Fall. Submissions for the open issues are accepted year round.

FORTHCOMING VOLUMES

The Poetry of J. H. Prynne.
Special Co-Editor: Ryan Dobran
Spring 2009
Contributors: Justin Katko, Sam Ladkin, Ian Patterson, Neil Pattison, Reitha Pattison, Robin Purves, Thomas Roebuck, Matthew Sperling, Josh Stanley, Michael Stone-Richards, Keston Sutherland, Mike Wallace-Hadrill, John Wilkinson.

Occitan Poetry
Special Co-Editors: Anna Kłosowska & Valerie Wilhite
Spring 2010
Contributions: Vincent Barletta, Bill Burgwinkle, Charles Fantazzi, Marisa Gálvez, Virginie Greene, Cary Howie, Erin Labbie, Deborah Lyons, Simone Marchesi, Jean-Jacques Poucel, Jesús Rodríguez-Velasco, Luke Sunderland, Valerie Wilhite.

Black Metal
Special Co-Editors: Nicola Masciandaro & Reza Negarestani
Spring 2012
Contributors: Lee Barron, Ray Brassier, Erik Butler, Dominic Fox, Nicola Masciandaro, Reza Negarestani, Benjamin Noys, Steven Shakespeare, Aspasia Stephanou, Eugene Thacker, James Trafford, Stewart Voegtlin, Scott Wilson, Alex Williams, Evan Calder Williams.

Made in the USA